# GENSHIKEN

4

## KIO SHIMOKU

TRANSLATED AND ADAPTED BY
### David Ury

LETTERED BY
### Retinal Graphics

BALLANTINE BOOKS • NEW YORK

*Genshiken*, volume 4 is a work of fiction.
Names, characters, places, and incidents are the
products of the author's imagination or are used
fictitiously. Any resemblance to actual events, locales,
or persons, living or dead, is entirely coincidental.

A Del Rey Trade Paperback Original

Genshiken copyright © 2003 by Kio Shimoku

English translation copyright © 2006 by Kio
Shimoku

All rights reserved.

Published in the United States by Del Rey Books, an
imprint of The Random House Publishing Group,
a division of Random House, Inc., New York.

Del Rey is a registered trademark and the Del Rey
colophon is a trademark of Random House, Inc.

Publication rights arranged through Kodansha Ltd.

First published in Japan in 2003 by
Kodansha Ltd., Tokyo

Library of Congress Control Number:
2005922043

ISBN 0-345-48242-5

Printed in the United States of America

www.delreymanga.com

5 7 9 10 8 6 4

Translated and adapted by David Ury

Lettered by Retinal Graphics

Text design by Retinal Graphics

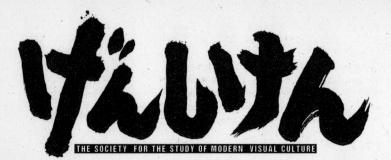

# げんいけん

THE SOCIETY FOR THE STUDY OF MODERN VISUAL CULTURE

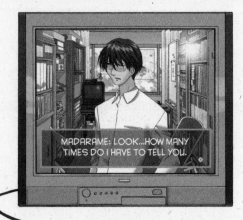

MADARAME: LOOK...HOW MANY TIMES DO I HAVE TO TELL YOU.

## KIO SHIMOKU

# Contents

## OUR FAVORITE GAME "ANOTHER STORIES"

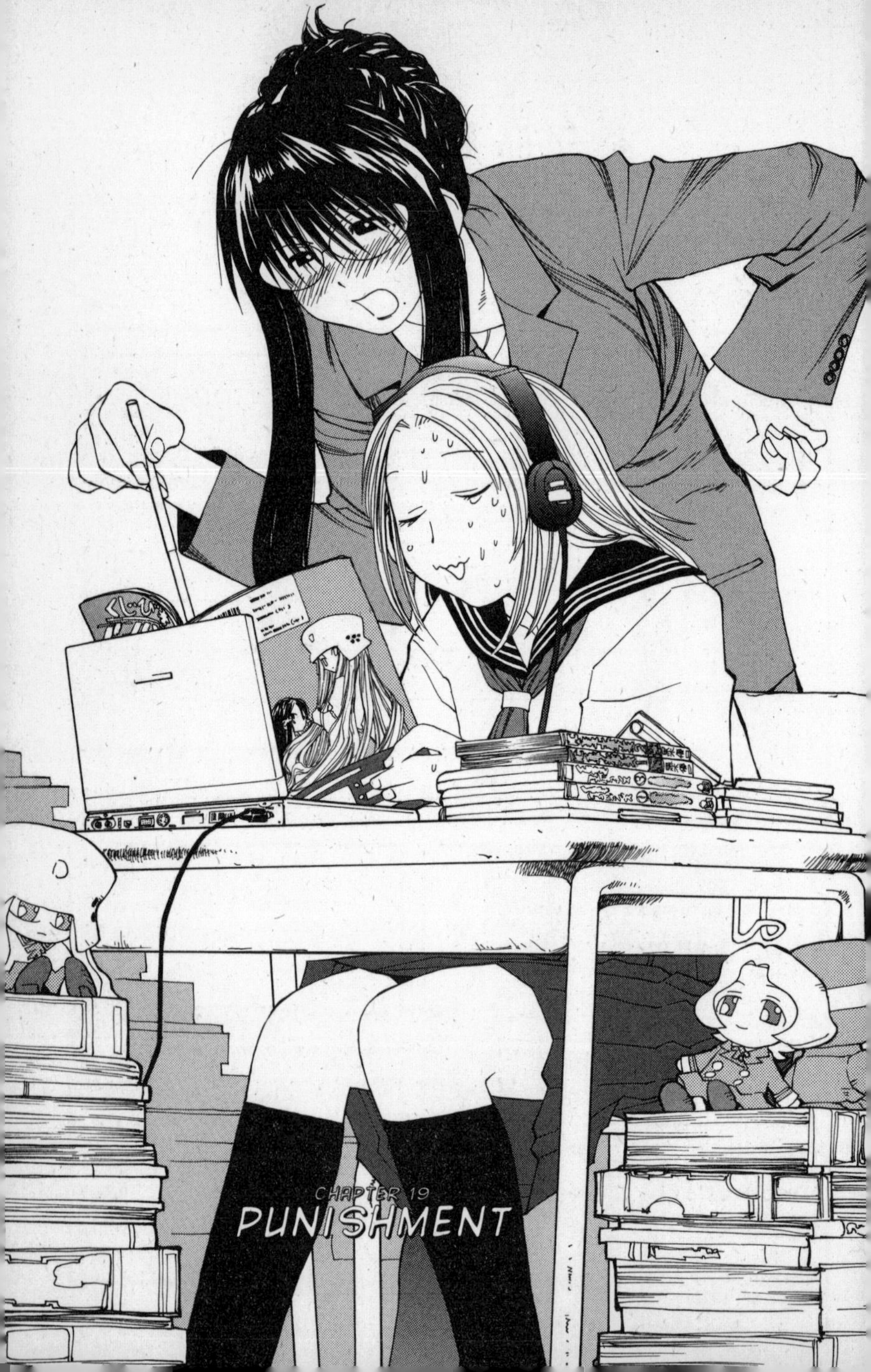
CHAPTER 19
PUNISHMENT

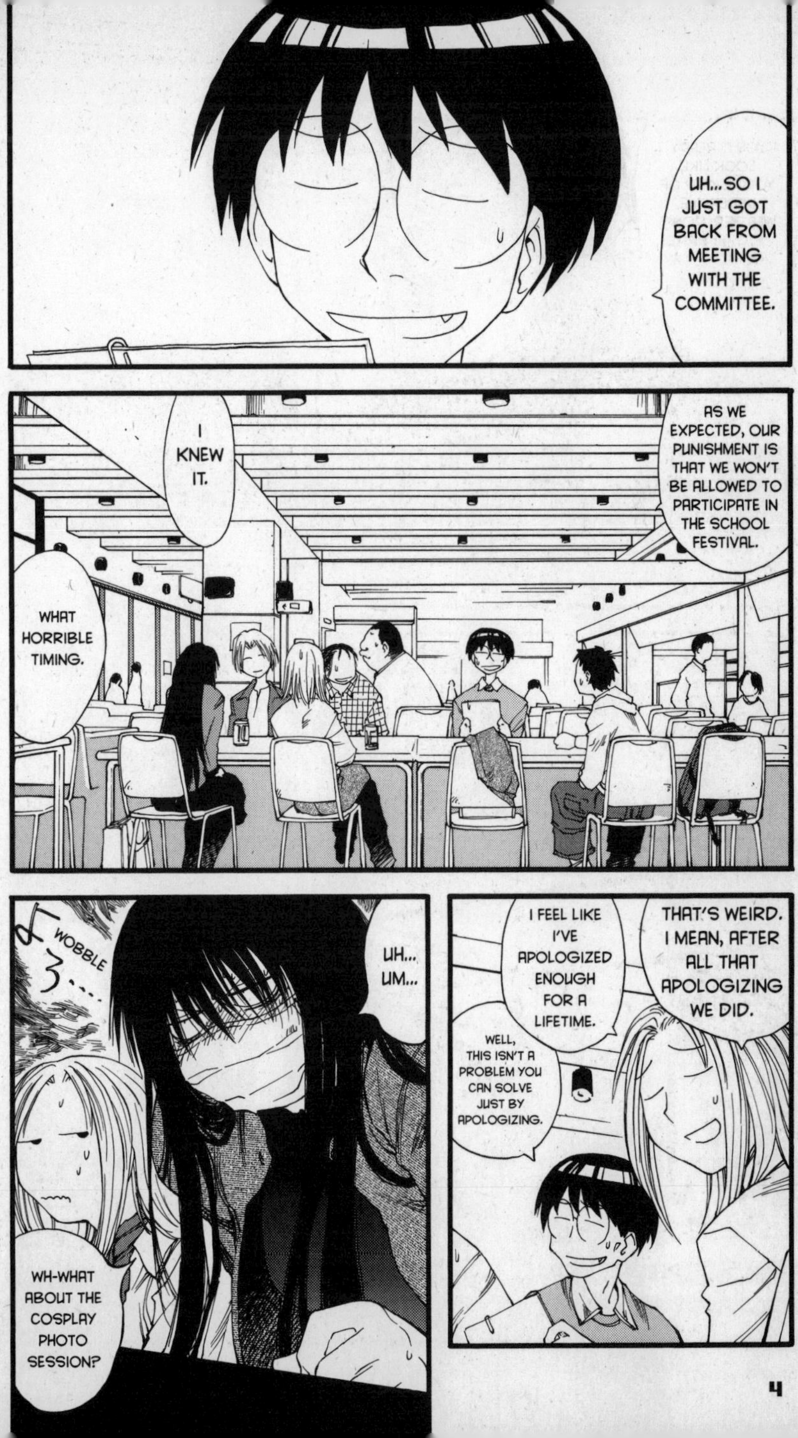
UH... SO I JUST GOT BACK FROM MEETING WITH THE COMMITTEE.
AS WE EXPECTED, OUR PUNISHMENT IS THAT WE WON'T BE ALLOWED TO PARTICIPATE IN THE SCHOOL FESTIVAL.
I KNEW IT.
WHAT HORRIBLE TIMING.
THAT'S WEIRD. I MEAN, AFTER ALL THAT APOLOGIZING WE DID.
I FEEL LIKE I'VE APOLOGIZED ENOUGH FOR A LIFETIME.
WELL, THIS ISN'T A PROBLEM YOU CAN SOLVE JUST BY APOLOGIZING.
UH... UM...
WOBBLE
WH-WHAT ABOUT THE COSPLAY PHOTO SESSION?

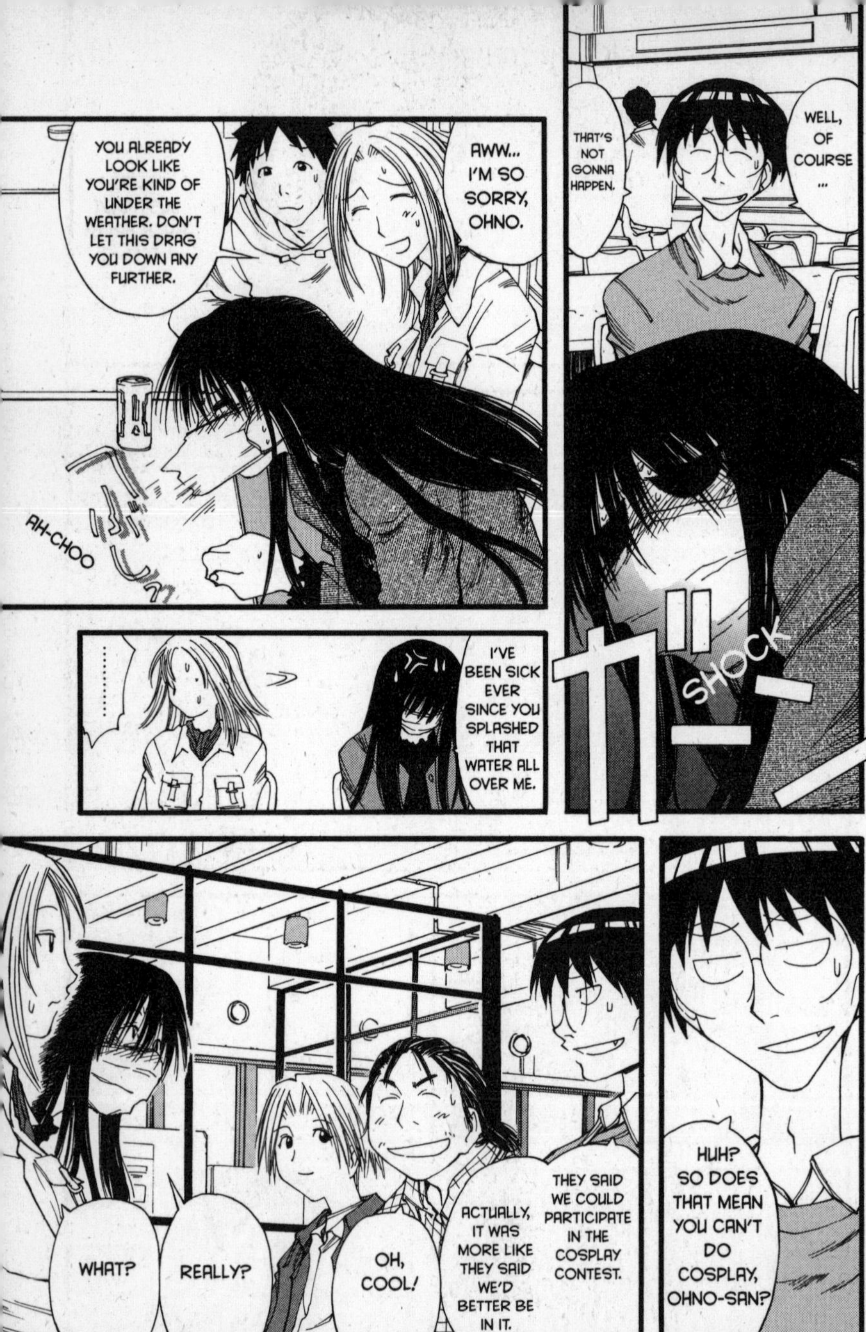
WELL, OF COURSE ...
THAT'S NOT GONNA HAPPEN.
SHOCK
AWW... I'M SO SORRY, OHNO.
YOU ALREADY LOOK LIKE YOU'RE KIND OF UNDER THE WEATHER. DON'T LET THIS DRAG YOU DOWN ANY FURTHER.
AH-CHOO
I'VE BEEN SICK EVER SINCE YOU SPLASHED THAT WATER ALL OVER ME.
......
HUH? SO DOES THAT MEAN YOU CAN'T DO COSPLAY, OHNO-SAN?
THEY SAID WE COULD PARTICIPATE IN THE COSPLAY CONTEST.
ACTUALLY, IT WAS MORE LIKE THEY SAID WE'D BETTER BE IN IT.
OH, COOL!
REALLY?
WHAT?

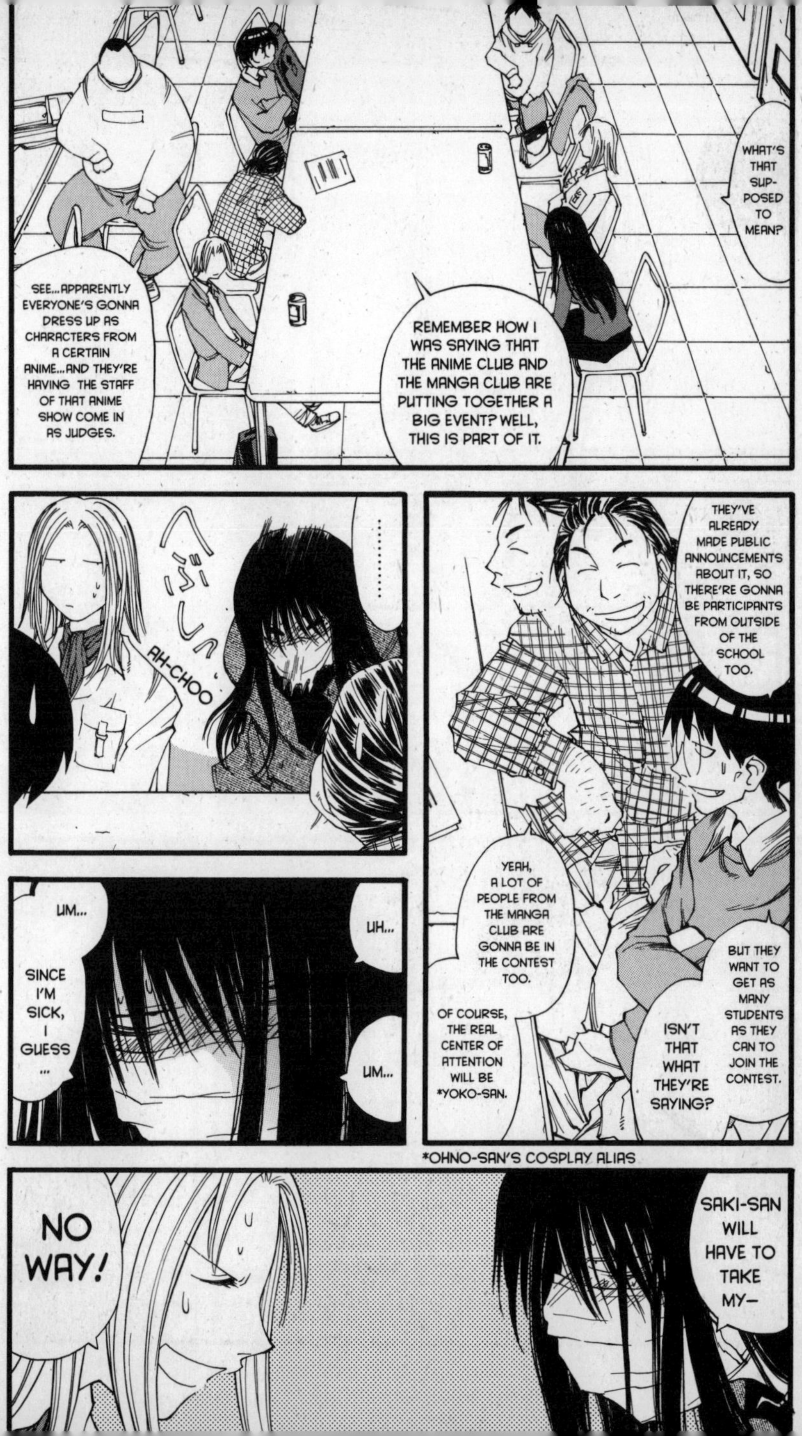
WHAT'S THAT SUPPOSED TO MEAN?
REMEMBER HOW I WAS SAYING THAT THE ANIME CLUB AND THE MANGA CLUB ARE PUTTING TOGETHER A BIG EVENT? WELL, THIS IS PART OF IT.
SEE...APPARENTLY EVERYONE'S GONNA DRESS UP AS CHARACTERS FROM A CERTAIN ANIME...AND THEY'RE HAVING THE STAFF OF THAT ANIME SHOW COME IN AS JUDGES.
THEY'VE ALREADY MADE PUBLIC ANNOUNCEMENTS ABOUT IT, SO THERE'RE GONNA BE PARTICIPANTS FROM OUTSIDE OF THE SCHOOL TOO.
YEAH, A LOT OF PEOPLE FROM THE MANGA CLUB ARE GONNA BE IN THE CONTEST TOO.
BUT THEY WANT TO GET AS MANY STUDENTS AS THEY CAN TO JOIN THE CONTEST.
ISN'T THAT WHAT THEY'RE SAYING?
OF COURSE, THE REAL CENTER OF ATTENTION WILL BE *YOKO-SAN.
......
AH-CHOO
UH...
UM...
UM...
SINCE I'M SICK, I GUESS...
*OHNO-SAN'S COSPLAY ALIAS
SAKI-SAN WILL HAVE TO TAKE MY—
NO WAY!

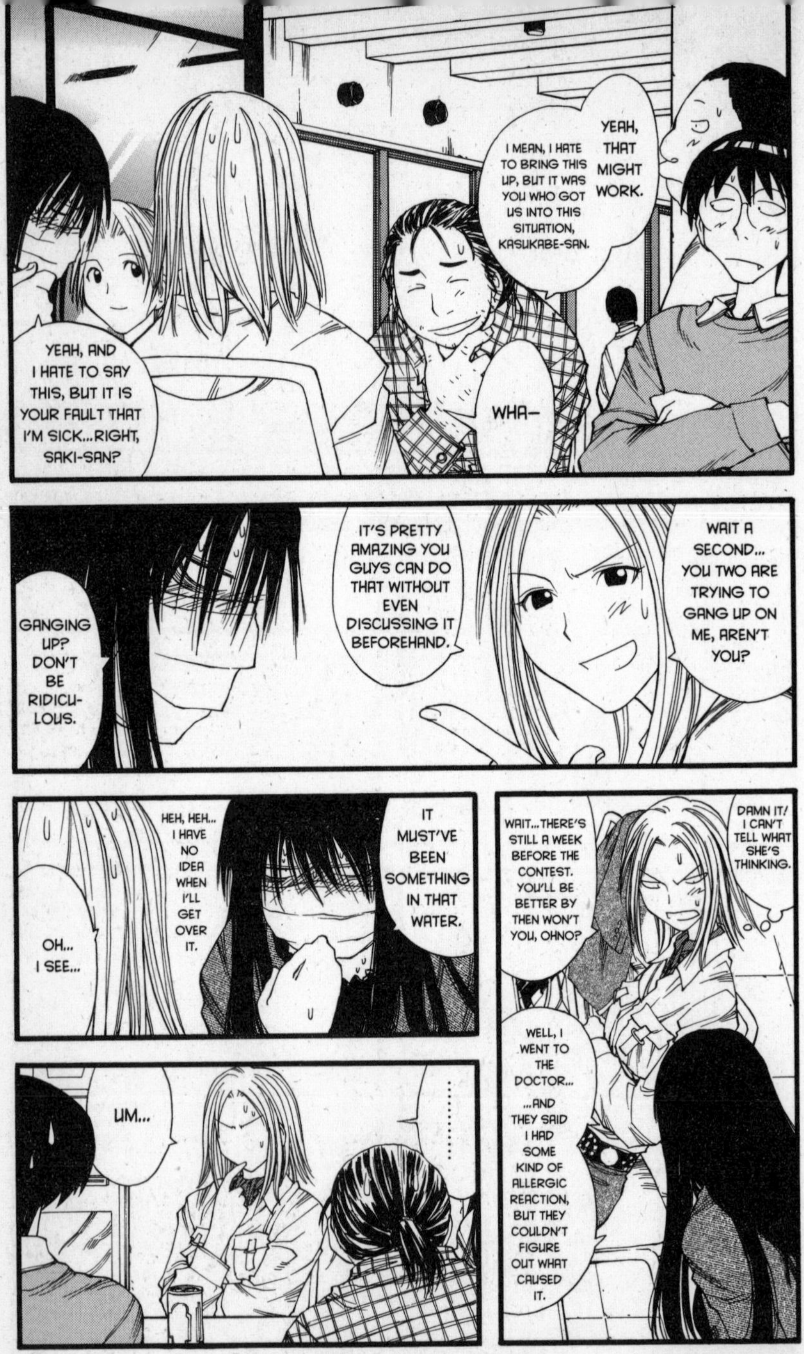
YEAH, THAT MIGHT WORK.
I MEAN, I HATE TO BRING THIS UP, BUT IT WAS YOU WHO GOT US INTO THIS SITUATION, KASUKABE-SAN.
WHA—
YEAH, AND I HATE TO SAY THIS, BUT IT IS YOUR FAULT THAT I'M SICK...RIGHT, SAKI-SAN?
WAIT A SECOND... YOU TWO ARE TRYING TO GANG UP ON ME, AREN'T YOU?
IT'S PRETTY AMAZING YOU GUYS CAN DO THAT WITHOUT EVEN DISCUSSING IT BEFOREHAND.
GANGING UP? DON'T BE RIDICU-LOUS.
DAMN IT! I CAN'T TELL WHAT SHE'S THINKING.
WAIT...THERE'S STILL A WEEK BEFORE THE CONTEST. YOU'LL BE BETTER BY THEN WON'T YOU, OHNO?
WELL, I WENT TO THE DOCTOR...
...AND THEY SAID I HAD SOME KIND OF ALLERGIC REACTION, BUT THEY COULDN'T FIGURE OUT WHAT CAUSED IT.
IT MUST'VE BEEN SOMETHING IN THAT WATER.
HEH, HEH... I HAVE NO IDEA WHEN I'LL GET OVER IT.
OH... I SEE...
........
UM...

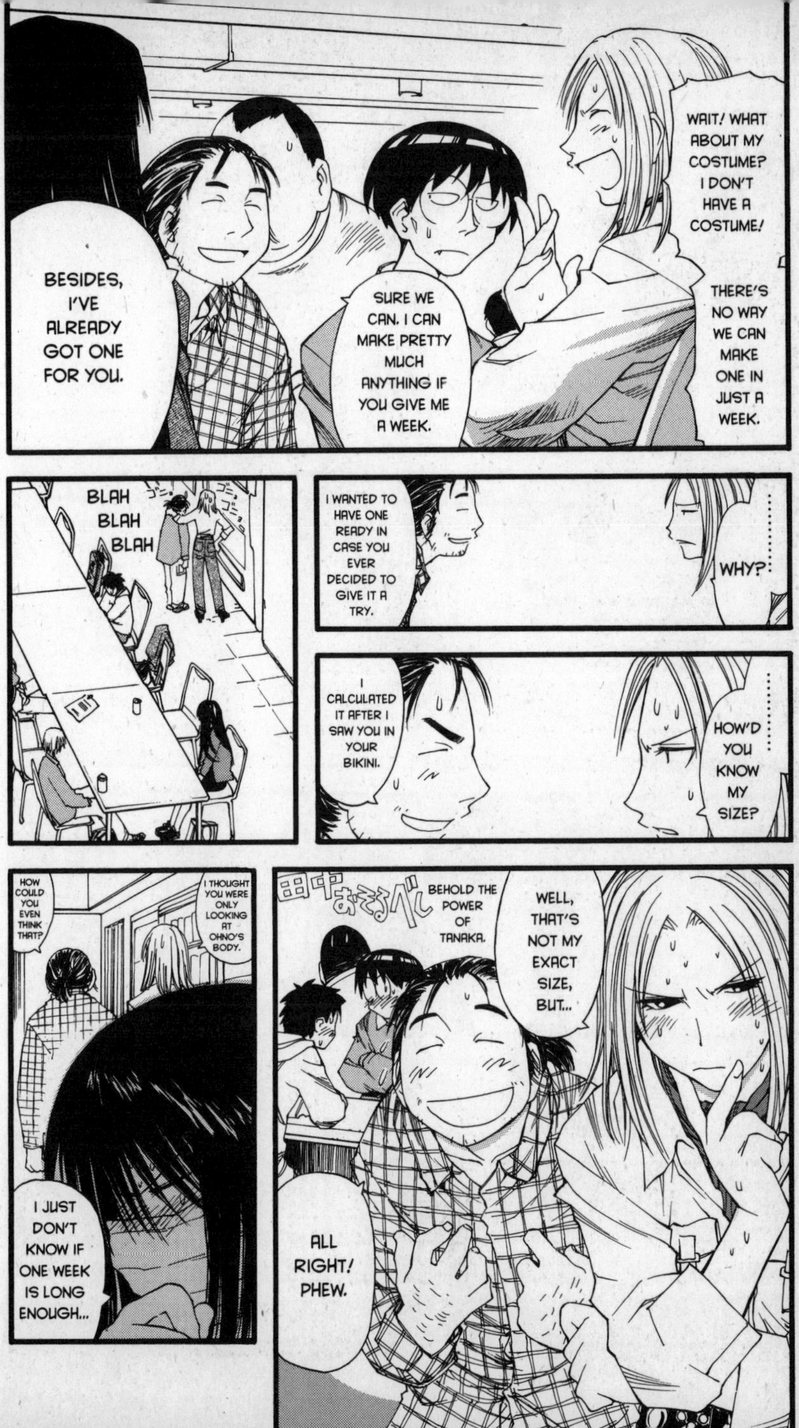
WAIT! WHAT ABOUT MY COSTUME? I DON'T HAVE A COSTUME!
THERE'S NO WAY WE CAN MAKE ONE IN JUST A WEEK.
SURE WE CAN. I CAN MAKE PRETTY MUCH ANYTHING IF YOU GIVE ME A WEEK.
BESIDES, I'VE ALREADY GOT ONE FOR YOU.
......
WHY?
I WANTED TO HAVE ONE READY IN CASE YOU EVER DECIDED TO GIVE IT A TRY.
......
HOW'D YOU KNOW MY SIZE?
I CALCULATED IT AFTER I SAW YOU IN YOUR BIKINI.
BLAH BLAH BLAH
WELL, THAT'S NOT MY EXACT SIZE, BUT...
田中おそるべし
BEHOLD THE POWER OF TANAKA.
ALL RIGHT! PHEW.
I THOUGHT YOU WERE ONLY LOOKING AT OHNO'S BODY.
HOW COULD YOU EVEN THINK THAT?
I JUST DON'T KNOW IF ONE WEEK IS LONG ENOUGH...

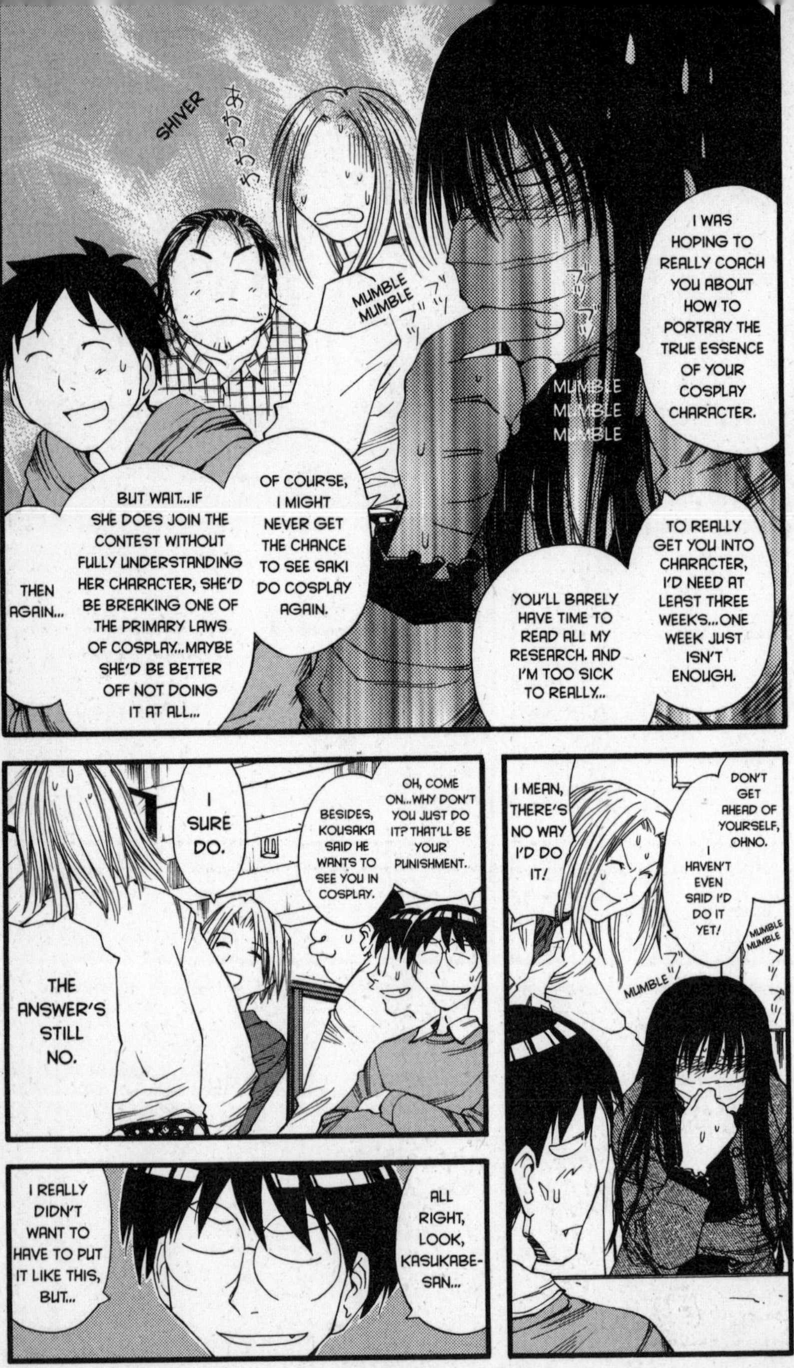
I WAS HOPING TO REALLY COACH YOU ABOUT HOW TO PORTRAY THE TRUE ESSENCE OF YOUR COSPLAY CHARACTER.
MUMBLE MUMBLE MUMBLE
MUMBLE MUMBLE
SHIVER
TO REALLY GET YOU INTO CHARACTER, I'D NEED AT LEAST THREE WEEKS...ONE WEEK JUST ISN'T ENOUGH.
YOU'LL BARELY HAVE TIME TO READ ALL MY RESEARCH. AND I'M TOO SICK TO REALLY...
OF COURSE, I MIGHT NEVER GET THE CHANCE TO SEE SAKI DO COSPLAY AGAIN.
BUT WAIT...IF SHE DOES JOIN THE CONTEST WITHOUT FULLY UNDERSTANDING HER CHARACTER, SHE'D BE BREAKING ONE OF THE PRIMARY LAWS OF COSPLAY...MAYBE SHE'D BE BETTER OFF NOT DOING IT AT ALL...
THEN AGAIN...
DON'T GET AHEAD OF YOURSELF, OHNO.
I HAVEN'T EVEN SAID I'D DO IT YET!
I MEAN, THERE'S NO WAY I'D DO IT!
MUMBLE MUMBLE
MUMBLE
OH, COME ON...WHY DON'T YOU JUST DO IT? THAT'LL BE YOUR PUNISHMENT.
BESIDES, KOUSAKA SAID HE WANTS TO SEE YOU IN COSPLAY.
I SURE DO.
THE ANSWER'S STILL NO.
ALL RIGHT, LOOK, KASUKABE-SAN...
I REALLY DIDN'T WANT TO HAVE TO PUT IT LIKE THIS, BUT...

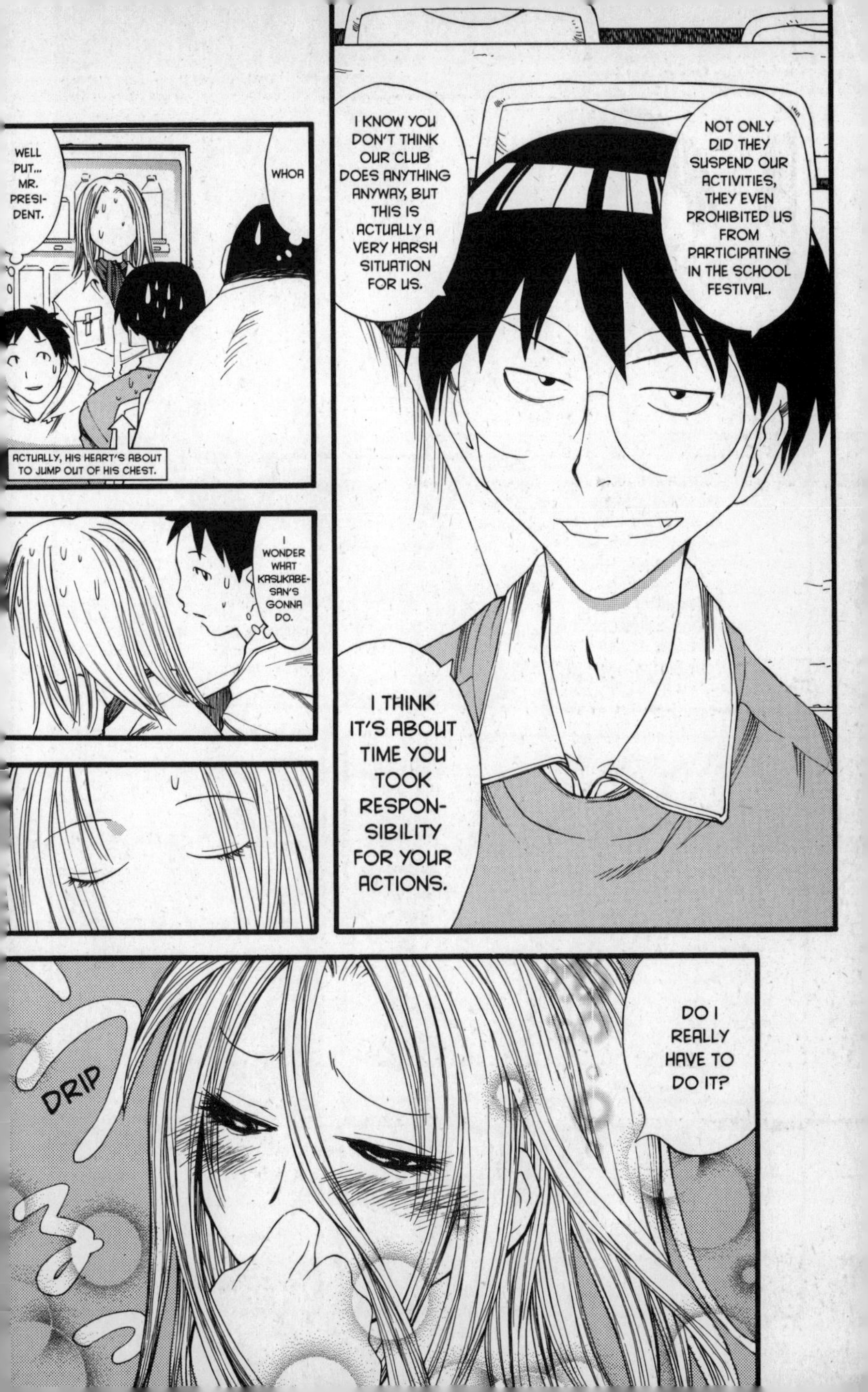
NOT ONLY DID THEY SUSPEND OUR ACTIVITIES, THEY EVEN PROHIBITED US FROM PARTICIPATING IN THE SCHOOL FESTIVAL.
I KNOW YOU DON'T THINK OUR CLUB DOES ANYTHING ANYWAY, BUT THIS IS ACTUALLY A VERY HARSH SITUATION FOR US.
I THINK IT'S ABOUT TIME YOU TOOK RESPON-SIBILITY FOR YOUR ACTIONS.
WHOA
WELL PUT... MR. PRESI-DENT.
ACTUALLY, HIS HEART'S ABOUT TO JUMP OUT OF HIS CHEST.
I WONDER WHAT KASUKABE-SAN'S GONNA DO.
DO I REALLY HAVE TO DO IT?
DRIP

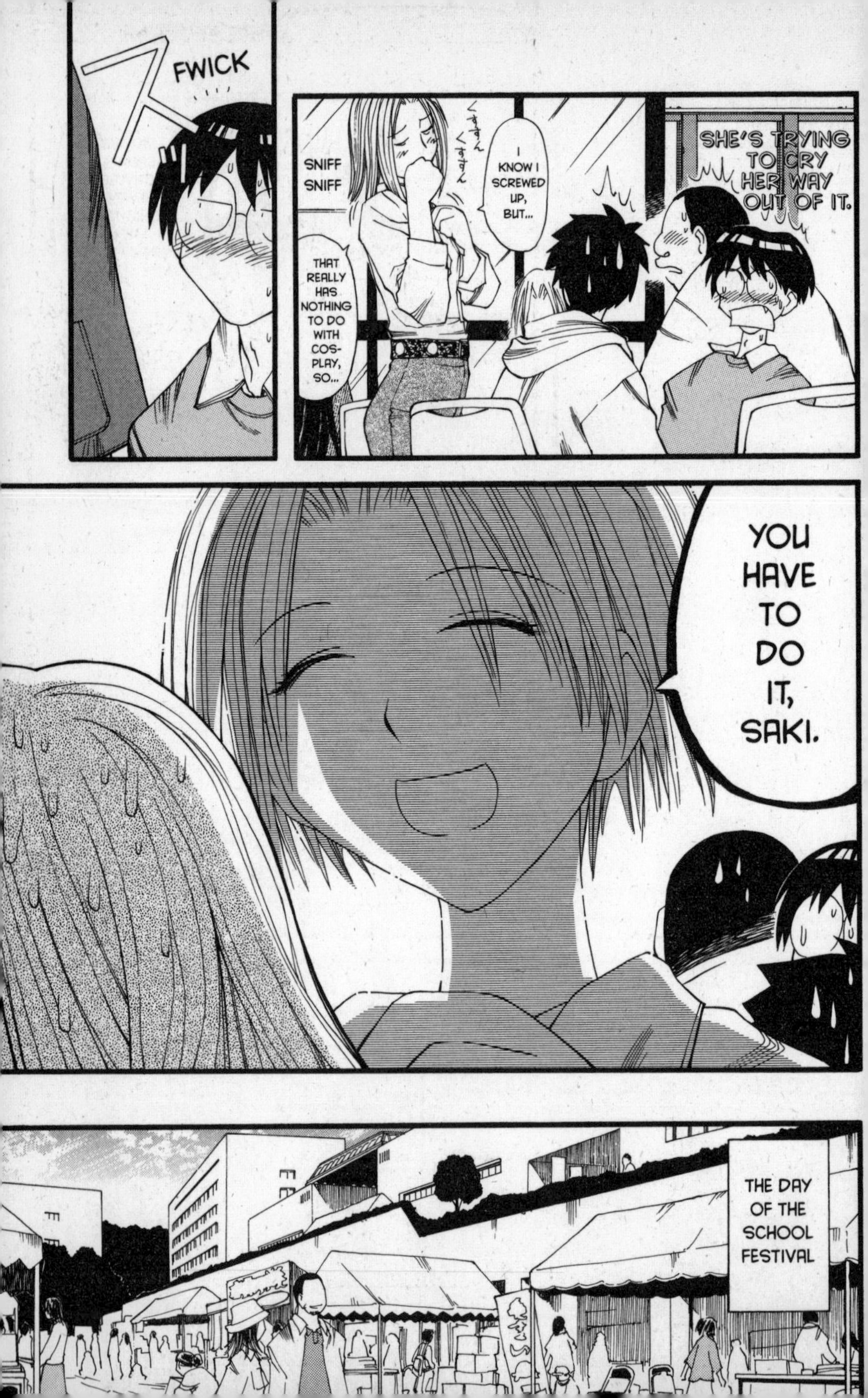
SHE'S TRYING TO CRY HER WAY OUT OF IT.
I KNOW I SCREWED UP, BUT...
くすすん
くすすん
SNIFF SNIFF
THAT REALLY HAS NOTHING TO DO WITH COS-PLAY, SO...
FWICK
YOU HAVE TO DO IT, SAKI.
THE DAY OF THE SCHOOL FESTIVAL

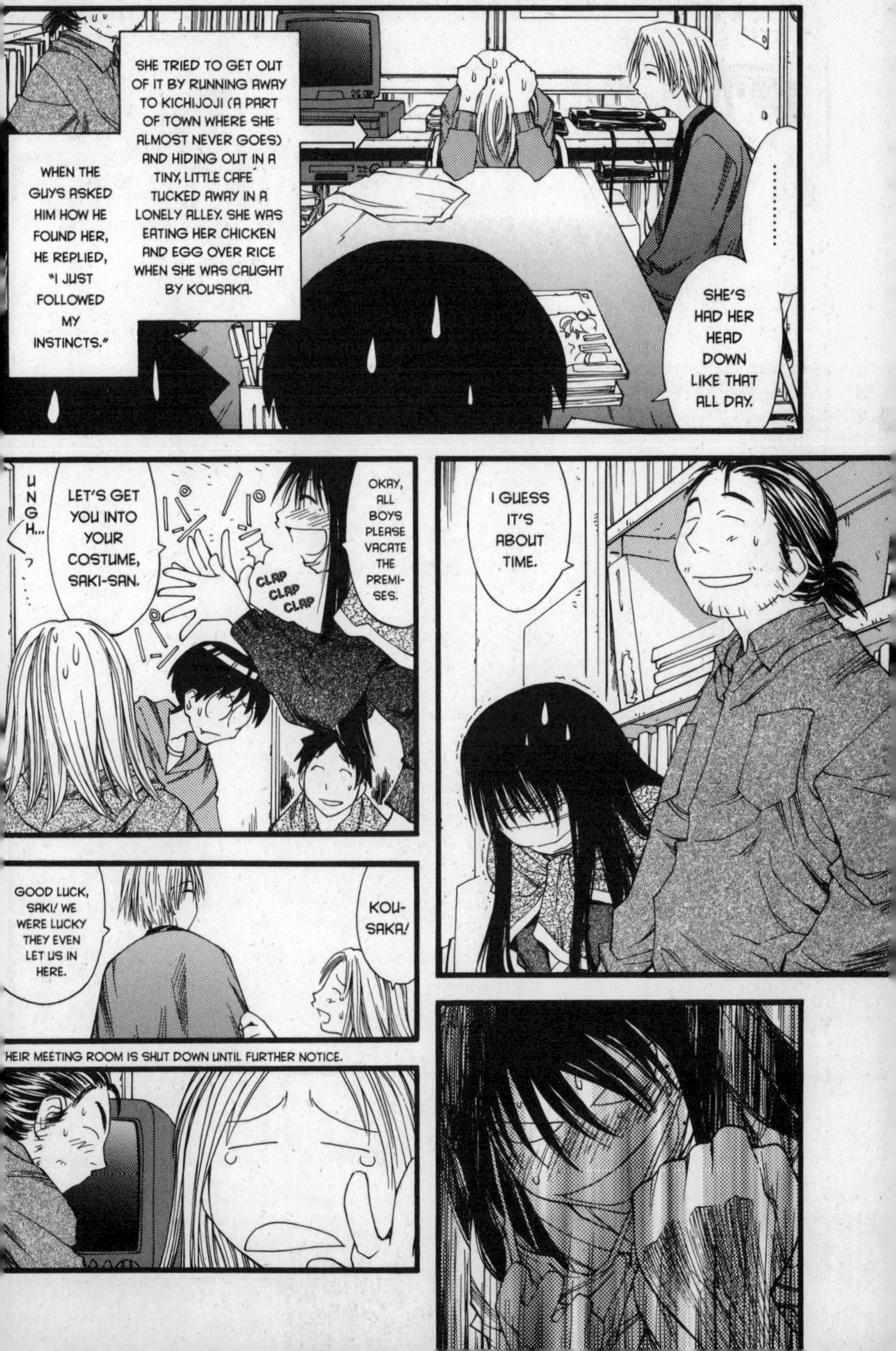
......
SHE'S HAD HER HEAD DOWN LIKE THAT ALL DAY.
SHE TRIED TO GET OUT OF IT BY RUNNING AWAY TO KICHIJOJI (A PART OF TOWN WHERE SHE ALMOST NEVER GOES) AND HIDING OUT IN A TINY, LITTLE CAFÉ TUCKED AWAY IN A LONELY ALLEY. SHE WAS EATING HER CHICKEN AND EGG OVER RICE WHEN SHE WAS CAUGHT BY KOUSAKA.
WHEN THE GUYS ASKED HIM HOW HE FOUND HER, HE REPLIED, "I JUST FOLLOWED MY INSTINCTS."
I GUESS IT'S ABOUT TIME.
OKAY, ALL BOYS PLEASE VACATE THE PREMISES.
CLAP CLAP CLAP
LET'S GET YOU INTO YOUR COSTUME, SAKI-SAN.
UNGH...
KOU-SAKA!
GOOD LUCK, SAKI! WE WERE LUCKY THEY EVEN LET US IN HERE.
HEIR MEETING ROOM IS SHUT DOWN UNTIL FURTHER NOTICE.

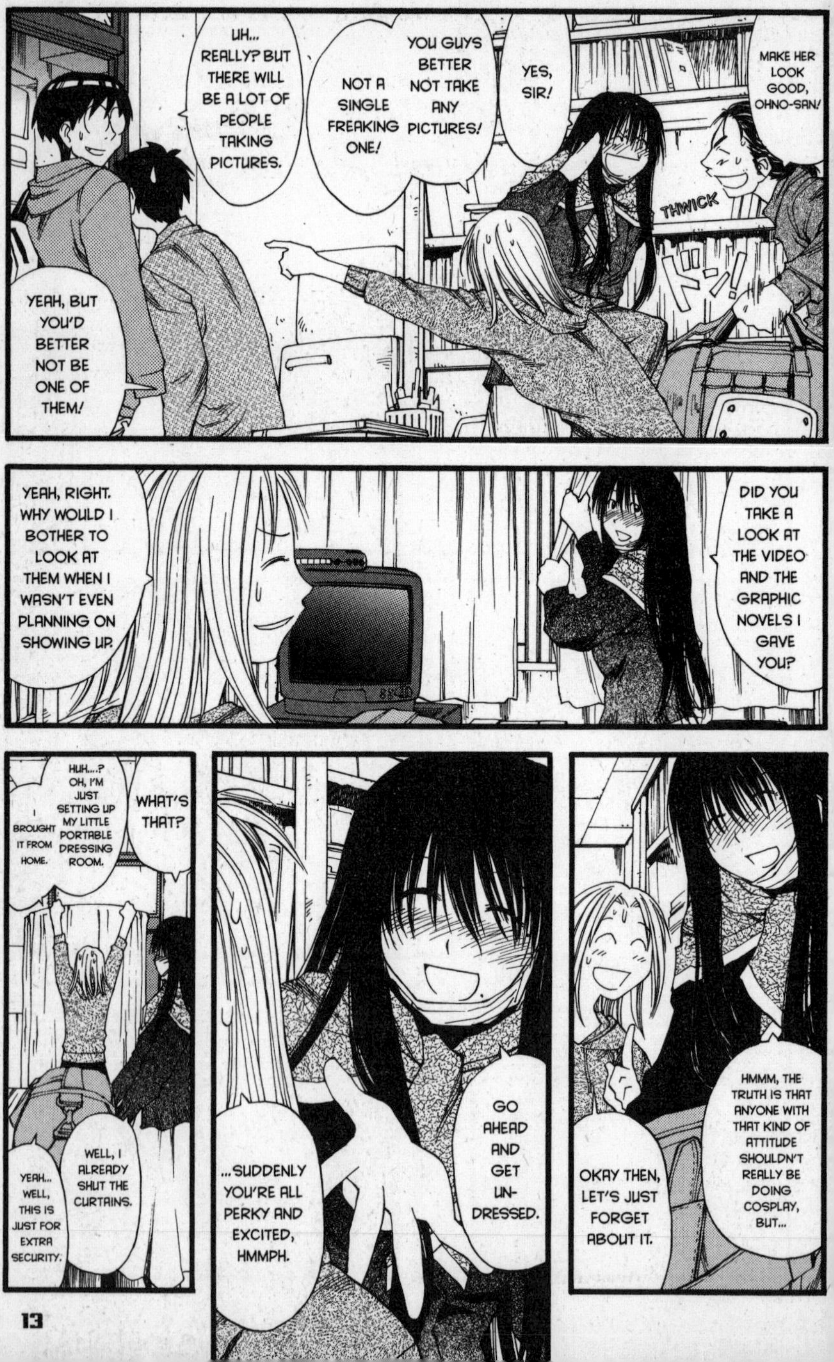
MAKE HER LOOK GOOD, OHNO-SAN!
THWICK
YES, SIR!
YOU GUYS BETTER NOT TAKE ANY PICTURES!
NOT A SINGLE FREAKING ONE!
UH... REALLY? BUT THERE WILL BE A LOT OF PEOPLE TAKING PICTURES.
YEAH, BUT YOU'D BETTER NOT BE ONE OF THEM!
DID YOU TAKE A LOOK AT THE VIDEO AND THE GRAPHIC NOVELS I GAVE YOU?
YEAH, RIGHT. WHY WOULD I BOTHER TO LOOK AT THEM WHEN I WASN'T EVEN PLANNING ON SHOWING UP.
HMMM, THE TRUTH IS THAT ANYONE WITH THAT KIND OF ATTITUDE SHOULDN'T REALLY BE DOING COSPLAY, BUT...
OKAY THEN, LET'S JUST FORGET ABOUT IT.
GO AHEAD AND GET UN-DRESSED.
...SUDDENLY YOU'RE ALL PERKY AND EXCITED, HMMPH.
WHAT'S THAT?
HUH...? OH, I'M JUST SETTING UP MY LITTLE PORTABLE DRESSING ROOM.
I BROUGHT IT FROM HOME.
WELL, I ALREADY SHUT THE CURTAINS.
YEAH... WELL, THIS IS JUST FOR EXTRA SECURITY.

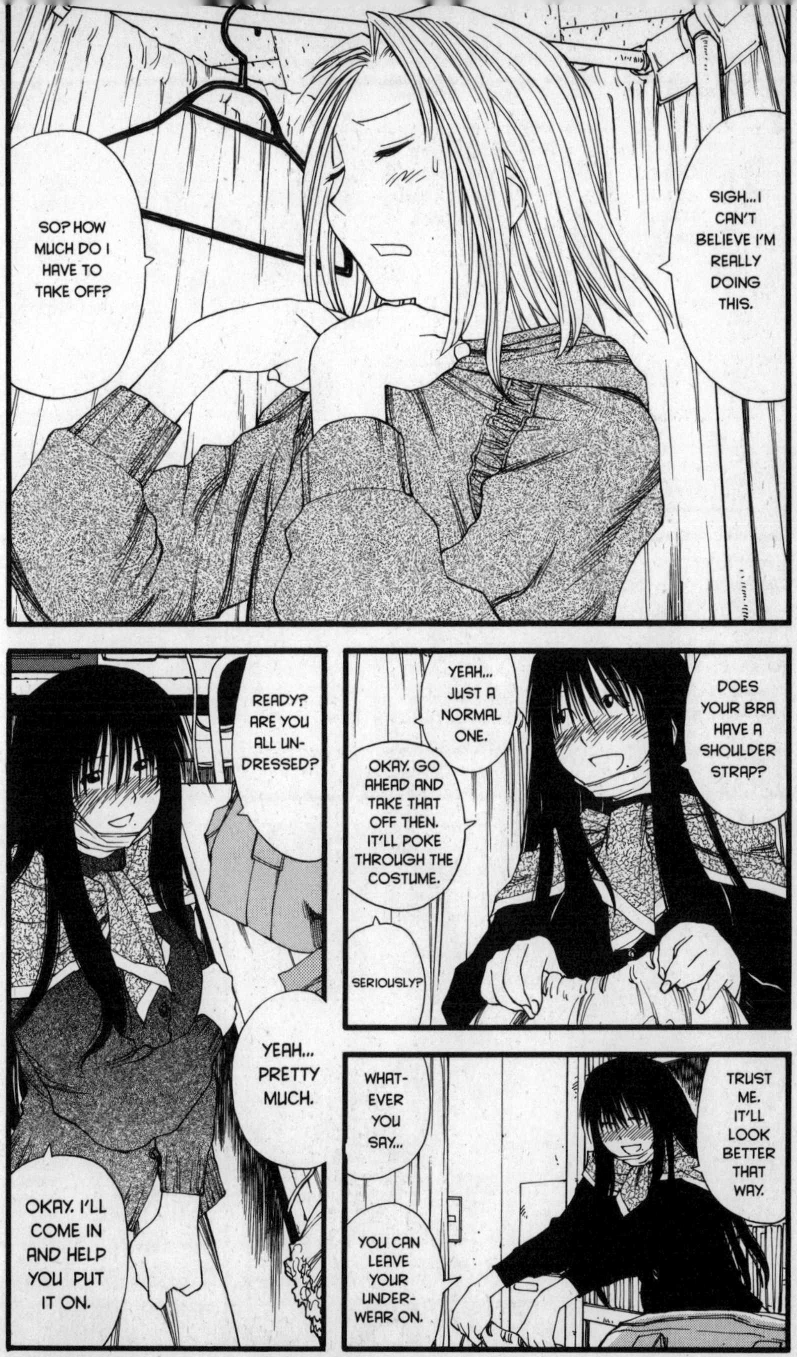
SIGH...I CAN'T BELIEVE I'M REALLY DOING THIS.
SO? HOW MUCH DO I HAVE TO TAKE OFF?
DOES YOUR BRA HAVE A SHOULDER STRAP?
YEAH... JUST A NORMAL ONE.
OKAY. GO AHEAD AND TAKE THAT OFF THEN. IT'LL POKE THROUGH THE COSTUME.
SERIOUSLY?
TRUST ME. IT'LL LOOK BETTER THAT WAY.
WHAT-EVER YOU SAY...
YOU CAN LEAVE YOUR UNDER-WEAR ON.
READY? ARE YOU ALL UN-DRESSED?
YEAH... PRETTY MUCH.
OKAY. I'LL COME IN AND HELP YOU PUT IT ON.

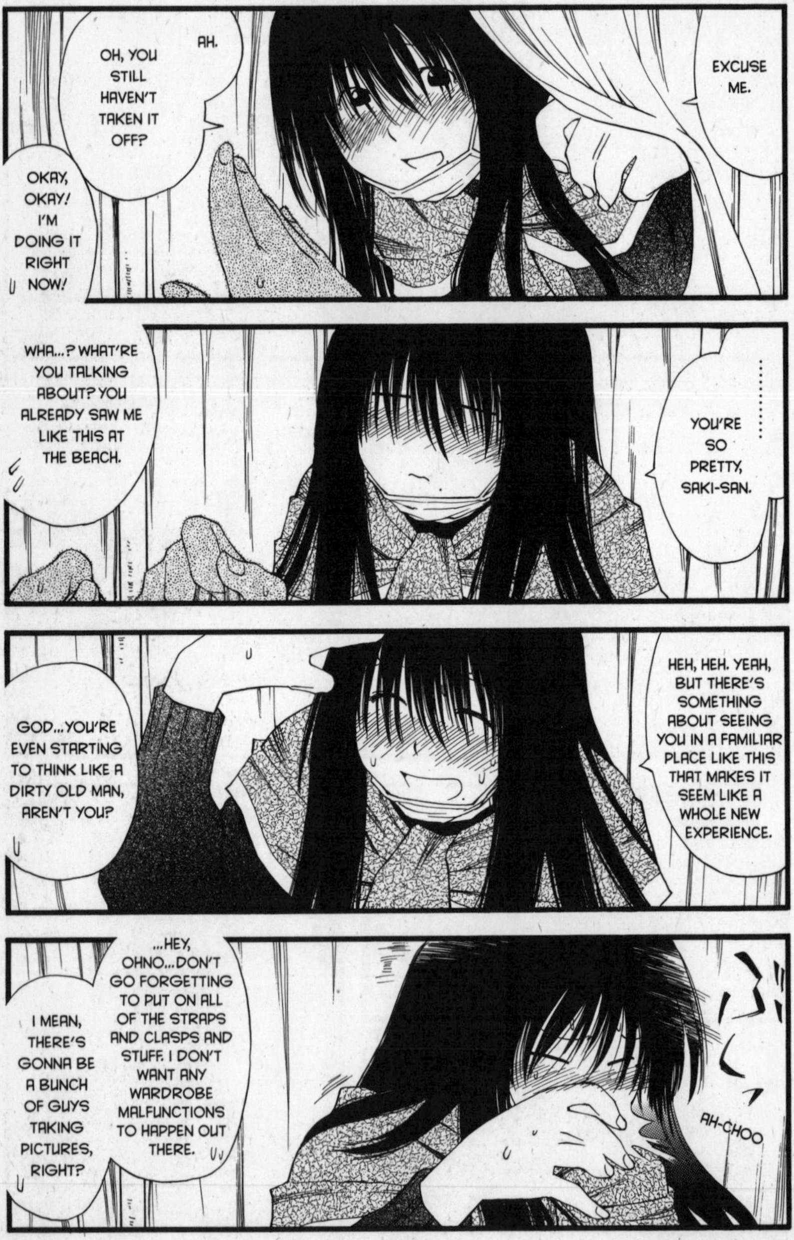
EXCUSE ME.
AH.
OH, YOU STILL HAVEN'T TAKEN IT OFF?
OKAY, OKAY! I'M DOING IT RIGHT NOW!
......
YOU'RE SO PRETTY, SAKI-SAN.
WHA...? WHAT'RE YOU TALKING ABOUT? YOU ALREADY SAW ME LIKE THIS AT THE BEACH.
HEH, HEH. YEAH, BUT THERE'S SOMETHING ABOUT SEEING YOU IN A FAMILIAR PLACE LIKE THIS THAT MAKES IT SEEM LIKE A WHOLE NEW EXPERIENCE.
GOD...YOU'RE EVEN STARTING TO THINK LIKE A DIRTY OLD MAN, AREN'T YOU?
AH-CHOO
...HEY, OHNO...DON'T GO FORGETTING TO PUT ON ALL OF THE STRAPS AND CLASPS AND STUFF. I DON'T WANT ANY WARDROBE MALFUNCTIONS TO HAPPEN OUT THERE.
I MEAN, THERE'S GONNA BE A BUNCH OF GUYS TAKING PICTURES, RIGHT?

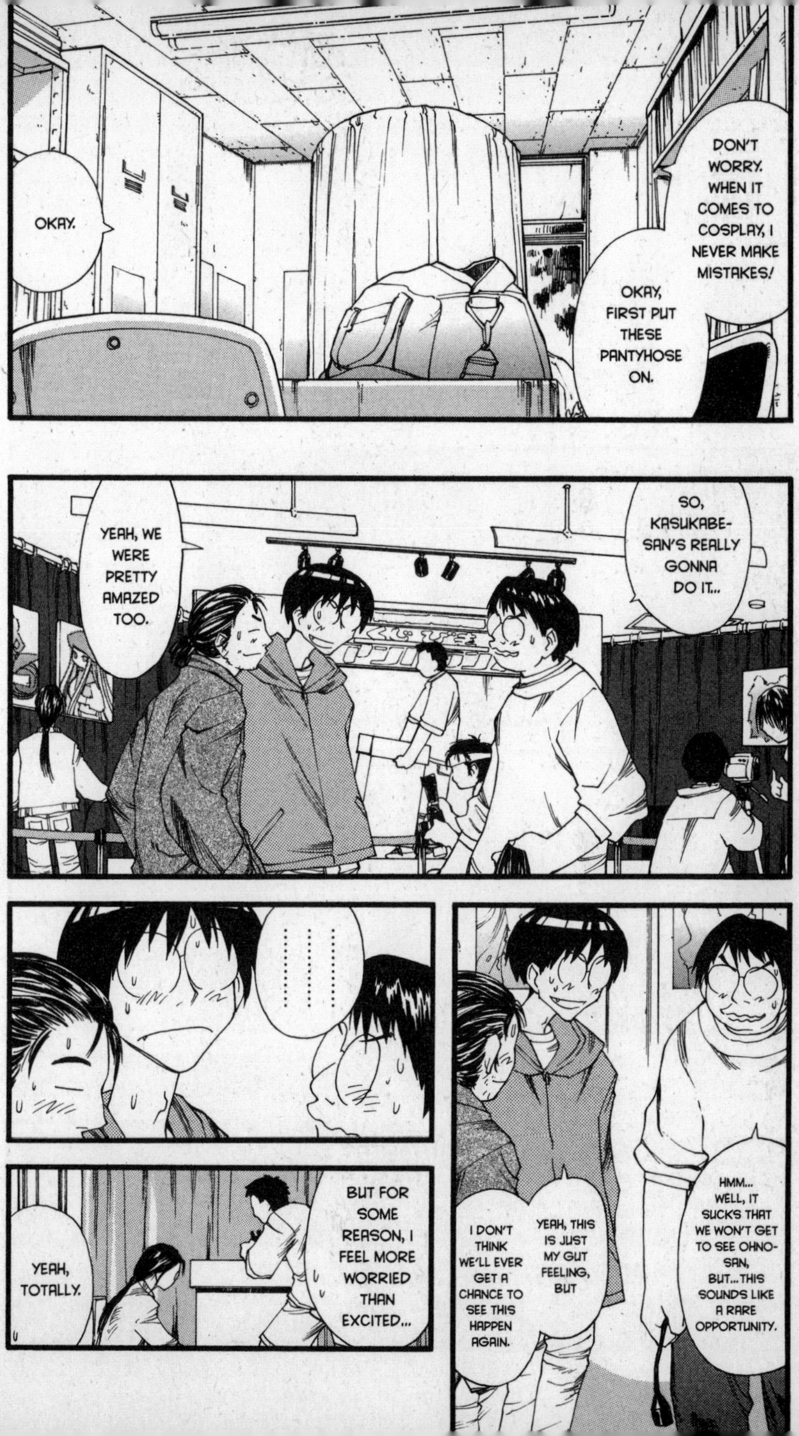
DON'T WORRY. WHEN IT COMES TO COSPLAY, I NEVER MAKE MISTAKES!
OKAY, FIRST PUT THESE PANTYHOSE ON.
OKAY.
SO, KASUKABE-SAN'S REALLY GONNA DO IT...
YEAH, WE WERE PRETTY AMAZED TOO.
HMM... WELL, IT SUCKS THAT WE WON'T GET TO SEE OHNO-SAN, BUT...THIS SOUNDS LIKE A RARE OPPORTUNITY.
YEAH, THIS IS JUST MY GUT FEELING, BUT
I DON'T THINK WE'LL EVER GET A CHANCE TO SEE THIS HAPPEN AGAIN.
......
BUT FOR SOME REASON, I FEEL MORE WORRIED THAN EXCITED...
YEAH, TOTALLY.

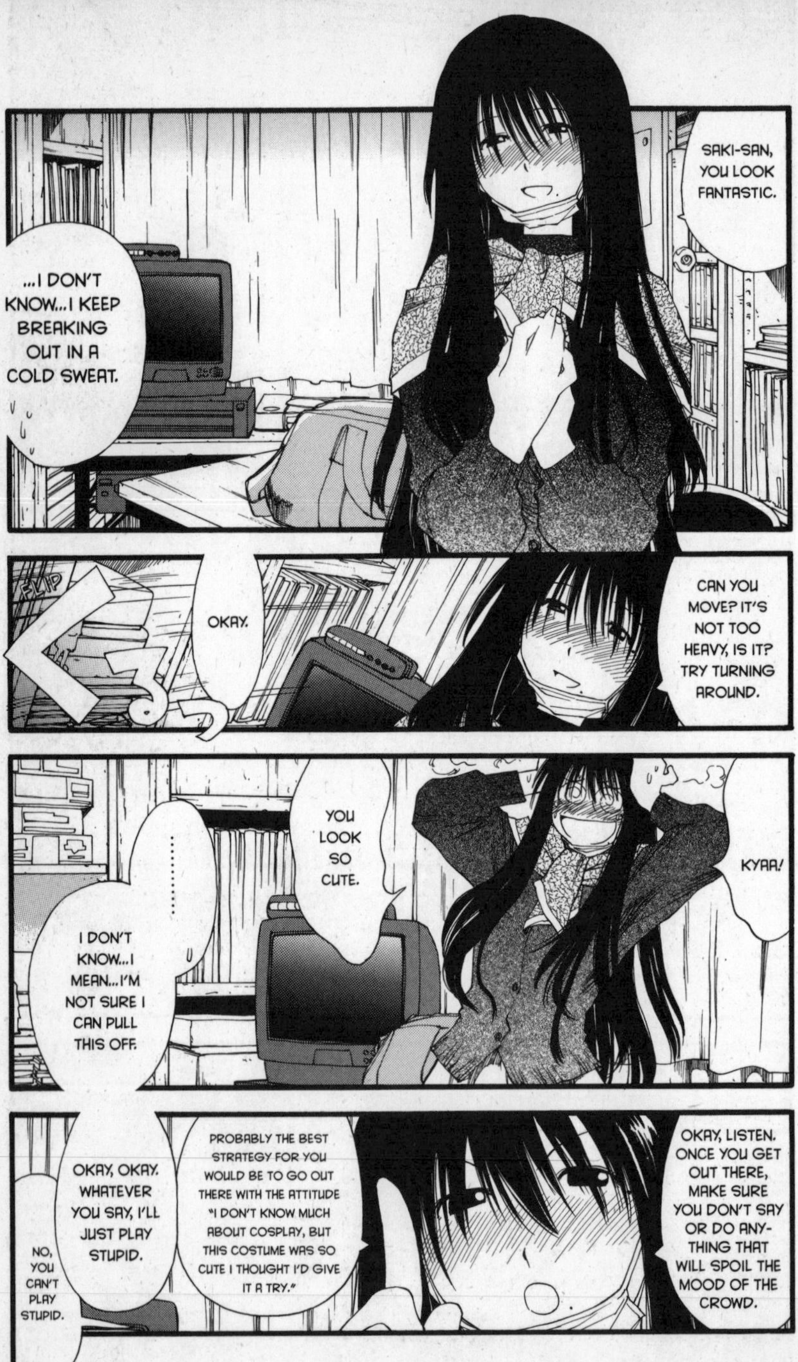
SAKI-SAN, YOU LOOK FANTASTIC.
...I DON'T KNOW...I KEEP BREAKING OUT IN A COLD SWEAT.
CAN YOU MOVE? IT'S NOT TOO HEAVY, IS IT? TRY TURNING AROUND.
OKAY.
FLIP
KYAA!
YOU LOOK SO CUTE.
......
I DON'T KNOW...I MEAN...I'M NOT SURE I CAN PULL THIS OFF.
OKAY, LISTEN. ONCE YOU GET OUT THERE, MAKE SURE YOU DON'T SAY OR DO ANY-THING THAT WILL SPOIL THE MOOD OF THE CROWD.
PROBABLY THE BEST STRATEGY FOR YOU WOULD BE TO GO OUT THERE WITH THE ATTITUDE "I DON'T KNOW MUCH ABOUT COSPLAY, BUT THIS COSTUME WAS SO CUTE I THOUGHT I'D GIVE IT A TRY."
OKAY, OKAY. WHATEVER YOU SAY, I'LL JUST PLAY STUPID.
NO, YOU CAN'T PLAY STUPID.

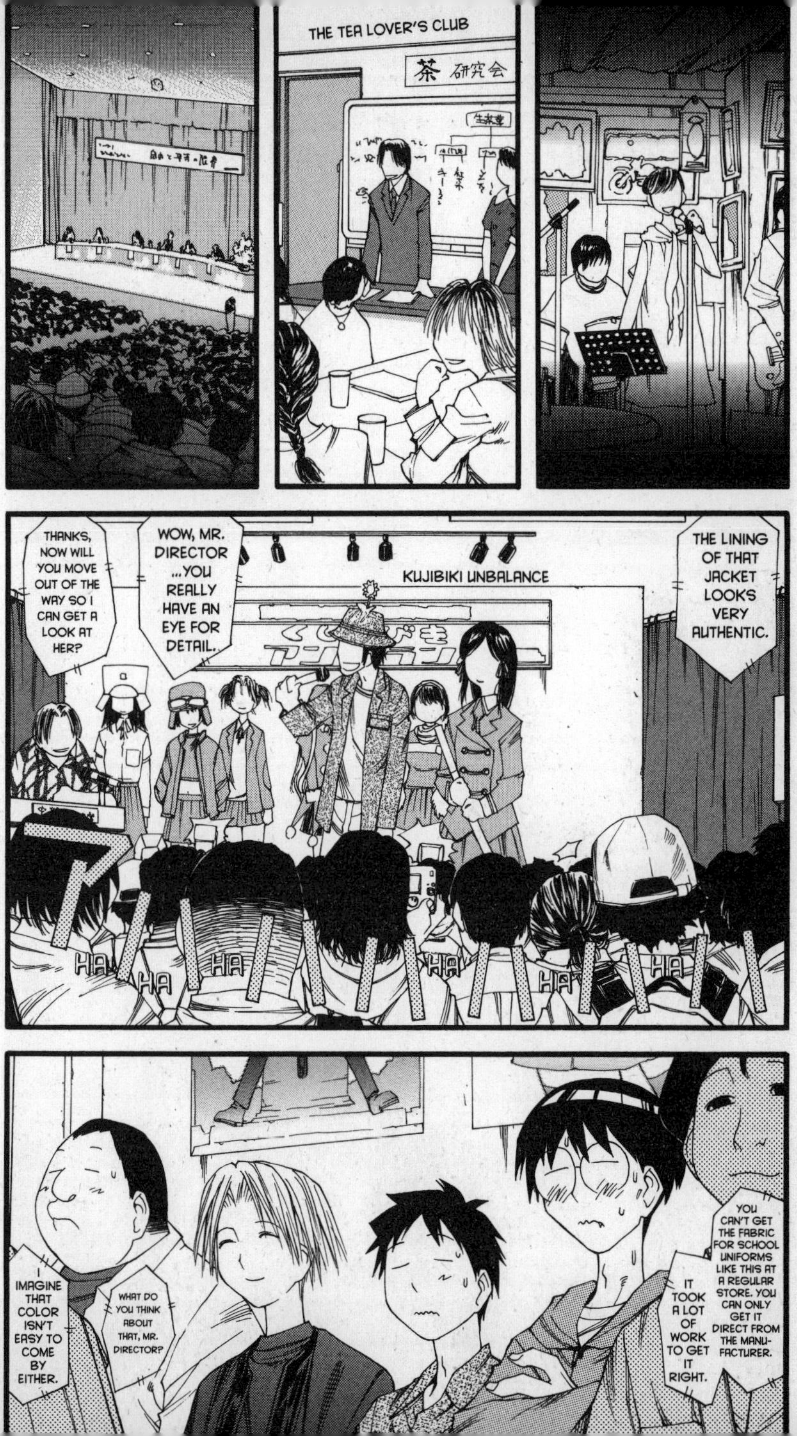
THE TEA LOVER'S CLUB
茶 研究会
THE LINING OF THAT JACKET LOOKS VERY AUTHENTIC.
KUJIBIKI UNBALANCE
WOW, MR. DIRECTOR ...YOU REALLY HAVE AN EYE FOR DETAIL.
THANKS, NOW WILL YOU MOVE OUT OF THE WAY SO I CAN GET A LOOK AT HER?
HA HA HA HA HA HA
YOU CAN'T GET THE FABRIC FOR SCHOOL UNIFORMS LIKE THIS AT A REGULAR STORE. YOU CAN ONLY GET IT DIRECT FROM THE MANUFACTURER.
IT TOOK A LOT OF WORK TO GET IT RIGHT.
WHAT DO YOU THINK ABOUT THAT, MR. DIRECTOR?
I IMAGINE THAT COLOR ISN'T EASY TO COME BY EITHER.

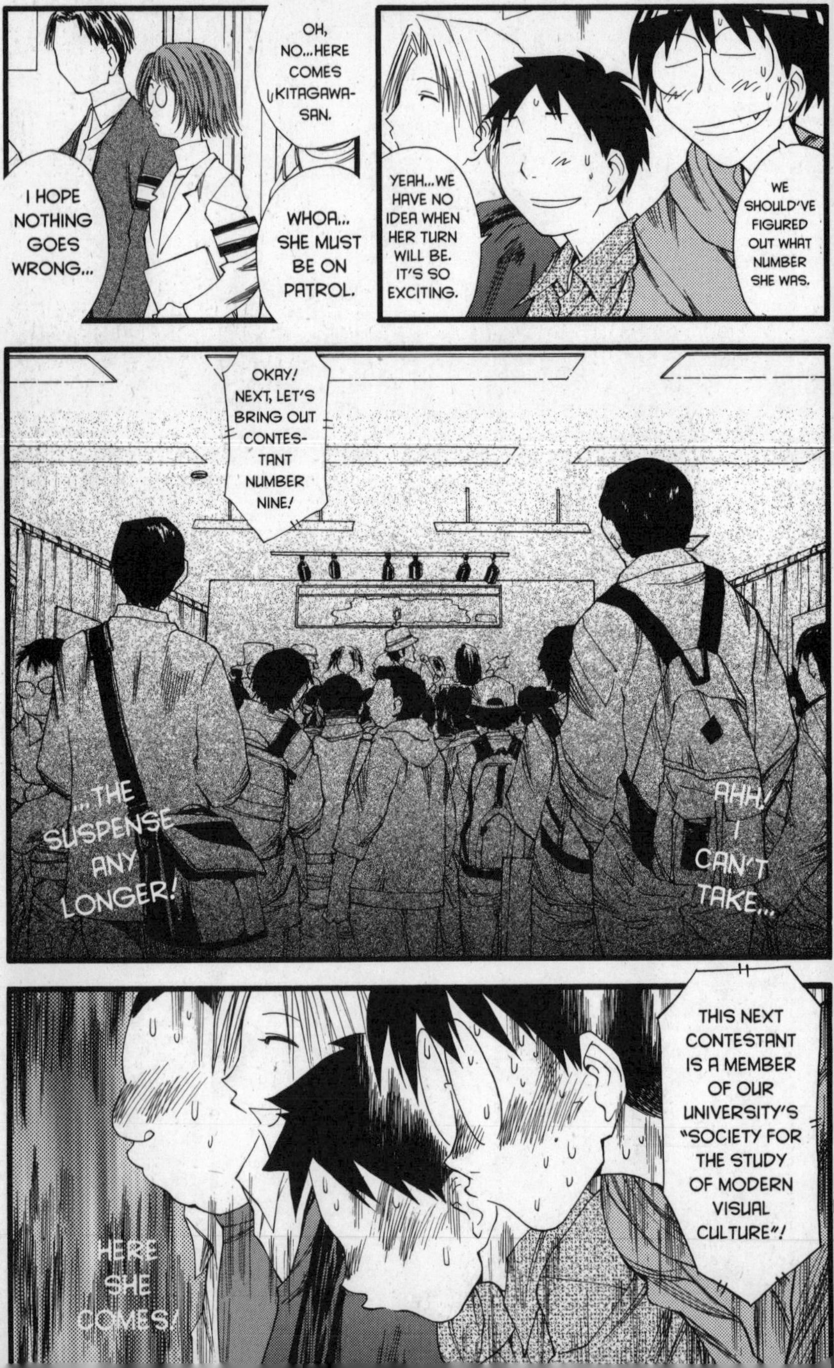
WE SHOULD'VE FIGURED OUT WHAT NUMBER SHE WAS.
YEAH...WE HAVE NO IDEA WHEN HER TURN WILL BE. IT'S SO EXCITING.
OH, NO...HERE COMES KITAGAWA-SAN.
WHOA... SHE MUST BE ON PATROL.
I HOPE NOTHING GOES WRONG...
OKAY! NEXT, LET'S BRING OUT CONTES-TANT NUMBER NINE!
AHH! I CAN'T TAKE...
...THE SUSPENSE ANY LONGER!
THIS NEXT CONTESTANT IS A MEMBER OF OUR UNIVERSITY'S "SOCIETY FOR THE STUDY OF MODERN VISUAL CULTURE"!
HERE SHE COMES!

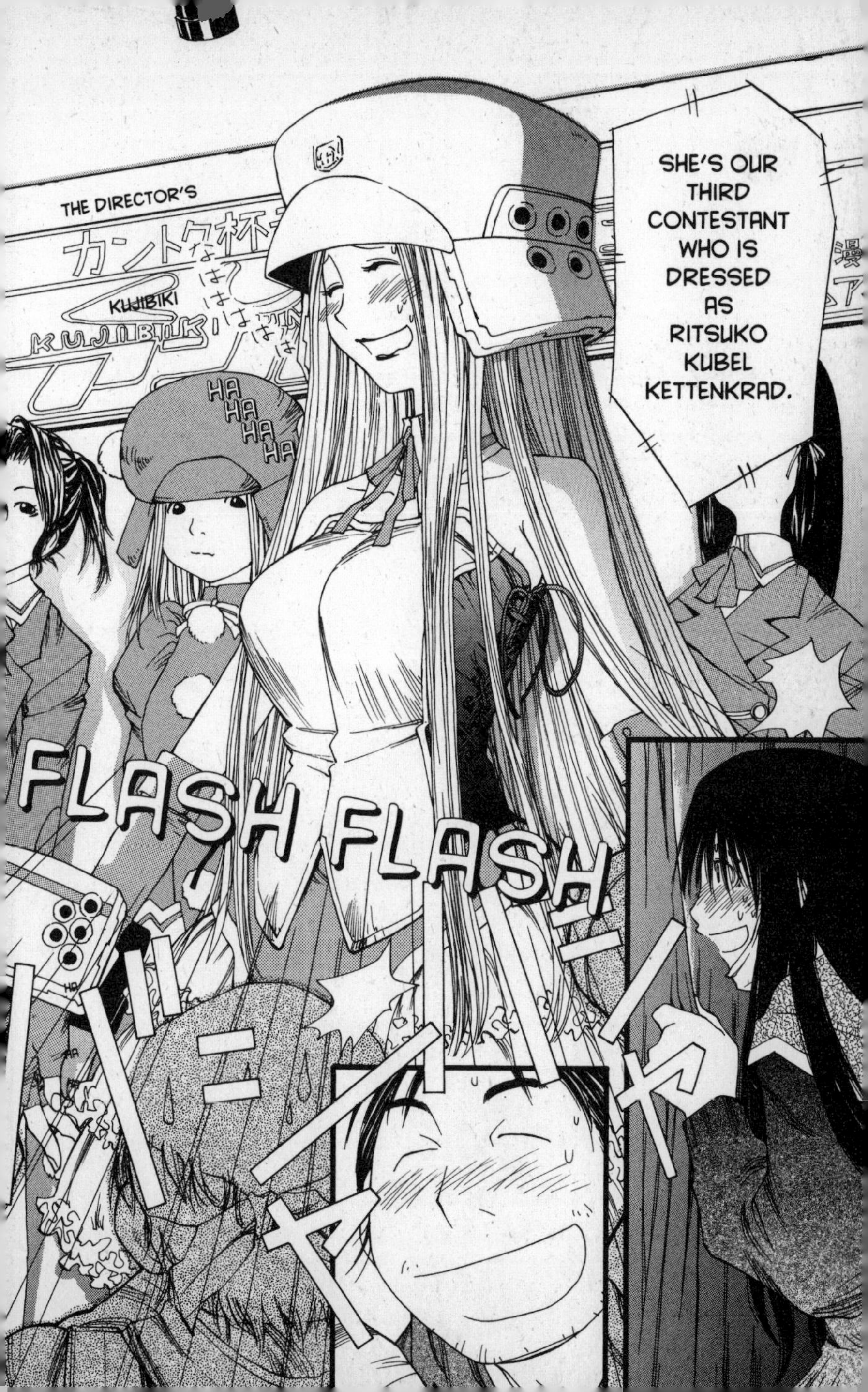
SHE'S OUR THIRD CONTESTANT WHO IS DRESSED AS RITSUKO KUBEL KETTENKRAD.
THE DIRECTOR'S
KUJIBIKI
HA HA HA HA
FLASH FLASH

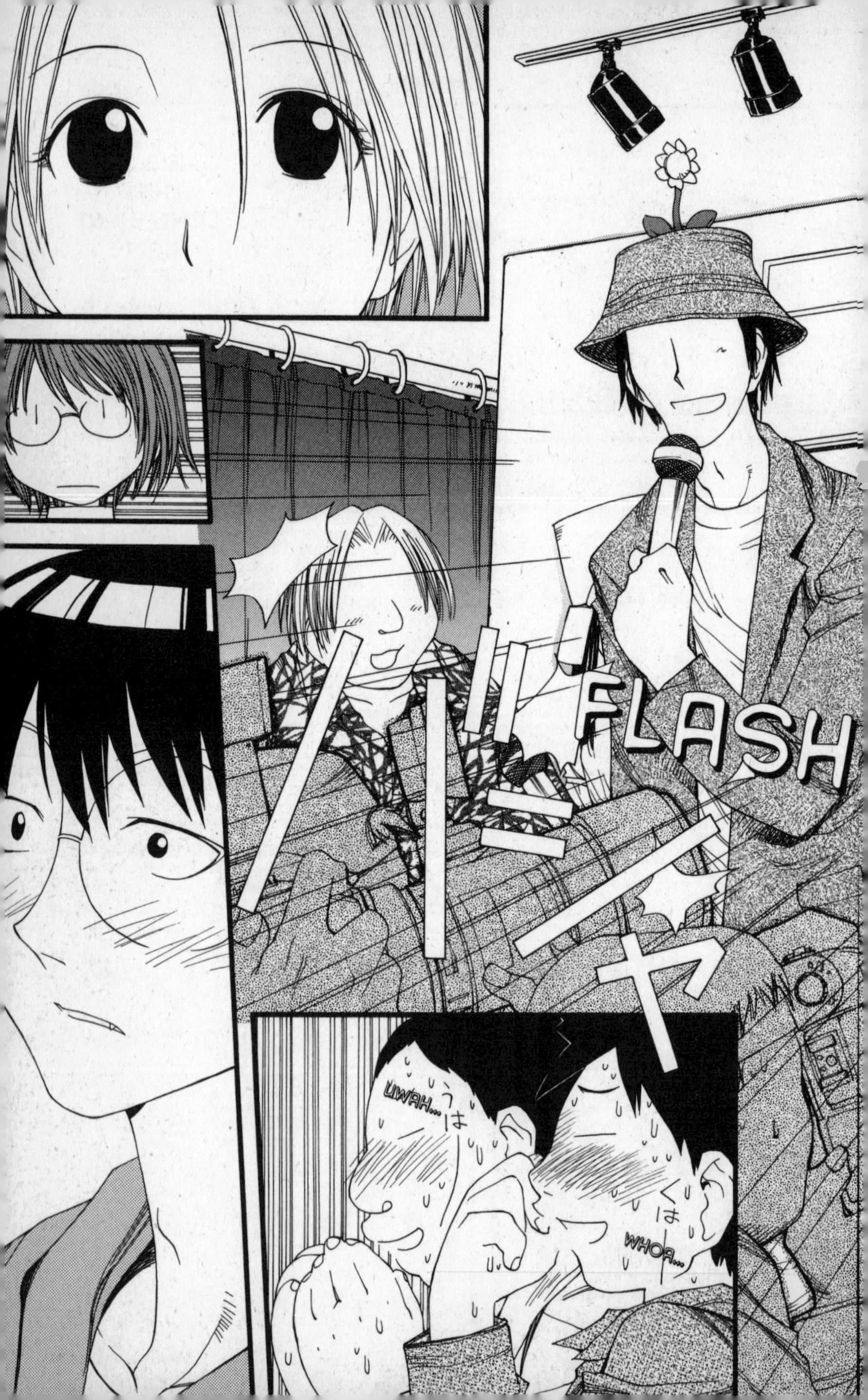
FLASH
くは
WHOA...
っは
UWAH...

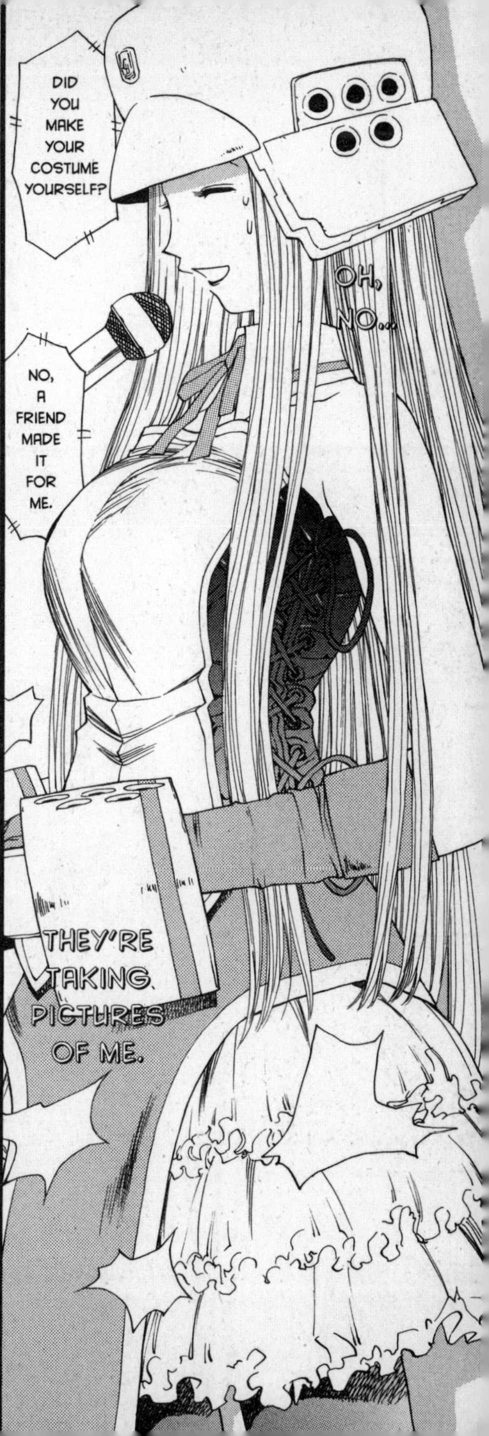
DID YOU MAKE YOUR COSTUME YOURSELF?
OH, NO...
NO, A FRIEND MADE IT FOR ME.
THEY'RE TAKING PICTURES OF ME.

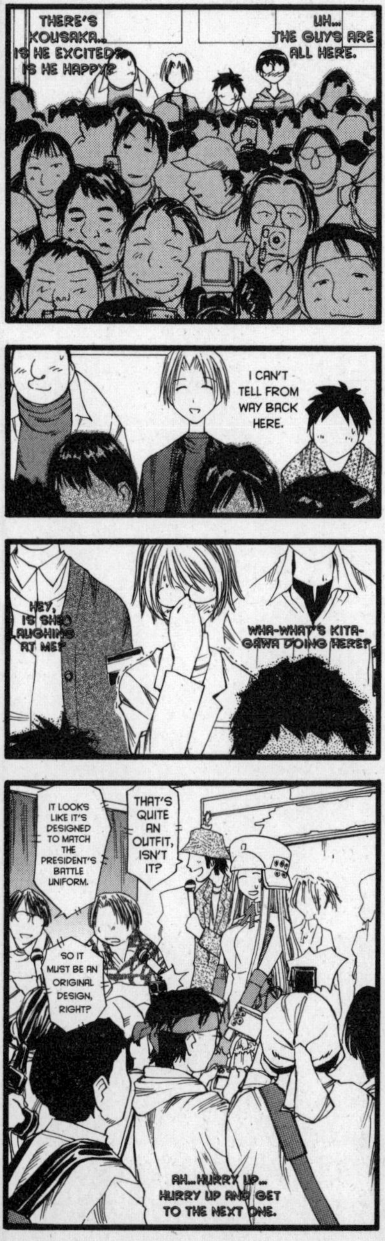
UH... THE GUYS ARE ALL HERE.
THERE'S KOUSAKA... IS HE EXCITED? IS HE HAPPY?
I CAN'T TELL FROM WAY BACK HERE.
WHA-WHAT'S KITA-GAWA DOING HERE?
HEY, IS SHE LAUGHING AT ME?
THAT'S QUITE AN OUTFIT, ISN'T IT?
IT LOOKS LIKE IT'S DESIGNED TO MATCH THE PRESIDENT'S BATTLE UNIFORM.
SO IT MUST BE AN ORIGINAL DESIGN, RIGHT?
AH...HURRY UP... HURRY UP AND GET TO THE NEXT ONE.

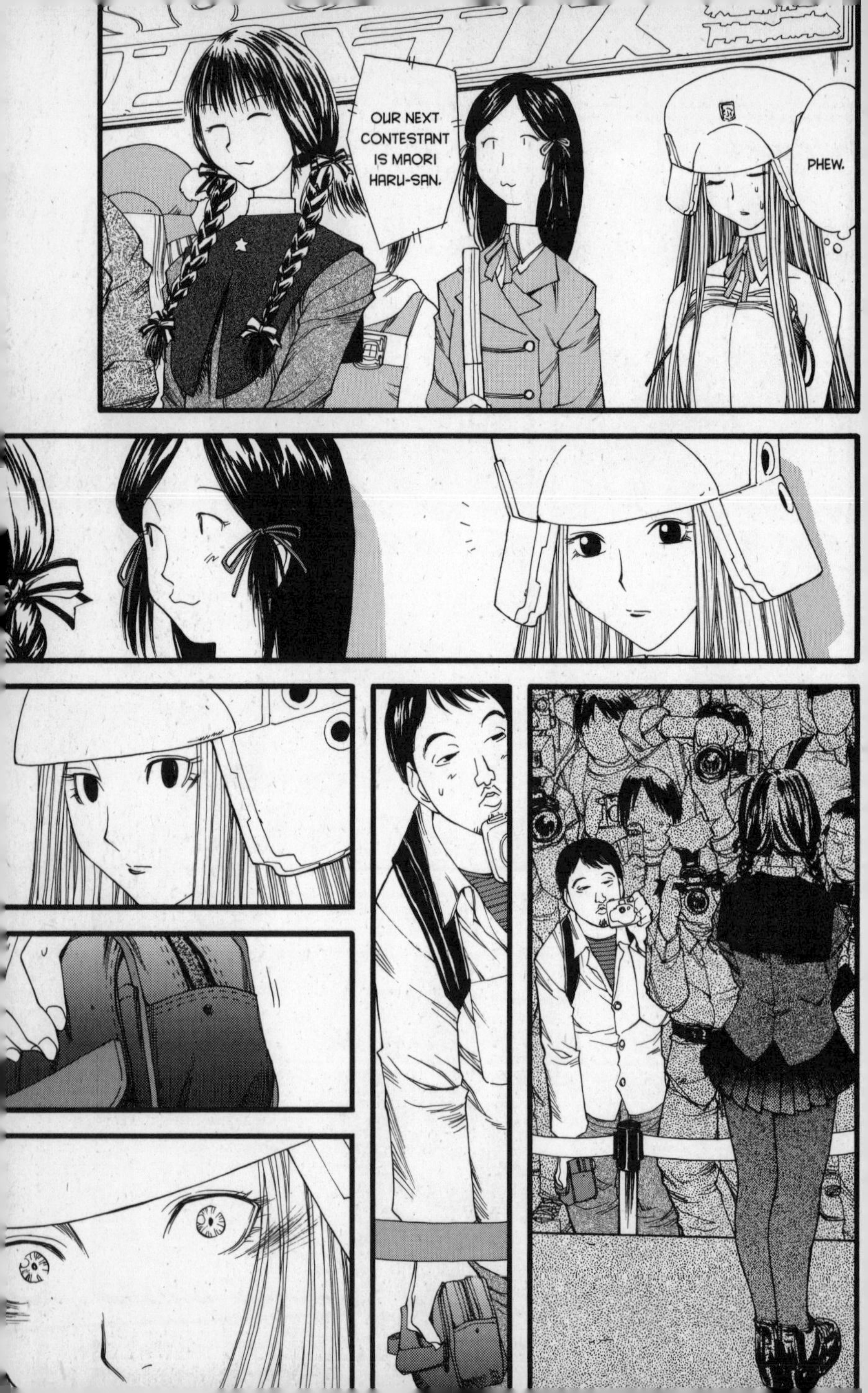
PHEW.
OUR NEXT CONTESTANT IS MAORI HARU-SAN.

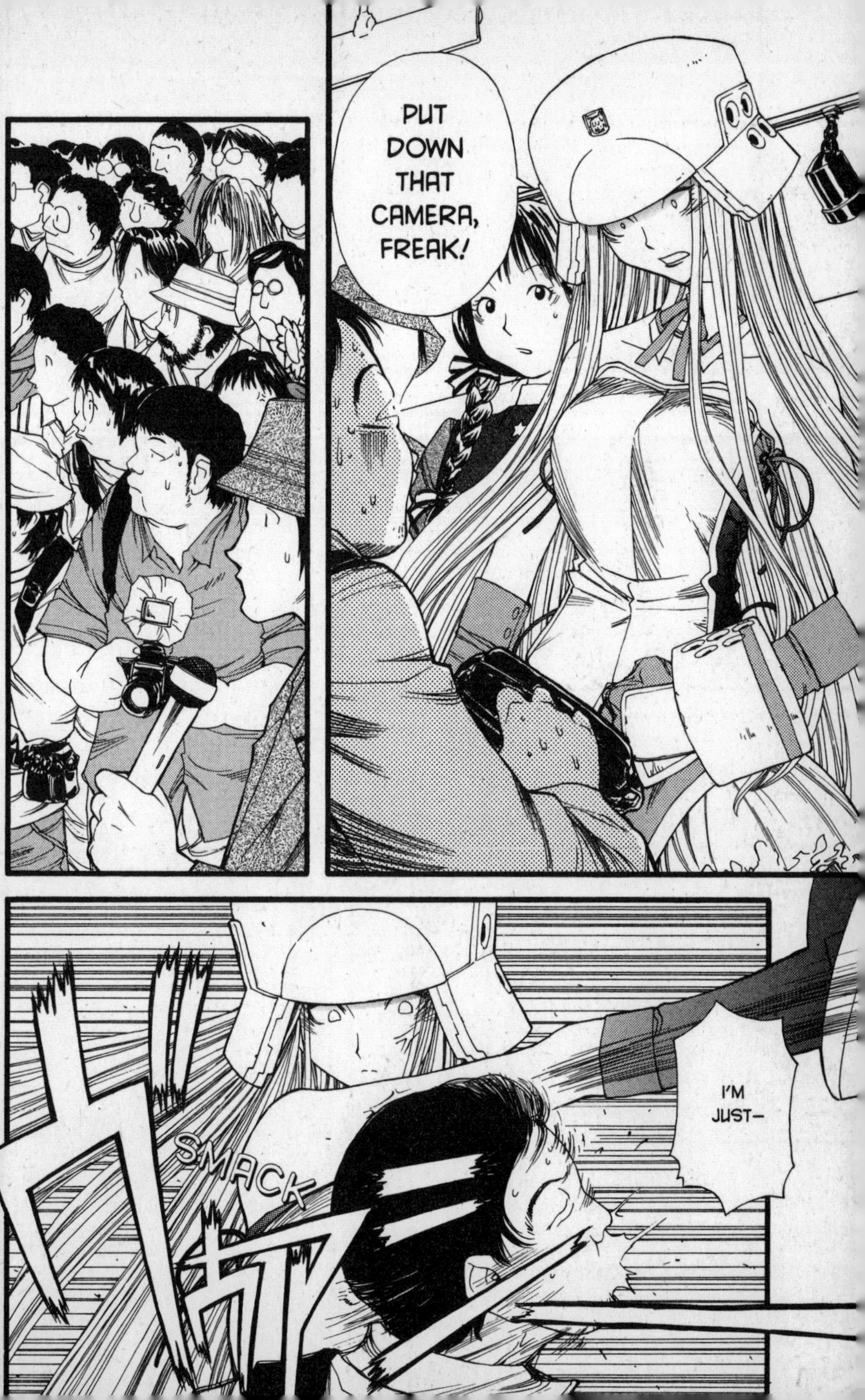
PUT DOWN THAT CAMERA, FREAK!
I'M JUST–
SMACK

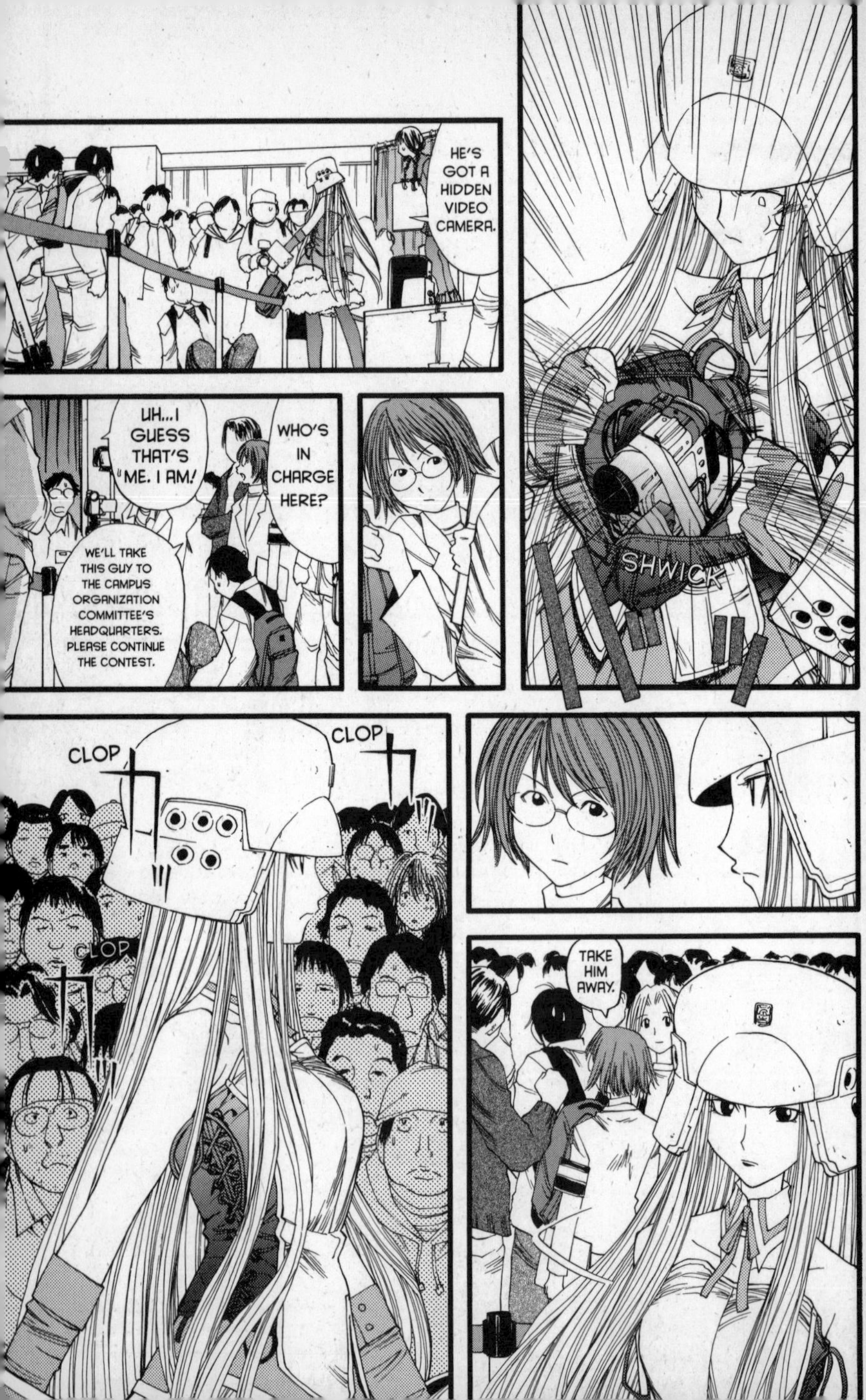
SHWICK
HE'S GOT A HIDDEN VIDEO CAMERA.
WHO'S IN CHARGE HERE?
UH...I GUESS THAT'S ME. I AM!
WE'LL TAKE THIS GUY TO THE CAMPUS ORGANIZATION COMMITTEE'S HEADQUARTERS. PLEASE CONTINUE THE CONTEST.
TAKE HIM AWAY.
CLOP
CLOP
CLOP

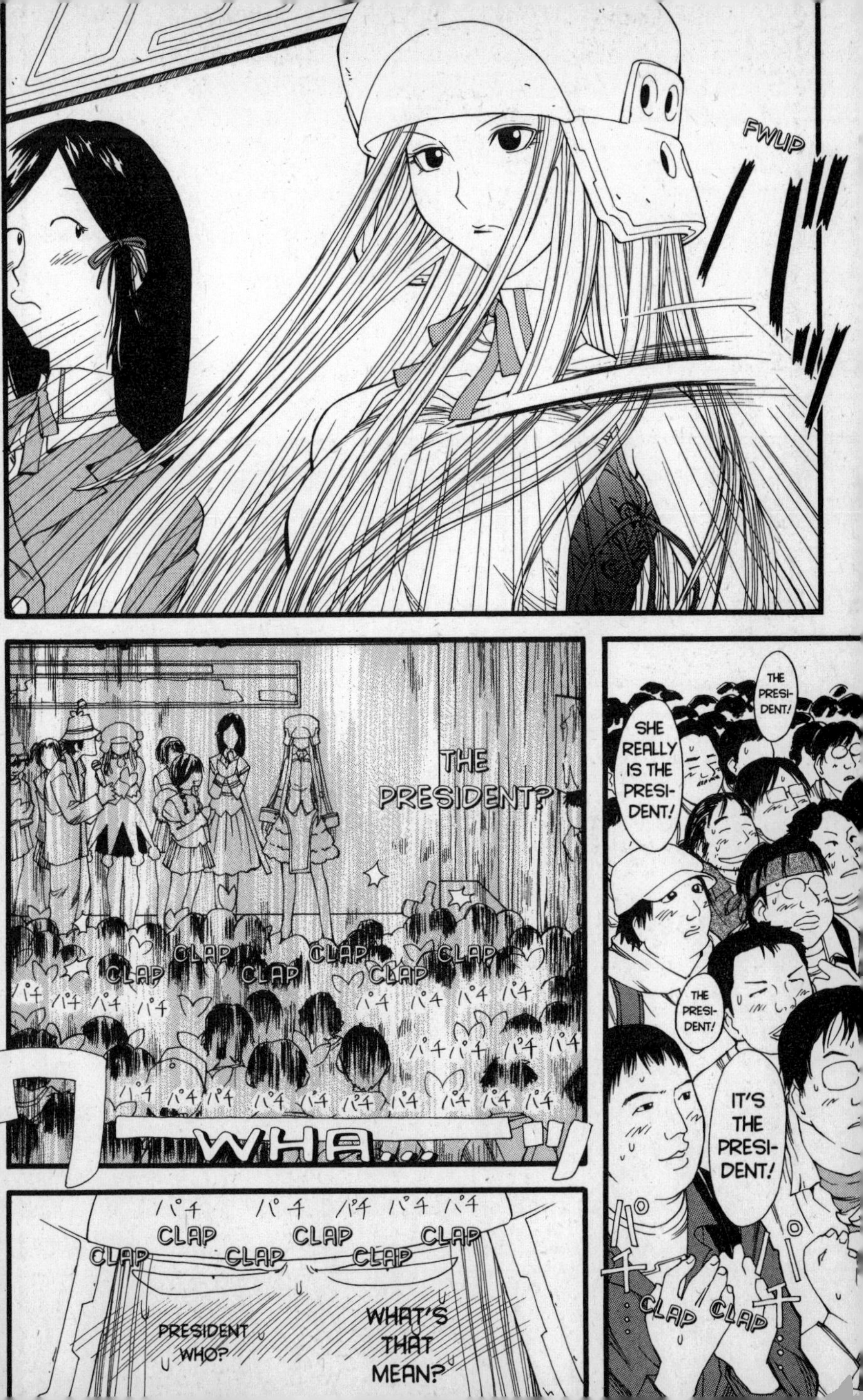
FWUP
THE PRESIDENT!
SHE REALLY IS THE PRESI-DENT!
THE PRESI-DENT!
IT'S THE PRESI-DENT!
CLAP CLAP
THE PRESIDENT?
CLAP CLAP CLAP CLAP CLAP CLAP
WHA...
CLAP CLAP CLAP CLAP CLAP CLAP
WHAT'S THAT MEAN?
PRESIDENT WHO?

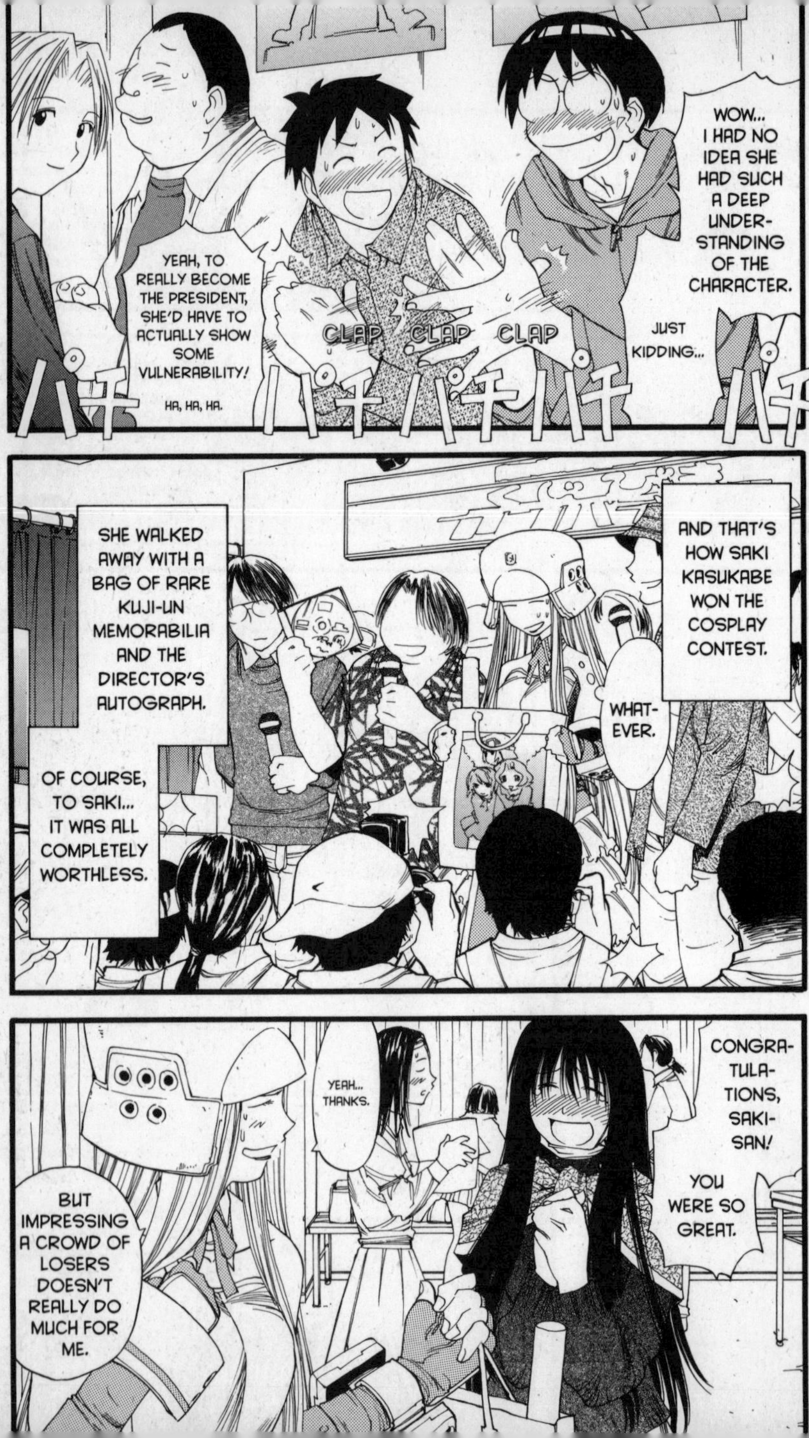
WOW... I HAD NO IDEA SHE HAD SUCH A DEEP UNDER-STANDING OF THE CHARACTER.
JUST KIDDING...
CLAP CLAP CLAP
パチ パチ パチ パチ
YEAH, TO REALLY BECOME THE PRESIDENT, SHE'D HAVE TO ACTUALLY SHOW SOME VULNERABILITY!
HA, HA, HA.
AND THAT'S HOW SAKI KASUKABE WON THE COSPLAY CONTEST.
WHAT-EVER.
SHE WALKED AWAY WITH A BAG OF RARE KUJI-UN MEMORABILIA AND THE DIRECTOR'S AUTOGRAPH.
OF COURSE, TO SAKI... IT WAS ALL COMPLETELY WORTHLESS.
CONGRA-TULA-TIONS, SAKI-SAN!
YOU WERE SO GREAT.
YEAH... THANKS.
BUT IMPRESSING A CROWD OF LOSERS DOESN'T REALLY DO MUCH FOR ME.

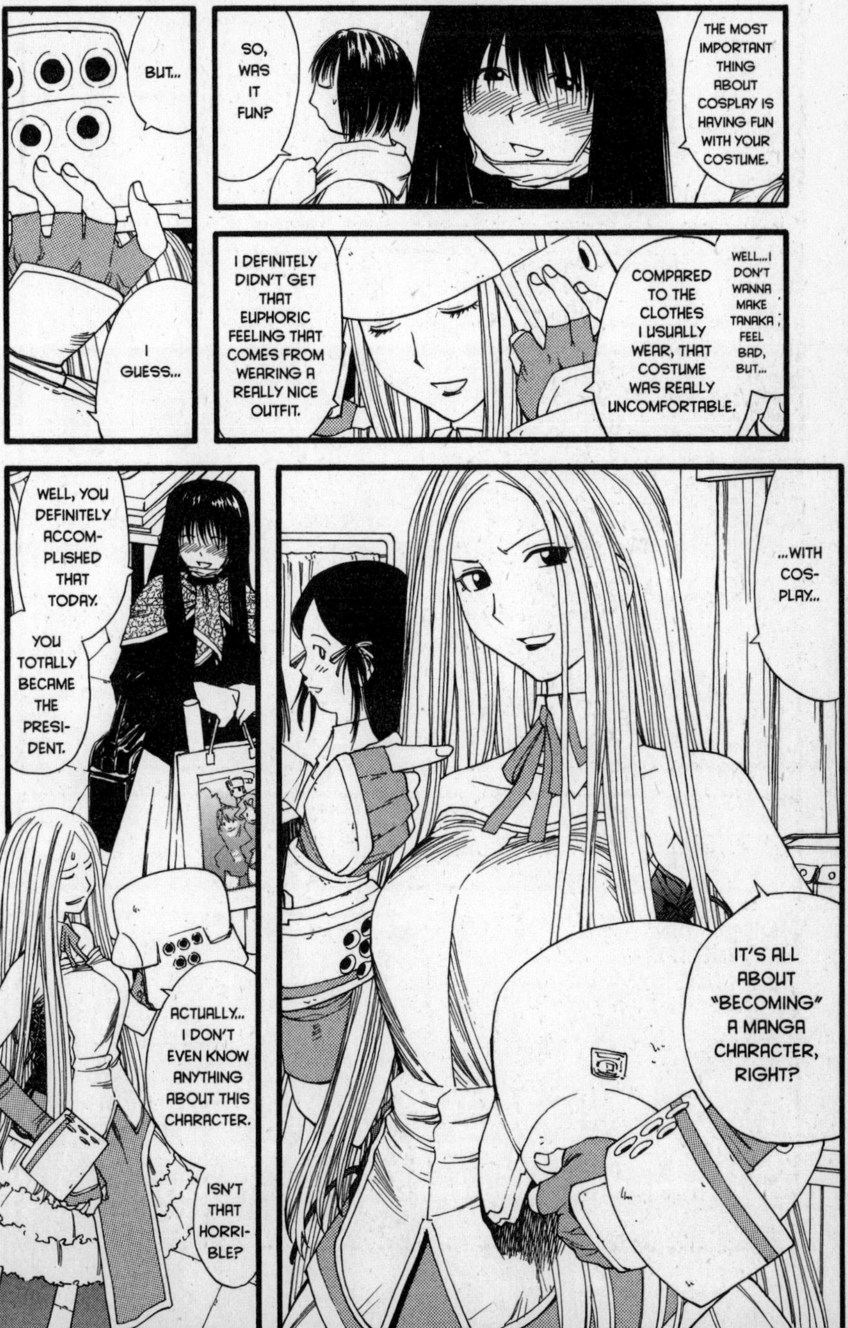
THE MOST IMPORTANT THING ABOUT COSPLAY IS HAVING FUN WITH YOUR COSTUME.
SO, WAS IT FUN?
WELL...I DON'T WANNA MAKE TANAKA FEEL BAD, BUT...
COMPARED TO THE CLOTHES I USUALLY WEAR, THAT COSTUME WAS REALLY UNCOMFORTABLE.
I DEFINITELY DIDN'T GET THAT EUPHORIC FEELING THAT COMES FROM WEARING A REALLY NICE OUTFIT.
BUT...
I GUESS...
...WITH COS-PLAY...
IT'S ALL ABOUT "BECOMING" A MANGA CHARACTER, RIGHT?
WELL, YOU DEFINITELY ACCOM-PLISHED THAT TODAY.
YOU TOTALLY BECAME THE PRESI-DENT.
ACTUALLY... I DON'T EVEN KNOW ANYTHING ABOUT THIS CHARACTER.
ISN'T THAT HORRI-BLE?

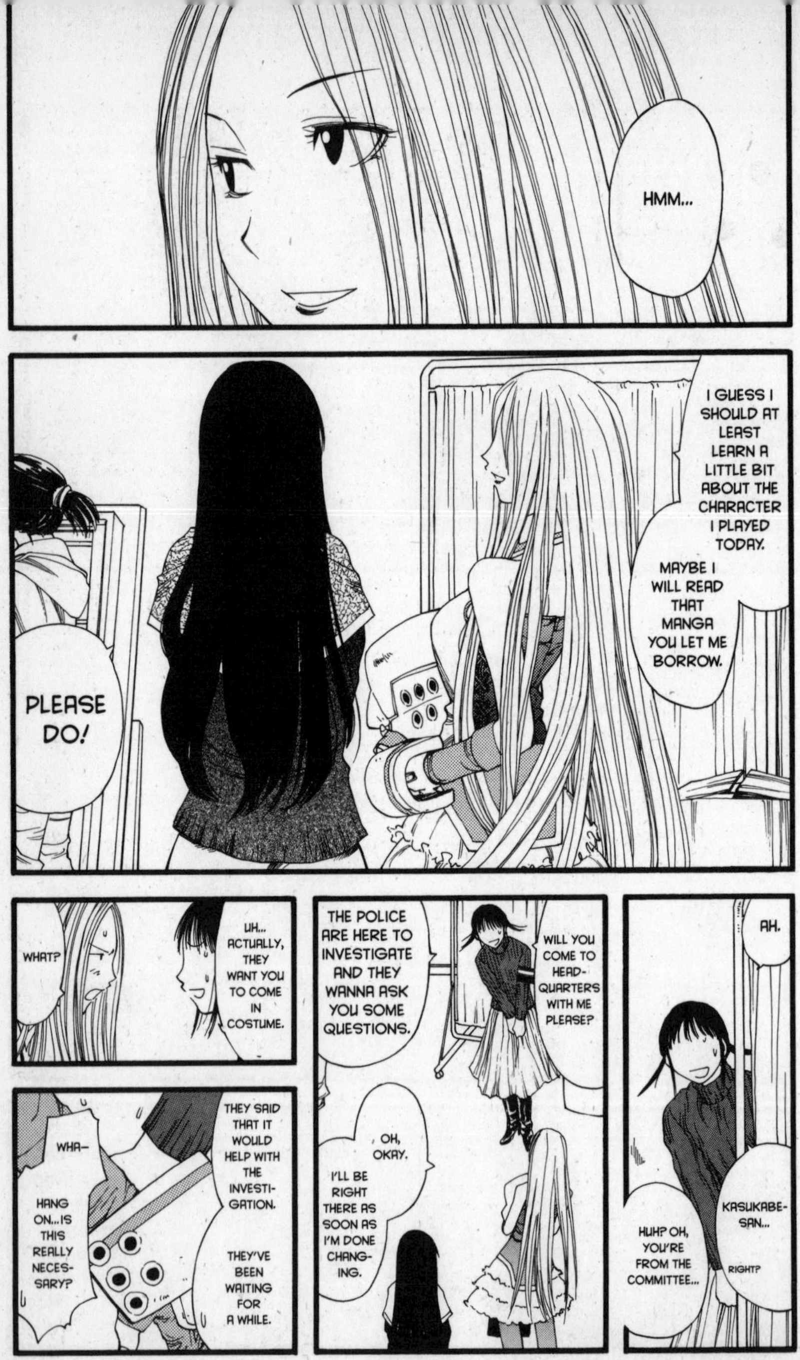
HMM...
I GUESS I SHOULD AT LEAST LEARN A LITTLE BIT ABOUT THE CHARACTER I PLAYED TODAY.
MAYBE I WILL READ THAT MANGA YOU LET ME BORROW.
PLEASE DO!
AH.
KASUKABE-SAN...
RIGHT?
HUH? OH, YOU'RE FROM THE COMMITTEE...
WILL YOU COME TO HEAD-QUARTERS WITH ME PLEASE?
THE POLICE ARE HERE TO INVESTIGATE AND THEY WANNA ASK YOU SOME QUESTIONS.
OH, OKAY.
I'LL BE RIGHT THERE AS SOON AS I'M DONE CHANG-ING.
UH... ACTUALLY, THEY WANT YOU TO COME IN COSTUME.
WHAT?
THEY SAID THAT IT WOULD HELP WITH THE INVESTI-GATION.
THEY'VE BEEN WAITING FOR A WHILE.
WHA-
HANG ON...IS THIS REALLY NECES-SARY?

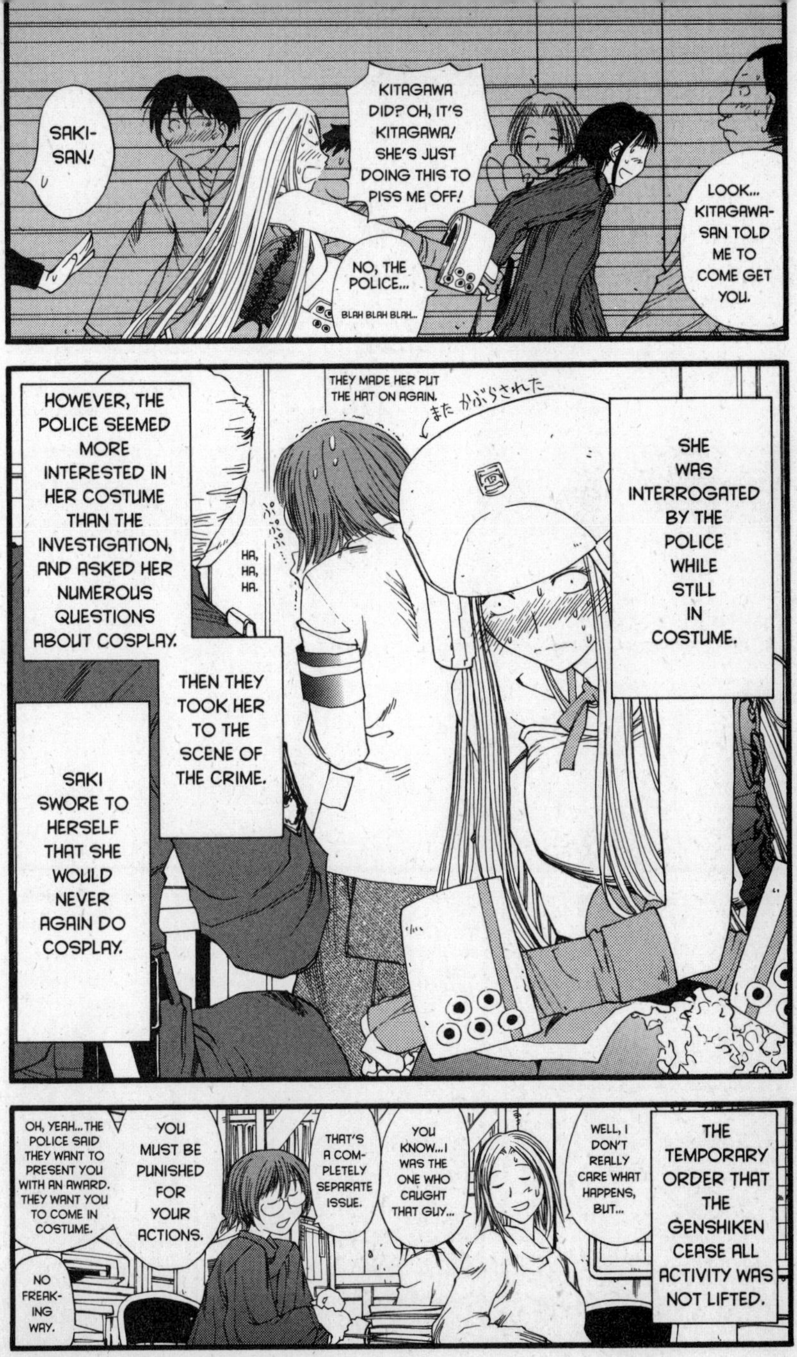
LOOK... KITAGAWA-SAN TOLD ME TO COME GET YOU.
KITAGAWA DID? OH, IT'S KITAGAWA! SHE'S JUST DOING THIS TO PISS ME OFF!
NO, THE POLICE...
BLAH BLAH BLAH...
SAKI-SAN!
THEY MADE HER PUT THE HAT ON AGAIN.
またかぶらされた
SHE WAS INTERROGATED BY THE POLICE WHILE STILL IN COSTUME.
HOWEVER, THE POLICE SEEMED MORE INTERESTED IN HER COSTUME THAN THE INVESTIGATION, AND ASKED HER NUMEROUS QUESTIONS ABOUT COSPLAY.
HA, HA, HA.
THEN THEY TOOK HER TO THE SCENE OF THE CRIME.
SAKI SWORE TO HERSELF THAT SHE WOULD NEVER AGAIN DO COSPLAY.
THE TEMPORARY ORDER THAT THE GENSHIKEN CEASE ALL ACTIVITY WAS NOT LIFTED.
WELL, I DON'T REALLY CARE WHAT HAPPENS, BUT...
YOU KNOW... I WAS THE ONE WHO CAUGHT THAT GUY...
THAT'S A COM-PLETELY SEPARATE ISSUE.
YOU MUST BE PUNISHED FOR YOUR ACTIONS.
OH, YEAH... THE POLICE SAID THEY WANT TO PRESENT YOU WITH AN AWARD. THEY WANT YOU TO COME IN COSTUME.
NO FREAK-ING WAY.

END OF CHAPTER 19

# OUR FAVORITE GAME ANOTHER STORIES

STORY 1

## RENKO KAMISHAKUJII

REVIEWED BY 72-YEAR-OLD PIT VIPER

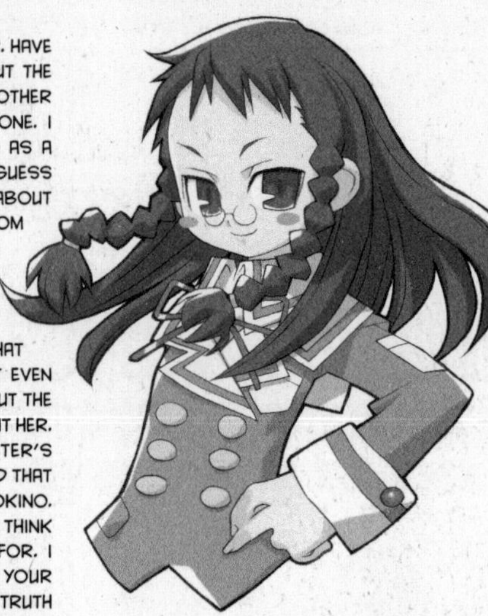

HELLO AGAIN! IT'S ME, THE PIT VIPER. HAVE YOU PLAYED IT YET? I'M TALKING ABOUT THE NEW KUJIBIKI UNBALANCE GAME "ANOTHER STORIES." YEAH...THIS IS A STRANGE ONE. I MEAN, THEY DON'T EVEN HAVE TOKINO AS A CHARACTER. [HA HA] UNBELIEVABLE. I GUESS THEY'RE TRYING TO SAY, GO READ ABOUT TOKINO ON YOUR OWN. THE STORIES FROM THE MANGA MAKE UP JUST A SMALL PART OF THE SCENARIOS THAT APPEAR IN THE GAME. THAT WAS A PRETTY GUTSY MOVE ON THE PART OF THE GAME'S CREATORS. IT'S AMAZING THAT THEY LET THEM MAKE A GAME WITHOUT EVEN USING THE SHOW'S MAIN CHARACTER, BUT THE SALES HAVE BEEN STRONG EVEN WITHOUT HER. [LAUGH] ACTUALLY, EACH CHARACTER'S SCENARIO IS SO COMPLEX AND DETAILED THAT I THINK IT'S A SUCCESS EVEN WITHOUT TOKINO. IT LITERALLY IS "ANOTHER STORY," AND I THINK IT'S WHAT THE FANS WERE LOOKING FOR. I THOUGHT IT WAS JUST GONNA BE YOUR TYPICAL "CHARACTER GAME," BUT THE TRUTH IS IT REALLY IMPRESSED ME.

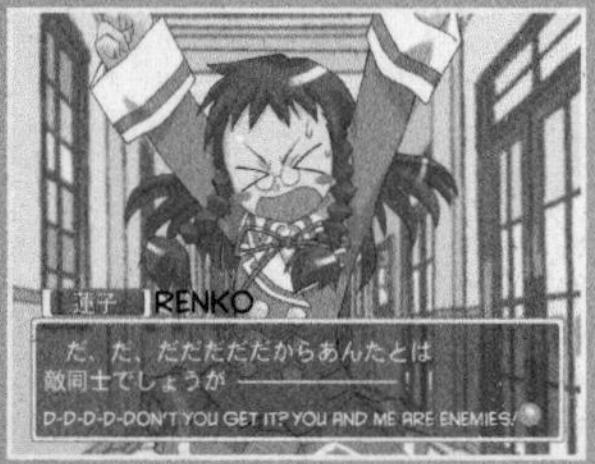
蓮子 RENKO
だ、た、だだだだだからあんたとは
敵同士でしょうが ――――!
D-D-D-D-DON'T YOU GET IT? YOU AND ME ARE ENEMIES!

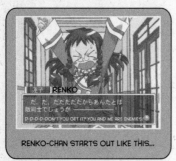

RENKO-CHAN STARTS OUT LIKE THIS...

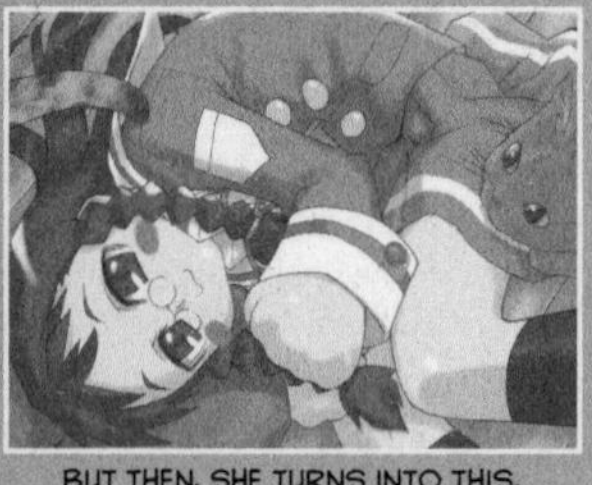

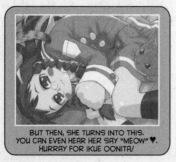

BUT THEN, SHE TURNS INTO THIS.
YOU CAN EVEN HEAR HER SAY "MEOW"♥.
HURRAY FOR IKUE OONITA!

...WELL, MY DETAILED ANALYSIS OF THE GAME IN GENERAL ENDS HERE. I'M ACTUALLY SUPPOSED TO BE REVIEWING THE RENKO-CHAN SCENARIO!

LET'S SEE...THERE'S ONE KITTY AND ANOTHER AND ANOTHER, AND A KITTY OVER THERE, AND A KITTY OVER THERE...PANT, PANT...SORRY, I'M GETTING AHEAD OF MYSELF. BUT SERIOUSLY, THE MAIN THING I REMEMBER ABOUT THE RENKO-CHAN SCENARIO IS ALL THE CATS. RENKO-CHAN HAS A LOT OF PET CATS IN HER HOUSE. ACTUALLY, I HAVE A CAT IN MY HOUSE TOO, AND THERE'RE A LOT OF SCENES IN THIS SCENARIO THAT CAT LOVERS WILL ENJOY. BUT AFTER A WHILE, EVEN RENKO-CHAN STARTS TO LOOK LIKE A CAT. WHEN YOU PLAY IT IN "RENKO KITTY CAT MODE," IT'S LIKE...WAHHHH! I SAW IT WITH MY OWN EYES RENKO'S EARS TURN INTO CAT EARS. VIVA THE CAT EARS!

THE SCENARIO TAKES PLACE ASSUMING THAT TOKINO AND RENKO-CHAN HAVE ALREADY WORKED OUT THEIR DIFFERENCES, AND RENKO-CHAN BECOMES THE NEXT PRESIDENT. THERE'RE SCENES WHERE SHE'S WEARING THE HELMET, BUT PERSONALLY, ALL I CAN REMEMBER ABOUT IT IS THE CATS. YUP...I WAS THINKING ABOUT HOW, IN THE MANGA, THERE'S NOT REALLY ANY CONNECTION BETWEEN RENKO-CHAN AND CHIHIRO. SO WHAT DOES THAT SAY ABOUT THE RELATIONSHIP BETWEEN TOKINO AND RENKO-CHAN? IN EPISODE 25 OF THE ANIME, RENKO TRIES TO PERSUADE TOKINO TO JOIN HER SIDE...RIGHT? MAYBE IT'S TOO LATE?

## CHAPTER 19 - MOMENTS LATER

THE DOWNSIDE OF BEING A BLONDE

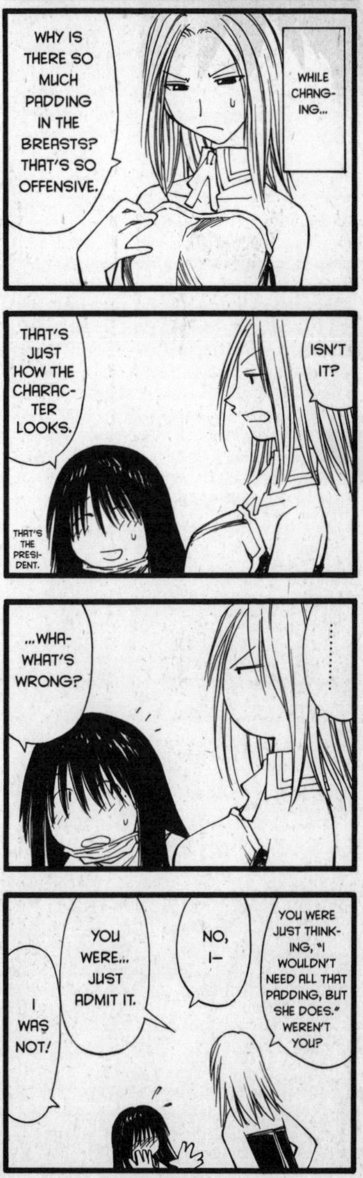
WHILE CHANGING...
WHY IS THERE SO MUCH PADDING IN THE BREASTS? THAT'S SO OFFENSIVE.
ISN'T IT?
THAT'S JUST HOW THE CHARACTER LOOKS.
THAT'S THE PRESIDENT.
...WHA-WHAT'S WRONG?
YOU WERE JUST THINKING, "I WOULDN'T NEED ALL THAT PADDING, BUT SHE DOES." WEREN'T YOU?
NO, I–
YOU WERE... JUST ADMIT IT.
I WAS NOT!

MATERIALS PROVIDED BY THE MANGA CLUB, ASSEMBLED BY KUGAYAMA

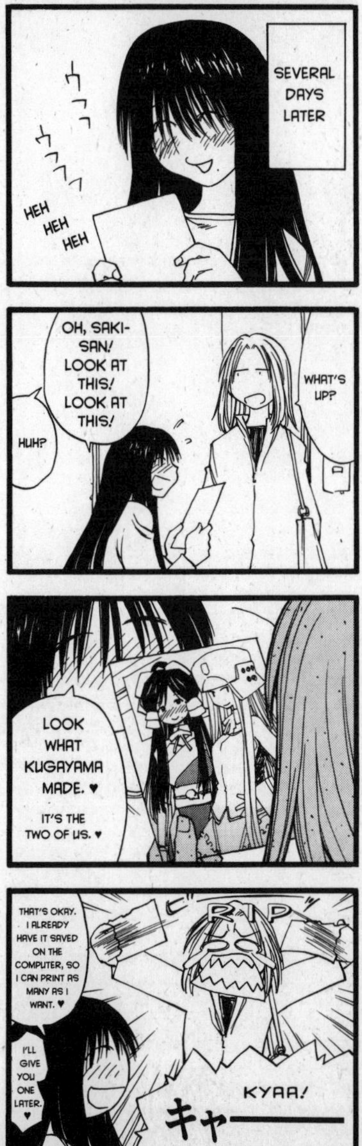
SEVERAL DAYS LATER
ウフフ
ウフフフ
HEH HEH HEH
WHAT'S UP?
OH, SAKI-SAN! LOOK AT THIS! LOOK AT THIS!
HUH?
LOOK WHAT KUGAYAMA MADE. ♥
IT'S THE TWO OF US. ♥
RIP
THAT'S OKAY. I ALREADY HAVE IT SAVED ON THE COMPUTER, SO I CAN PRINT AS MANY AS I WANT. ♥
KYAA!
キャー
I'LL GIVE YOU ONE LATER. ♥

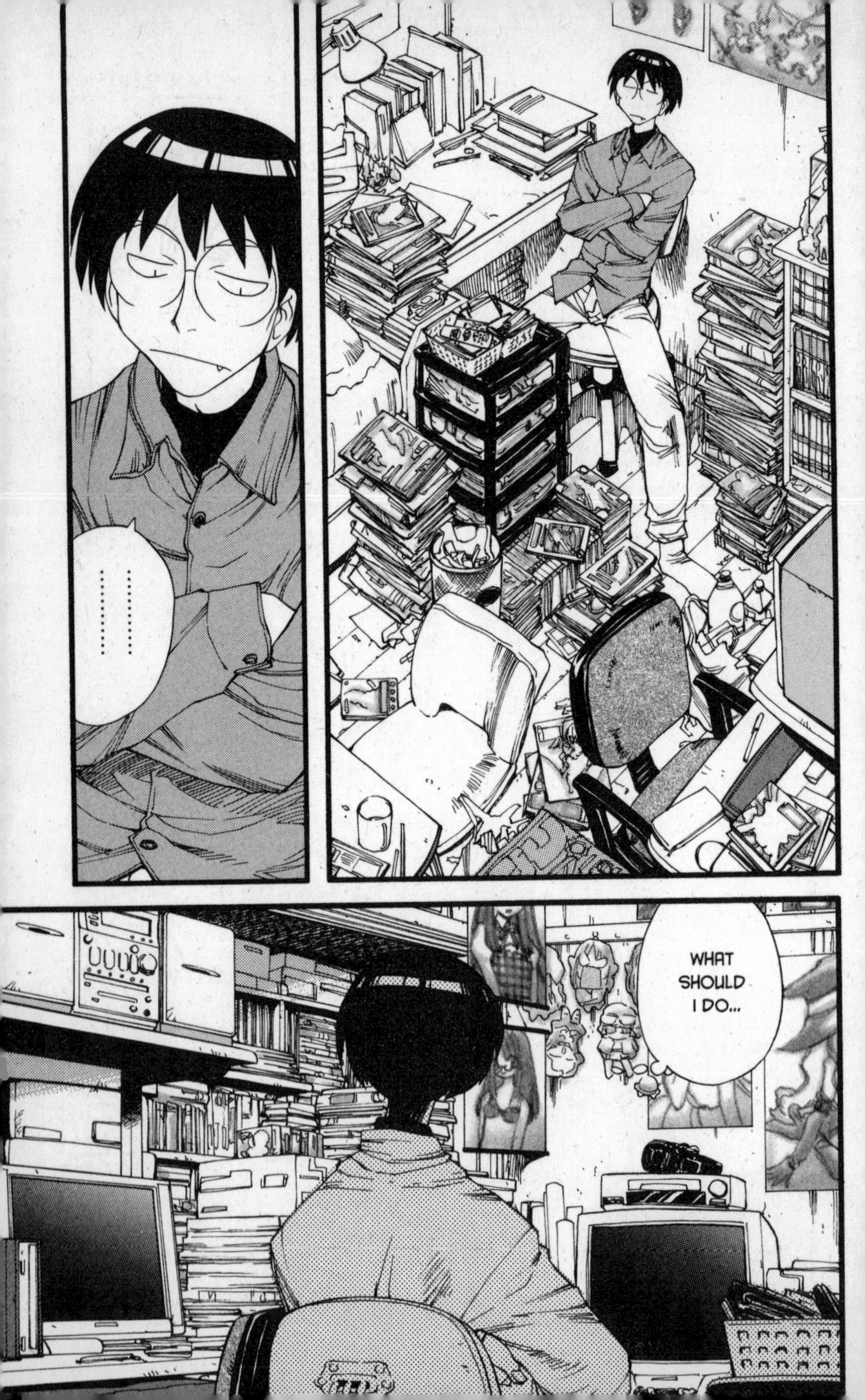
……
WHAT SHOULD I DO...

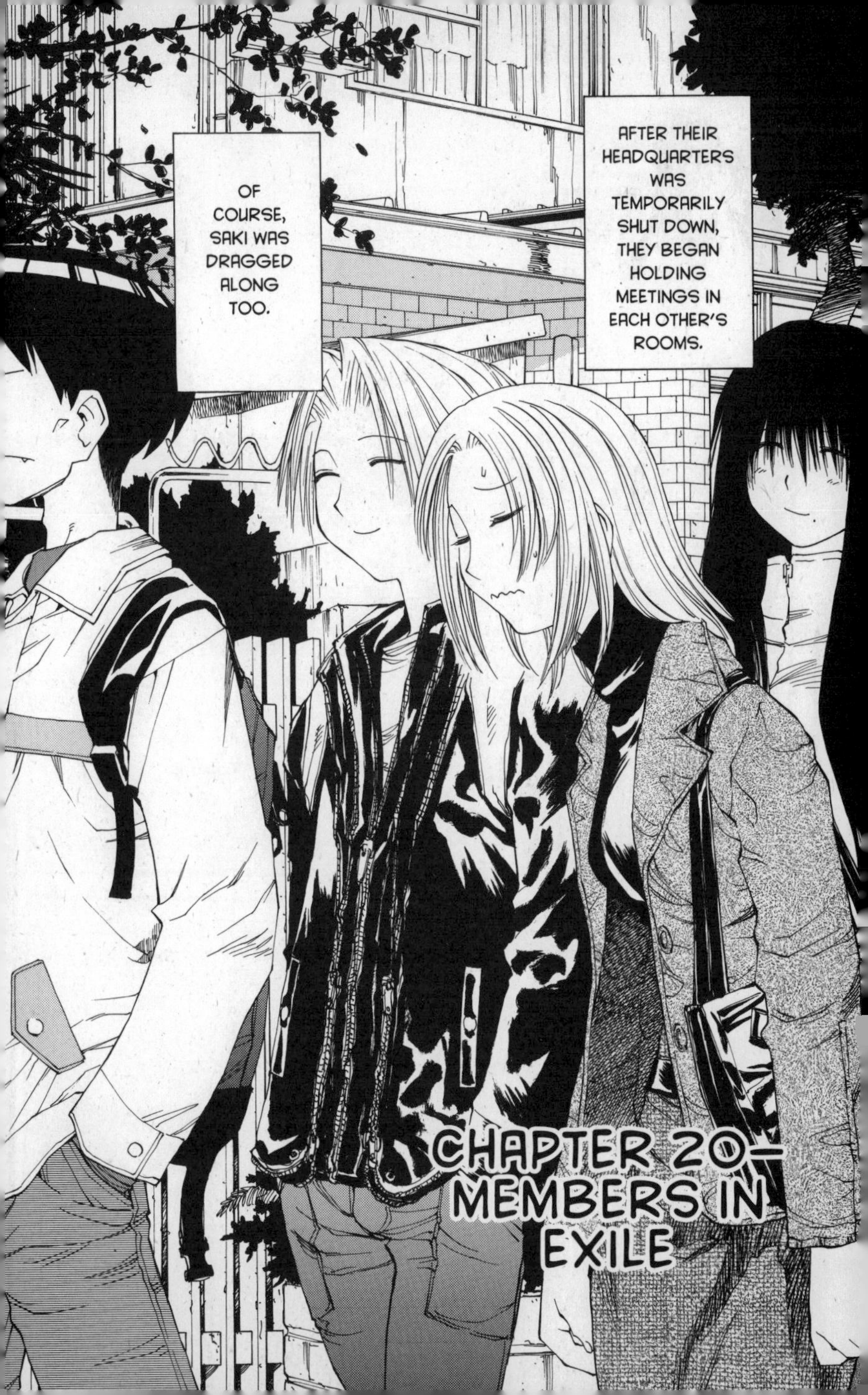
AFTER THEIR HEADQUARTERS WAS TEMPORARILY SHUT DOWN, THEY BEGAN HOLDING MEETINGS IN EACH OTHER'S ROOMS.
OF COURSE, SAKI WAS DRAGGED ALONG TOO.
CHAPTER 20—MEMBERS IN EXILE

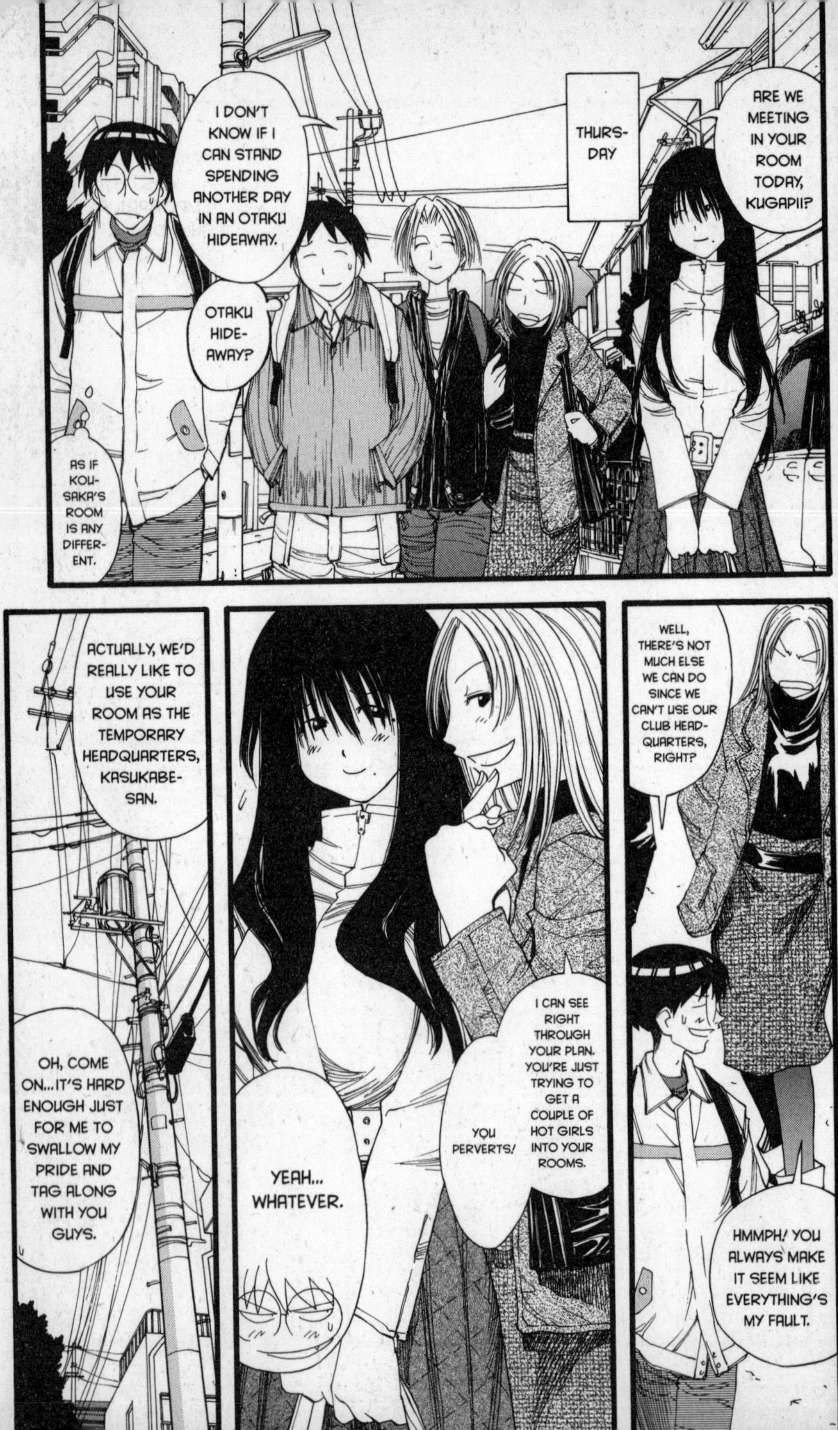
ARE WE MEETING IN YOUR ROOM TODAY, KUGAPII?
THURS-DAY
I DON'T KNOW IF I CAN STAND SPENDING ANOTHER DAY IN AN OTAKU HIDEAWAY.
OTAKU HIDE-AWAY?
AS IF KOU-SAKA'S ROOM IS ANY DIFFER-ENT.
WELL, THERE'S NOT MUCH ELSE WE CAN DO SINCE WE CAN'T USE OUR CLUB HEAD-QUARTERS, RIGHT?
HMMPH! YOU ALWAYS MAKE IT SEEM LIKE EVERYTHING'S MY FAULT.
I CAN SEE RIGHT THROUGH YOUR PLAN. YOU'RE JUST TRYING TO GET A COUPLE OF HOT GIRLS INTO YOUR ROOMS.
YOU PERVERTS!
YEAH... WHATEVER.
ACTUALLY, WE'D REALLY LIKE TO USE YOUR ROOM AS THE TEMPORARY HEADQUARTERS, KASUKABE-SAN.
OH, COME ON...IT'S HARD ENOUGH JUST FOR ME TO SWALLOW MY PRIDE AND TAG ALONG WITH YOU GUYS.

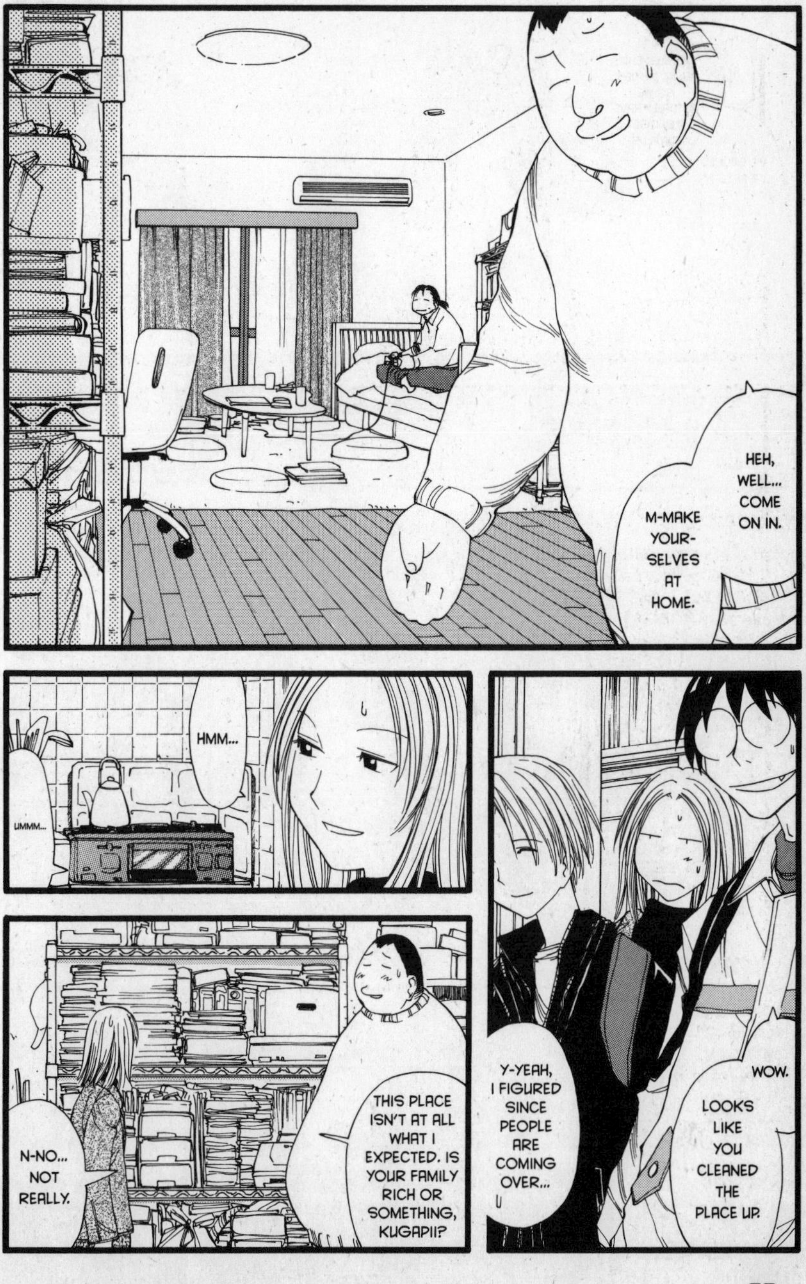
HEH, WELL... COME ON IN.
M-MAKE YOUR-SELVES AT HOME.
WOW.
LOOKS LIKE YOU CLEANED THE PLACE UP.
Y-YEAH, I FIGURED SINCE PEOPLE ARE COMING OVER...
HMM...
UMMM...
THIS PLACE ISN'T AT ALL WHAT I EXPECTED. IS YOUR FAMILY RICH OR SOMETHING, KUGAPII?
N-NO... NOT REALLY.

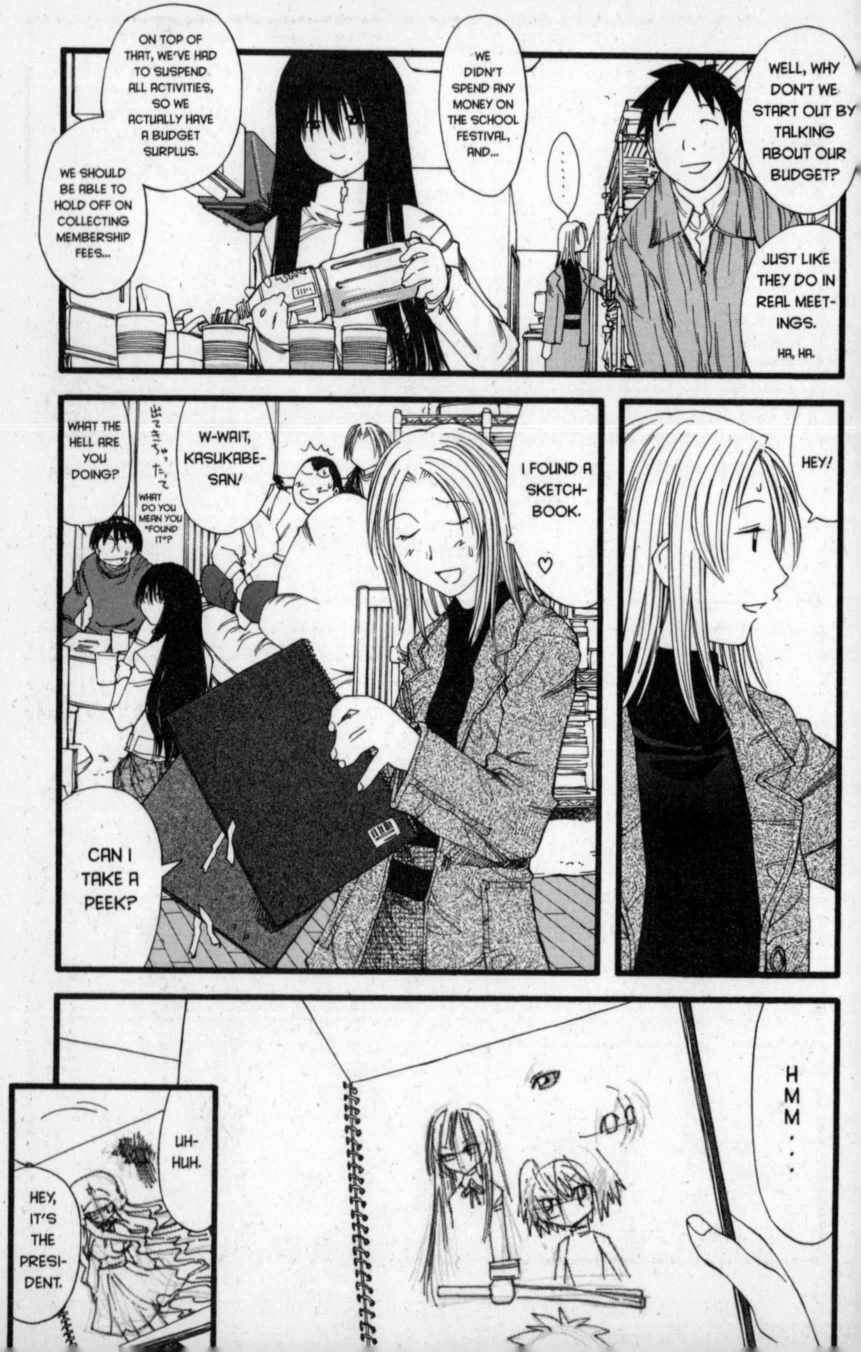
WELL, WHY DON'T WE START OUT BY TALKING ABOUT OUR BUDGET?
JUST LIKE THEY DO IN REAL MEETINGS.
HA, HA.
......
WE DIDN'T SPEND ANY MONEY ON THE SCHOOL FESTIVAL, AND...
ON TOP OF THAT, WE'VE HAD TO SUSPEND ALL ACTIVITIES, SO WE ACTUALLY HAVE A BUDGET SURPLUS.
WE SHOULD BE ABLE TO HOLD OFF ON COLLECTING MEMBERSHIP FEES...
HEY!
I FOUND A SKETCH-BOOK. ♡
W-WAIT, KASUKABE-SAN!
出てきちゃったって
WHAT DO YOU MEAN YOU "FOUND IT"?
WHAT THE HELL ARE YOU DOING?
CAN I TAKE A PEEK?
HMM...
UH-HUH.
HEY, IT'S THE PRESIDENT.

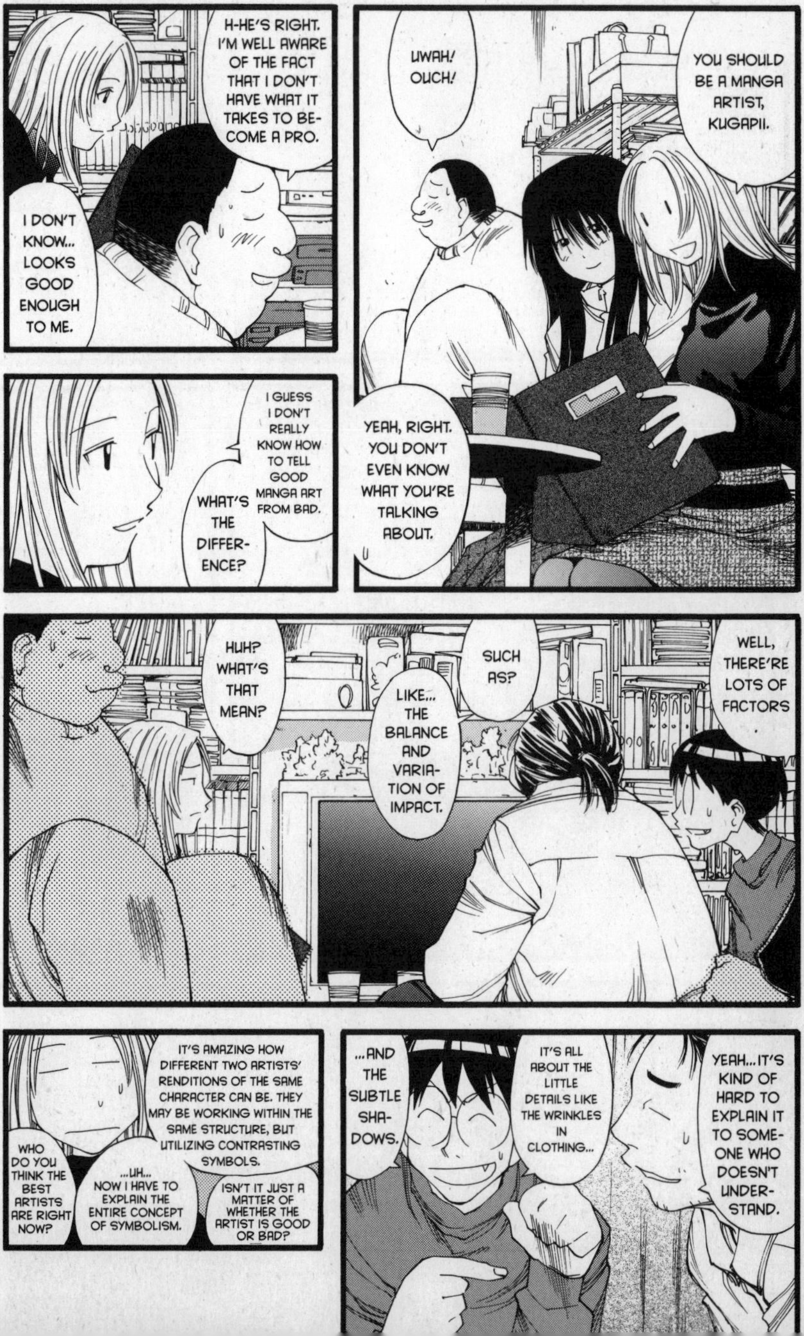
YOU SHOULD BE A MANGA ARTIST, KUGAPII.
UWAH! OUCH!
YEAH, RIGHT. YOU DON'T EVEN KNOW WHAT YOU'RE TALKING ABOUT.
H-HE'S RIGHT. I'M WELL AWARE OF THE FACT THAT I DON'T HAVE WHAT IT TAKES TO BECOME A PRO.
I DON'T KNOW... LOOKS GOOD ENOUGH TO ME.
I GUESS I DON'T REALLY KNOW HOW TO TELL GOOD MANGA ART FROM BAD.
WHAT'S THE DIFFERENCE?
WELL, THERE'RE LOTS OF FACTORS.
SUCH AS?
LIKE... THE BALANCE AND VARIATION OF IMPACT.
HUH? WHAT'S THAT MEAN?
YEAH... IT'S KIND OF HARD TO EXPLAIN IT TO SOMEONE WHO DOESN'T UNDERSTAND.
IT'S ALL ABOUT THE LITTLE DETAILS LIKE THE WRINKLES IN CLOTHING...
...AND THE SUBTLE SHADOWS.
IT'S AMAZING HOW DIFFERENT TWO ARTISTS' RENDITIONS OF THE SAME CHARACTER CAN BE. THEY MAY BE WORKING WITHIN THE SAME STRUCTURE, BUT UTILIZING CONTRASTING SYMBOLS.
ISN'T IT JUST A MATTER OF WHETHER THE ARTIST IS GOOD OR BAD?
...UH... NOW I HAVE TO EXPLAIN THE ENTIRE CONCEPT OF SYMBOLISM.
WHO DO YOU THINK THE BEST ARTISTS ARE RIGHT NOW?

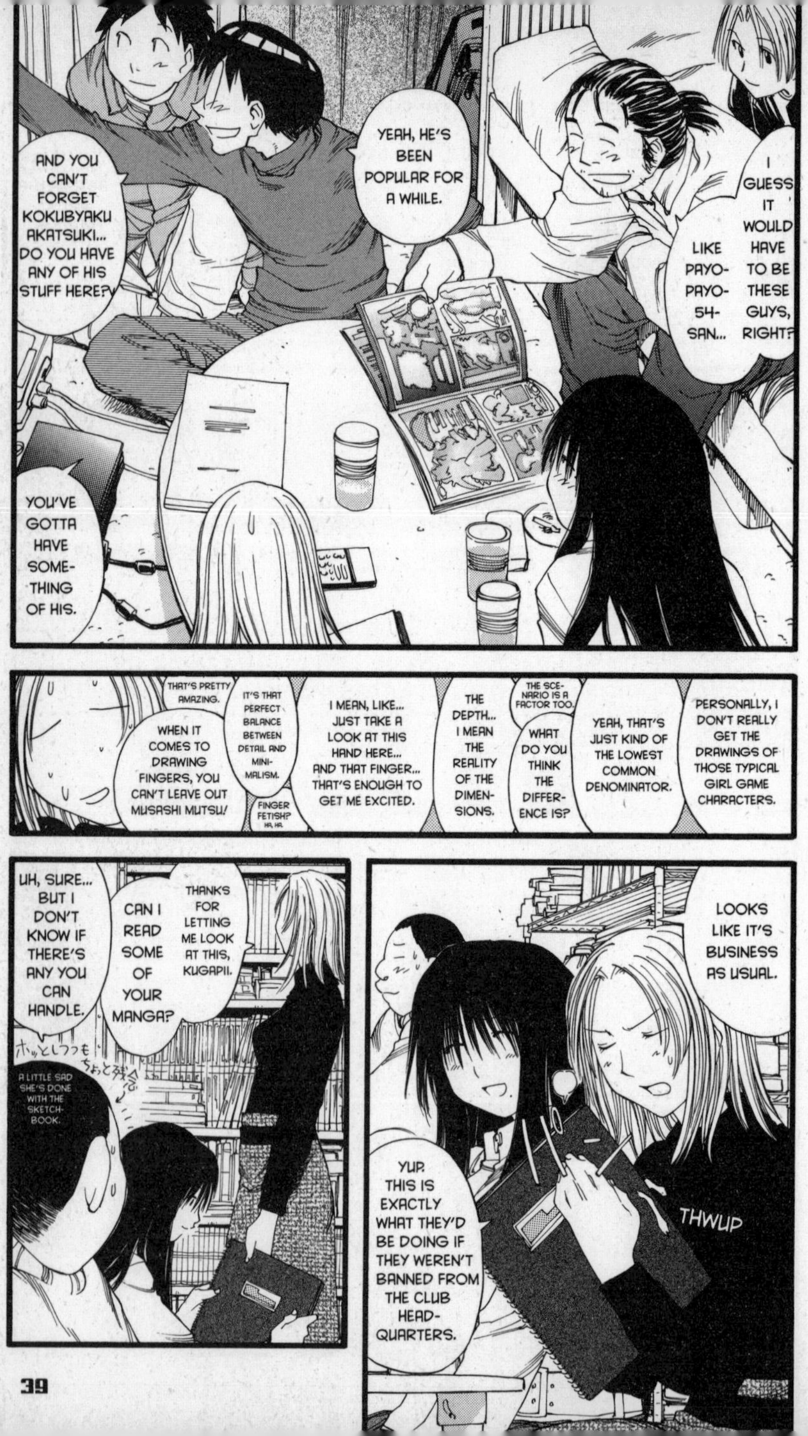
I GUESS IT WOULD HAVE TO BE THESE GUYS, RIGHT?
LIKE PAYO-PAYO-54-SAN...
YEAH, HE'S BEEN POPULAR FOR A WHILE.
AND YOU CAN'T FORGET KOKUBYAKU AKATSUKI... DO YOU HAVE ANY OF HIS STUFF HERE?
YOU'VE GOTTA HAVE SOMETHING OF HIS.
PERSONALLY, I DON'T REALLY GET THE DRAWINGS OF THOSE TYPICAL GIRL GAME CHARACTERS.
YEAH, THAT'S JUST KIND OF THE LOWEST COMMON DENOMINATOR.
THE SCENARIO IS A FACTOR TOO.
WHAT DO YOU THINK THE DIFFERENCE IS?
THE DEPTH... I MEAN THE REALITY OF THE DIMENSIONS.
I MEAN, LIKE... JUST TAKE A LOOK AT THIS HAND HERE... AND THAT FINGER... THAT'S ENOUGH TO GET ME EXCITED.
IT'S THAT PERFECT BALANCE BETWEEN DETAIL AND MINIMALISM.
FINGER FETISH? HA, HA.
THAT'S PRETTY AMAZING.
WHEN IT COMES TO DRAWING FINGERS, YOU CAN'T LEAVE OUT MUSASHI MUTSU!
LOOKS LIKE IT'S BUSINESS AS USUAL.
YUP. THIS IS EXACTLY WHAT THEY'D BE DOING IF THEY WEREN'T BANNED FROM THE CLUB HEADQUARTERS.
THWUP
THANKS FOR LETTING ME LOOK AT THIS, KUGAPII.
CAN I READ SOME OF YOUR MANGA?
UH, SURE... BUT I DON'T KNOW IF THERE'S ANY YOU CAN HANDLE.
ホッとしつつもちょっと残念
A LITTLE SAD SHE'S DONE WITH THE SKETCHBOOK.

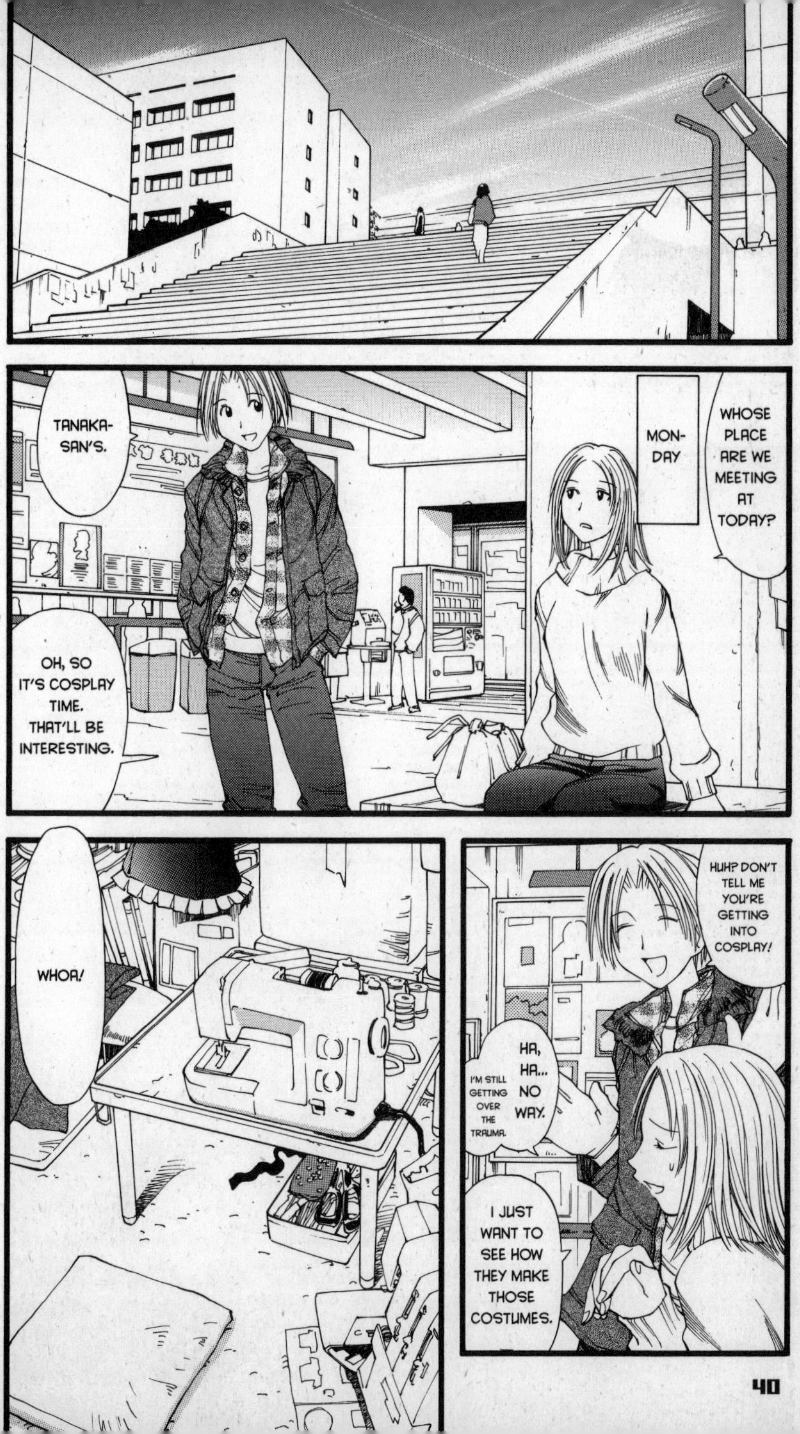
WHOSE PLACE ARE WE MEETING AT TODAY?
MON-DAY
TANAKA-SAN'S.
OH, SO IT'S COSPLAY TIME. THAT'LL BE INTERESTING.
HUH? DON'T TELL ME YOU'RE GETTING INTO COSPLAY!
HA, HA... NO WAY.
I'M STILL GETTING OVER THE TRAUMA.
I JUST WANT TO SEE HOW THEY MAKE THOSE COSTUMES.
WHOA!

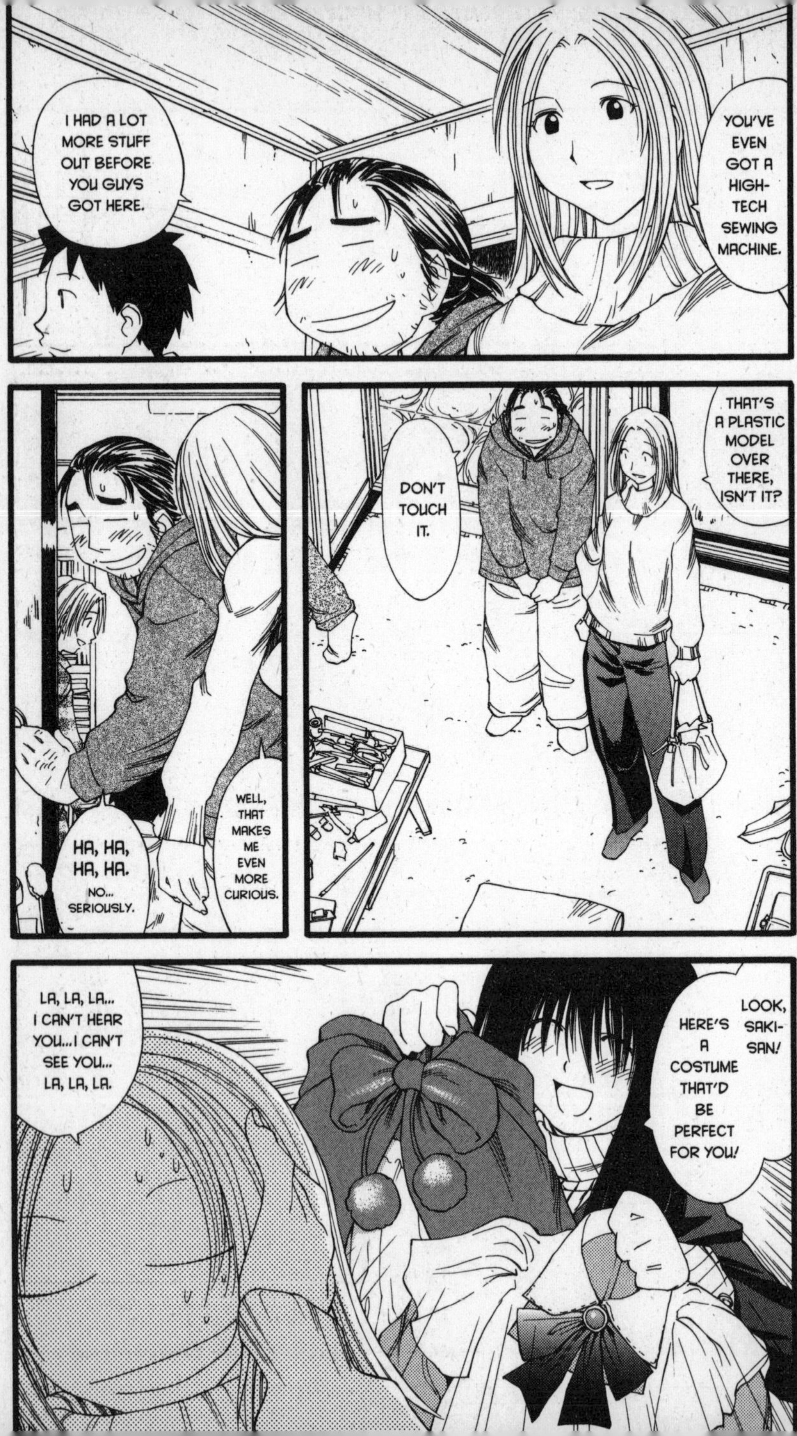
YOU'VE EVEN GOT A HIGH-TECH SEWING MACHINE.
I HAD A LOT MORE STUFF OUT BEFORE YOU GUYS GOT HERE.
THAT'S A PLASTIC MODEL OVER THERE, ISN'T IT?
DON'T TOUCH IT.
WELL, THAT MAKES ME EVEN MORE CURIOUS.
HA, HA, HA, HA. NO... SERIOUSLY.
LOOK, SAKI-SAN! HERE'S A COSTUME THAT'D BE PERFECT FOR YOU!
LA, LA, LA... I CAN'T HEAR YOU...I CAN'T SEE YOU... LA, LA, LA.

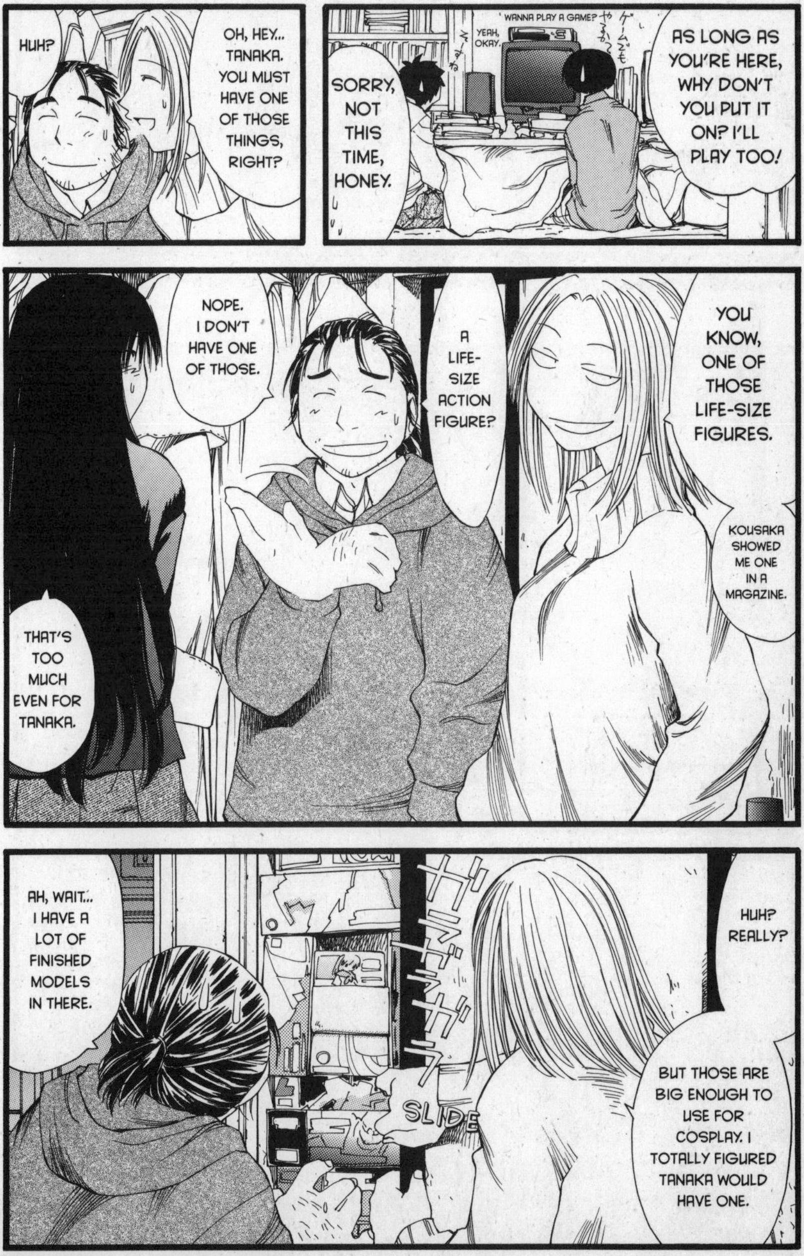
WANNA PLAY A GAME?
YEAH, OKAY.
AS LONG AS YOU'RE HERE, WHY DON'T YOU PUT IT ON? I'LL PLAY TOO!
SORRY, NOT THIS TIME, HONEY.
OH, HEY... TANAKA. YOU MUST HAVE ONE OF THOSE THINGS, RIGHT?
HUH?
YOU KNOW, ONE OF THOSE LIFE-SIZE FIGURES.
KOUSAKA SHOWED ME ONE IN A MAGAZINE.
A LIFE-SIZE ACTION FIGURE?
NOPE. I DON'T HAVE ONE OF THOSE.
THAT'S TOO MUCH EVEN FOR TANAKA.
HUH? REALLY?
BUT THOSE ARE BIG ENOUGH TO USE FOR COSPLAY. I TOTALLY FIGURED TANAKA WOULD HAVE ONE.
SLIDE
AH, WAIT... I HAVE A LOT OF FINISHED MODELS IN THERE.

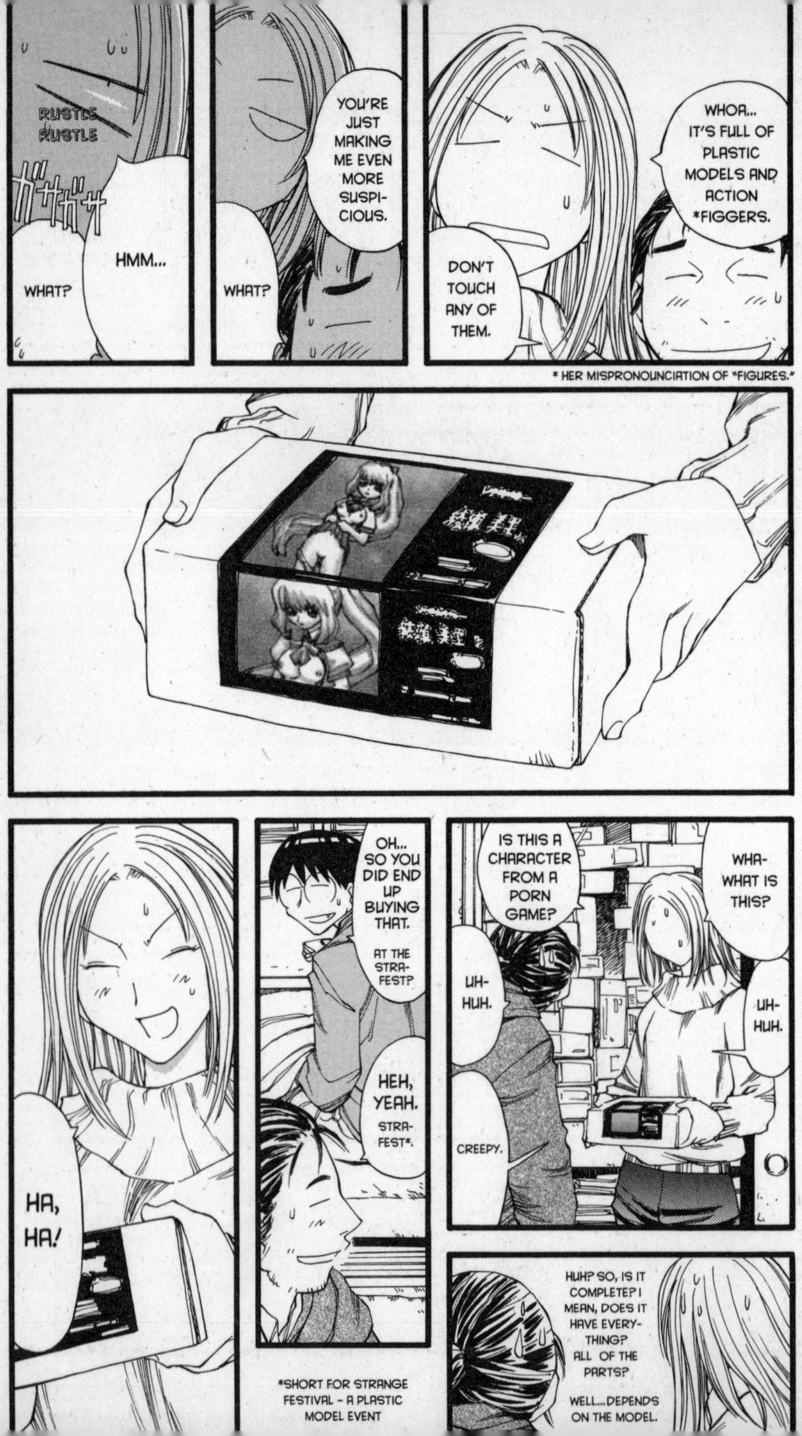
WHOA... IT'S FULL OF PLASTIC MODELS AND ACTION *FIGGERS.
DON'T TOUCH ANY OF THEM.
YOU'RE JUST MAKING ME EVEN MORE SUSPICIOUS.
WHAT?
RUSTLE RUSTLE
ガサガサ
HMM...
WHAT?
WHA-WHAT IS THIS?
IS THIS A CHARACTER FROM A PORN GAME?
UH-HUH.
UH-HUH.
CREEPY.
HUH? SO, IS IT COMPLETE? I MEAN, DOES IT HAVE EVERYTHING? ALL OF THE PARTS?
WELL...DEPENDS ON THE MODEL.
OH... SO YOU DID END UP BUYING THAT.
AT THE STRA-FEST?
HEH, YEAH.
STRA-FEST*.
HA, HA!

* HER MISPRONOUNCIATION OF "FIGURES."

*SHORT FOR STRANGE FESTIVAL - A PLASTIC MODEL EVENT

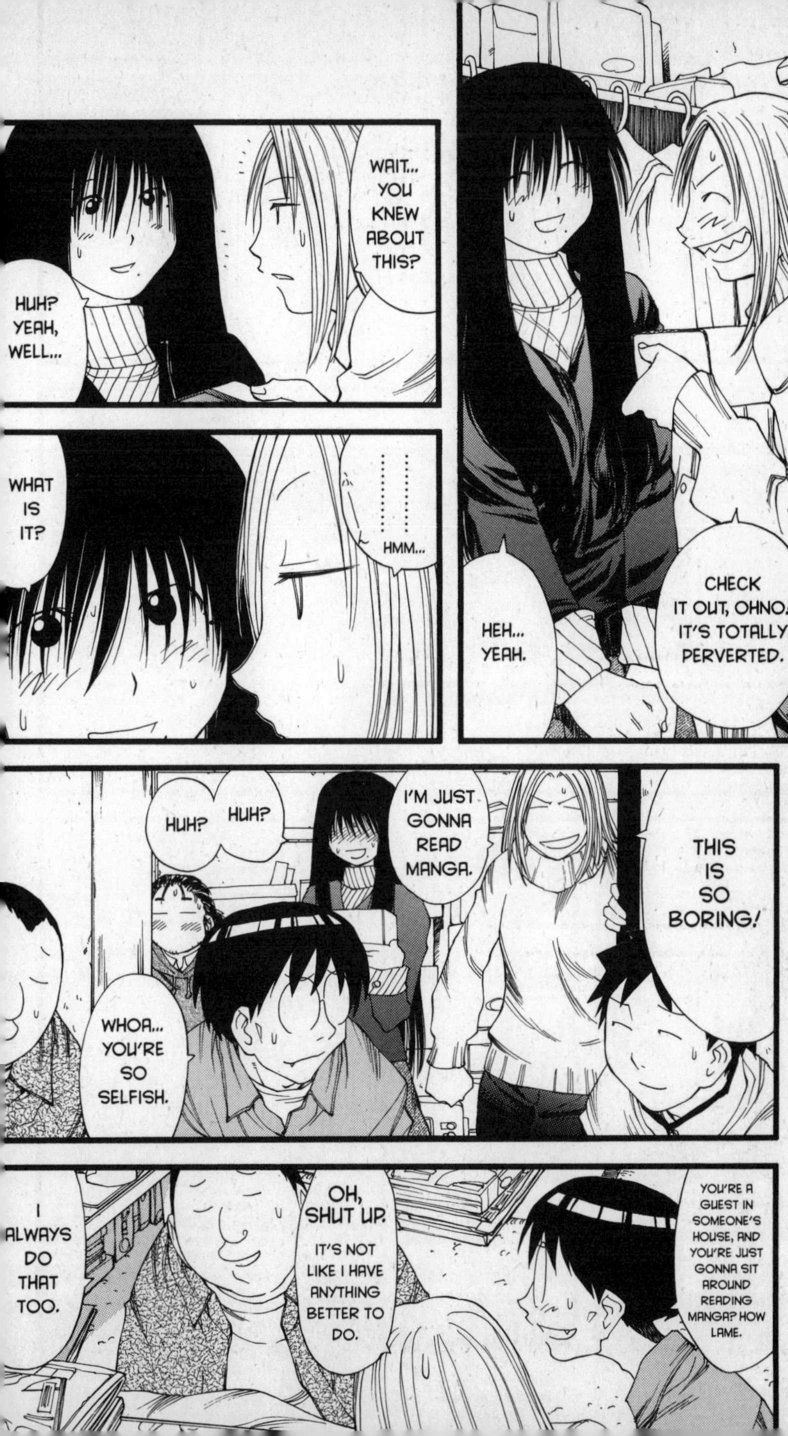
CHECK IT OUT, OHNO! IT'S TOTALLY PERVERTED.
HEH... YEAH.
WAIT... YOU KNEW ABOUT THIS?
HUH? YEAH, WELL...
...... HMM...
WHAT IS IT?
THIS IS SO BORING!
I'M JUST GONNA READ MANGA.
HUH?
HUH?
WHOA... YOU'RE SO SELFISH.
YOU'RE A GUEST IN SOMEONE'S HOUSE, AND YOU'RE JUST GONNA SIT AROUND READING MANGA? HOW LAME.
OH, SHUT UP.
IT'S NOT LIKE I HAVE ANYTHING BETTER TO DO.
I ALWAYS DO THAT TOO.

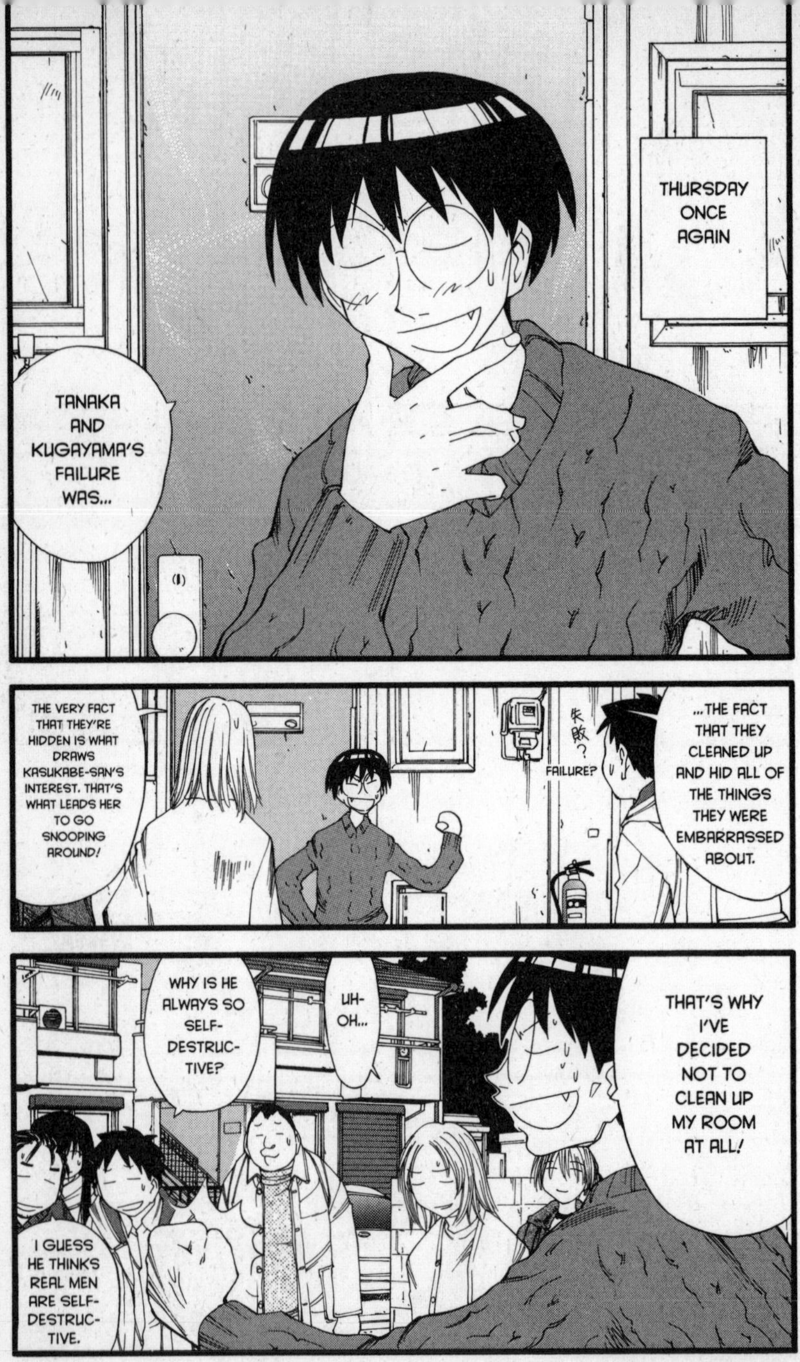
THURSDAY ONCE AGAIN
TANAKA AND KUGAYAMA'S FAILURE WAS...
...THE FACT THAT THEY CLEANED UP AND HID ALL OF THE THINGS THEY WERE EMBARRASSED ABOUT.
失敗？
FAILURE?
THE VERY FACT THAT THEY'RE HIDDEN IS WHAT DRAWS KASUKABE-SAN'S INTEREST. THAT'S WHAT LEADS HER TO GO SNOOPING AROUND!
THAT'S WHY I'VE DECIDED NOT TO CLEAN UP MY ROOM AT ALL!
UH-OH...
WHY IS HE ALWAYS SO SELF-DESTRUCTIVE?
I GUESS HE THINKS REAL MEN ARE SELF-DESTRUCTIVE.

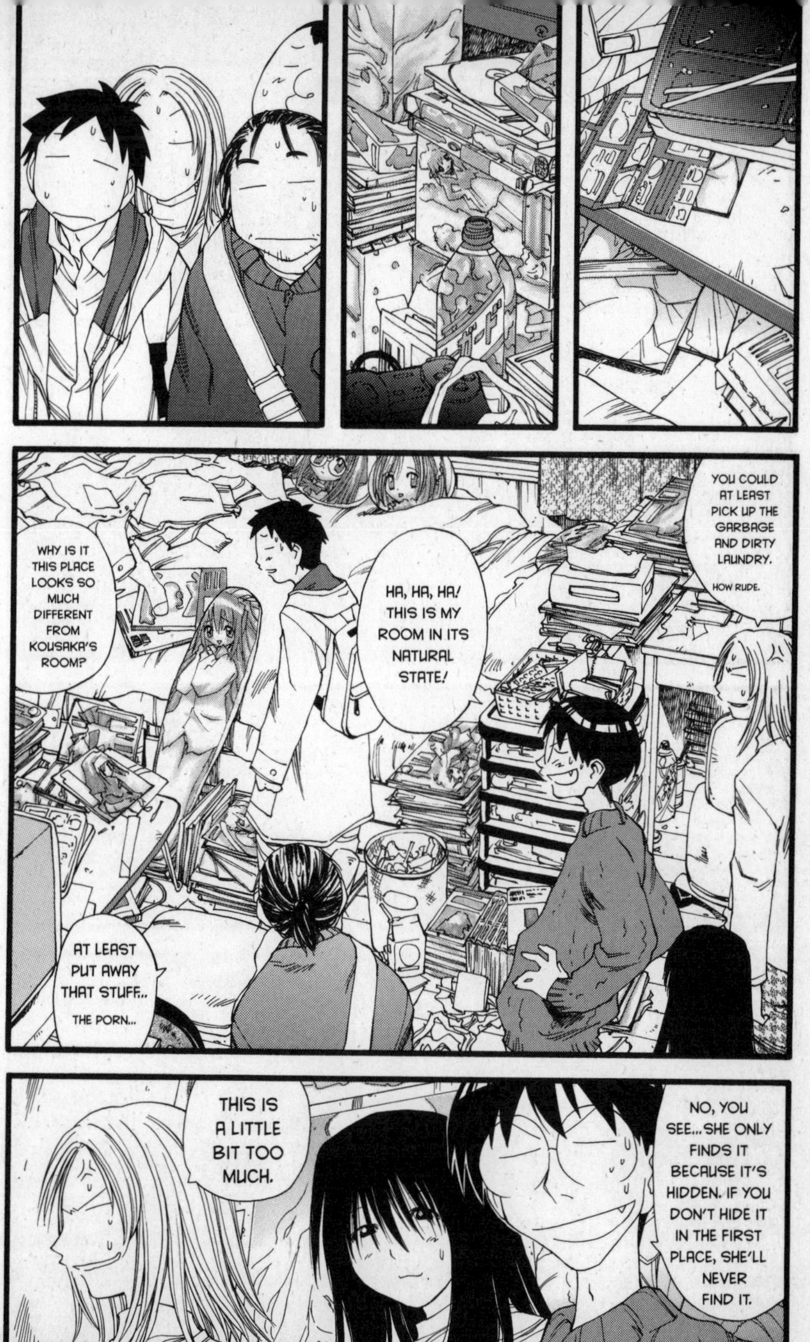
YOU COULD AT LEAST PICK UP THE GARBAGE AND DIRTY LAUNDRY.
HOW RUDE.
HA, HA, HA! THIS IS MY ROOM IN ITS NATURAL STATE!
WHY IS IT THIS PLACE LOOKS SO MUCH DIFFERENT FROM KOUSAKA'S ROOM?
AT LEAST PUT AWAY THAT STUFF...
THE PORN...
NO, YOU SEE... SHE ONLY FINDS IT BECAUSE IT'S HIDDEN. IF YOU DON'T HIDE IT IN THE FIRST PLACE, SHE'LL NEVER FIND IT.
THIS IS A LITTLE BIT TOO MUCH.

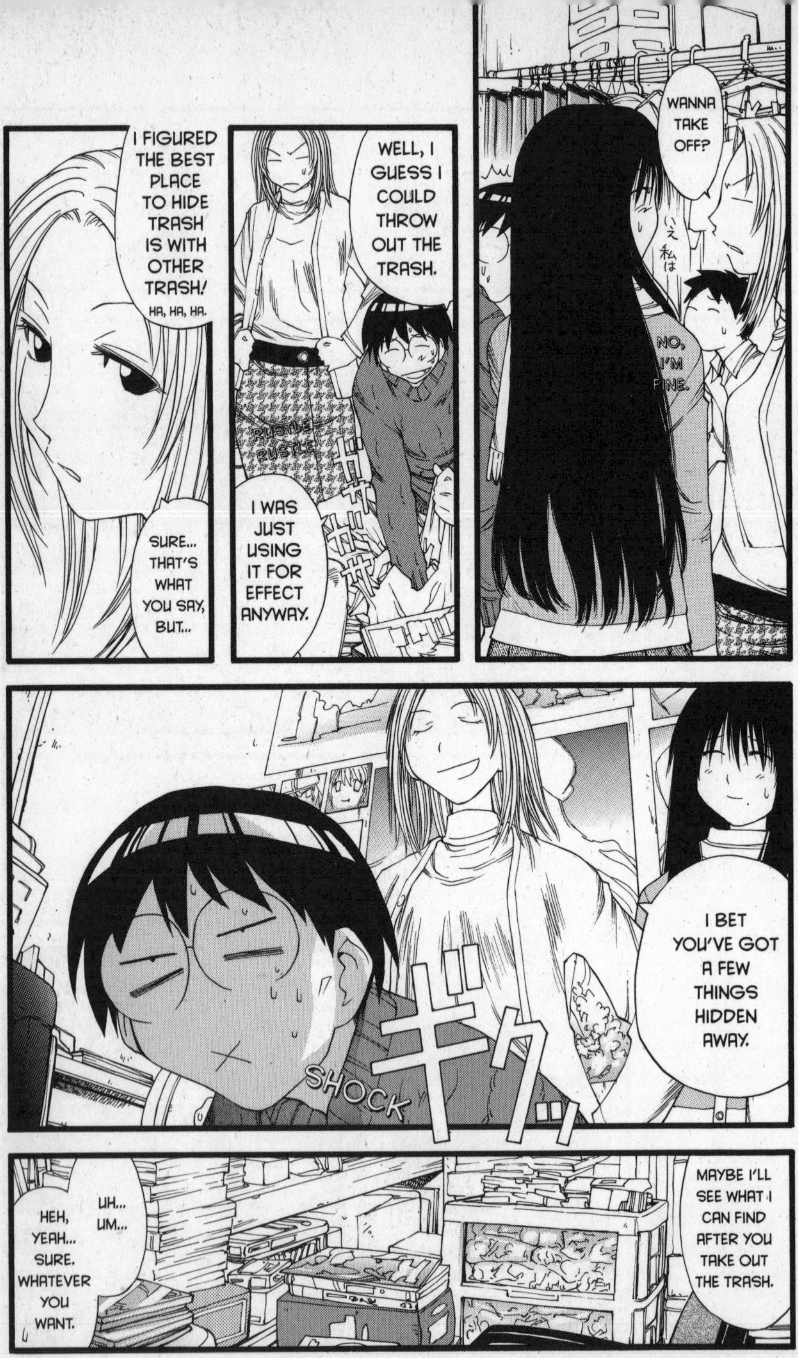
WANNA TAKE OFF?
いえ 私は
NO, I'M FINE.
WELL, I GUESS I COULD THROW OUT THE TRASH.
RUSTLE RUSTLE
I WAS JUST USING IT FOR EFFECT ANYWAY.
I FIGURED THE BEST PLACE TO HIDE TRASH IS WITH OTHER TRASH!
HA, HA, HA.
SURE... THAT'S WHAT YOU SAY, BUT...
I BET YOU'VE GOT A FEW THINGS HIDDEN AWAY.
SHOCK
MAYBE I'LL SEE WHAT I CAN FIND AFTER YOU TAKE OUT THE TRASH.
UH... UM...
HEH, YEAH... SURE. WHATEVER YOU WANT.

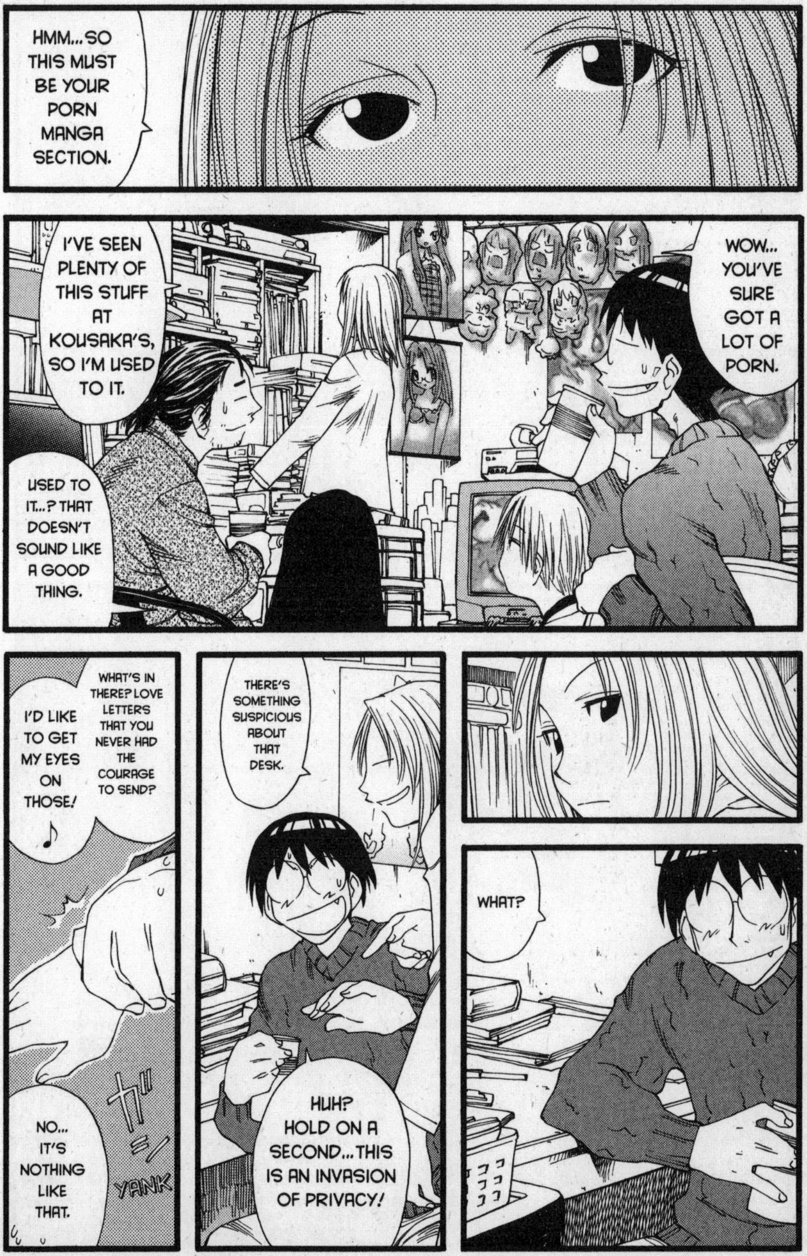
HMM...SO THIS MUST BE YOUR PORN MANGA SECTION.
WOW... YOU'VE SURE GOT A LOT OF PORN.
I'VE SEEN PLENTY OF THIS STUFF AT KOUSAKA'S, SO I'M USED TO IT.
USED TO IT...? THAT DOESN'T SOUND LIKE A GOOD THING.
WHAT?
THERE'S SOMETHING SUSPICIOUS ABOUT THAT DESK.
HUH? HOLD ON A SECOND...THIS IS AN INVASION OF PRIVACY!
WHAT'S IN THERE? LOVE LETTERS THAT YOU NEVER HAD THE COURAGE TO SEND?
I'D LIKE TO GET MY EYES ON THOSE! ♪
YANK
NO... IT'S NOTHING LIKE THAT.

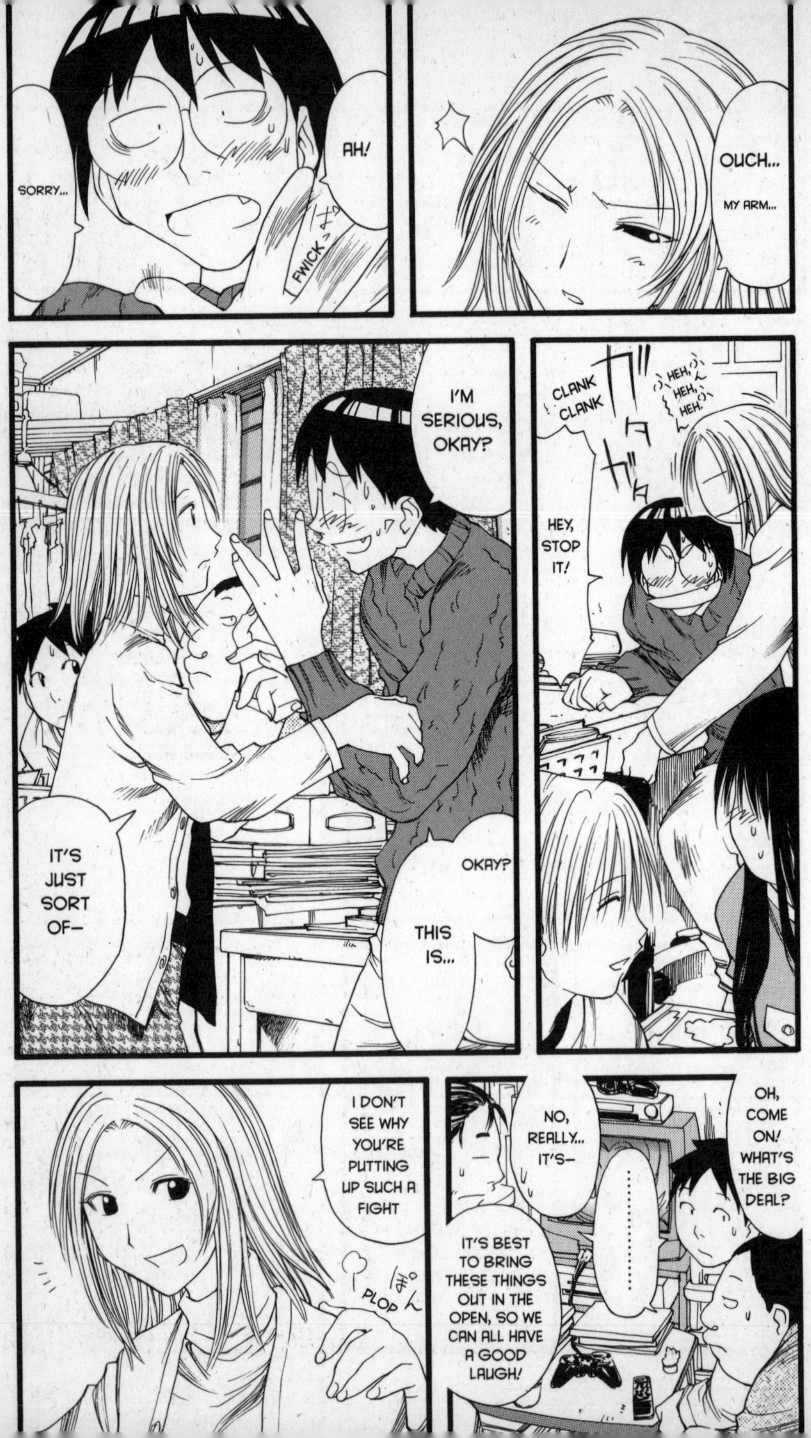
OUCH...
MY ARM...
AH!
FWICK
SORRY...
HEH, HEH, HEH.
CLANK CLANK
HEY, STOP IT!
I'M SERIOUS, OKAY?
OKAY?
THIS IS...
IT'S JUST SORT OF—
OH, COME ON! WHAT'S THE BIG DEAL?
NO, REALLY... IT'S—
......
IT'S BEST TO BRING THESE THINGS OUT IN THE OPEN, SO WE CAN ALL HAVE A GOOD LAUGH!
I DON'T SEE WHY YOU'RE PUTTING UP SUCH A FIGHT
PLOP

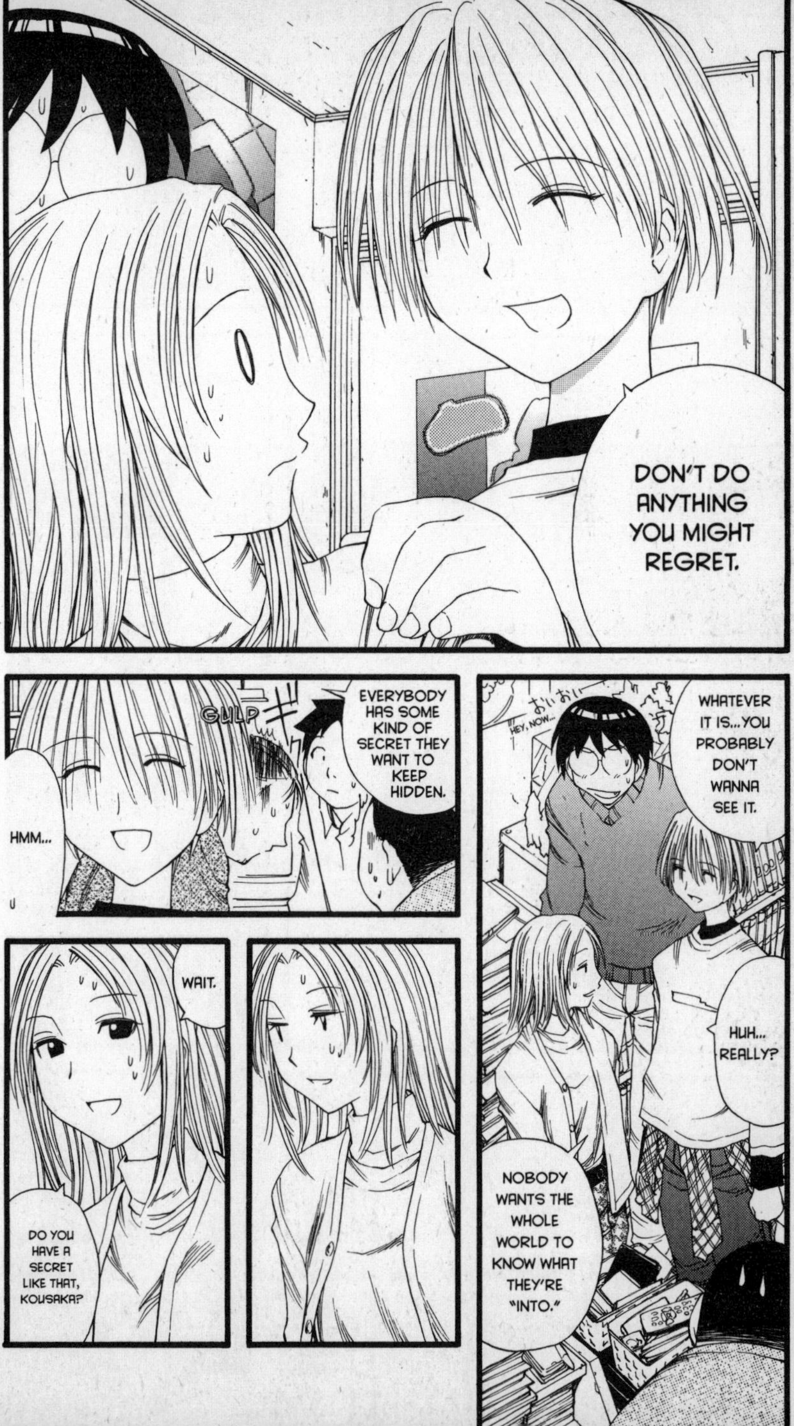
DON'T DO ANYTHING YOU MIGHT REGRET.
WHATEVER IT IS...YOU PROBABLY DON'T WANNA SEE IT.
おいおい
HEY, NOW...
HUH... REALLY?
NOBODY WANTS THE WHOLE WORLD TO KNOW WHAT THEY'RE "INTO."
GULP
EVERYBODY HAS SOME KIND OF SECRET THEY WANT TO KEEP HIDDEN.
HMM...
WAIT.
DO YOU HAVE A SECRET LIKE THAT, KOUSAKA?

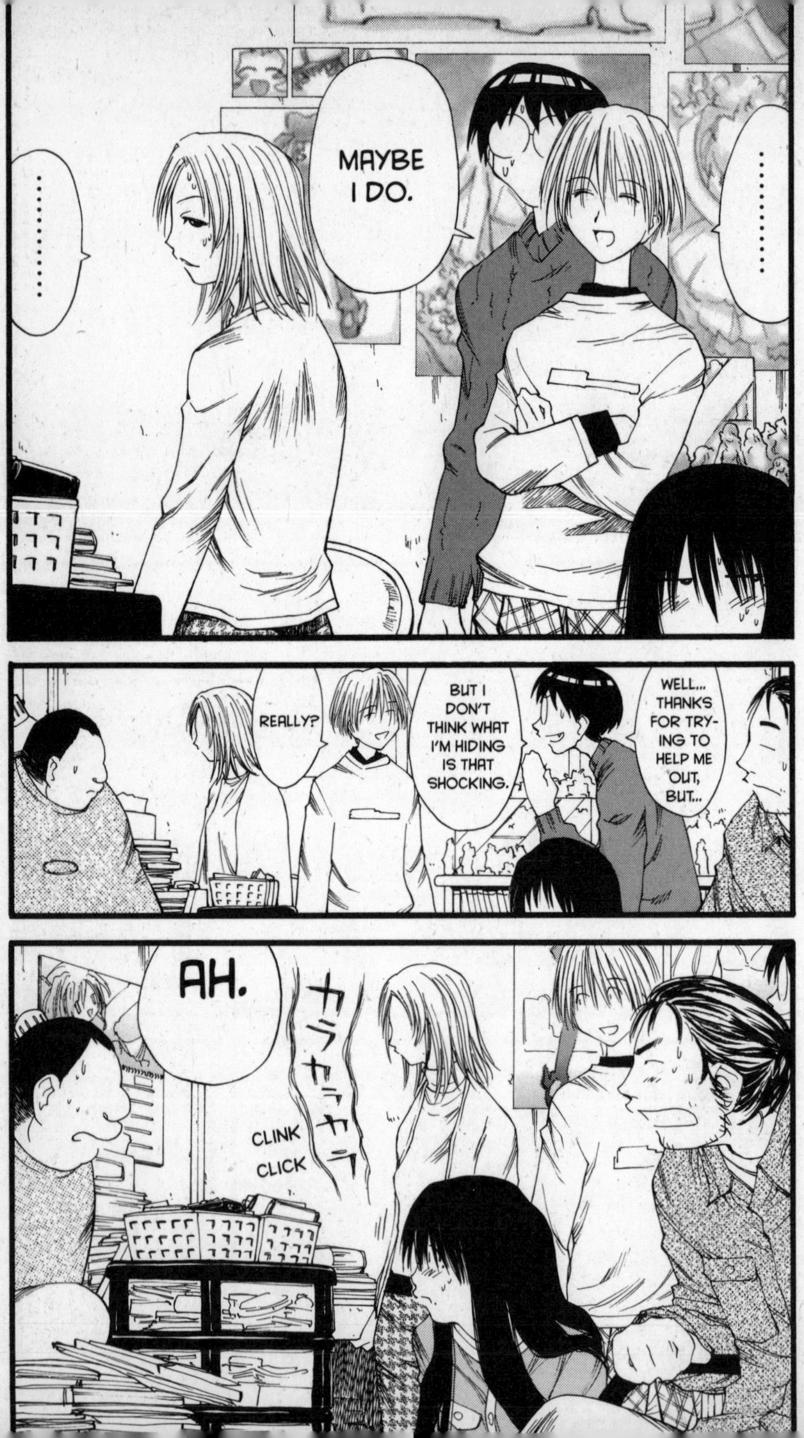
......
MAYBE I DO.
......
WELL... THANKS FOR TRY-ING TO HELP ME OUT, BUT...
BUT I DON'T THINK WHAT I'M HIDING IS THAT SHOCKING.
REALLY?
AH.
カラカラカラ
CLINK CLICK

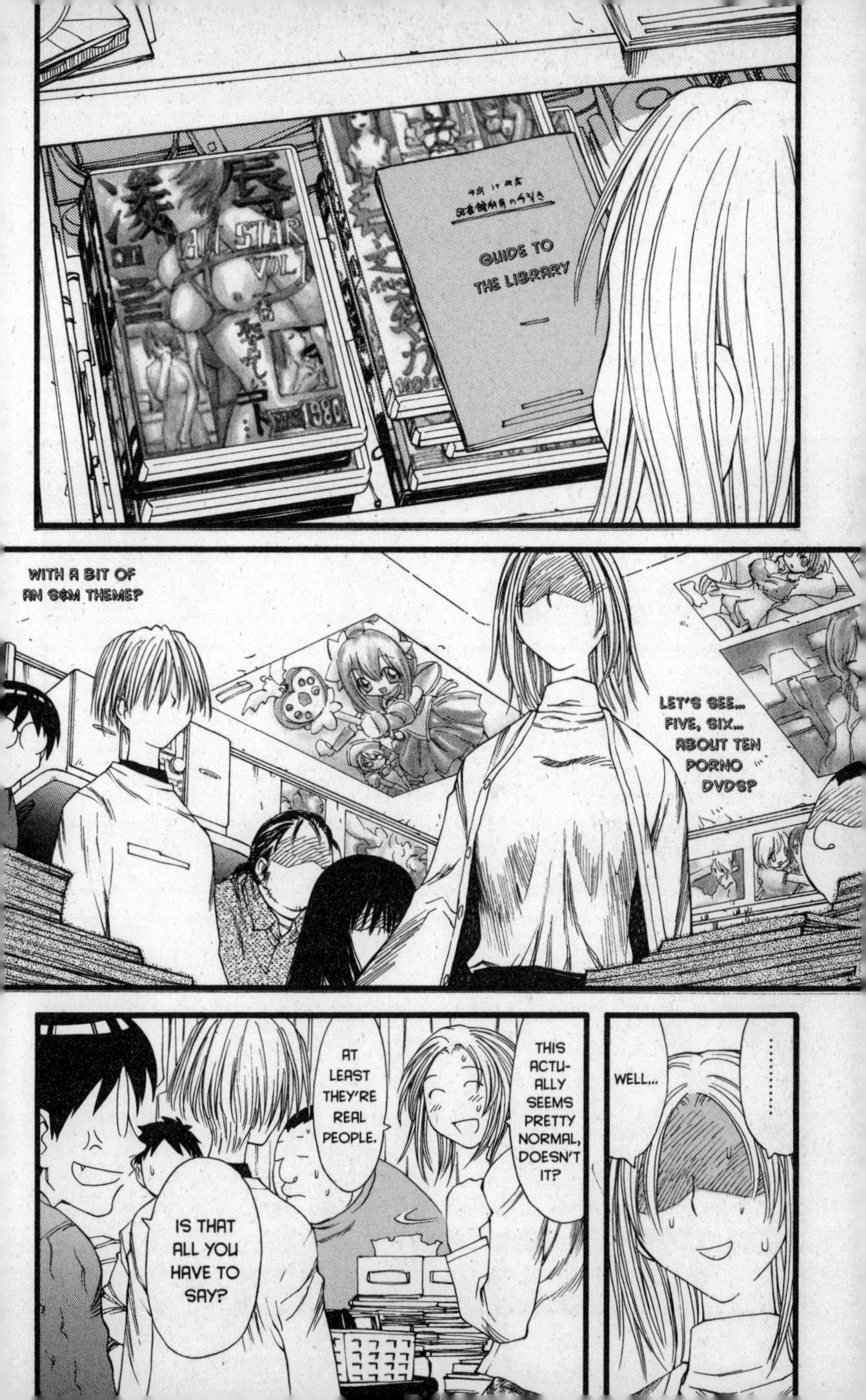
GUIDE TO THE LIBRARY
LET'S SEE... FIVE, SIX... ABOUT TEN PORNO DVDS?
WITH A BIT OF AN S&M THEME?
......
WELL,...
THIS ACTUALLY SEEMS PRETTY NORMAL, DOESN'T IT?
AT LEAST THEY'RE REAL PEOPLE.
IS THAT ALL YOU HAVE TO SAY?

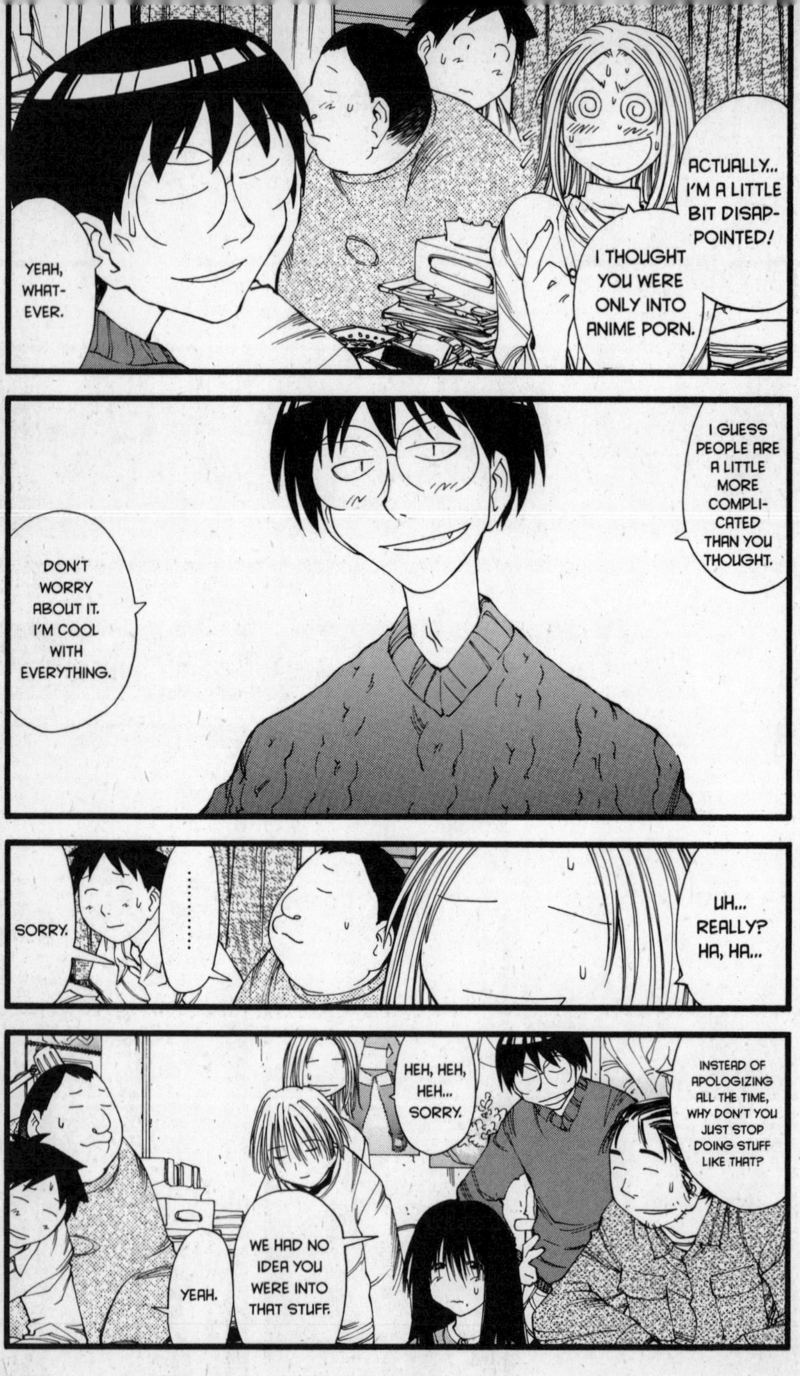
ACTUALLY... I'M A LITTLE BIT DISAPPOINTED!
I THOUGHT YOU WERE ONLY INTO ANIME PORN.
YEAH, WHATEVER.
I GUESS PEOPLE ARE A LITTLE MORE COMPLICATED THAN YOU THOUGHT.
DON'T WORRY ABOUT IT. I'M COOL WITH EVERYTHING.
UH... REALLY? HA, HA...
......
SORRY.
INSTEAD OF APOLOGIZING ALL THE TIME, WHY DON'T YOU JUST STOP DOING STUFF LIKE THAT?
HEH, HEH, HEH... SORRY.
WE HAD NO IDEA YOU WERE INTO THAT STUFF.
YEAH.

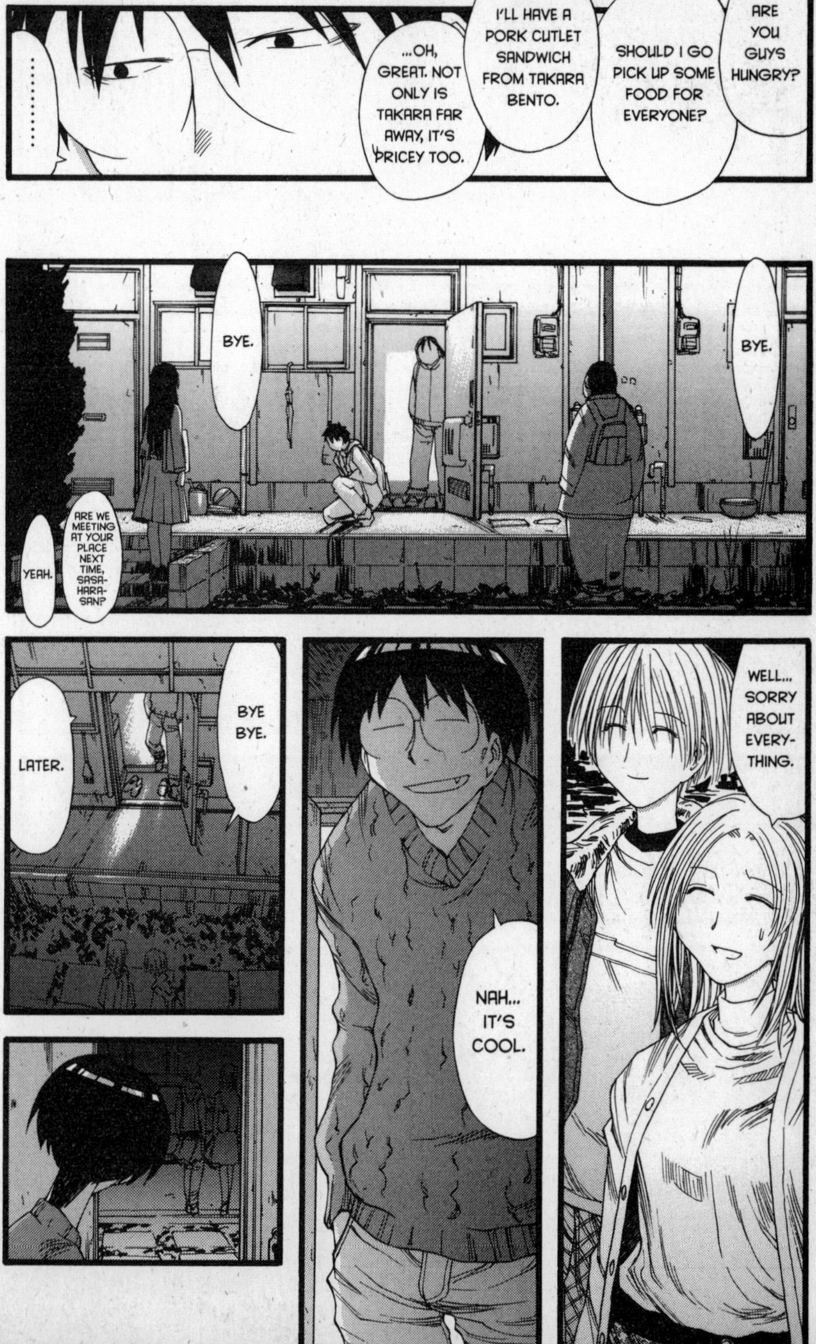
ARE YOU GUYS HUNGRY?
SHOULD I GO PICK UP SOME FOOD FOR EVERYONE?
I'LL HAVE A PORK CUTLET SANDWICH FROM TAKARA BENTO.
...OH, GREAT. NOT ONLY IS TAKARA FAR AWAY, IT'S PRICEY TOO.
......
BYE.
BYE.
ARE WE MEETING AT YOUR PLACE NEXT TIME, SASA-HARA-SAN?
YEAH.
WELL... SORRY ABOUT EVERY-THING.
NAH... IT'S COOL.
BYE BYE.
LATER.

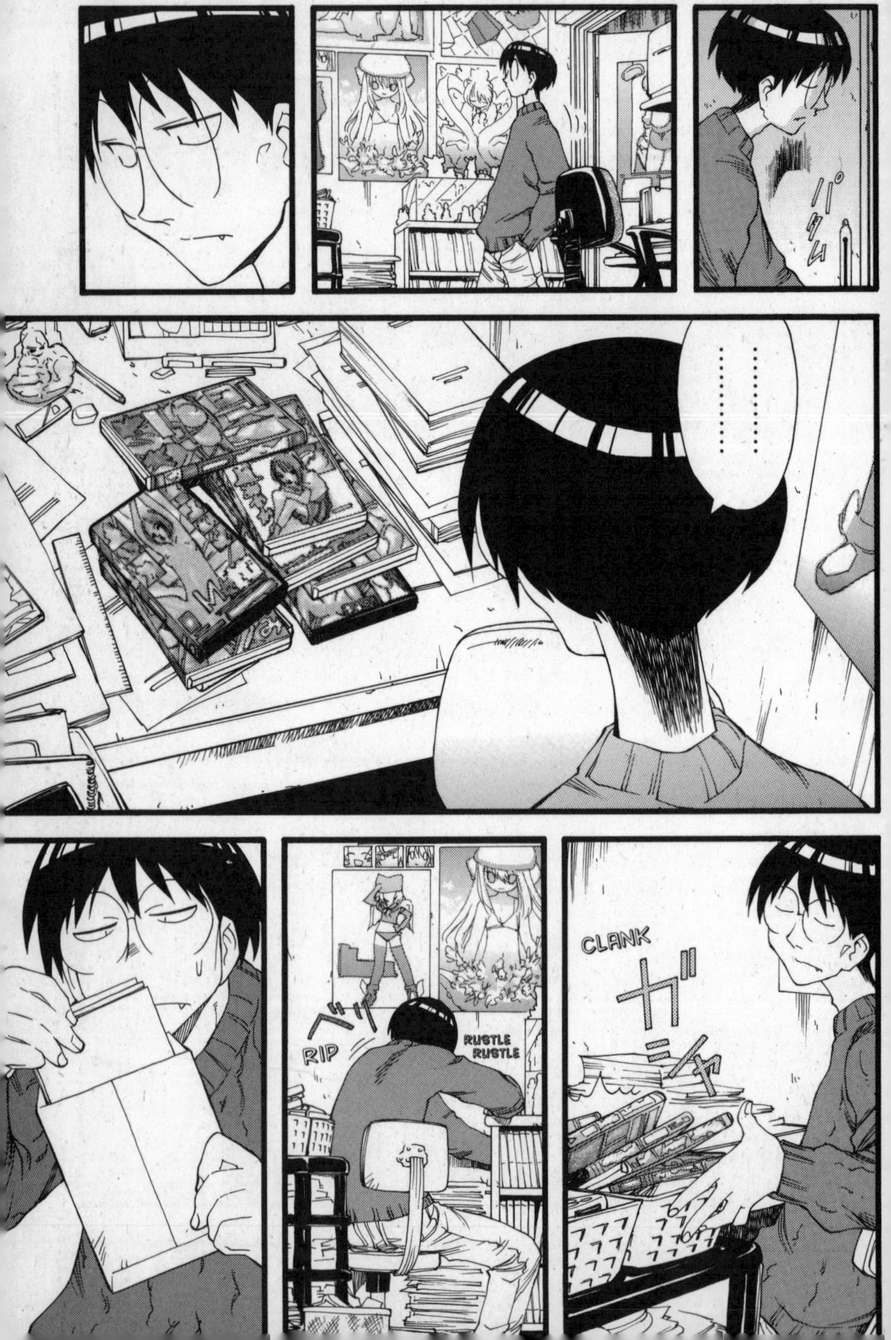
パタム
……
CLANK
RUSTLE
RUSTLE
RIP

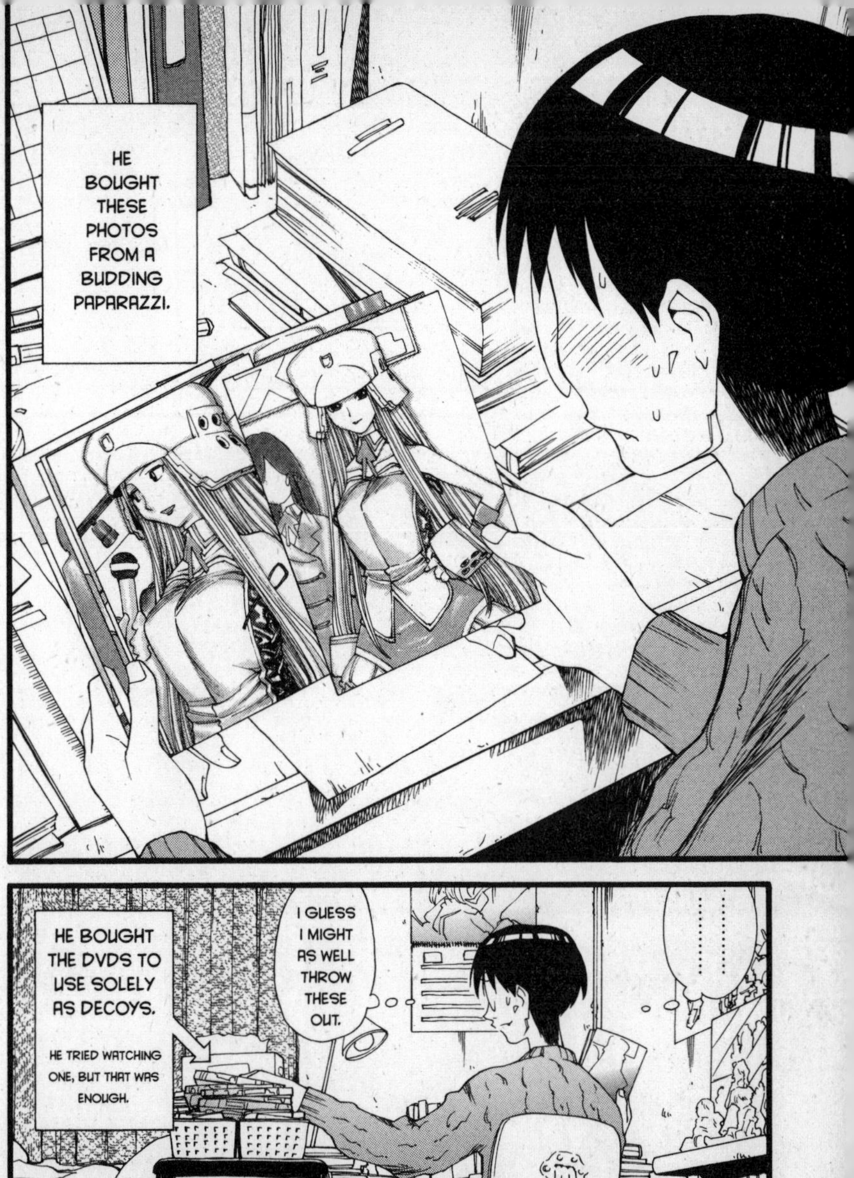
HE BOUGHT THESE PHOTOS FROM A BUDDING PAPARAZZI.
......
I GUESS I MIGHT AS WELL THROW THESE OUT.
HE BOUGHT THE DVDS TO USE SOLELY AS DECOYS.
HE TRIED WATCHING ONE, BUT THAT WAS ENOUGH.

END OF CHAPTER 20

# OUR FAVORITE GAME ANOTHER STORIES

STORY 2

RITSUKO KUBEL KETTENKRAD REVIEWED BY BENJAMIN TAKEYO

YEAH, I REALLY LONGED FOR A GAME LIKE THIS. IT STARTS OUT FOLLOWING THE BASIC STORY LINE OF THE SERIES WITH A FEW ADDITIONS. BUT I GOT REALLY EXCITED AS I WATCHED THE STORY GRADUALLY DEVELOP INTO SOMETHING COMPLETELY NEW. IT'S COOL THAT THE GAME SPANS THE COURSE OF A YEAR, AND ENDS WITH THE STUDENT BODY PRESIDENTIAL RACE. THE STORY IS ACTUALLY MORE EVOLVED THAN THAT OF THE ANIME OR THE ORIGINAL MANGA! NOW, IF ONLY IT WERE AN 18 AND OVER GAME. [LAUGH]

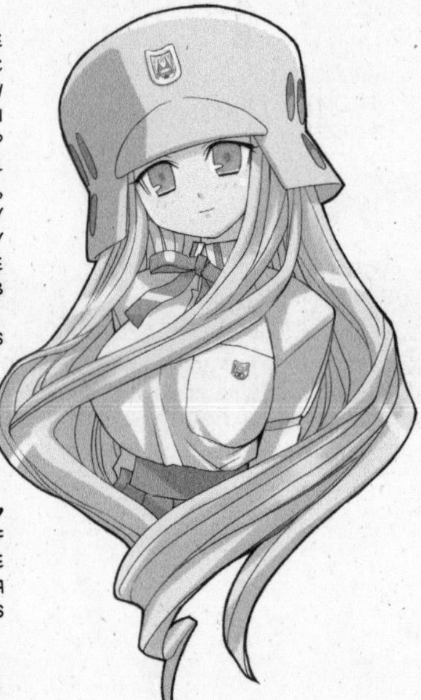

ANYWAY, I CHOSE THE PRESIDENT. THAT'S RIGHT...THE PRESIDENT! OKAY, EVERYBODY? THE PRESIDENT AND THE PRESIDENT...I'M TALKING ABOUT THE PRESIDENT...YOU HEARD ME...THE PRESIDENT...HEH, HEH, HEH...SORRY, I WAS JUST TRYING TO IMITATE WHAT THE PIT VIPER WROTE. FINALLY, I GET MY CHANCE TO HOOK UP WITH THE PRESIDENT. ♥ AND AS I LOOK BACK ON ALL MY MEMORIES OF THE PRESIDENT (I'M TALKING ABOUT REAL-TIME MEMORIES), IT MAKES ME GLAD TO BE ALIVE. [HA HA] ...OH, NO...JUST THINKING ABOUT IT BRINGS A LOOK OF JOY TO MY FACE. [HA HA] EVER SINCE SHE WAS A CHILD, HER PARENTS' DYSFUNCTIONAL RELATIONSHIP HAS CAST A SHADOW UPON HER MENTAL STATE, BUT IT MAKES ME SO HAPPY TO SEE HER STARTING TO MOVE IN A POSITIVE DIRECTION. IT'S SO PERFECT, I DON'T KNOW HOW THE MANGA'S GONNA TOP THIS STORY LINE. [HA HA] ACTUALLY, NOW THAT I THINK ABOUT IT, THE ONLY KUJI-UN CHARACTER WHOSE PARENTS ARE AROUND IS TOKINO. THESE CHARACTERS LEAD TOUGH LIVES. OH, YEAH...SHE STARTS CALLING CHIHIRO "CHIHIRO-CHAN" AFTER THE "MEMORIES IN THE PARK" EVENT DURING SUMMER VACATION. THIS STORY LINE EXISTS IN THE ORIGINAL MANGA TOO, BUT THE DIALOGUE IS DIFFERENT, AND IT'S MUCH LESS DETAILED. THEY HAD TO CHANGE IT BECAUSE THE STORY LEADING UP TO IT WAS SO DIFFERENT. YUP. IT'S COOL. [BENJAMIN]

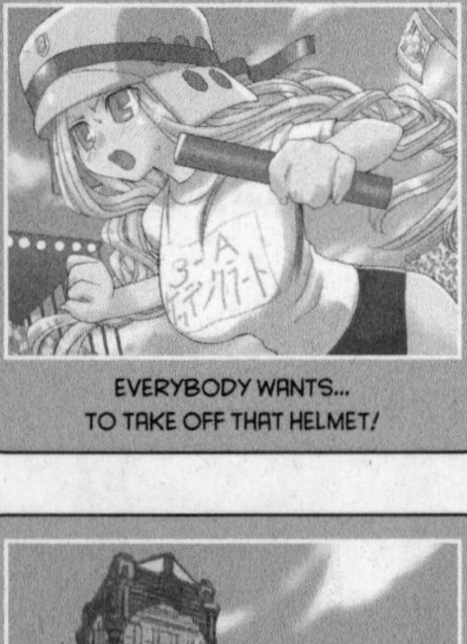
3-A

EVERYBODY WANTS...
TO TAKE OFF THAT HELMET!

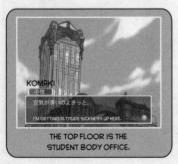

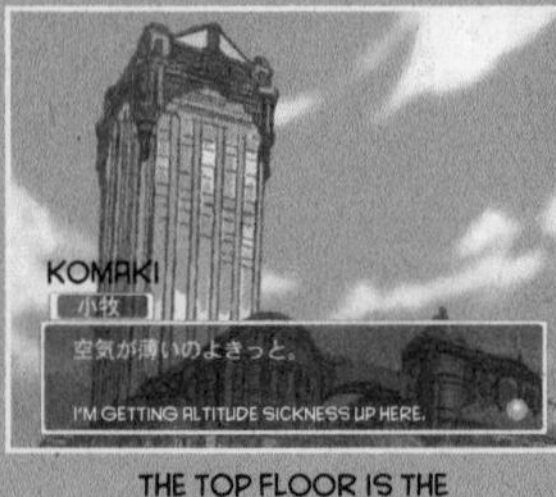
KOMAKI
小牧
空気が薄いのよきっと。
I'M GETTING ALTITUDE SICKNESS UP HERE.

THE TOP FLOOR IS THE
STUDENT BODY OFFICE.

★

WELL, YOU DIDN'T REALLY LEAVE ME MUCH ROOM TO WRITE. YEAH...EVERYONE LOVES THE PRESIDENT. SHE'S PROBABLY THE CHARACTER WITH THE MOST STORY LINES. PERSONALLY, I THINK THAT THE PRESIDENT LOOKS SO CUTE WHEN THEY SHOW HER AS A YOUNG GIRL. I COULD HARDLY CONTROL MYSELF. [HA HA] [PIT VIPER]

CHAPTER 20 - MOMENTS LATER

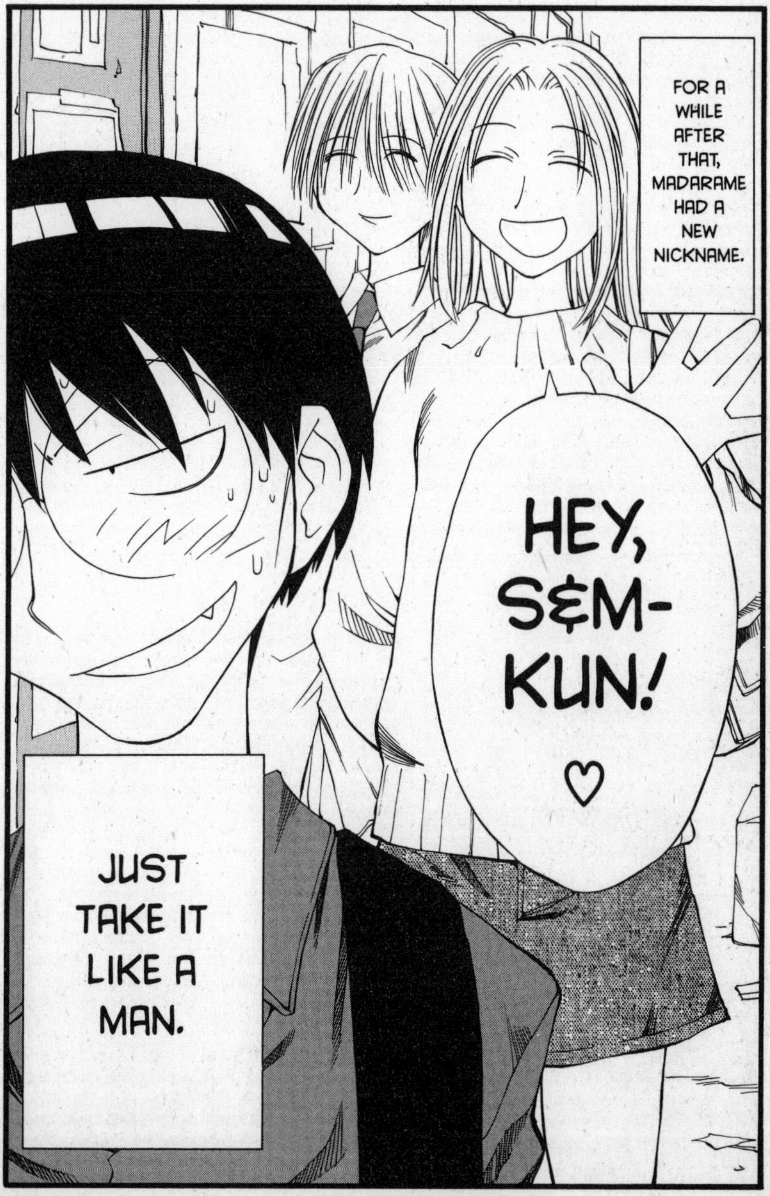
FOR A WHILE AFTER THAT, MADARAME HAD A NEW NICKNAME.
HEY, S&M-KUN! ♡
JUST TAKE IT LIKE A MAN.

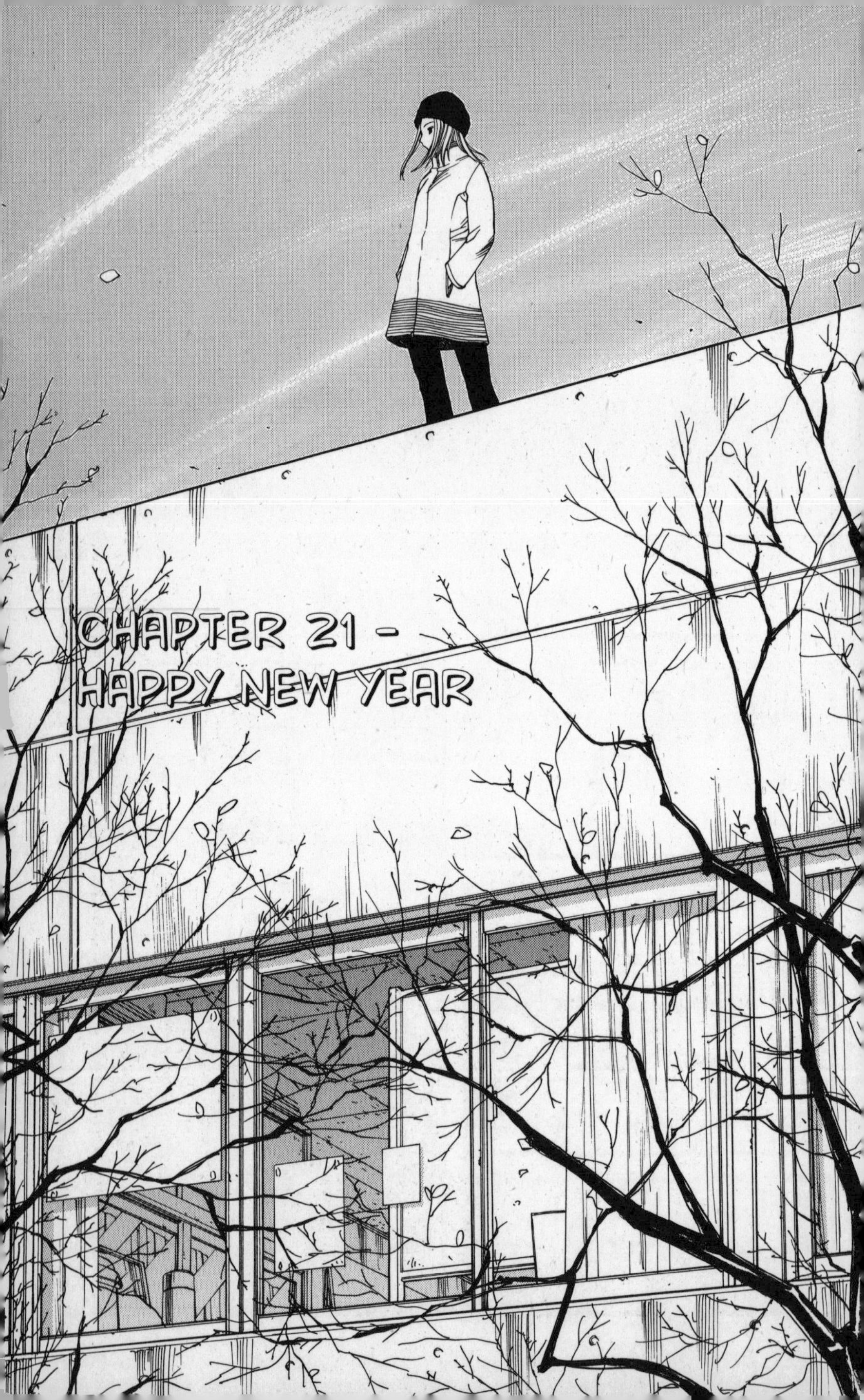
CHAPTER 21 -
HAPPY NEW YEAR

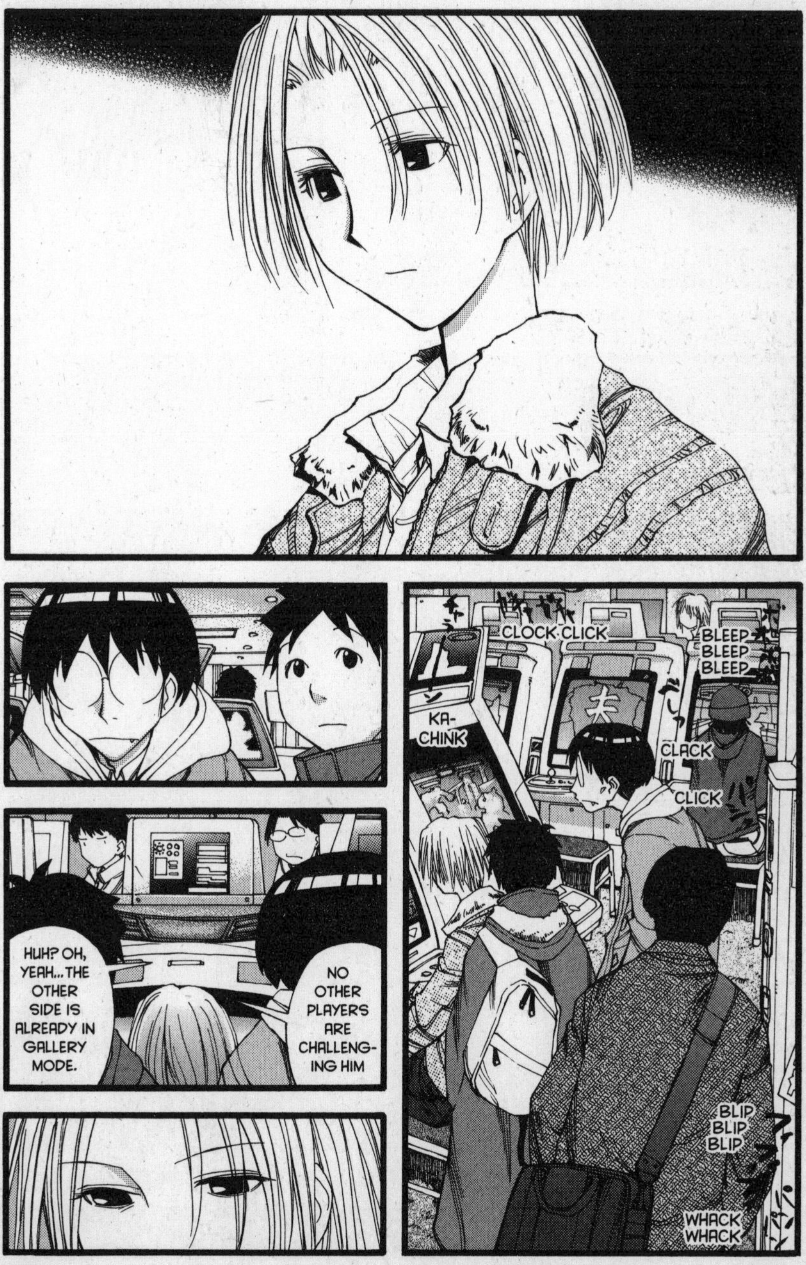
BLEEP BLEEP BLEEP
CLOCK CLICK
KA-CHINK
CLACK
CLICK
BLIP BLIP BLIP
WHACK WHACK
NO OTHER PLAYERS ARE CHALLENGING HIM
HUH? OH, YEAH... THE OTHER SIDE IS ALREADY IN GALLERY MODE.

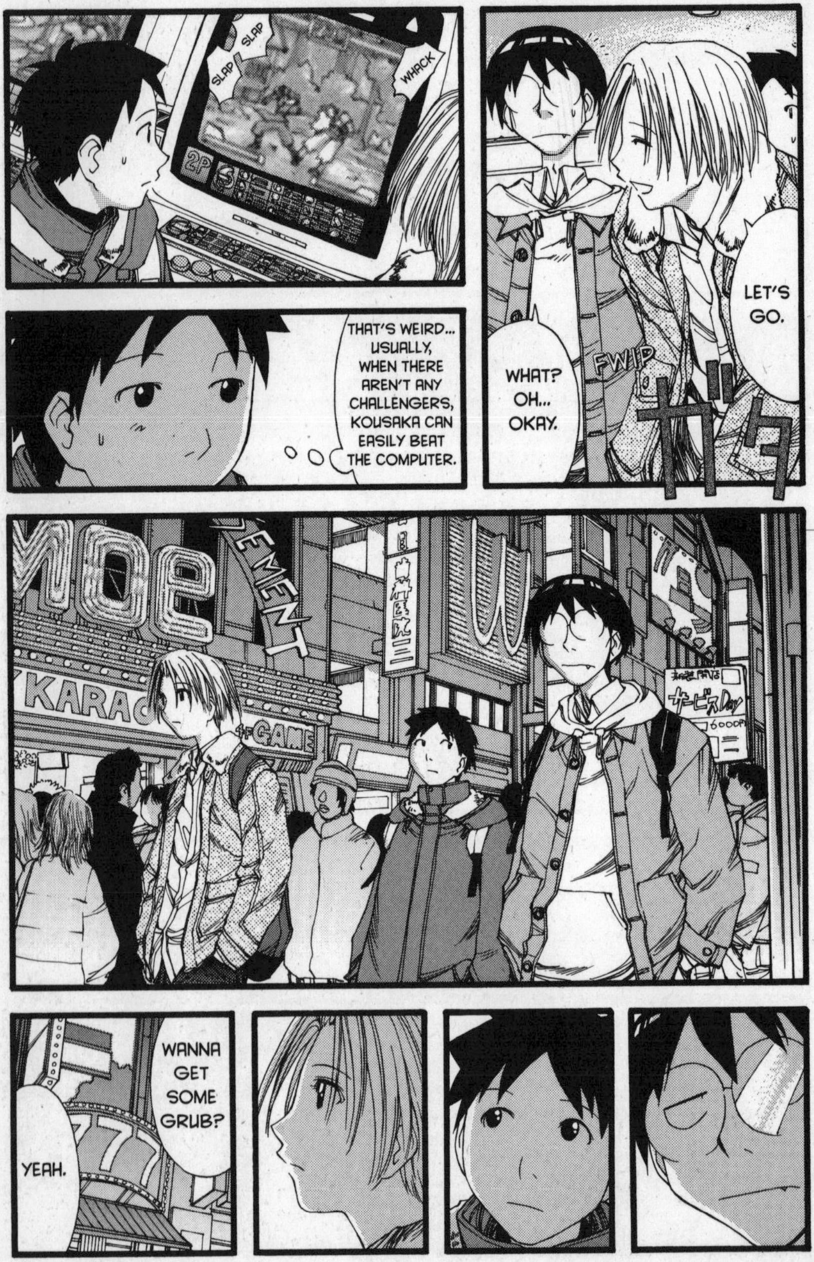
LET'S GO.
FWIP
ガタ
WHAT? OH... OKAY.
SLAP SLAP
SLAP
WHACK
THAT'S WEIRD... USUALLY, WHEN THERE AREN'T ANY CHALLENGERS, KOUSAKA CAN EASILY BEAT THE COMPUTER.
MOE
GAME
サービスDay
WANNA GET SOME GRUB?
YEAH.

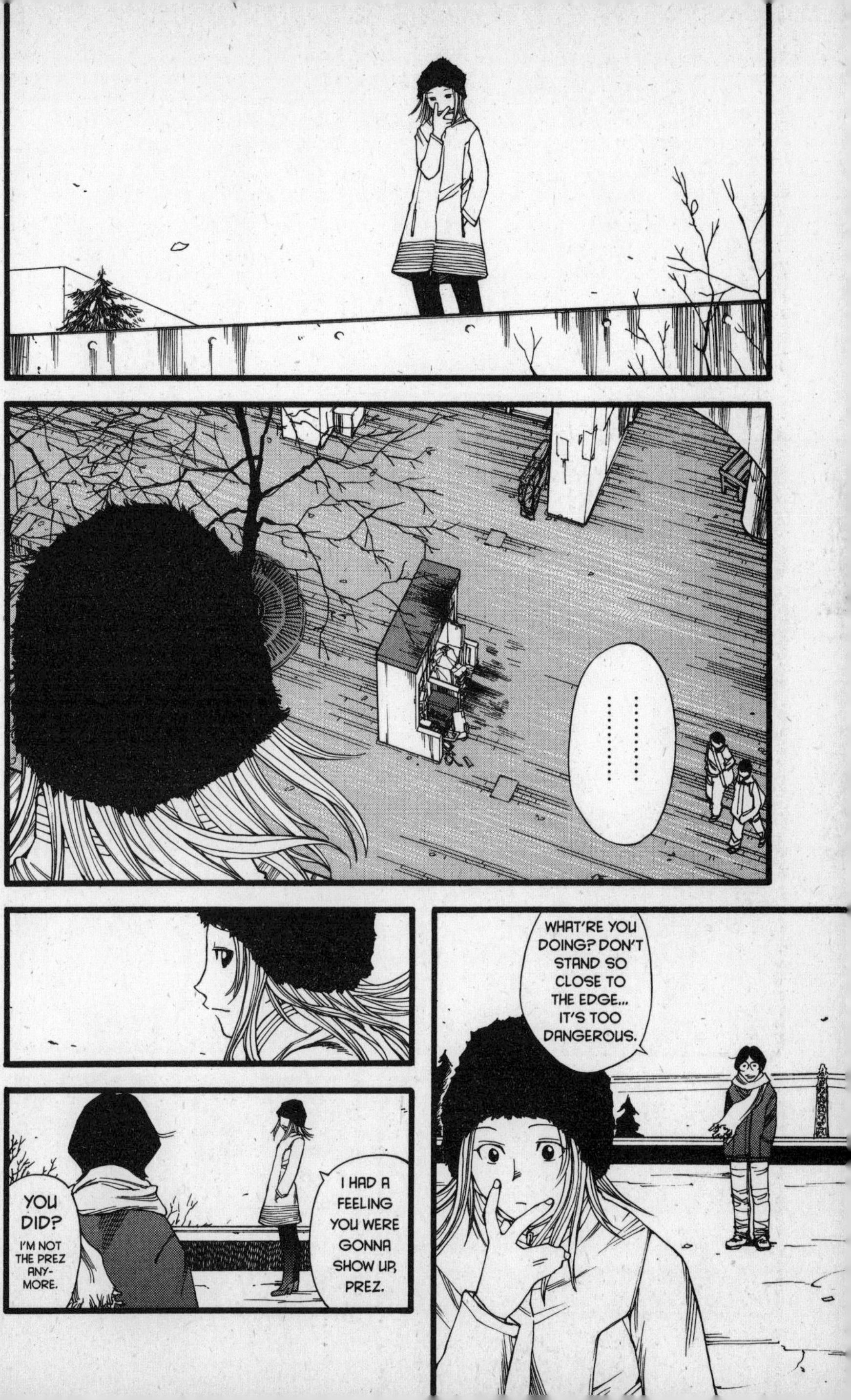
......
......
WHAT'RE YOU DOING? DON'T STAND SO CLOSE TO THE EDGE... IT'S TOO DANGEROUS.
I HAD A FEELING YOU WERE GONNA SHOW UP, PREZ.
YOU DID?
I'M NOT THE PREZ ANY-MORE.

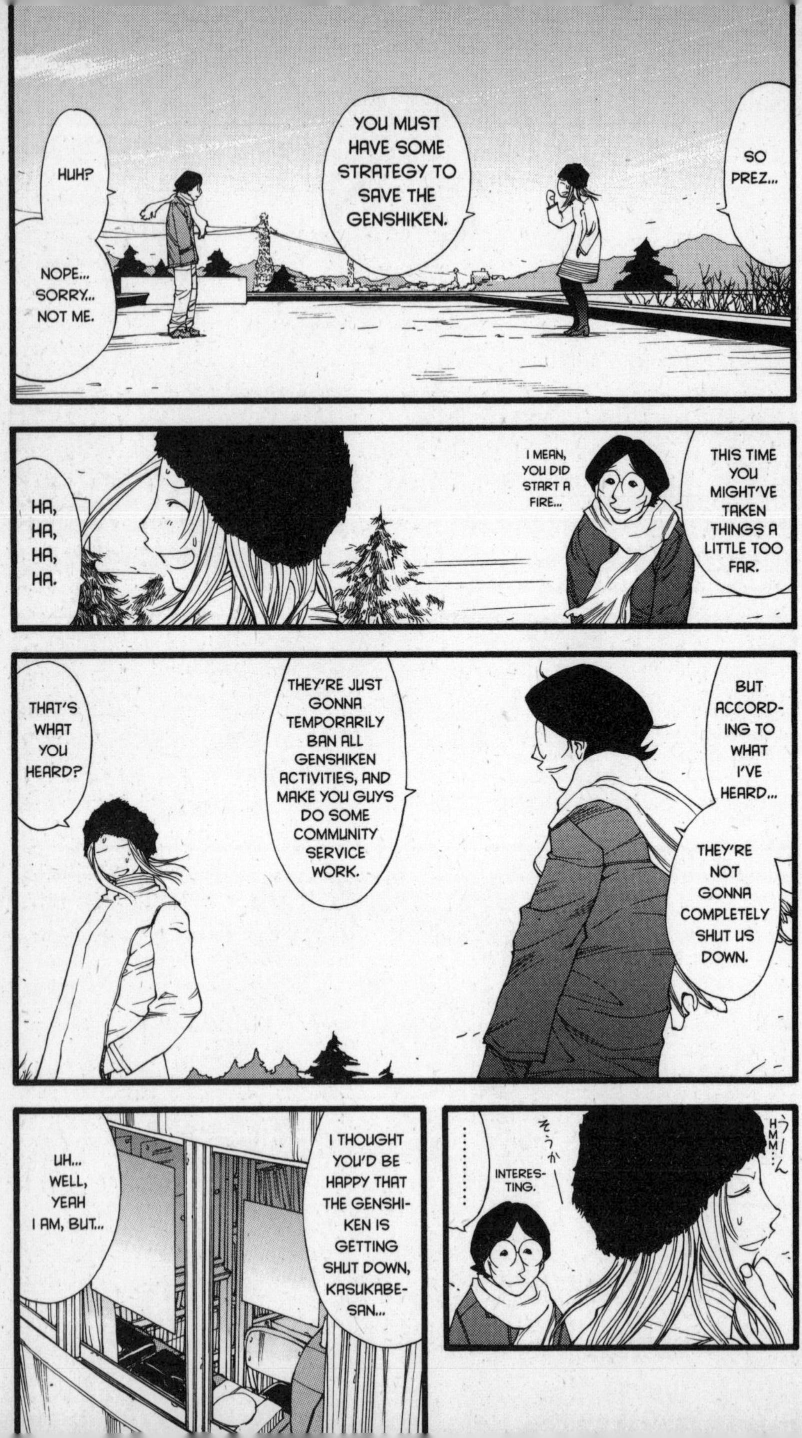
SO PREZ...
YOU MUST HAVE SOME STRATEGY TO SAVE THE GENSHIKEN.
HUH?
NOPE... SORRY... NOT ME.
THIS TIME YOU MIGHT'VE TAKEN THINGS A LITTLE TOO FAR.
I MEAN, YOU DID START A FIRE...
HA, HA, HA, HA.
BUT ACCORDING TO WHAT I'VE HEARD...
THEY'RE NOT GONNA COMPLETELY SHUT US DOWN.
THEY'RE JUST GONNA TEMPORARILY BAN ALL GENSHIKEN ACTIVITIES, AND MAKE YOU GUYS DO SOME COMMUNITY SERVICE WORK.
THAT'S WHAT YOU HEARD?
うーん HMM...
そうか
INTERESTING.
......
I THOUGHT YOU'D BE HAPPY THAT THE GENSHIKEN IS GETTING SHUT DOWN, KASUKABE-SAN...
UH... WELL, YEAH I AM, BUT...

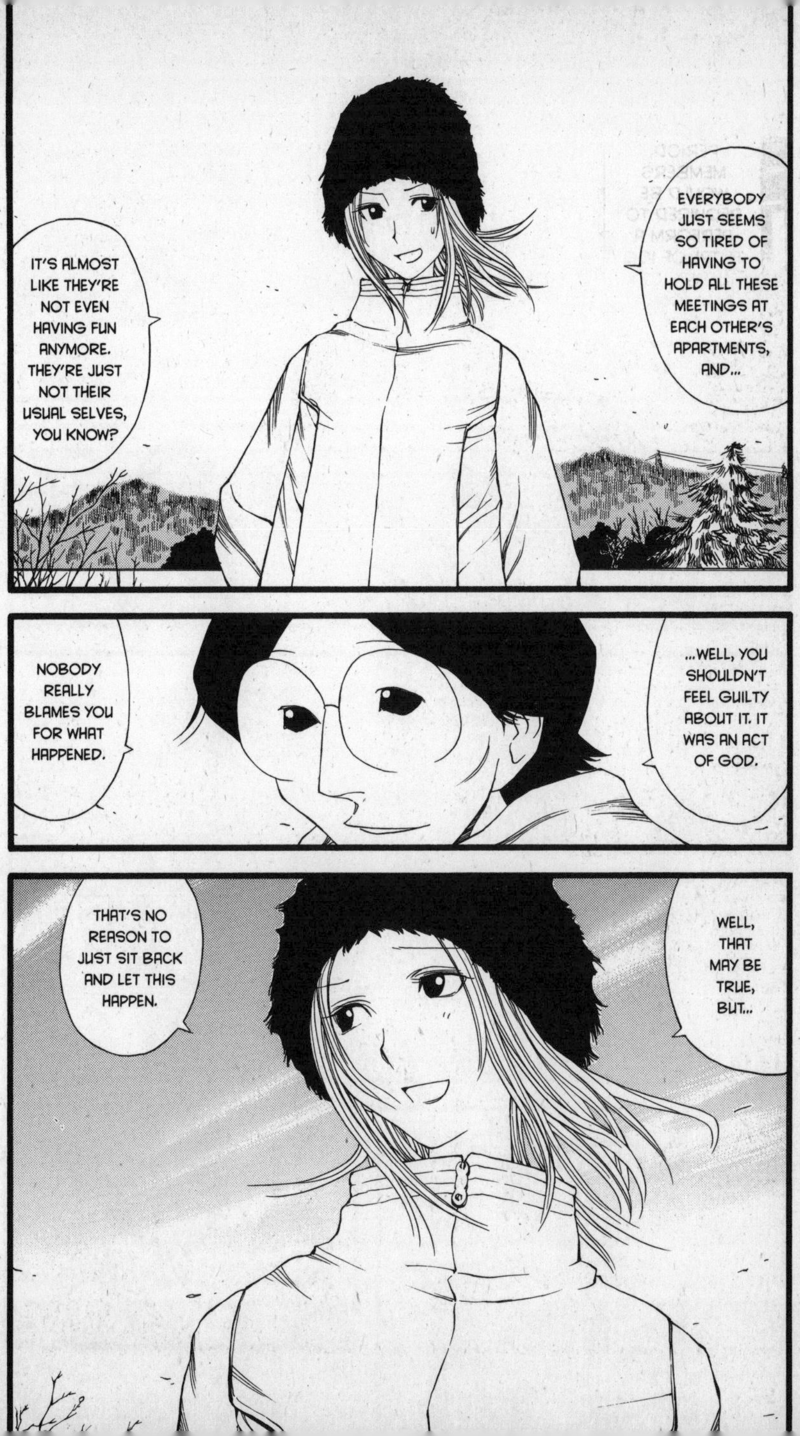
EVERYBODY JUST SEEMS SO TIRED OF HAVING TO HOLD ALL THESE MEETINGS AT EACH OTHER'S APARTMENTS, AND...
IT'S ALMOST LIKE THEY'RE NOT EVEN HAVING FUN ANYMORE. THEY'RE JUST NOT THEIR USUAL SELVES, YOU KNOW?
...WELL, YOU SHOULDN'T FEEL GUILTY ABOUT IT. IT WAS AN ACT OF GOD.
NOBODY REALLY BLAMES YOU FOR WHAT HAPPENED.
WELL, THAT MAY BE TRUE, BUT...
THAT'S NO REASON TO JUST SIT BACK AND LET THIS HAPPEN.

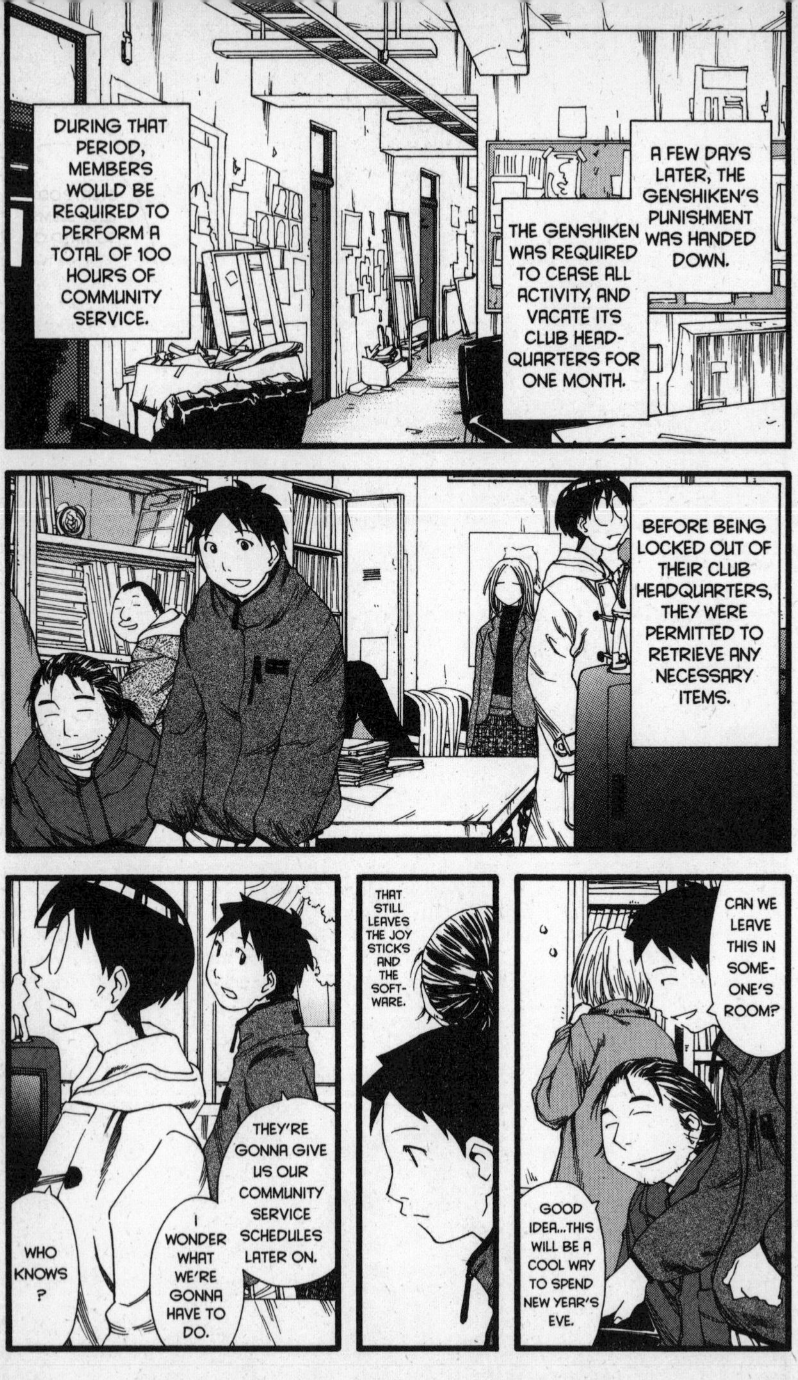
A FEW DAYS LATER, THE GENSHIKEN'S PUNISHMENT WAS HANDED DOWN.
THE GENSHIKEN WAS REQUIRED TO CEASE ALL ACTIVITY, AND VACATE ITS CLUB HEAD-QUARTERS FOR ONE MONTH.
DURING THAT PERIOD, MEMBERS WOULD BE REQUIRED TO PERFORM A TOTAL OF 100 HOURS OF COMMUNITY SERVICE.
BEFORE BEING LOCKED OUT OF THEIR CLUB HEADQUARTERS, THEY WERE PERMITTED TO RETRIEVE ANY NECESSARY ITEMS.
CAN WE LEAVE THIS IN SOME-ONE'S ROOM?
GOOD IDEA...THIS WILL BE A COOL WAY TO SPEND NEW YEAR'S EVE.
THAT STILL LEAVES THE JOY STICKS AND THE SOFT-WARE.
THEY'RE GONNA GIVE US OUR COMMUNITY SERVICE SCHEDULES LATER ON.
I WONDER WHAT WE'RE GONNA HAVE TO DO.
WHO KNOWS ?

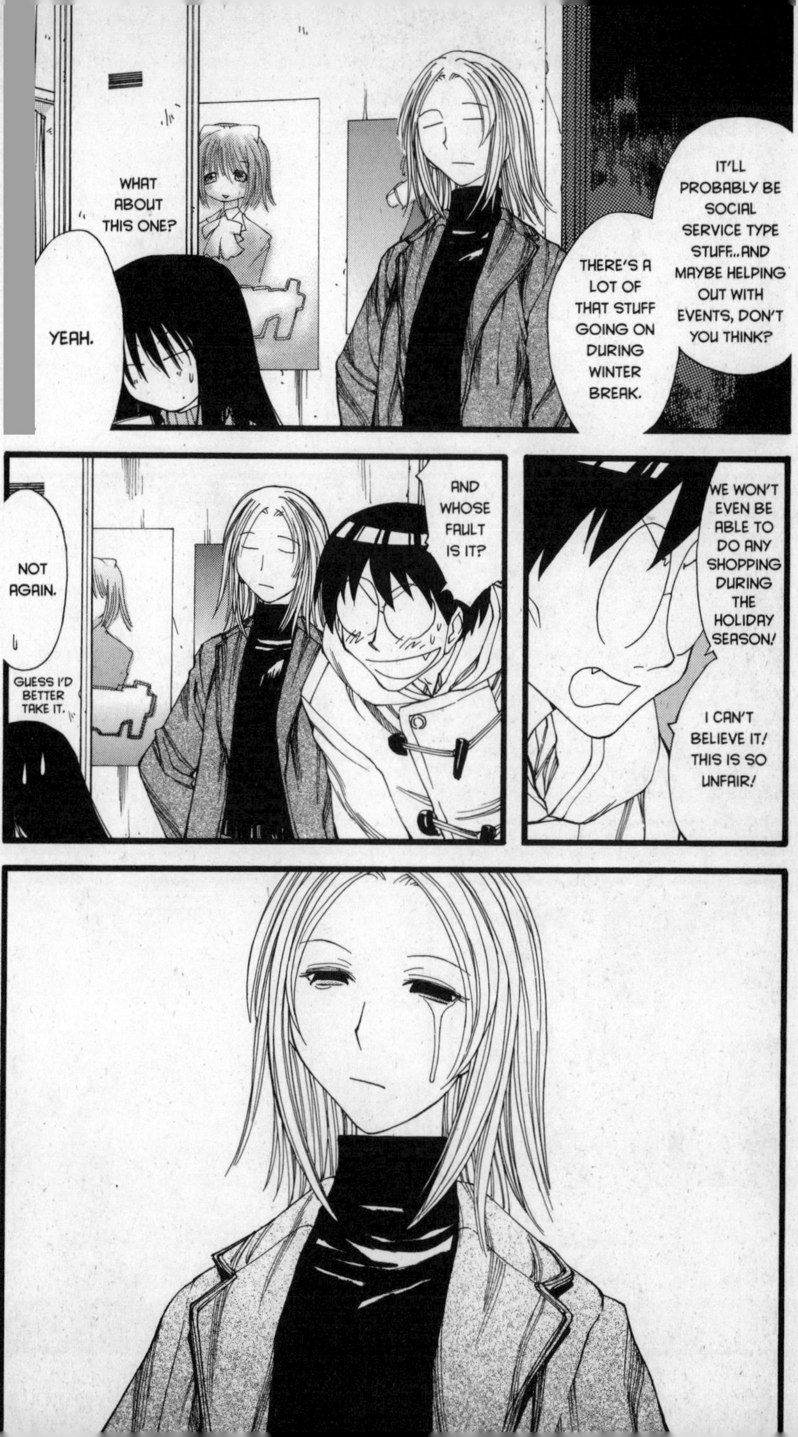
IT'LL PROBABLY BE SOCIAL SERVICE TYPE STUFF...AND MAYBE HELPING OUT WITH EVENTS, DON'T YOU THINK?
THERE'S A LOT OF THAT STUFF GOING ON DURING WINTER BREAK.
WHAT ABOUT THIS ONE?
YEAH.
WE WON'T EVEN BE ABLE TO DO ANY SHOPPING DURING THE HOLIDAY SEASON!
I CAN'T BELIEVE IT! THIS IS SO UNFAIR!
AND WHOSE FAULT IS IT?
NOT AGAIN.
GUESS I'D BETTER TAKE IT.

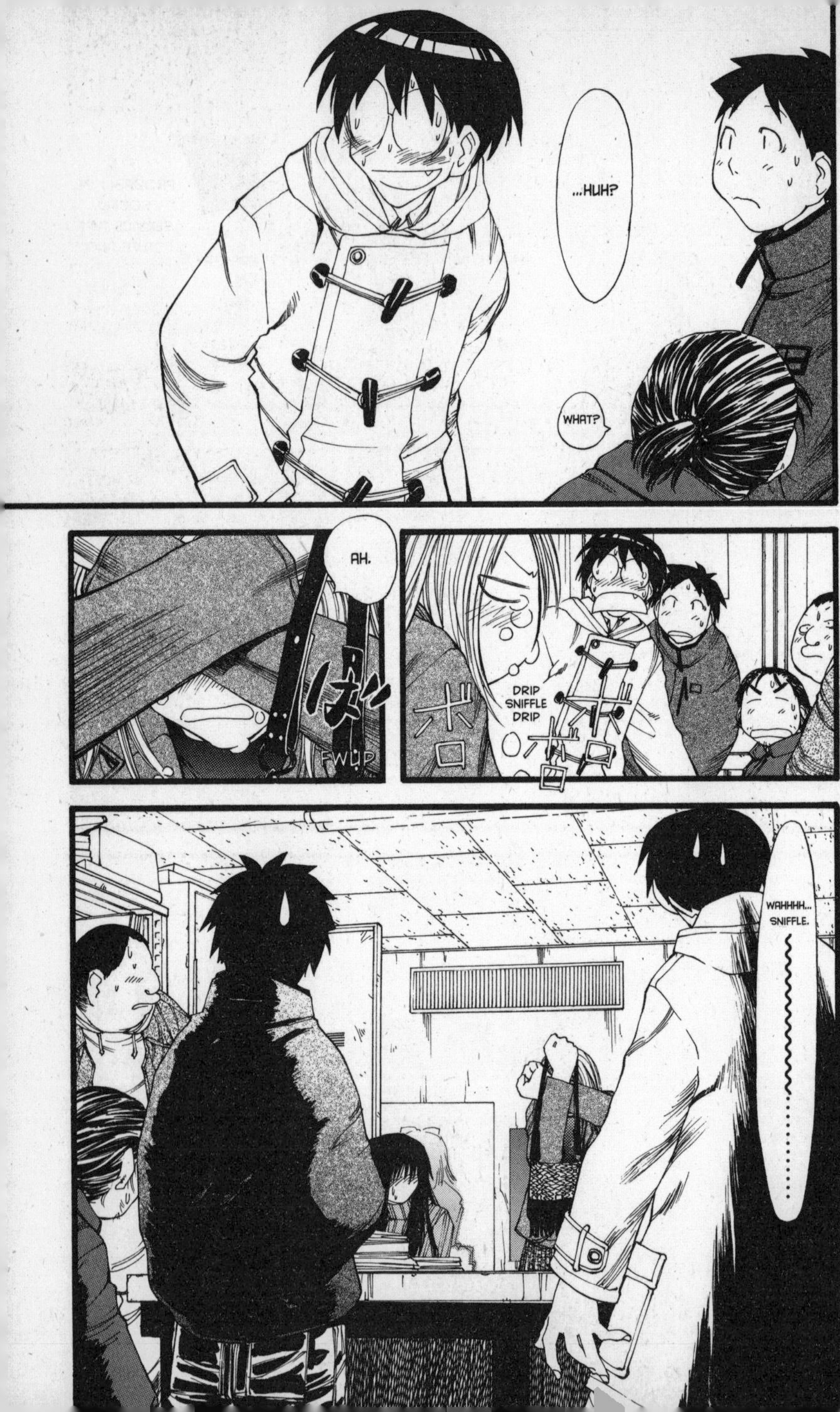
...HUH?
WHAT?
DRIP
SNIFFLE
DRIP
AH.
FWUP
WAHHHH... SNIFFLE.

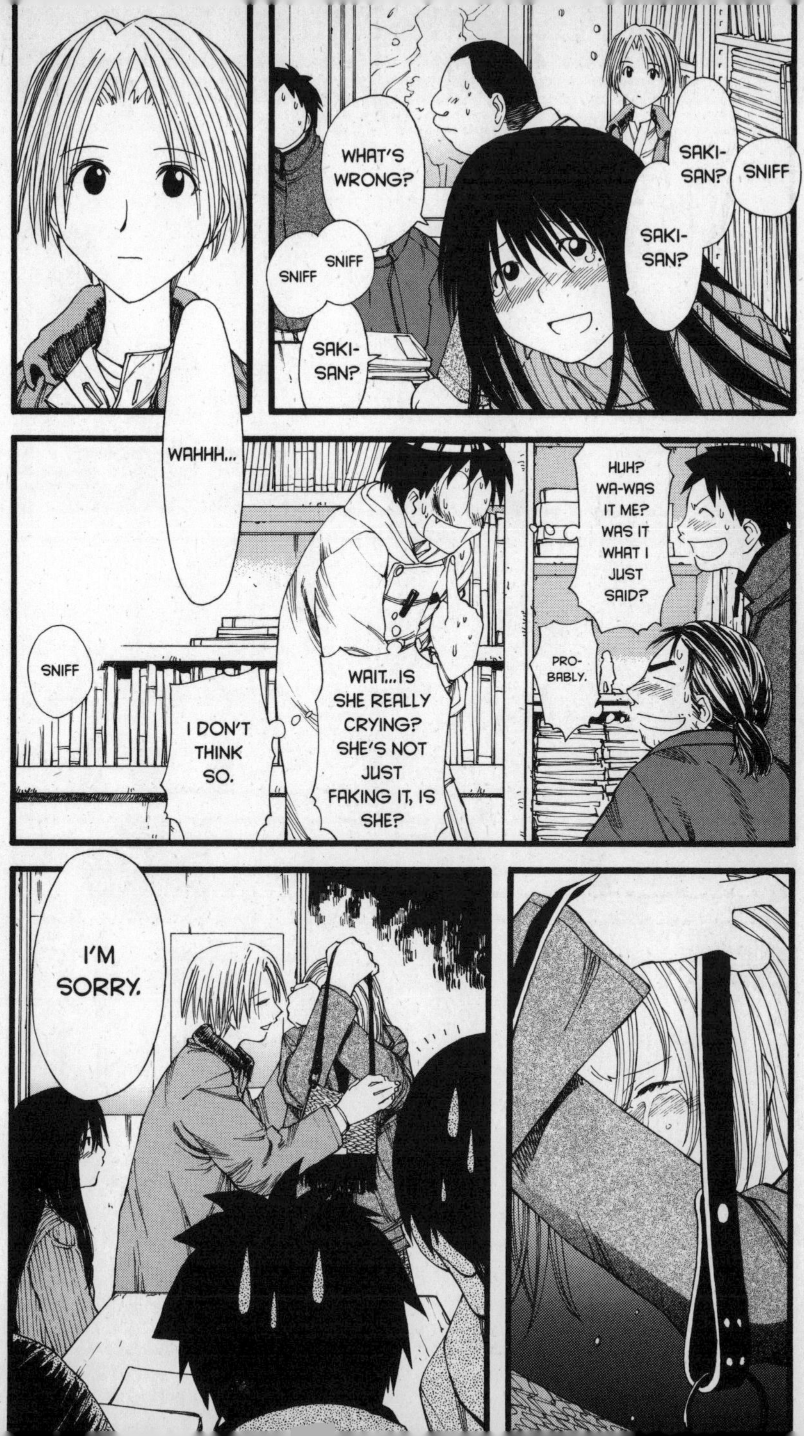
SNIFF
SAKI-SAN?
SAKI-SAN?
WHAT'S WRONG?
SNIFF SNIFF
SAKI-SAN?
WAHHH...
HUH? WA-WAS IT ME? WAS IT WHAT I JUST SAID?
PRO-BABLY.
WAIT...IS SHE REALLY CRYING? SHE'S NOT JUST FAKING IT, IS SHE?
I DON'T THINK SO.
SNIFF
I'M SORRY.

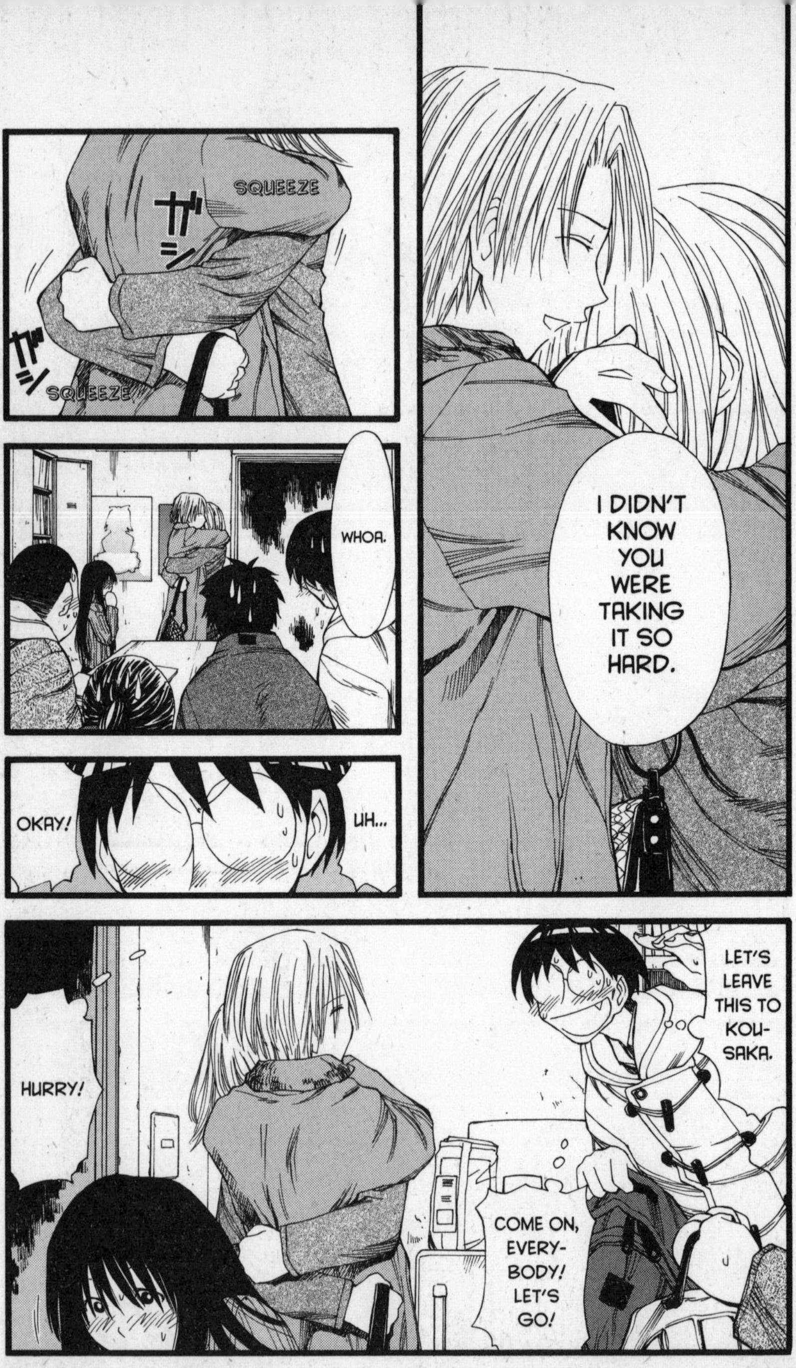
I DIDN'T KNOW YOU WERE TAKING IT SO HARD.
ガシ
SQUEEZE
ガシ
SQUEEZE
WHOA.
UH...
OKAY!
LET'S LEAVE THIS TO KOU-SAKA.
COME ON, EVERY-BODY! LET'S GO!
HURRY!

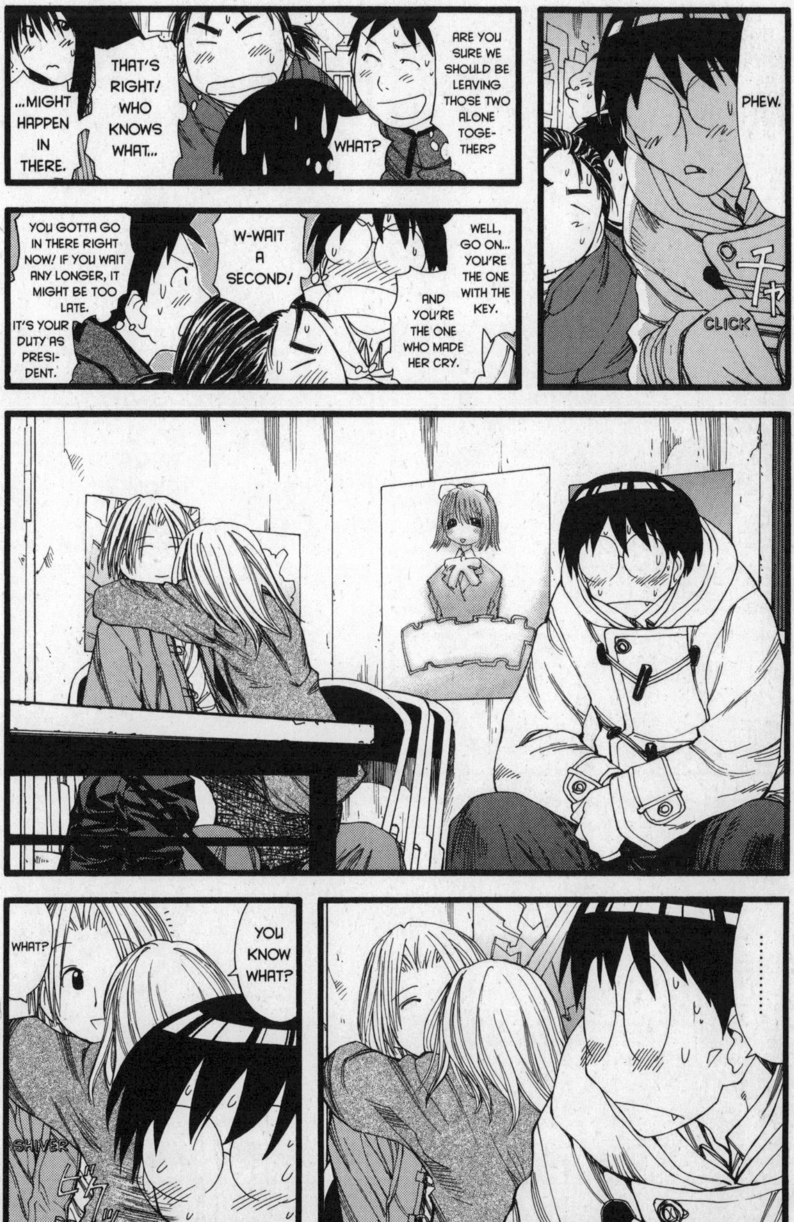
PHEW.
チャ
CLICK
ARE YOU SURE WE SHOULD BE LEAVING THOSE TWO ALONE TOGE-THER?
WHAT?
THAT'S RIGHT! WHO KNOWS WHAT...
...MIGHT HAPPEN IN THERE.
WELL, GO ON... YOU'RE THE ONE WITH THE KEY.
AND YOU'RE THE ONE WHO MADE HER CRY.
W-WAIT A SECOND!
YOU GOTTA GO IN THERE RIGHT NOW! IF YOU WAIT ANY LONGER, IT MIGHT BE TOO LATE.
IT'S YOUR DUTY AS PRESI-DENT.
.........
YOU KNOW WHAT?
WHAT?
SHIVER

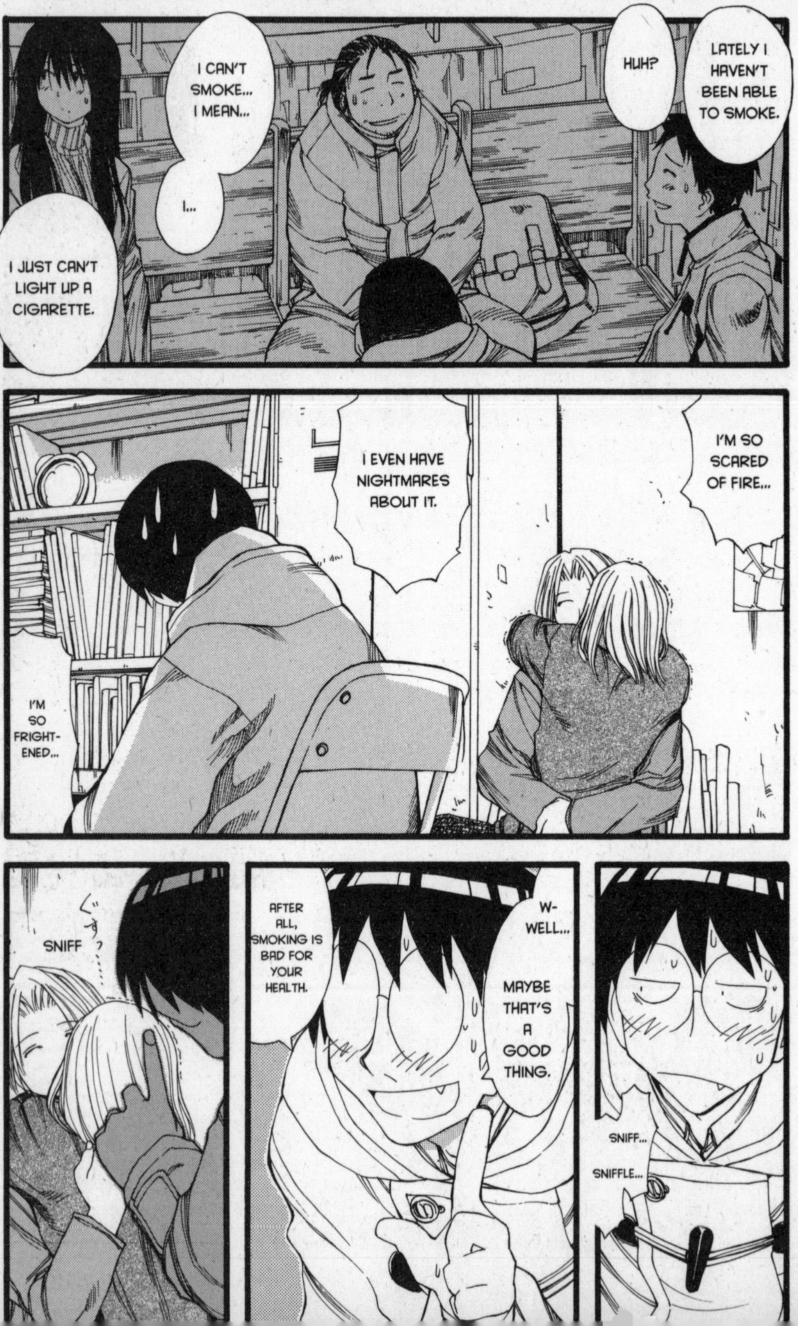
LATELY I HAVEN'T BEEN ABLE TO SMOKE.
HUH?
I CAN'T SMOKE... I MEAN...
I...
I JUST CAN'T LIGHT UP A CIGARETTE.
I'M SO SCARED OF FIRE...
I EVEN HAVE NIGHTMARES ABOUT IT.
I'M SO FRIGHT-ENED...
SNIFF...
SNIFFLE...
W-WELL...
MAYBE THAT'S A GOOD THING.
AFTER ALL, SMOKING IS BAD FOR YOUR HEALTH.
ぐすっ
SNIFF

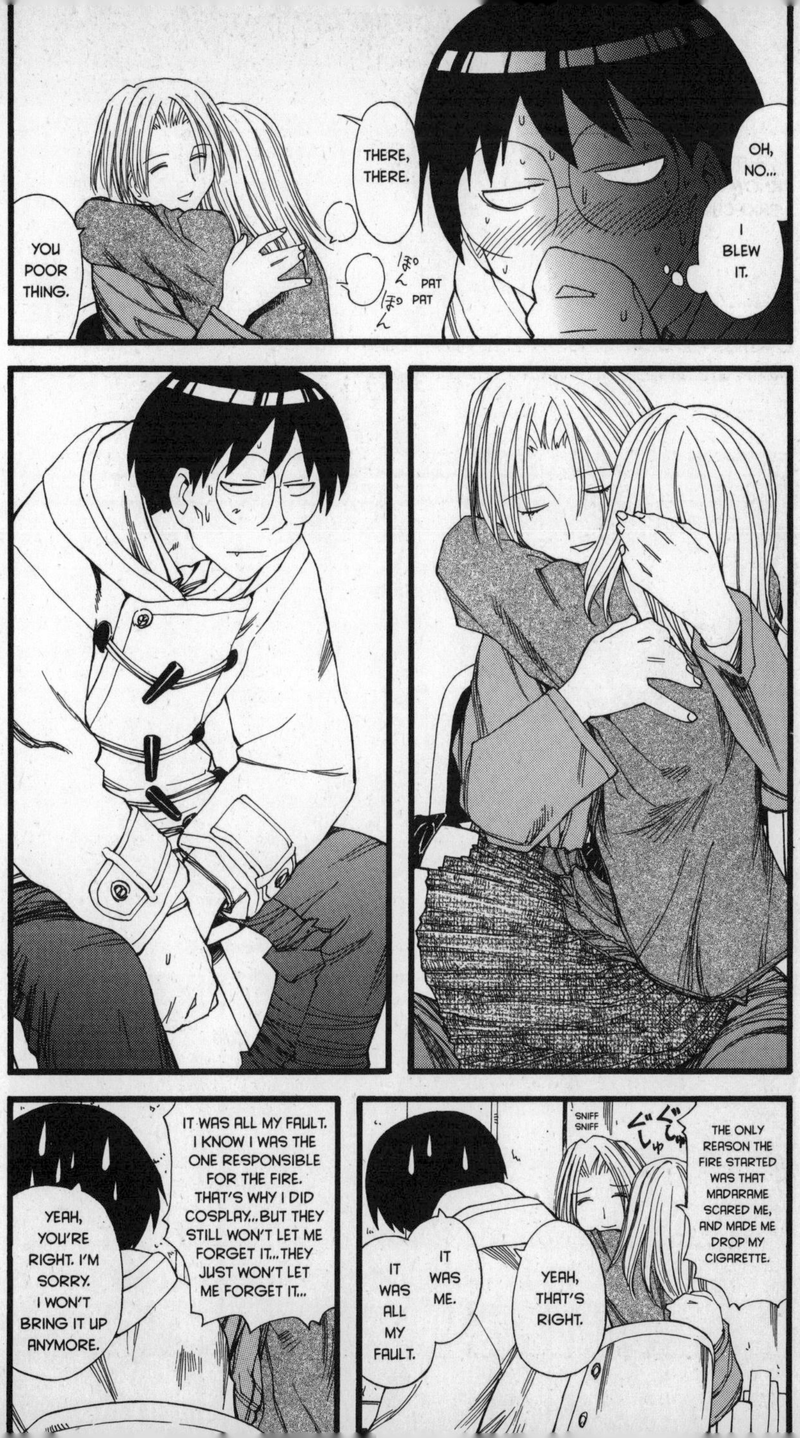
OH, NO... I BLEW IT.
THERE, THERE.
ぽんぽん
PAT PAT
YOU POOR THING.
THE ONLY REASON THE FIRE STARTED WAS THAT MADARAME SCARED ME, AND MADE ME DROP MY CIGARETTE.
ぐじゅぐじゅ
SNIFF SNIFF
YEAH, THAT'S RIGHT.
IT WAS ME.
IT WAS ALL MY FAULT.
IT WAS ALL MY FAULT. I KNOW I WAS THE ONE RESPONSIBLE FOR THE FIRE. THAT'S WHY I DID COSPLAY...BUT THEY STILL WON'T LET ME FORGET IT...THEY JUST WON'T LET ME FORGET IT...
YEAH, YOU'RE RIGHT. I'M SORRY. I WON'T BRING IT UP ANYMORE.

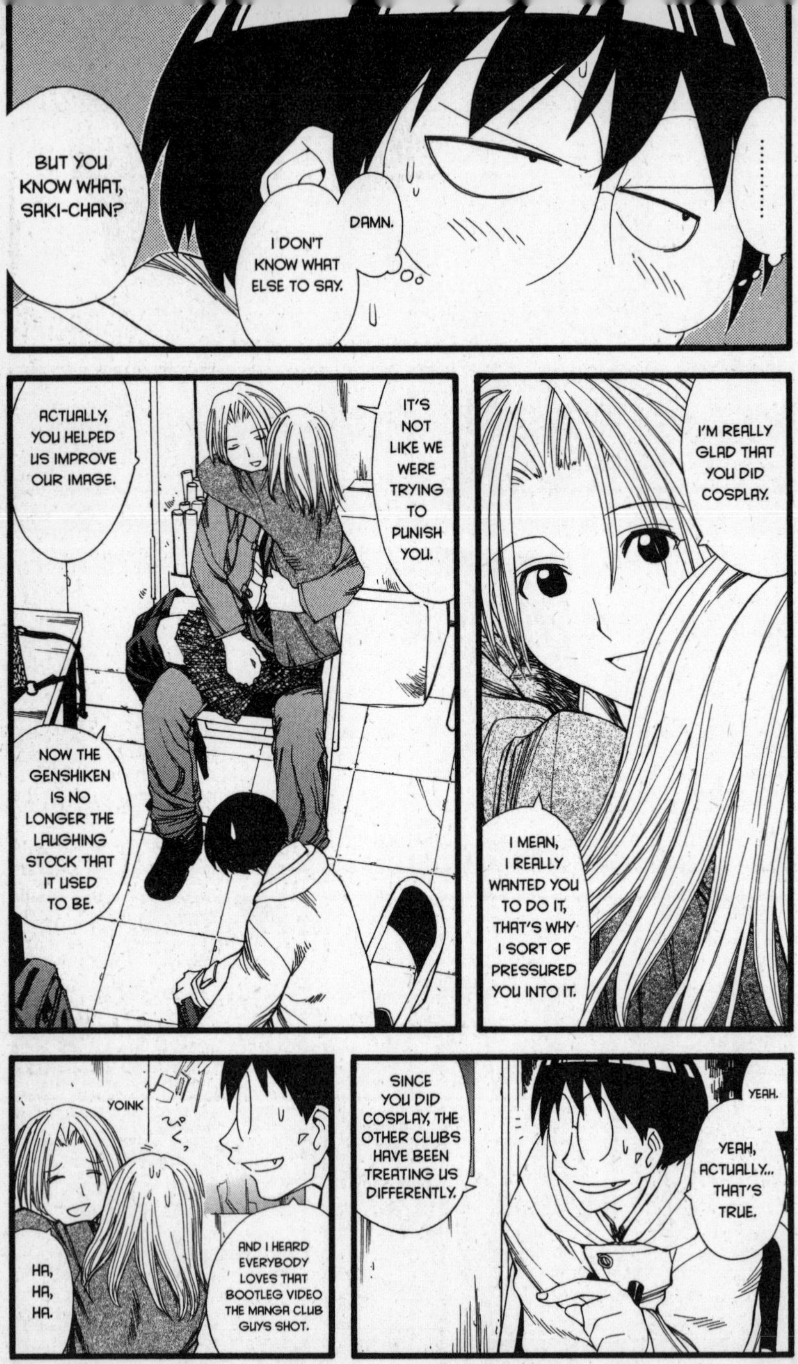
......
DAMN.
I DON'T KNOW WHAT ELSE TO SAY.
BUT YOU KNOW WHAT, SAKI-CHAN?
I'M REALLY GLAD THAT YOU DID COSPLAY.
I MEAN, I REALLY WANTED YOU TO DO IT, THAT'S WHY I SORT OF PRESSURED YOU INTO IT.
IT'S NOT LIKE WE WERE TRYING TO PUNISH YOU.
ACTUALLY, YOU HELPED US IMPROVE OUR IMAGE.
NOW THE GENSHIKEN IS NO LONGER THE LAUGHING STOCK THAT IT USED TO BE.
YEAH.
YEAH, ACTUALLY... THAT'S TRUE.
SINCE YOU DID COSPLAY, THE OTHER CLUBS HAVE BEEN TREATING US DIFFERENTLY.
YOINK
AND I HEARD EVERYBODY LOVES THAT BOOTLEG VIDEO THE MANGA CLUB GUYS SHOT.
HA, HA, HA.

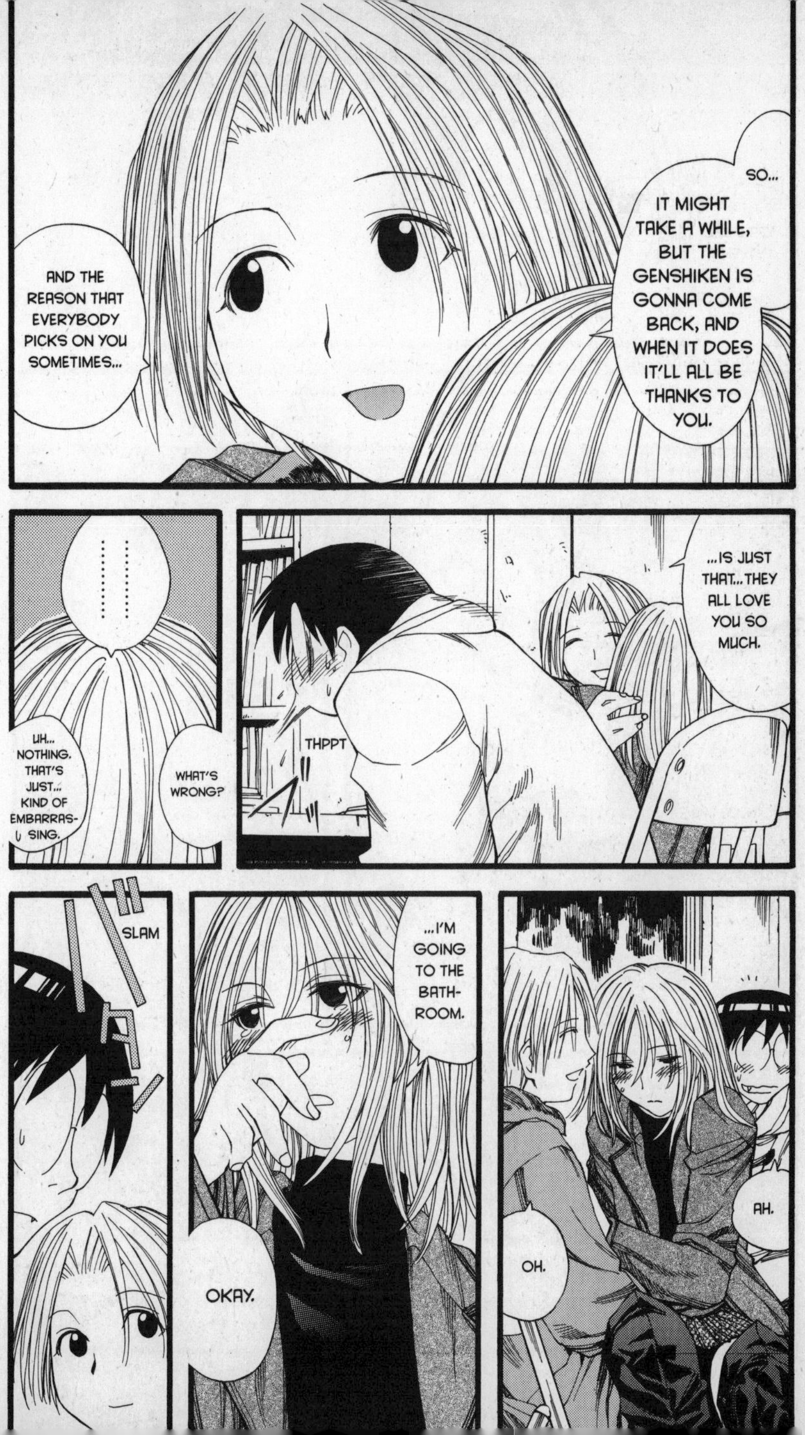
SO...
IT MIGHT TAKE A WHILE, BUT THE GENSHIKEN IS GONNA COME BACK, AND WHEN IT DOES IT'LL ALL BE THANKS TO YOU.
AND THE REASON THAT EVERYBODY PICKS ON YOU SOMETIMES...
...IS JUST THAT...THEY ALL LOVE YOU SO MUCH.
THPPT
......
WHAT'S WRONG?
UH... NOTHING. THAT'S JUST... KIND OF EMBARRAS-SING.
AH.
OH.
...I'M GOING TO THE BATH-ROOM.
OKAY.
SLAM

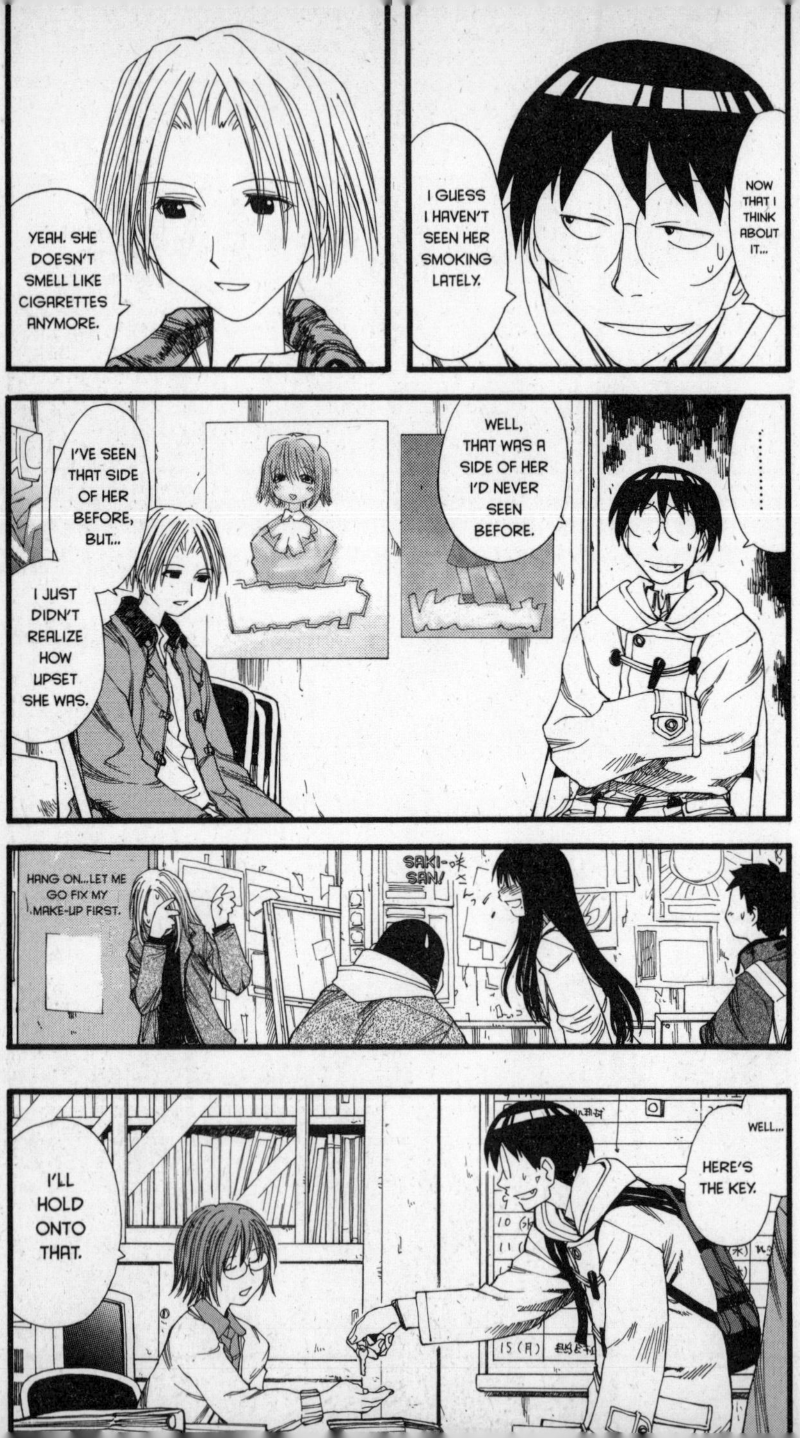
NOW THAT I THINK ABOUT IT...
I GUESS I HAVEN'T SEEN HER SMOKING LATELY.
YEAH. SHE DOESN'T SMELL LIKE CIGARETTES ANYMORE.
......
WELL, THAT WAS A SIDE OF HER I'D NEVER SEEN BEFORE.
I'VE SEEN THAT SIDE OF HER BEFORE, BUT...
I JUST DIDN'T REALIZE HOW UPSET SHE WAS.
SAKI-SAN!
HANG ON...LET ME GO FIX MY MAKE-UP FIRST.
WELL...
HERE'S THE KEY.
I'LL HOLD ONTO THAT.

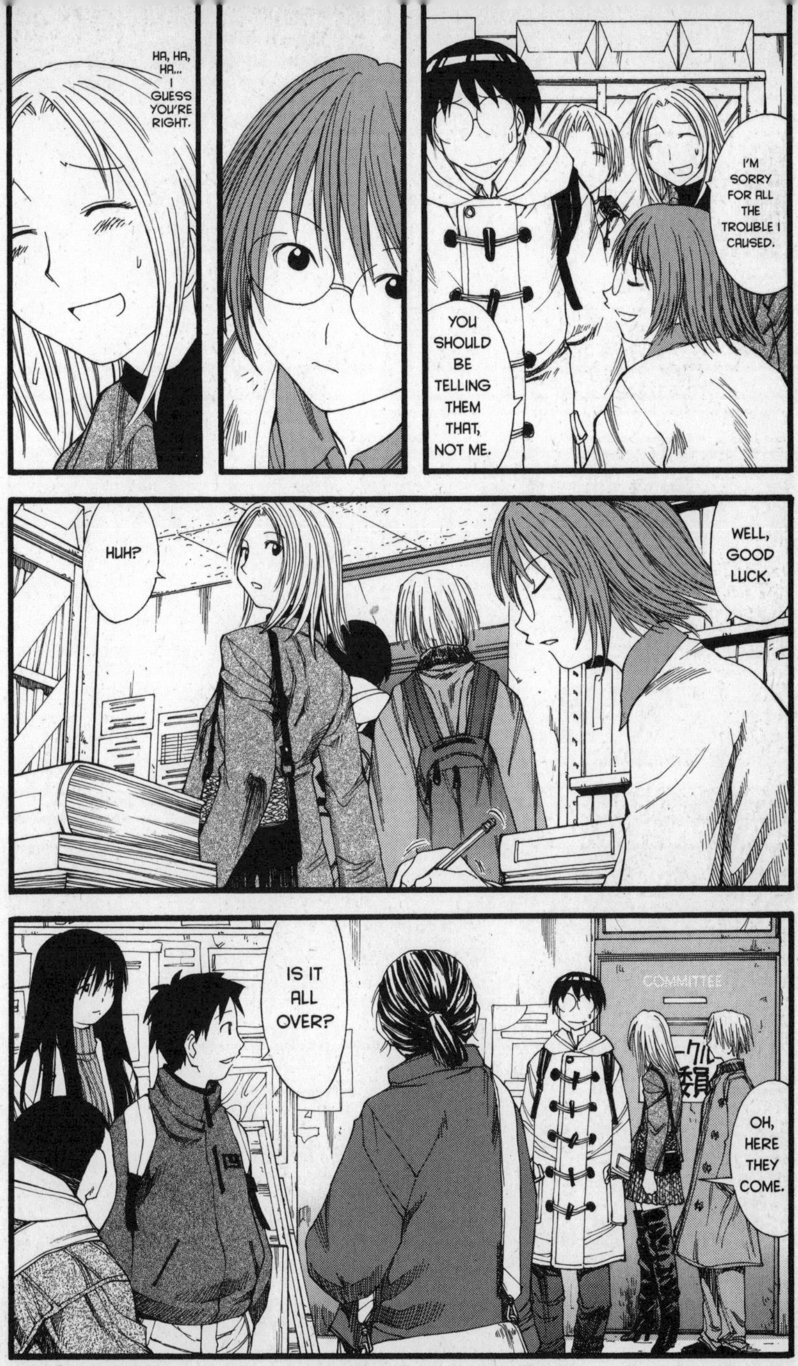
I'M SORRY FOR ALL THE TROUBLE I CAUSED.
YOU SHOULD BE TELLING THEM THAT, NOT ME.
HA, HA, HA... I GUESS YOU'RE RIGHT.
WELL, GOOD LUCK.
HUH?
COMMITTEE
OH, HERE THEY COME.
IS IT ALL OVER?

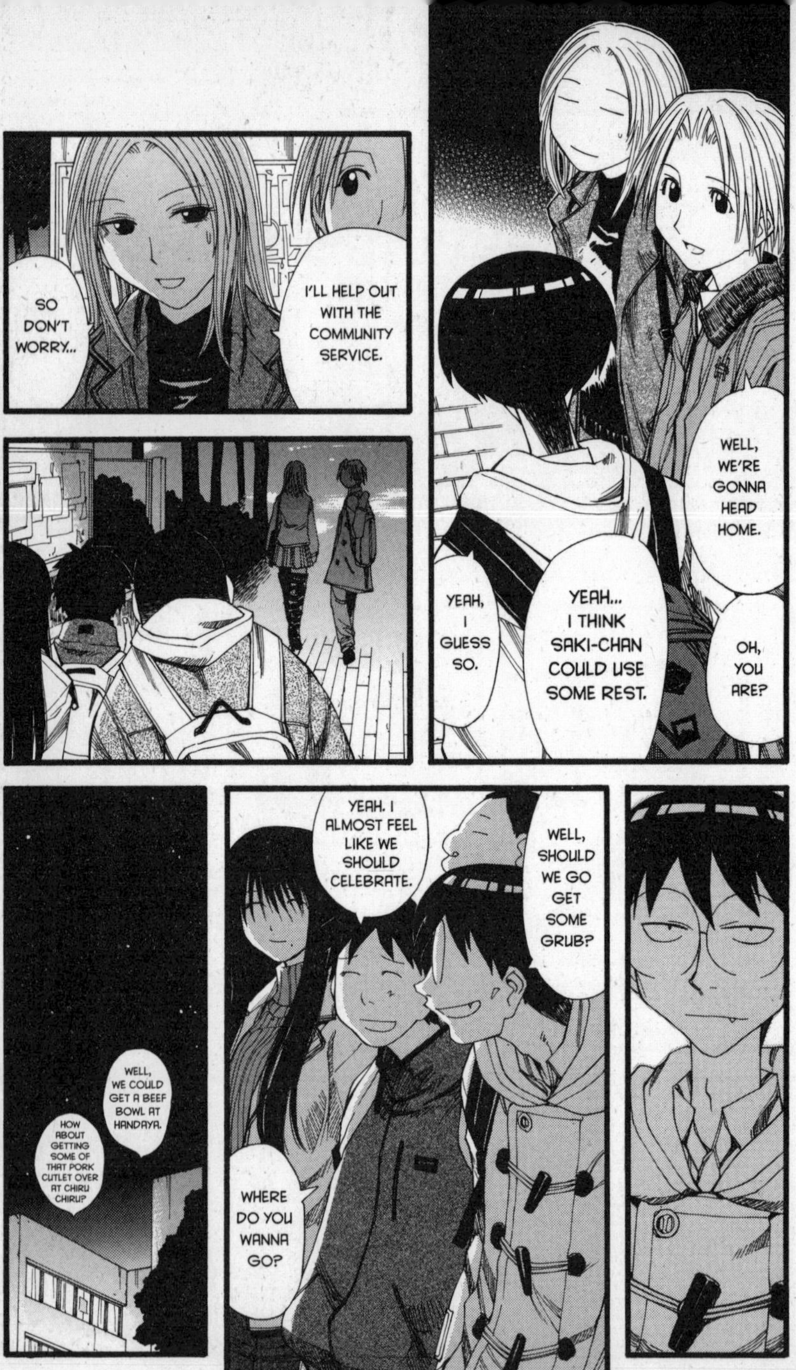
WELL, WE'RE GONNA HEAD HOME.
OH, YOU ARE?
YEAH... I THINK SAKI-CHAN COULD USE SOME REST.
YEAH, I GUESS SO.
I'LL HELP OUT WITH THE COMMUNITY SERVICE.
SO DON'T WORRY...
WELL, SHOULD WE GO GET SOME GRUB?
YEAH. I ALMOST FEEL LIKE WE SHOULD CELEBRATE.
WHERE DO YOU WANNA GO?
WELL, WE COULD GET A BEEF BOWL AT HANDAYA.
HOW ABOUT GETTING SOME OF THAT PORK CUTLET OVER AT CHIRU CHIRU?

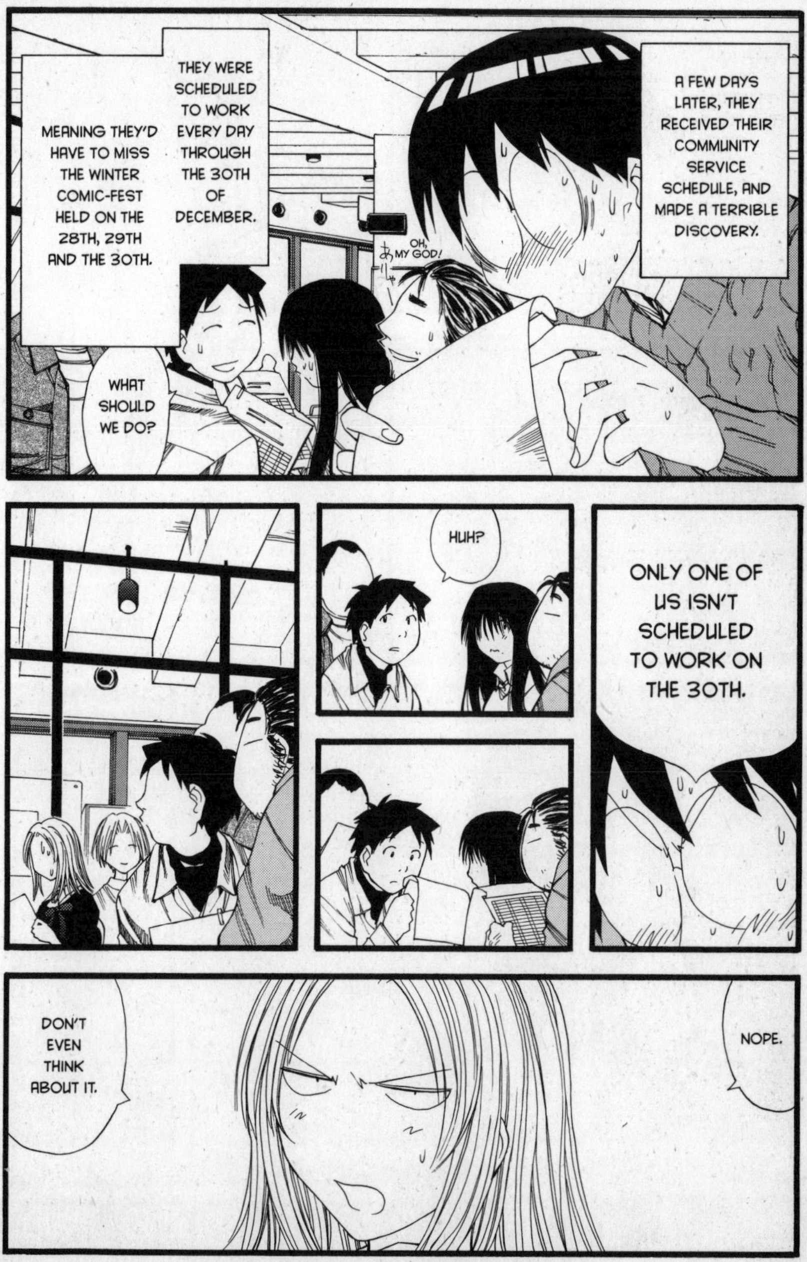
A FEW DAYS LATER, THEY RECEIVED THEIR COMMUNITY SERVICE SCHEDULE, AND MADE A TERRIBLE DISCOVERY.
THEY WERE SCHEDULED TO WORK EVERY DAY THROUGH THE 30TH OF DECEMBER.
MEANING THEY'D HAVE TO MISS THE WINTER COMIC-FEST HELD ON THE 28TH, 29TH AND THE 30TH.
OH, MY GOD!
WHAT SHOULD WE DO?
ONLY ONE OF US ISN'T SCHEDULED TO WORK ON THE 30TH.
HUH?
NOPE.
DON'T EVEN THINK ABOUT IT.

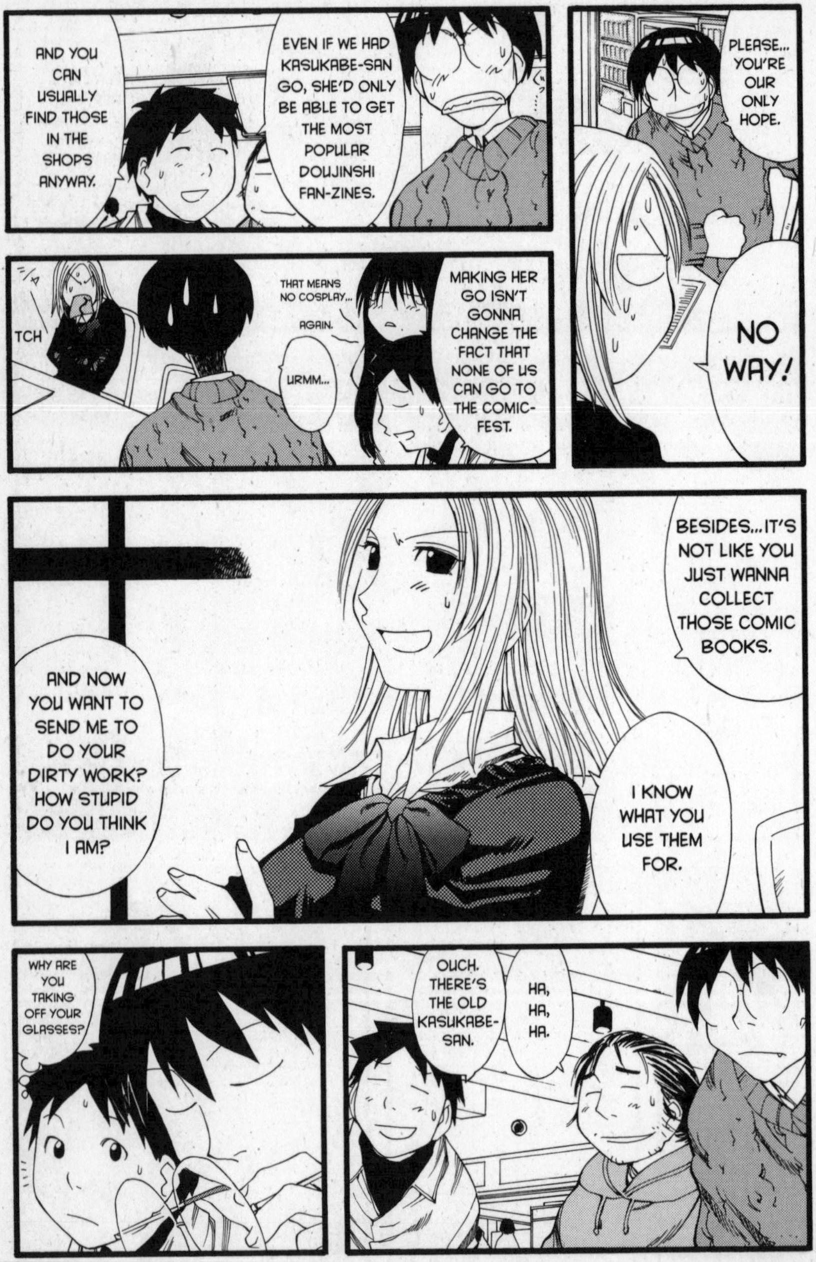
PLEASE... YOU'RE OUR ONLY HOPE.
NO WAY!
EVEN IF WE HAD KASUKABE-SAN GO, SHE'D ONLY BE ABLE TO GET THE MOST POPULAR DOUJINSHI FAN-ZINES.
AND YOU CAN USUALLY FIND THOSE IN THE SHOPS ANYWAY.
MAKING HER GO ISN'T GONNA CHANGE THE FACT THAT NONE OF US CAN GO TO THE COMIC-FEST.
THAT MEANS NO COSPLAY...
AGAIN.
URMM...
TCH
BESIDES...IT'S NOT LIKE YOU JUST WANNA COLLECT THOSE COMIC BOOKS.
I KNOW WHAT YOU USE THEM FOR.
AND NOW YOU WANT TO SEND ME TO DO YOUR DIRTY WORK? HOW STUPID DO YOU THINK I AM?
HA, HA, HA.
OUCH. THERE'S THE OLD KASUKABE-SAN.
WHY ARE YOU TAKING OFF YOUR GLASSES?

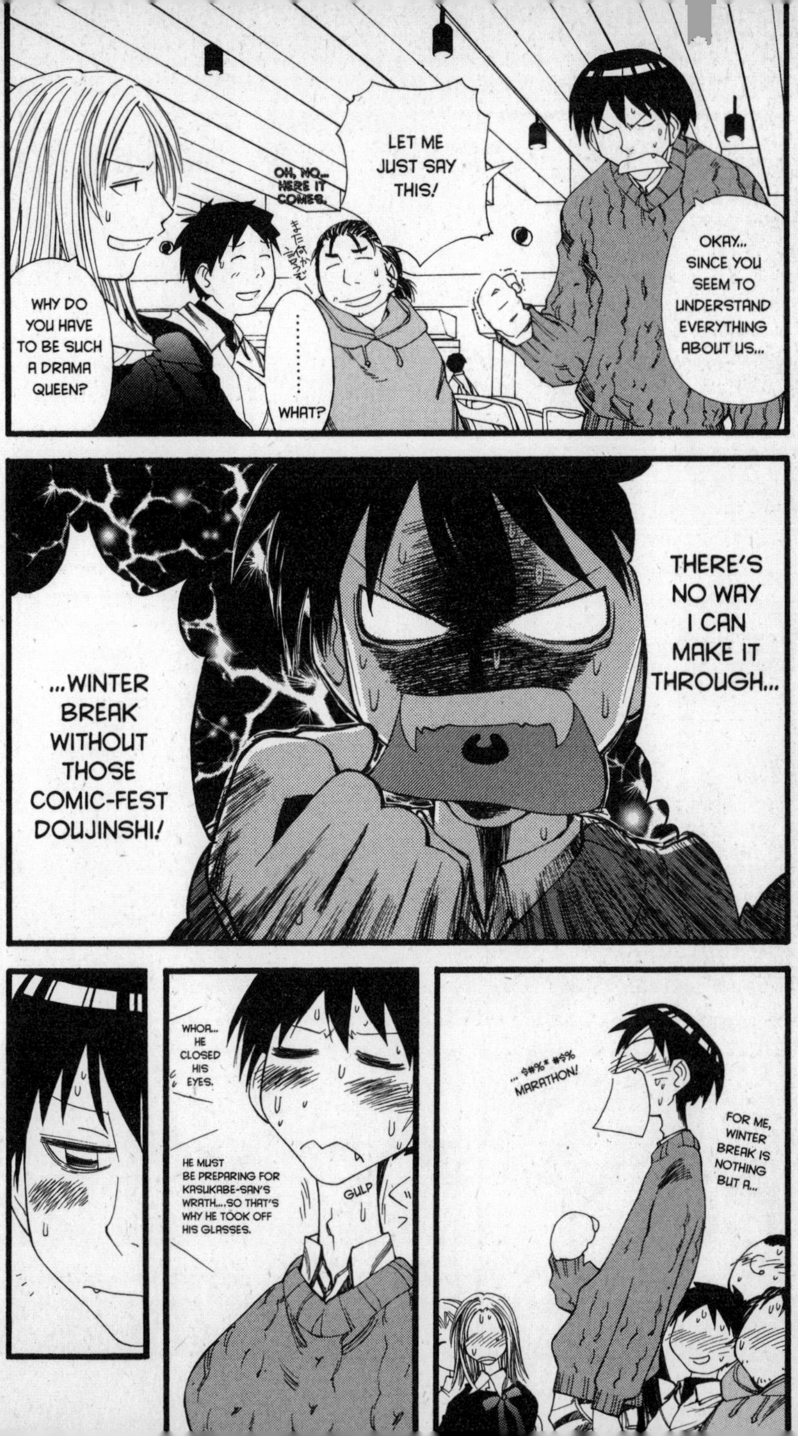
OKAY... SINCE YOU SEEM TO UNDERSTAND EVERYTHING ABOUT US...
LET ME JUST SAY THIS!
OH, NO... HERE IT COMES.
......... WHAT?
WHY DO YOU HAVE TO BE SUCH A DRAMA QUEEN?
THERE'S NO WAY I CAN MAKE IT THROUGH...
...WINTER BREAK WITHOUT THOSE COMIC-FEST DOUJINSHI!
FOR ME, WINTER BREAK IS NOTHING BUT A...
... $#%* #$% MARATHON!
WHOA... HE CLOSED HIS EYES.
HE MUST BE PREPARING FOR KASUKABE-SAN'S WRATH....SO THAT'S WHY HE TOOK OFF HIS GLASSES.
GULP

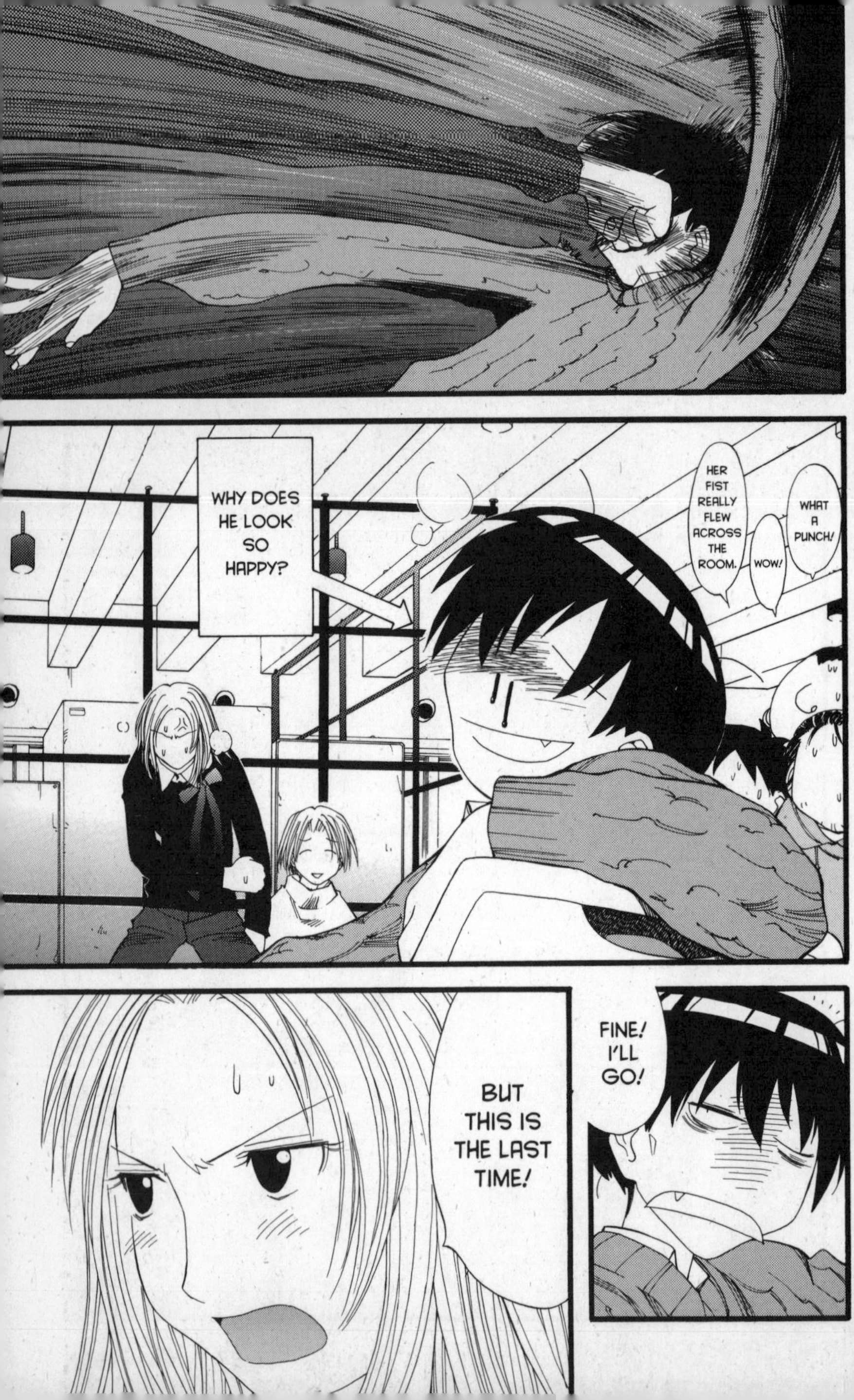
WHAT A PUNCH!
WOW!
HER FIST REALLY FLEW ACROSS THE ROOM.
WHY DOES HE LOOK SO HAPPY?
FINE! I'LL GO!
BUT THIS IS THE LAST TIME!

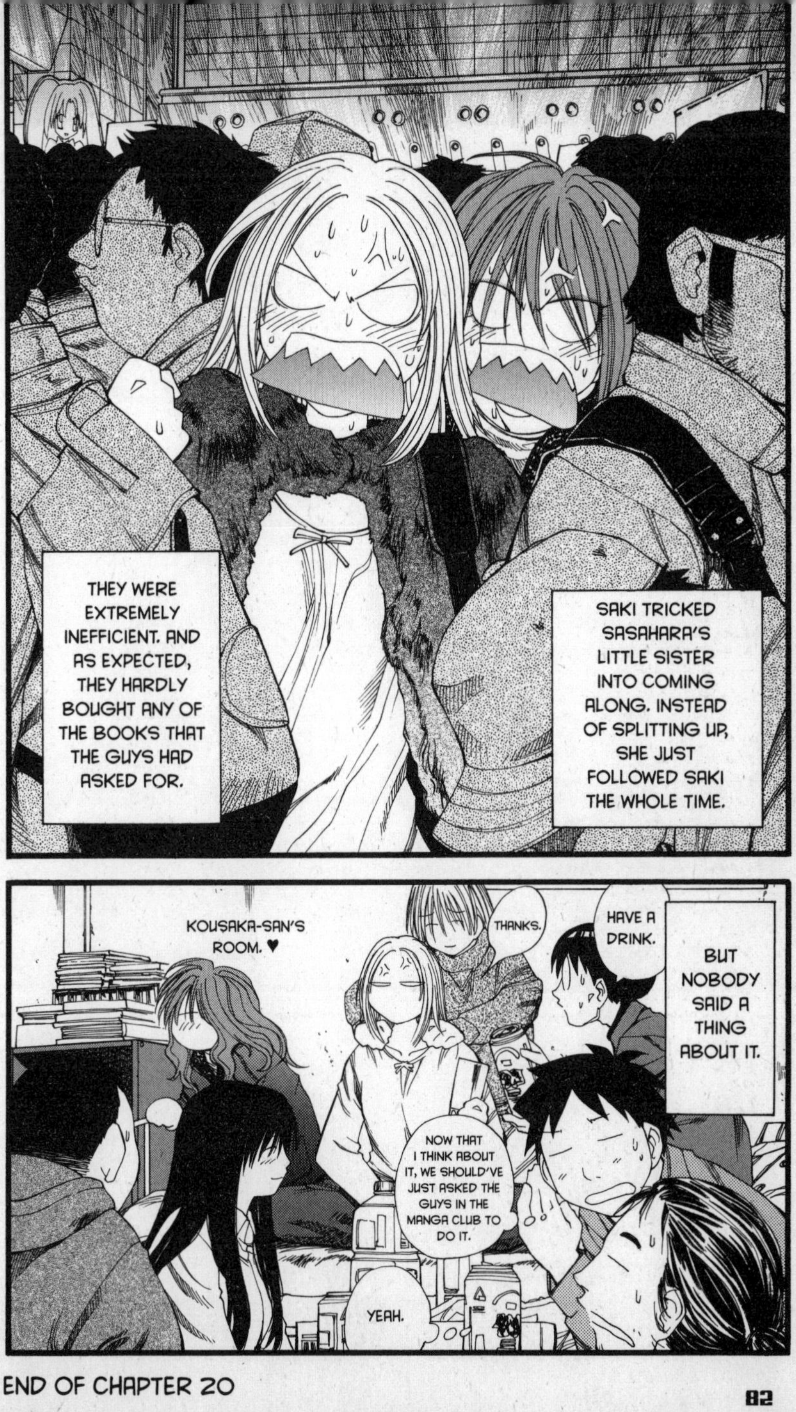
SAKI TRICKED SASAHARA'S LITTLE SISTER INTO COMING ALONG. INSTEAD OF SPLITTING UP, SHE JUST FOLLOWED SAKI THE WHOLE TIME.
THEY WERE EXTREMELY INEFFICIENT. AND AS EXPECTED, THEY HARDLY BOUGHT ANY OF THE BOOKS THAT THE GUYS HAD ASKED FOR.
BUT NOBODY SAID A THING ABOUT IT.
HAVE A DRINK.
THANKS.
KOUSAKA-SAN'S ROOM. ♥
NOW THAT I THINK ABOUT IT, WE SHOULD'VE JUST ASKED THE GUYS IN THE MANGA CLUB TO DO IT.
YEAH.

END OF CHAPTER 20

# OUR FAVORITE GAME ANOTHER STORIES

STORY 3

IZUMI TACHIBANA

REVIEWED BY THE OWL

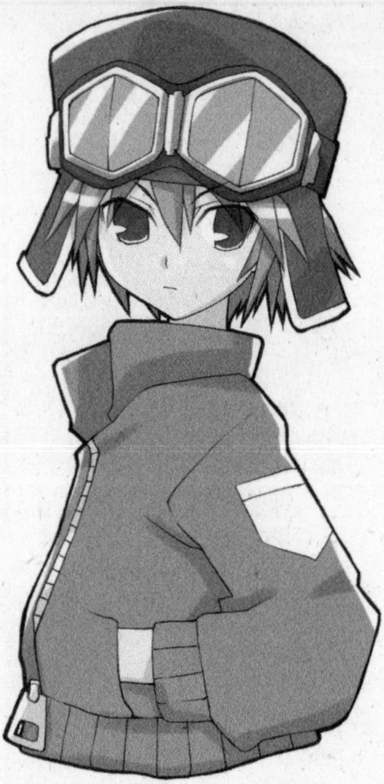

IZUMI'S SCENARIO IS THE ONE THAT REALLY GRABBED ME. THE BLEND OF EXCITEMENT AND SEXUAL AROUSAL WAS PERFECT. IZUMI IS KNOWN AS A CHARACTER WHO IS AT HOME IN THE DARK UNDERWORLD. IN THIS SCENARIO, HER MISSION IS TO FIND HER MISSING FATHER. IN THE ORIGINAL MANGA, THEY BRIEFLY TOUCH ON THIS TOPIC, BUT IN THE GAME, THEY REALLY DIVE RIGHT INTO IT. IN FACT, THEY CREATE A WHOLE NEW STORY LINE, BUT USE ALL THE DETAILS FROM THE ORIGINAL WORK. [LAUGH] BENJAMIN MENTIONED THIS IN HIS REVIEW OF THE PRESIDENT, BUT...WHAT'S GONNA HAPPEN WITH THE MANGA'S STORYLINE NOW?

HER FATHER GETS INVOLVED IN A BATTLE BETWEEN THE KISARAGI CLAN AND THE KIKYUU GANG. THEY GET INTO A MAHJONG MATCH IN WHICH A MYSTERIOUS SACRED ARTIFACT IS AT STAKE. JUST LIKE IZUMI, THE VICE PRESIDENT HAS ALSO LOST HER PARENTS TO A BATTLE. AMIDST AN ATMOSPHERE OF FEUDING AND UNAVOIDABLE DESTINY, IZUMI AND CHIHIRO BATTLE SIDE BY SIDE. YEAH...IT GETS PRETTY EXCITING.

SHE FINALLY FINDS OUT WHAT HAPPENED TO HER FATHER. AFTER THE FINAL BATTLE, SHE RETURNS HER GOGGLES TO THE HEAD OF THE KISARAGI CLAN AND GIVES UP HER NICKNAME "THE FOURTH BRIDGE." THAT SCENE HAS A VERY STRONG IMPACT. SHE THEN VOWS TO GIVE UP GAMBLING, AND BEGIN A NEW LIFE...AND CHIHIRO IS RIGHT THERE ALONGSIDE HER. IT'S FANTASTIC! [HA HA]

OH, AND NOW FOR THE SEXUALLY AROUSING PART...IT'S SO AWESOME THAT THERE ARE TWO AMUSEMENT PARK DATING EVENTS. DURING THE FIRST EVENT SHE WEARS HER USUAL ATTIRE, BUT ON THE SECOND ONE, TOKINO HELPS HER GET ALL DRESSED UP. THE WAY SHE ACTS ALL SHY IS SO CUTE...AND THE FACT THAT THEY USE THE SAME SITUATION TWICE IS VERY EFFECTIVE. WHEN IZUMI BUYS A BRAND-NEW PAIR OF GOGGLES, IT REALLY REFLECTS ON HER CHARACTER'S PERSONALITY. HEY, KUROKI! WHAT'RE YOU GONNA DO NOW? [HA HA] [THE OWL]

★

GEEZ...THERE'S NO ROOM FOR ME TO WRITE AGAIN. YOU WENT ON TOO LONG. [PIT VIPER]

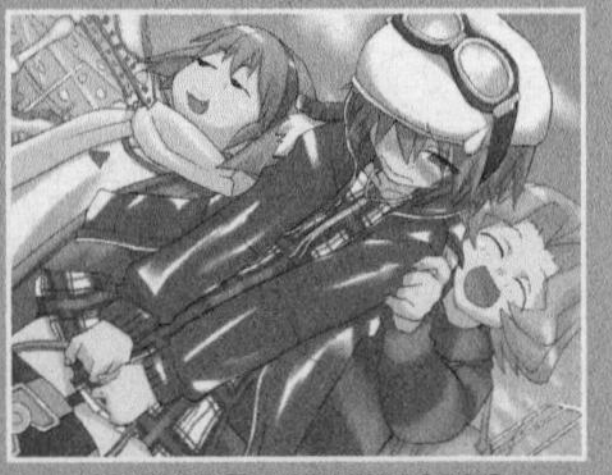

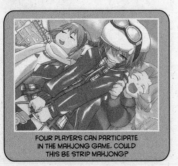

FOUR PLAYERS CAN PARTICIPATE IN THE MAHJONG GAME. COULD THIS BE STRIP MAHJONG?

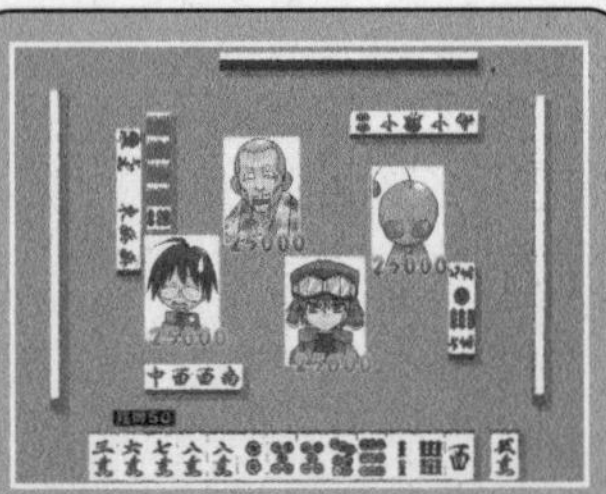

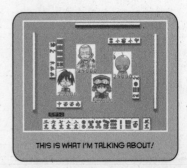

THIS IS WHAT I'M TALKING ABOUT!

CHAPTER 21 - MOMENTS LATER

KOUSAKA'S ROOM

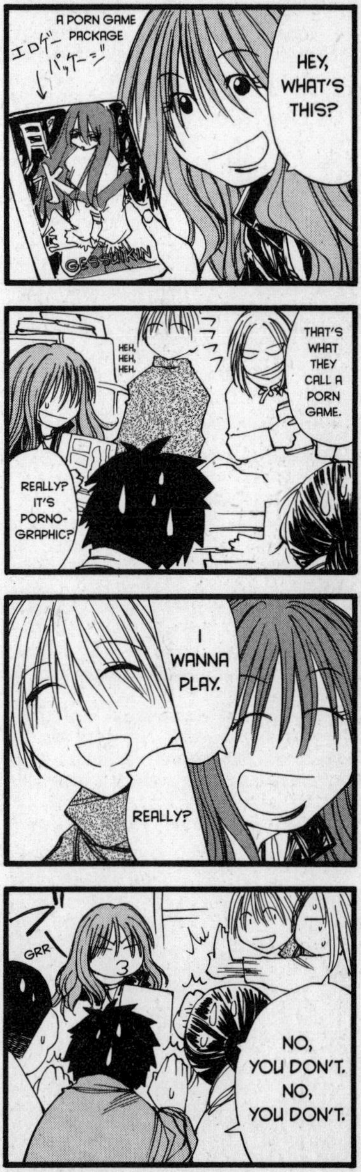
HEY, WHAT'S THIS?
A PORN GAME PACKAGE
エロゲーパッケージ
GESSUIKIN
THAT'S WHAT THEY CALL A PORN GAME.
HEH, HEH, HEH.
REALLY? IT'S PORNO-GRAPHIC?
I WANNA PLAY.
REALLY?
NO, YOU DON'T. NO, YOU DON'T.
GRR

IN FULL SWING

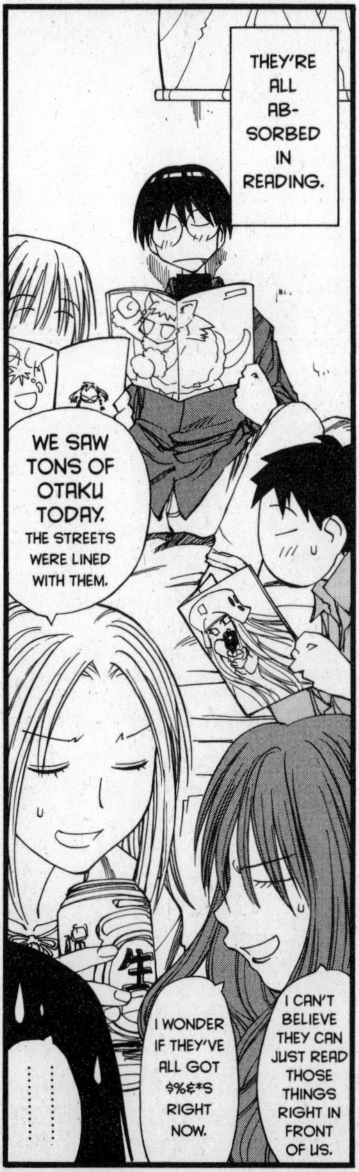
THEY'RE ALL AB-SORBED IN READING.
WE SAW TONS OF OTAKU TODAY. THE STREETS WERE LINED WITH THEM.
I CAN'T BELIEVE THEY CAN JUST READ THOSE THINGS RIGHT IN FRONT OF US.
I WONDER IF THEY'VE ALL GOT $%&*S RIGHT NOW.
......

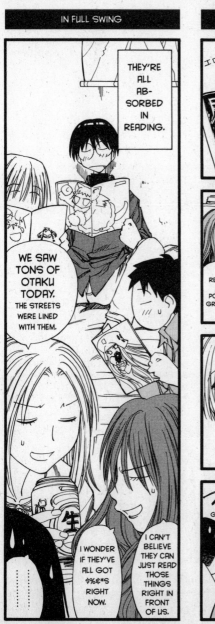

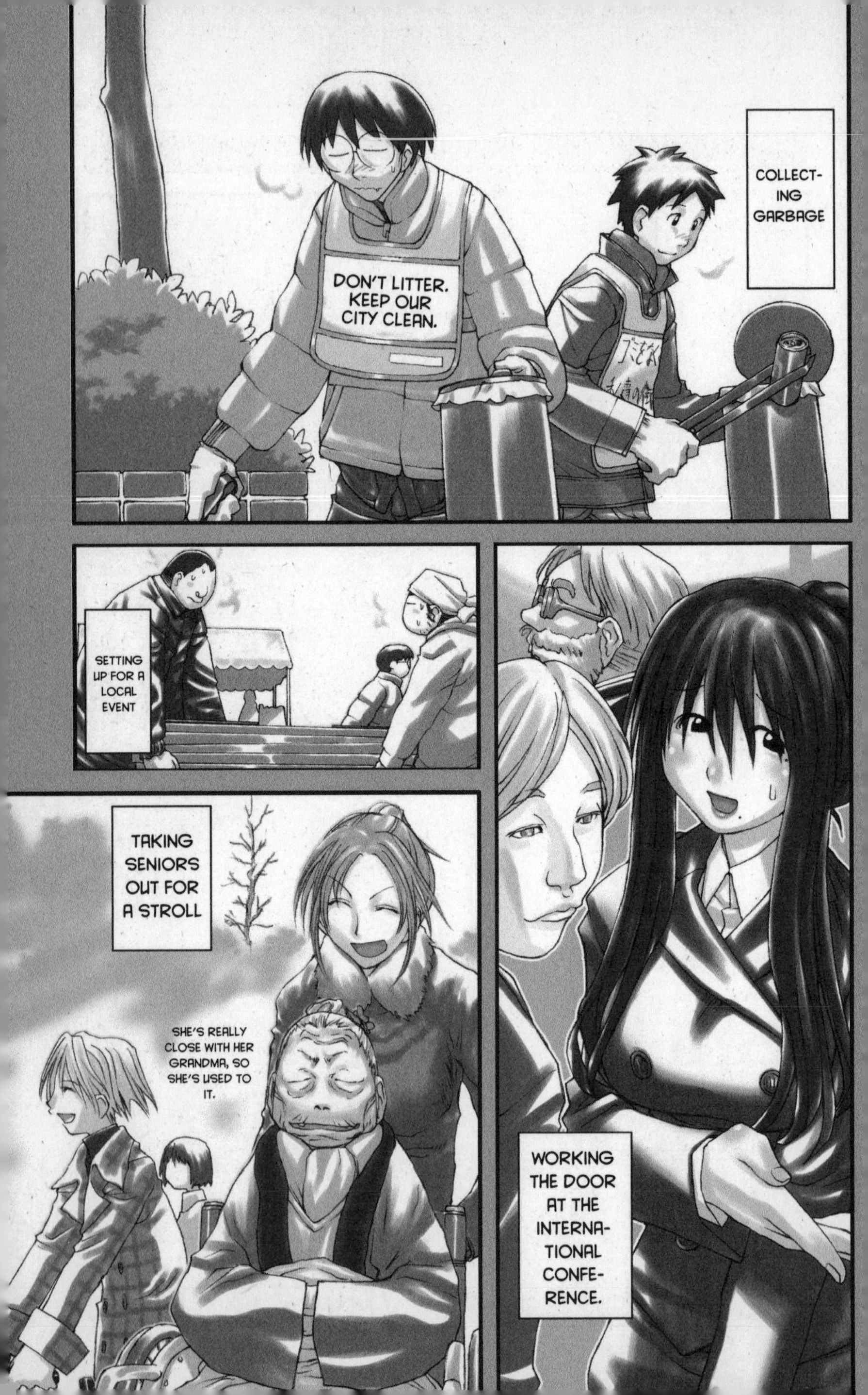
COLLECTING GARBAGE
DON'T LITTER. KEEP OUR CITY CLEAN.
WORKING THE DOOR AT THE INTERNATIONAL CONFERENCE.
SETTING UP FOR A LOCAL EVENT
TAKING SENIORS OUT FOR A STROLL
SHE'S REALLY CLOSE WITH HER GRANDMA, SO SHE'S USED TO IT.

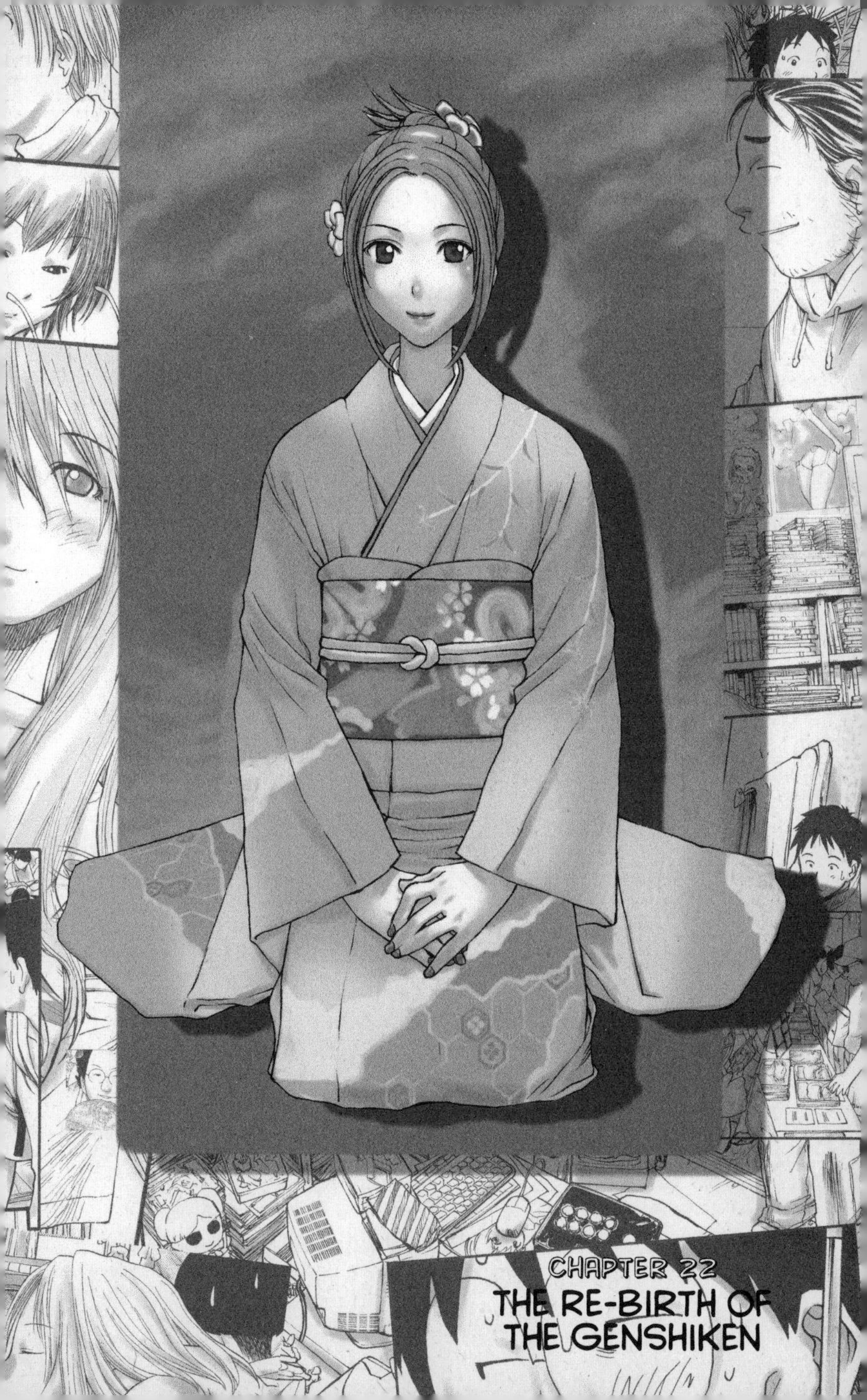
CHAPTER 22
THE RE-BIRTH OF THE GENSHIKEN

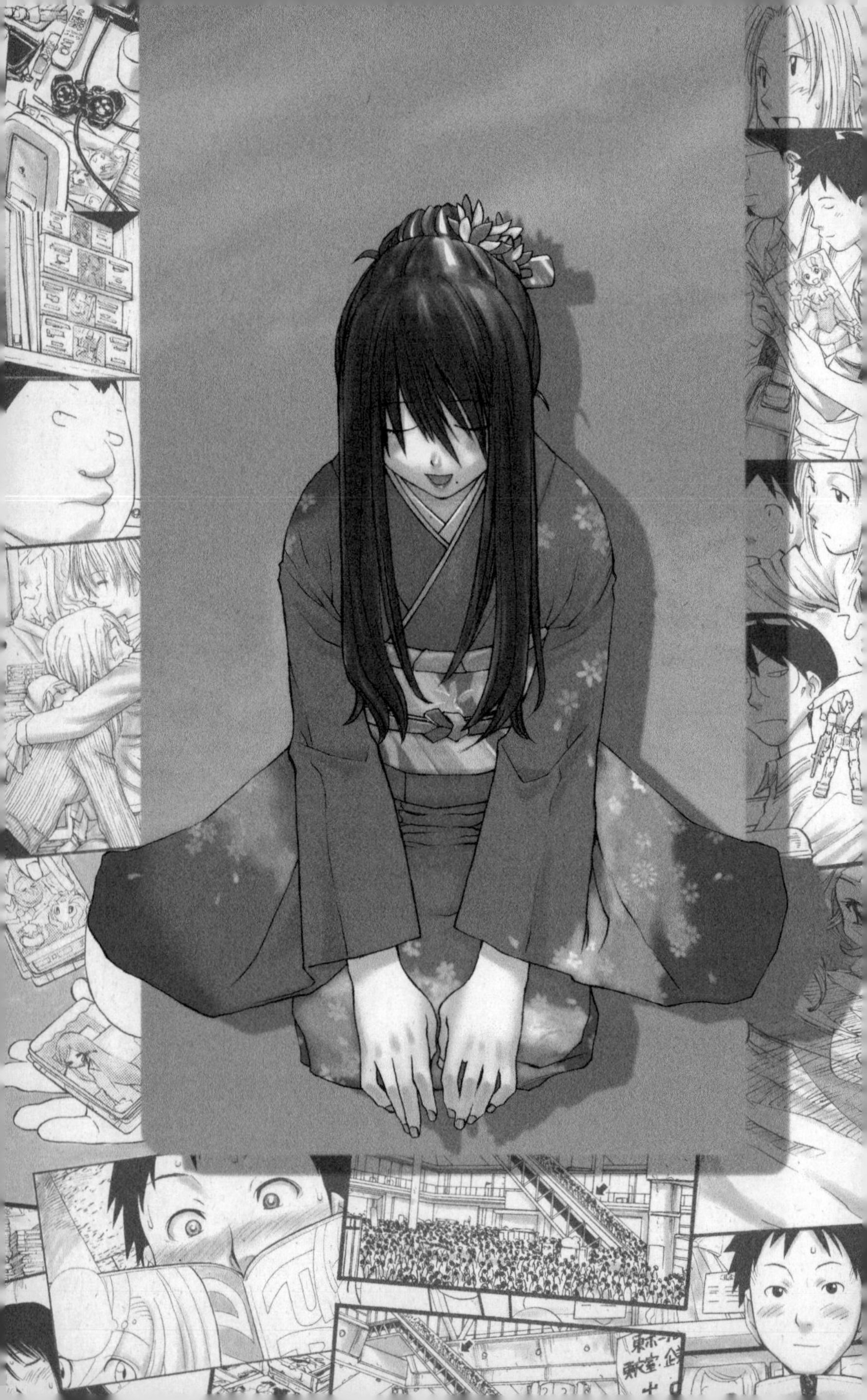

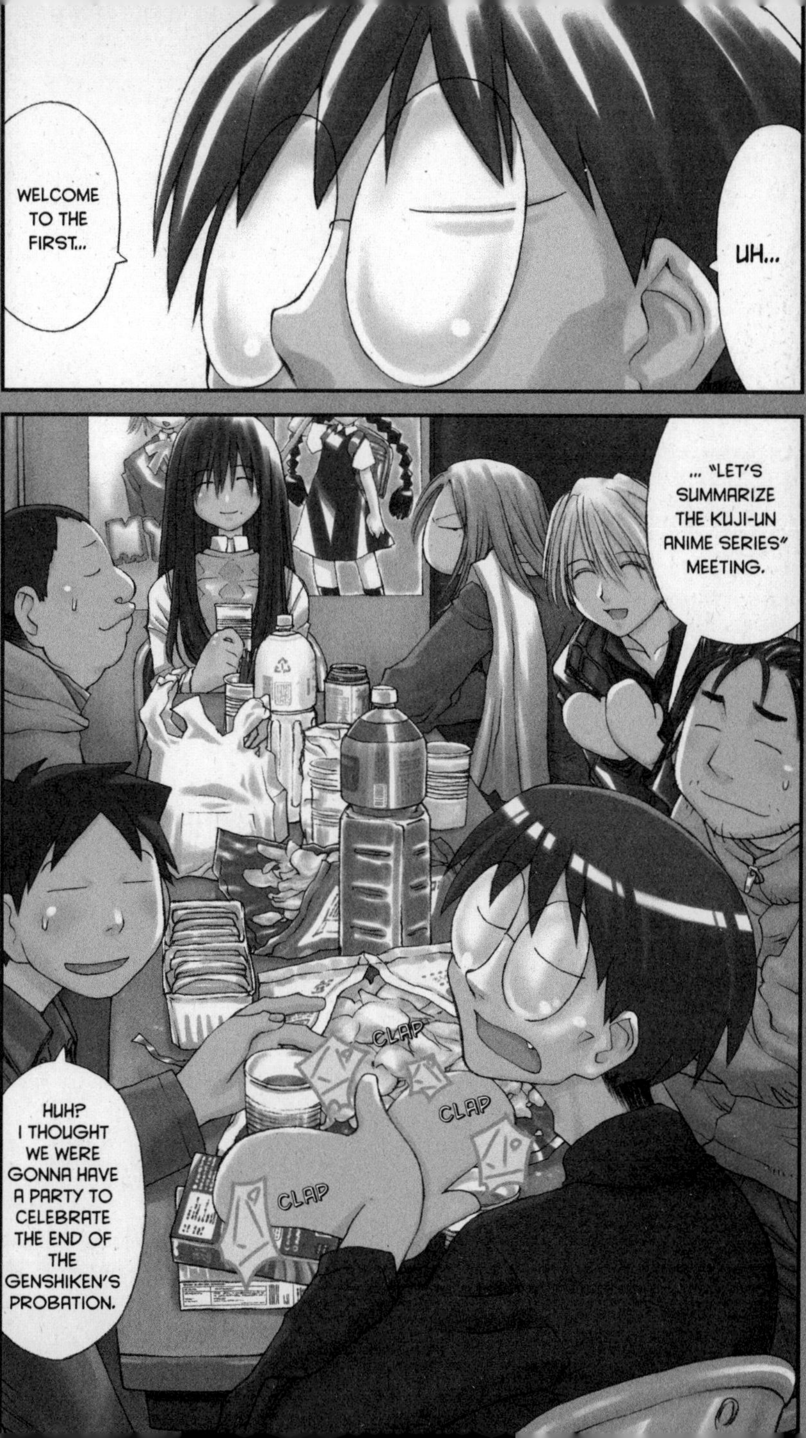
UH...
WELCOME TO THE FIRST...
... "LET'S SUMMARIZE THE KUJI-UN ANIME SERIES" MEETING.
CLAP
CLAP
CLAP
HUH? I THOUGHT WE WERE GONNA HAVE A PARTY TO CELEBRATE THE END OF THE GENSHIKEN'S PROBATION.

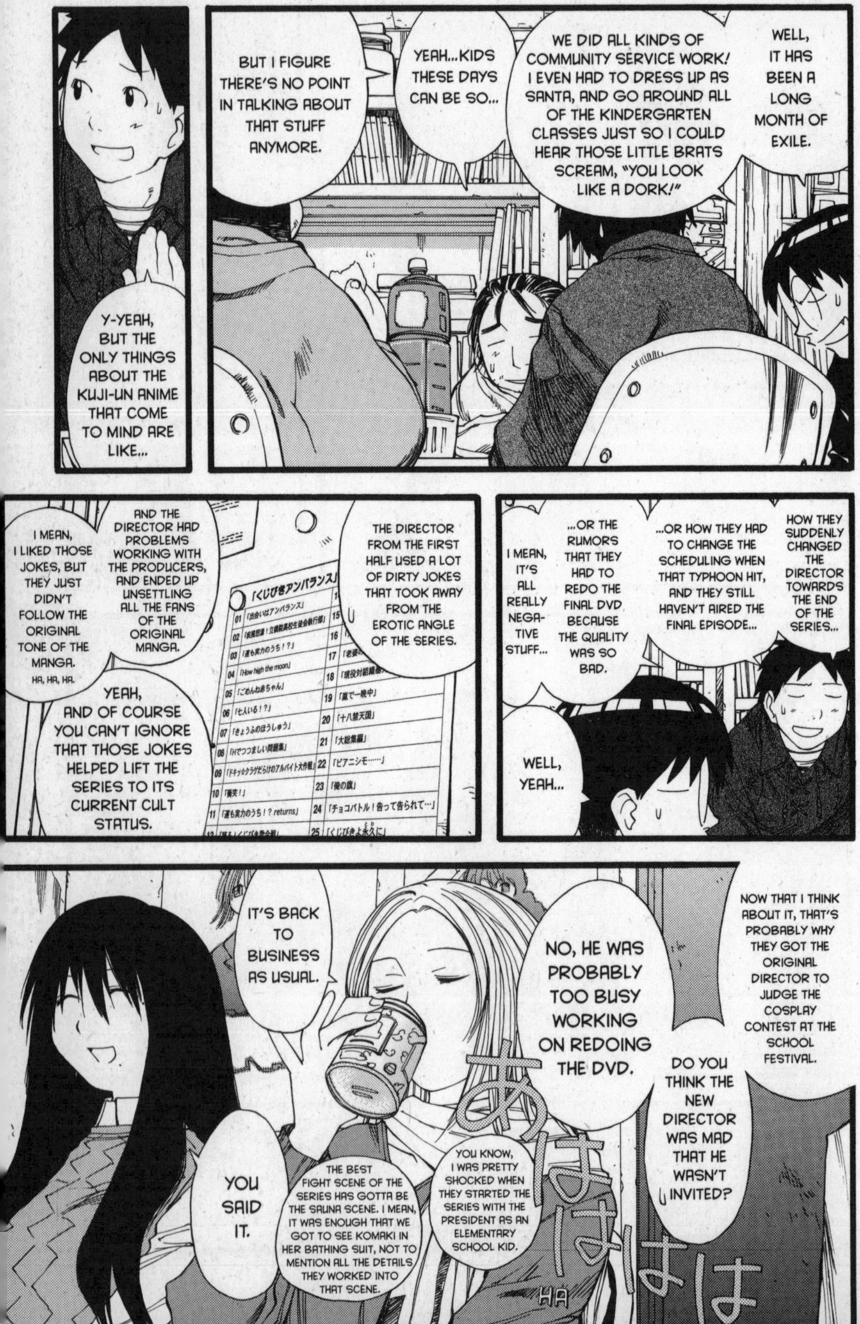
WELL, IT HAS BEEN A LONG MONTH OF EXILE.
WE DID ALL KINDS OF COMMUNITY SERVICE WORK! I EVEN HAD TO DRESS UP AS SANTA, AND GO AROUND ALL OF THE KINDERGARTEN CLASSES JUST SO I COULD HEAR THOSE LITTLE BRATS SCREAM, "YOU LOOK LIKE A DORK!"
YEAH...KIDS THESE DAYS CAN BE SO...
BUT I FIGURE THERE'S NO POINT IN TALKING ABOUT THAT STUFF ANYMORE.
Y-YEAH, BUT THE ONLY THINGS ABOUT THE KUJI-UN ANIME THAT COME TO MIND ARE LIKE...
HOW THEY SUDDENLY CHANGED THE DIRECTOR TOWARDS THE END OF THE SERIES...
...OR HOW THEY HAD TO CHANGE THE SCHEDULING WHEN THAT TYPHOON HIT, AND THEY STILL HAVEN'T AIRED THE FINAL EPISODE...
...OR THE RUMORS THAT THEY HAD TO REDO THE FINAL DVD BECAUSE THE QUALITY WAS SO BAD.
I MEAN, IT'S ALL REALLY NEGA-TIVE STUFF...
WELL, YEAH...
THE DIRECTOR FROM THE FIRST HALF USED A LOT OF DIRTY JOKES THAT TOOK AWAY FROM THE EROTIC ANGLE OF THE SERIES.
AND THE DIRECTOR HAD PROBLEMS WORKING WITH THE PRODUCERS, AND ENDED UP UNSETTLING ALL THE FANS OF THE ORIGINAL MANGA.
I MEAN, I LIKED THOSE JOKES, BUT THEY JUST DIDN'T FOLLOW THE ORIGINAL TONE OF THE MANGA.
HA, HA, HA.
YEAH, AND OF COURSE YOU CAN'T IGNORE THAT THOSE JOKES HELPED LIFT THE SERIES TO ITS CURRENT CULT STATUS.
「くじびきアンバランス」
01 「出会いはアンバランス」
03 「運も実力のうち！？」
04 「How high the moon」
05 「ごめんねあちゃん」
06 「七人いる！？」
07 「きょうふのほうしゅう」
08 「Hでつつましい問題集」
09 「ドキッ☆クラゲだらけのアルバイト大作戦」
10 「衝突！」
11 「運も実力のうち！？returns」
19 「嵐で一晩中」
20 「十八禁天国」
21 「大総集編」
22 「ピアニシモ……」
23 「俺の旗」
24 「チョコバトル！告って告られて…」
25 「くじびきよ永久に」
NOW THAT I THINK ABOUT IT, THAT'S PROBABLY WHY THEY GOT THE ORIGINAL DIRECTOR TO JUDGE THE COSPLAY CONTEST AT THE SCHOOL FESTIVAL.
DO YOU THINK THE NEW DIRECTOR WAS MAD THAT HE WASN'T INVITED?
NO, HE WAS PROBABLY TOO BUSY WORKING ON REDOING THE DVD.
IT'S BACK TO BUSINESS AS USUAL.
あははは
HA
YOU KNOW, I WAS PRETTY SHOCKED WHEN THEY STARTED THE SERIES WITH THE PRESIDENT AS AN ELEMENTARY SCHOOL KID.
THE BEST FIGHT SCENE OF THE SERIES HAS GOTTA BE THE SAUNA SCENE. I MEAN, IT WAS ENOUGH THAT WE GOT TO SEE KOMAKI IN HER BATHING SUIT, NOT TO MENTION ALL THE DETAILS THEY WORKED INTO THAT SCENE.
YOU SAID IT.

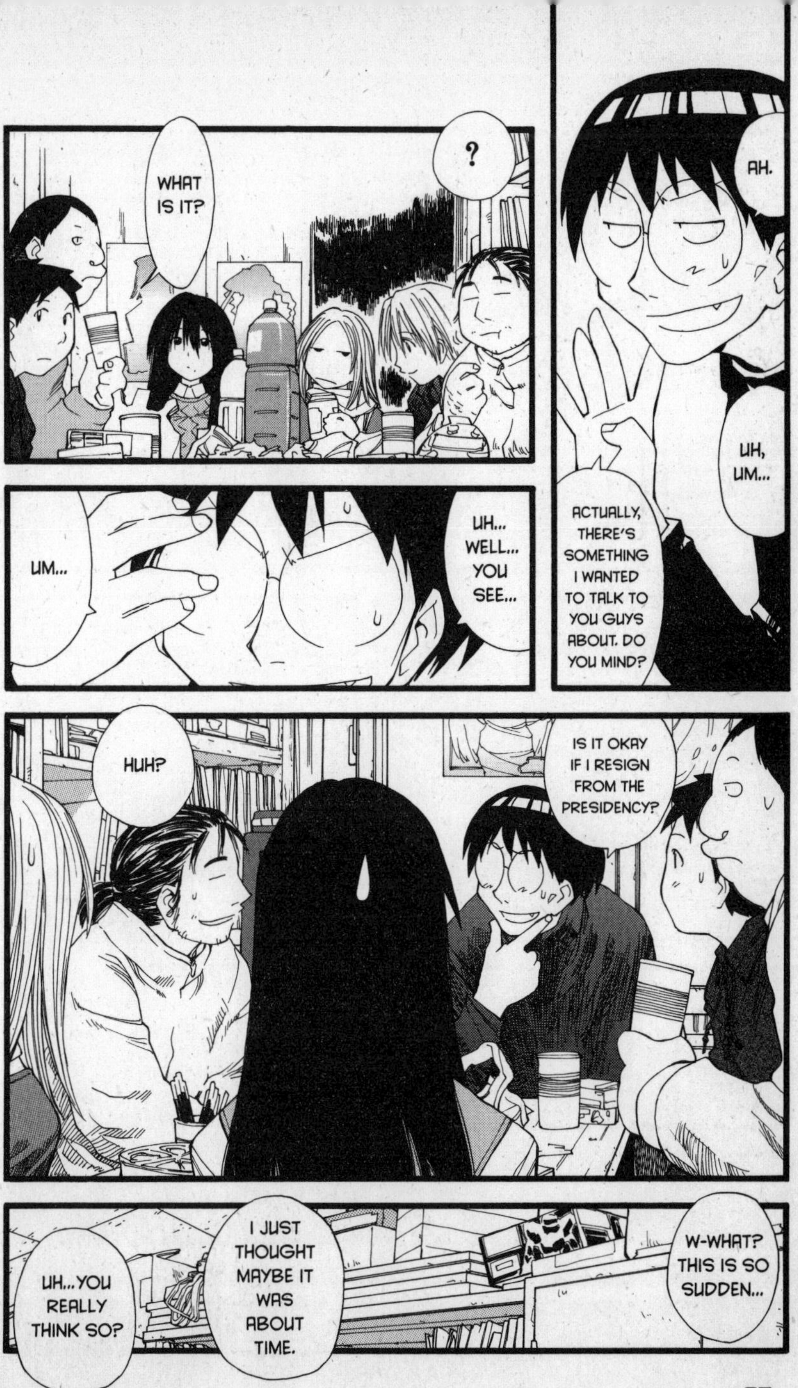
AH.
UH, UM...
ACTUALLY, THERE'S SOMETHING I WANTED TO TALK TO YOU GUYS ABOUT. DO YOU MIND?
?
WHAT IS IT?
UH... WELL... YOU SEE...
UM...
IS IT OKAY IF I RESIGN FROM THE PRESIDENCY?
HUH?
W-WHAT? THIS IS SO SUDDEN...
I JUST THOUGHT MAYBE IT WAS ABOUT TIME.
UH...YOU REALLY THINK SO?

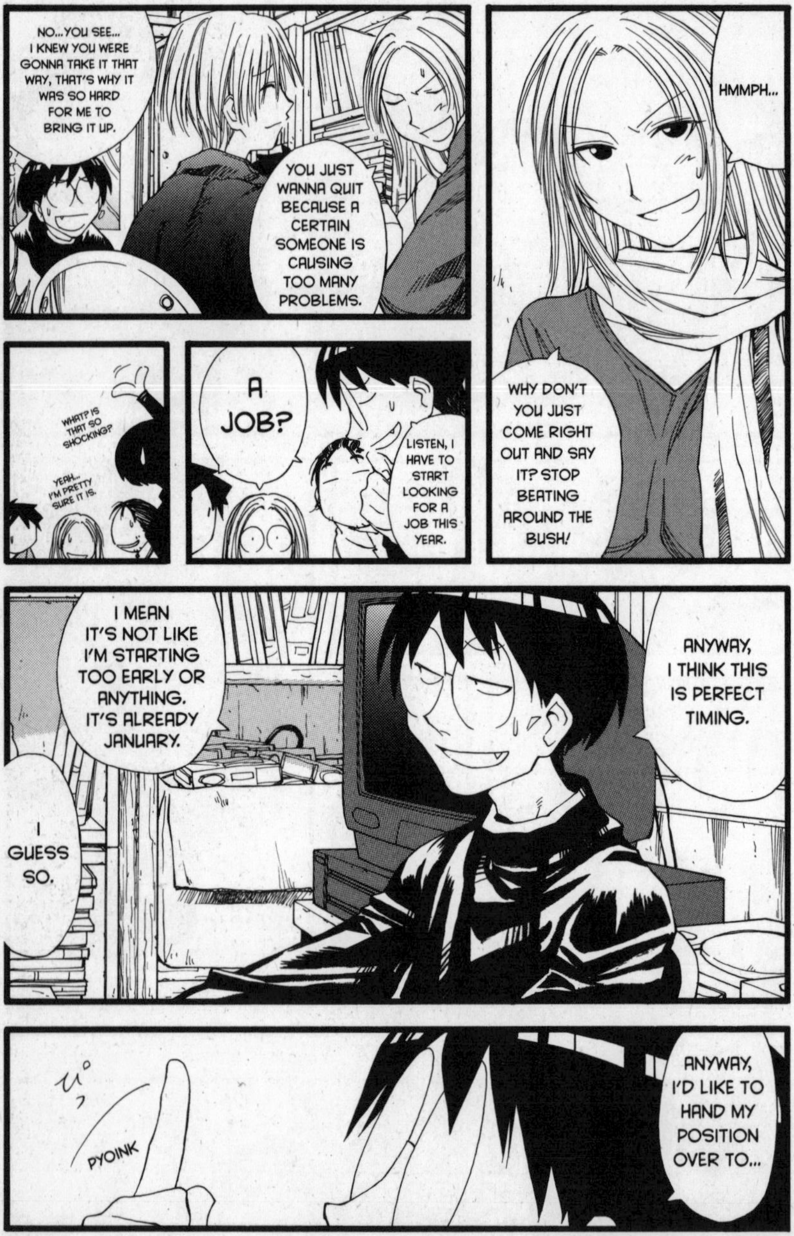
HMMPH...
WHY DON'T YOU JUST COME RIGHT OUT AND SAY IT? STOP BEATING AROUND THE BUSH!
YOU JUST WANNA QUIT BECAUSE A CERTAIN SOMEONE IS CAUSING TOO MANY PROBLEMS.
NO...YOU SEE... I KNEW YOU WERE GONNA TAKE IT THAT WAY, THAT'S WHY IT WAS SO HARD FOR ME TO BRING IT UP.
LISTEN, I HAVE TO START LOOKING FOR A JOB THIS YEAR.
A JOB?
WHAT? IS THAT SO SHOCKING?
YEAH... I'M PRETTY SURE IT IS.
ANYWAY, I THINK THIS IS PERFECT TIMING.
I MEAN IT'S NOT LIKE I'M STARTING TOO EARLY OR ANYTHING. IT'S ALREADY JANUARY.
I GUESS SO.
ANYWAY, I'D LIKE TO HAND MY POSITION OVER TO...
ぴっ
PYOINK

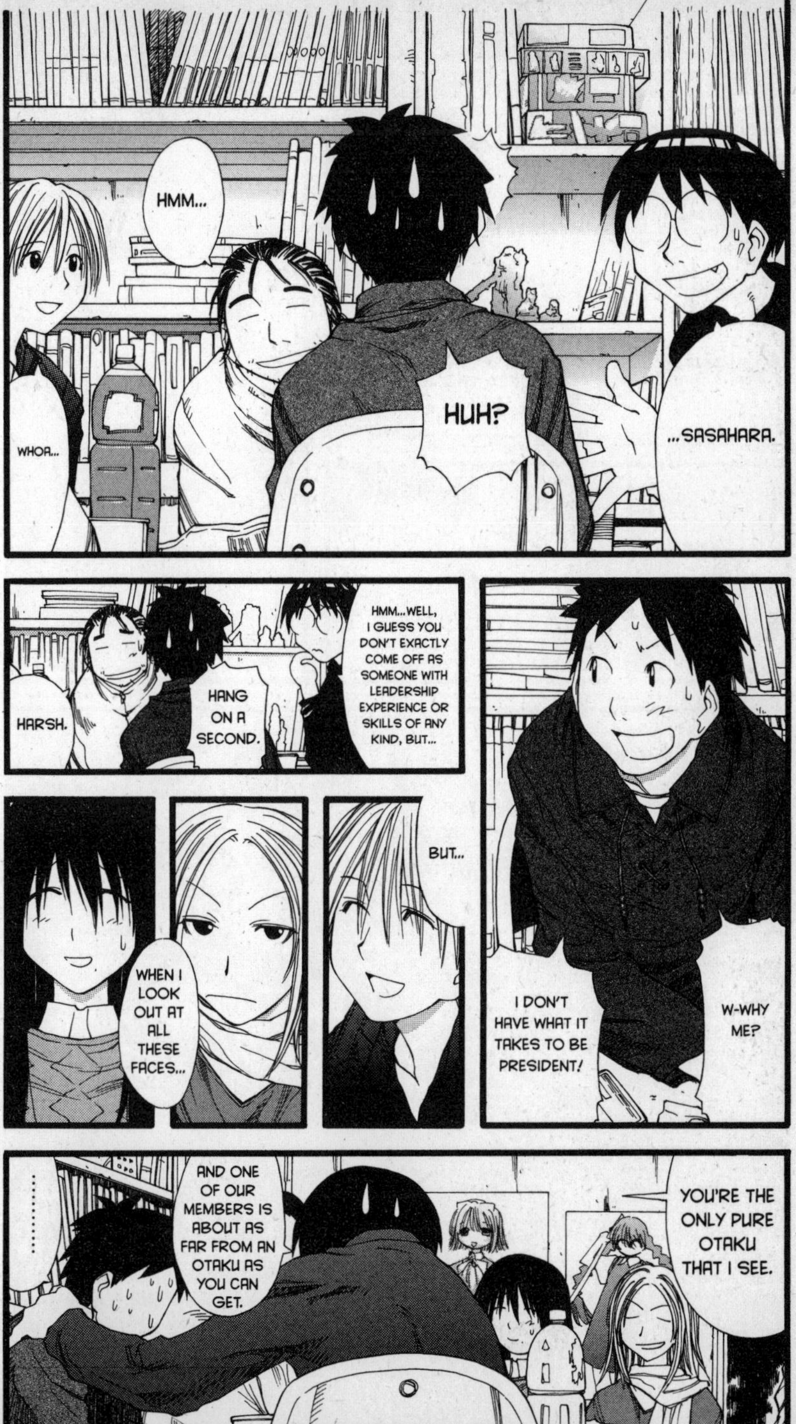
...SASAHARA.
HUH?
HMM...
WHOA...
W-WHY ME?
I DON'T HAVE WHAT IT TAKES TO BE PRESIDENT!
HMM...WELL, I GUESS YOU DON'T EXACTLY COME OFF AS SOMEONE WITH LEADERSHIP EXPERIENCE OR SKILLS OF ANY KIND, BUT...
HANG ON A SECOND.
HARSH.
BUT...
WHEN I LOOK OUT AT ALL THESE FACES...
YOU'RE THE ONLY PURE OTAKU THAT I SEE.
AND ONE OF OUR MEMBERS IS ABOUT AS FAR FROM AN OTAKU AS YOU CAN GET.
........

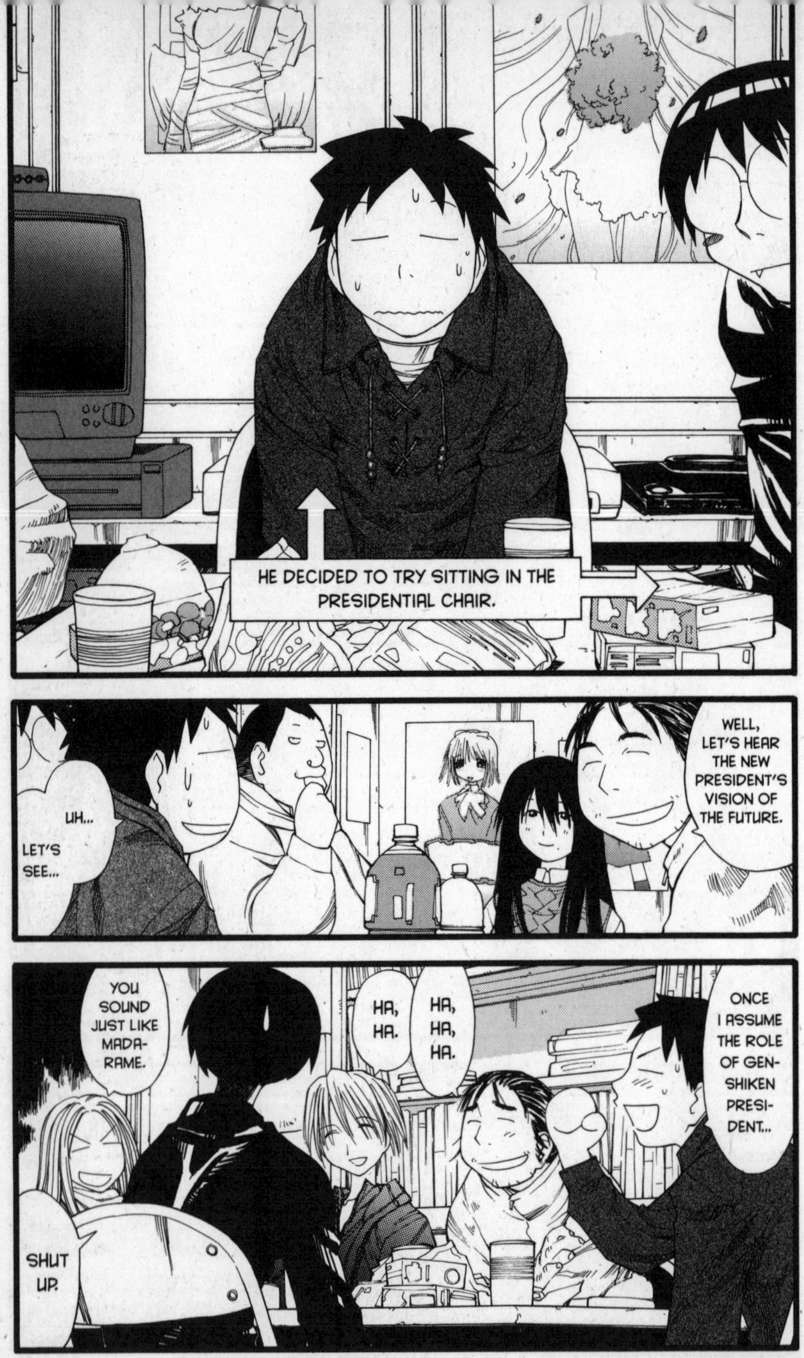
HE DECIDED TO TRY SITTING IN THE PRESIDENTIAL CHAIR.
WELL, LET'S HEAR THE NEW PRESIDENT'S VISION OF THE FUTURE.
UH... LET'S SEE...
ONCE I ASSUME THE ROLE OF GEN-SHIKEN PRESI-DENT...
HA, HA, HA.
HA, HA.
YOU SOUND JUST LIKE MADA-RAME.
SHUT UP.

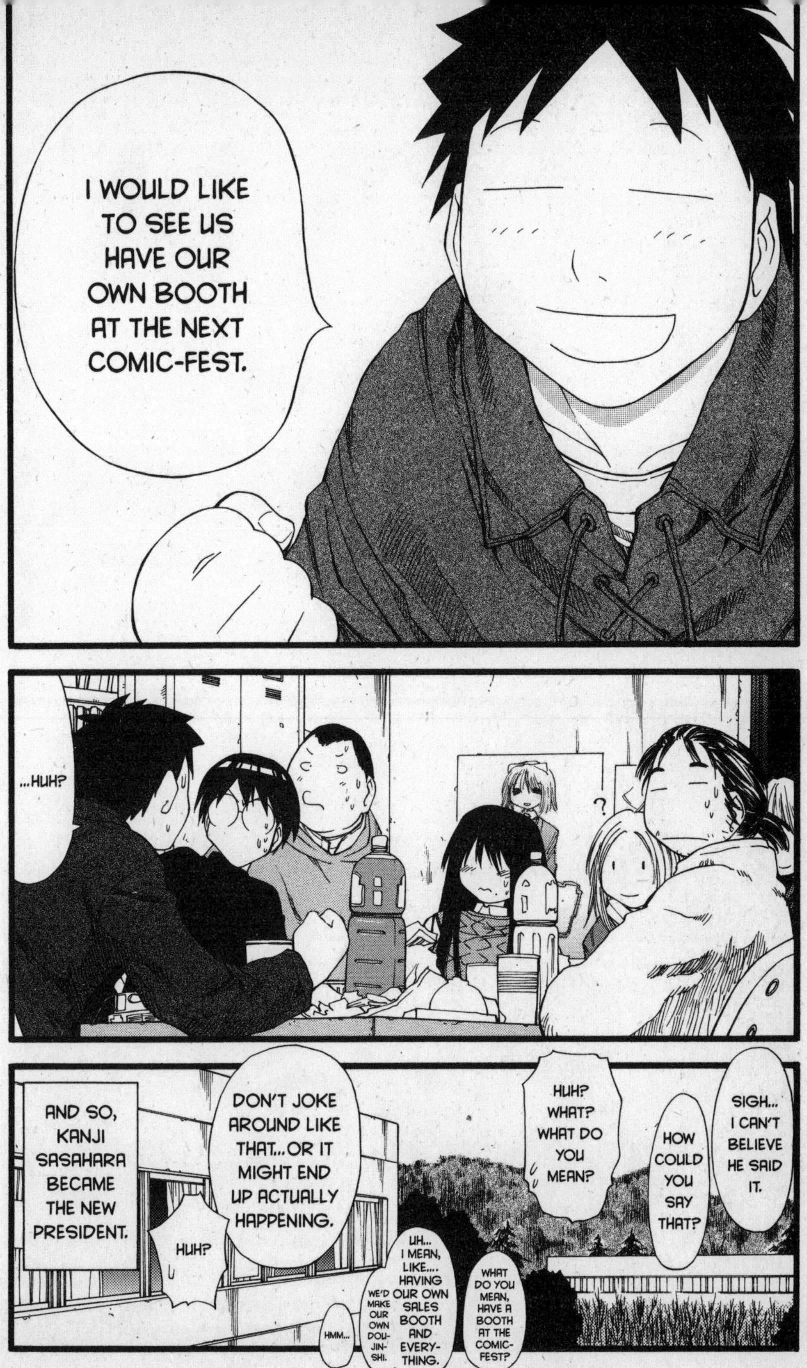
I WOULD LIKE TO SEE US HAVE OUR OWN BOOTH AT THE NEXT COMIC-FEST.
...HUH?
SIGH... I CAN'T BELIEVE HE SAID IT.
HOW COULD YOU SAY THAT?
HUH? WHAT? WHAT DO YOU MEAN?
WHAT DO YOU MEAN, HAVE A BOOTH AT THE COMIC-FEST?
UH... I MEAN, LIKE.... HAVING OUR OWN SALES BOOTH AND EVERY-THING.
WE'D MAKE OUR OWN DOU-JIN-SHI.
HMM...
DON'T JOKE AROUND LIKE THAT...OR IT MIGHT END UP ACTUALLY HAPPENING.
HUH?
AND SO, KANJI SASAHARA BECAME THE NEW PRESIDENT.

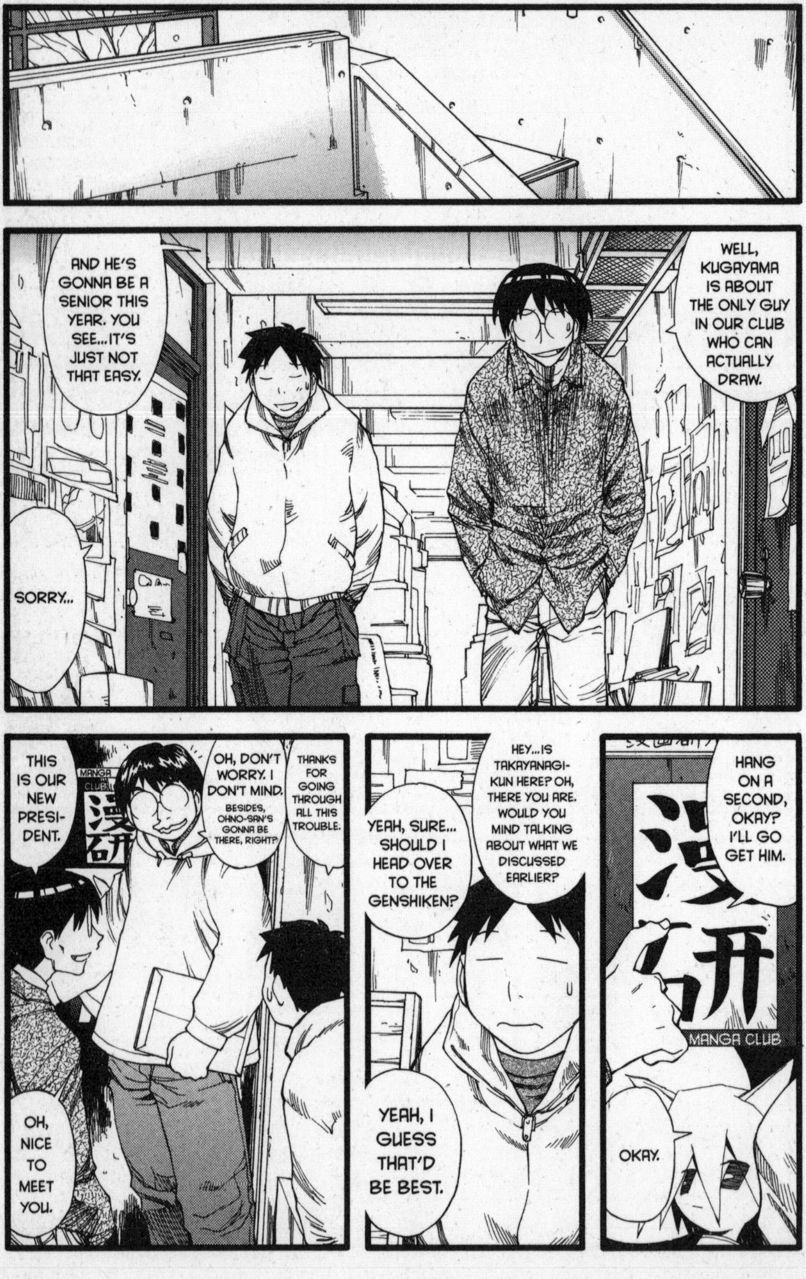
WELL, KUGAYAMA IS ABOUT THE ONLY GUY IN OUR CLUB WHO CAN ACTUALLY DRAW.
AND HE'S GONNA BE A SENIOR THIS YEAR. YOU SEE...IT'S JUST NOT THAT EASY.
SORRY...
HANG ON A SECOND, OKAY? I'LL GO GET HIM.
漫研
MANGA CLUB
OKAY.
HEY...IS TAKAYANAGI-KUN HERE? OH, THERE YOU ARE. WOULD YOU MIND TALKING ABOUT WHAT WE DISCUSSED EARLIER?
YEAH, SURE... SHOULD I HEAD OVER TO THE GENSHIKEN?
YEAH, I GUESS THAT'D BE BEST.
THANKS FOR GOING THROUGH ALL THIS TROUBLE.
OH, DON'T WORRY. I DON'T MIND. BESIDES, OHNO-SAN'S GONNA BE THERE, RIGHT?
THIS IS OUR NEW PRESIDENT.
OH, NICE TO MEET YOU.

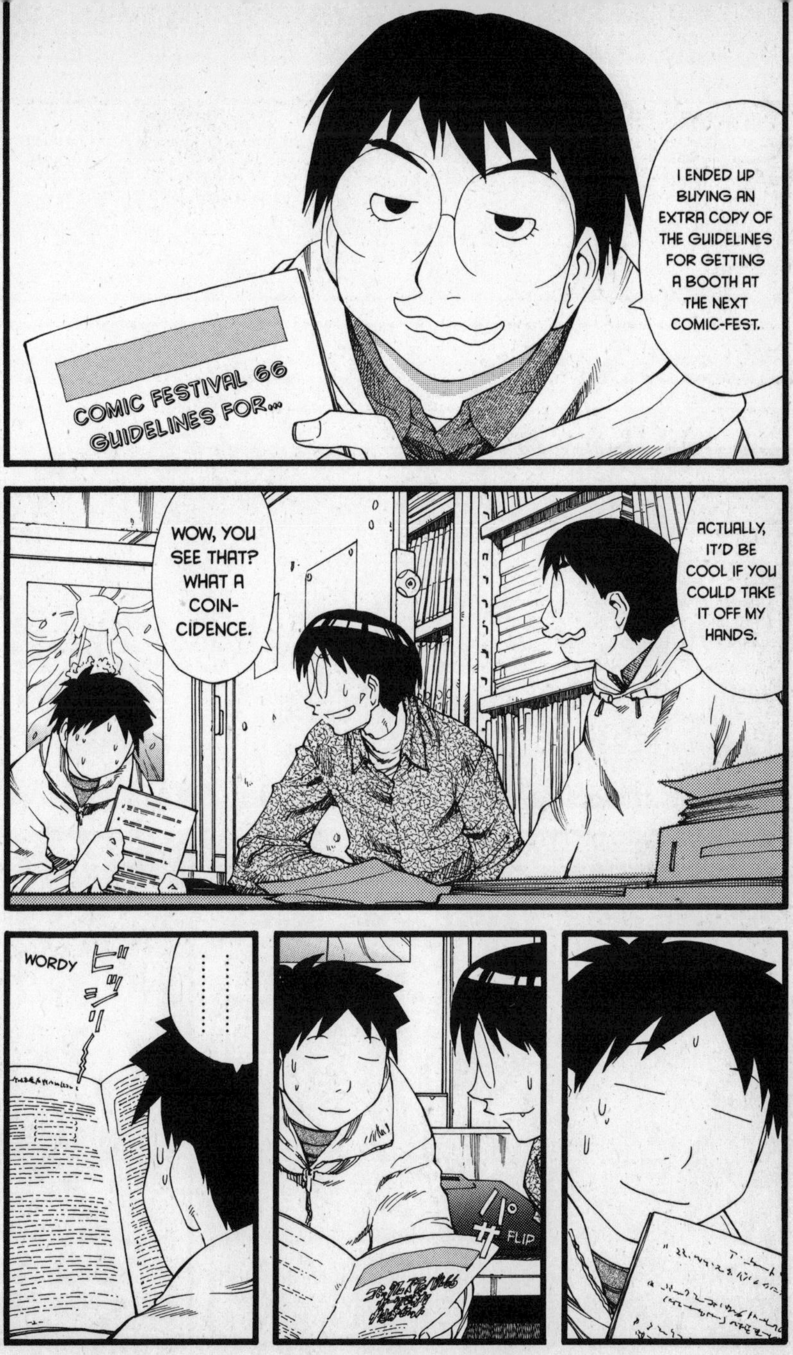
I ENDED UP BUYING AN EXTRA COPY OF THE GUIDELINES FOR GETTING A BOOTH AT THE NEXT COMIC-FEST.
COMIC FESTIVAL 66 GUIDELINES FOR...
ACTUALLY, IT'D BE COOL IF YOU COULD TAKE IT OFF MY HANDS.
WOW, YOU SEE THAT? WHAT A COINCIDENCE.
FLIP
WORDY
......

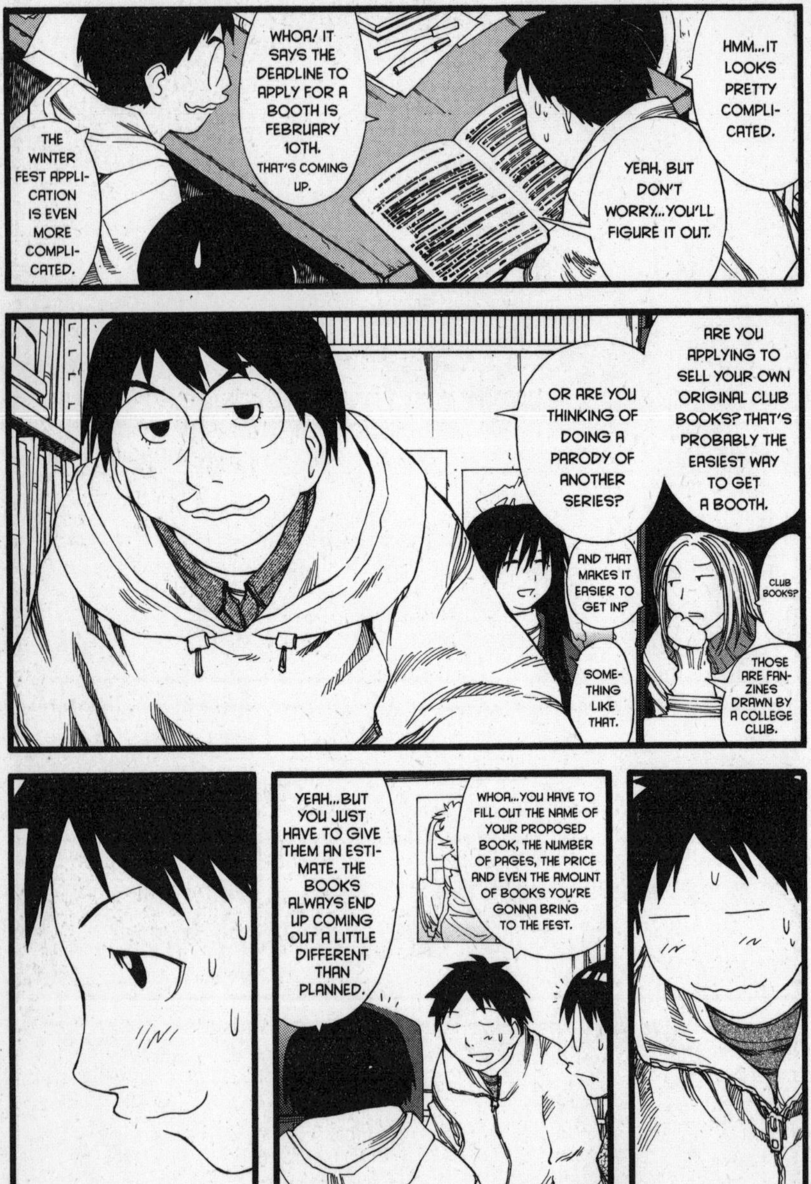
HMM...IT LOOKS PRETTY COMPLI-CATED.
YEAH, BUT DON'T WORRY...YOU'LL FIGURE IT OUT.
WHOA! IT SAYS THE DEADLINE TO APPLY FOR A BOOTH IS FEBRUARY 10TH.
THAT'S COMING UP.
THE WINTER FEST APPLI-CATION IS EVEN MORE COMPLI-CATED.
ARE YOU APPLYING TO SELL YOUR OWN ORIGINAL CLUB BOOKS? THAT'S PROBABLY THE EASIEST WAY TO GET A BOOTH.
OR ARE YOU THINKING OF DOING A PARODY OF ANOTHER SERIES?
CLUB BOOKS?
THOSE ARE FAN-ZINES DRAWN BY A COLLEGE CLUB.
AND THAT MAKES IT EASIER TO GET IN?
SOME-THING LIKE THAT.
WHOA...YOU HAVE TO FILL OUT THE NAME OF YOUR PROPOSED BOOK, THE NUMBER OF PAGES, THE PRICE AND EVEN THE AMOUNT OF BOOKS YOU'RE GONNA BRING TO THE FEST.
YEAH...BUT YOU JUST HAVE TO GIVE THEM AN ESTI-MATE. THE BOOKS ALWAYS END UP COMING OUT A LITTLE DIFFERENT THAN PLANNED.

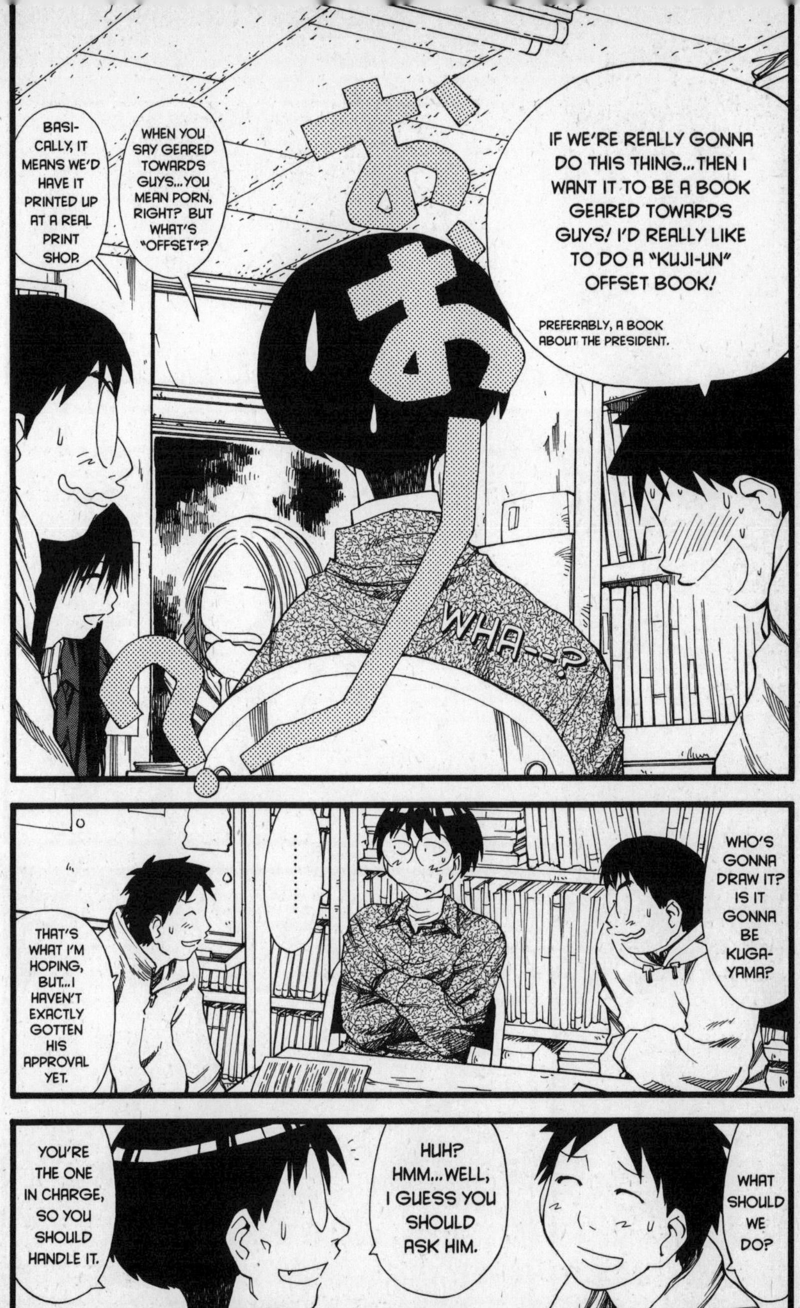
IF WE'RE REALLY GONNA DO THIS THING...THEN I WANT IT TO BE A BOOK GEARED TOWARDS GUYS! I'D REALLY LIKE TO DO A "KUJI-UN" OFFSET BOOK!
PREFERABLY, A BOOK ABOUT THE PRESIDENT.
WHA--?
WHEN YOU SAY GEARED TOWARDS GUYS...YOU MEAN PORN, RIGHT? BUT WHAT'S "OFFSET"?
BASI-CALLY, IT MEANS WE'D HAVE IT PRINTED UP AT A REAL PRINT SHOP.
WHO'S GONNA DRAW IT? IS IT GONNA BE KUGA-YAMA?
......
THAT'S WHAT I'M HOPING, BUT...I HAVEN'T EXACTLY GOTTEN HIS APPROVAL YET.
WHAT SHOULD WE DO?
HUH? HMM...WELL, I GUESS YOU SHOULD ASK HIM.
YOU'RE THE ONE IN CHARGE, SO YOU SHOULD HANDLE IT.

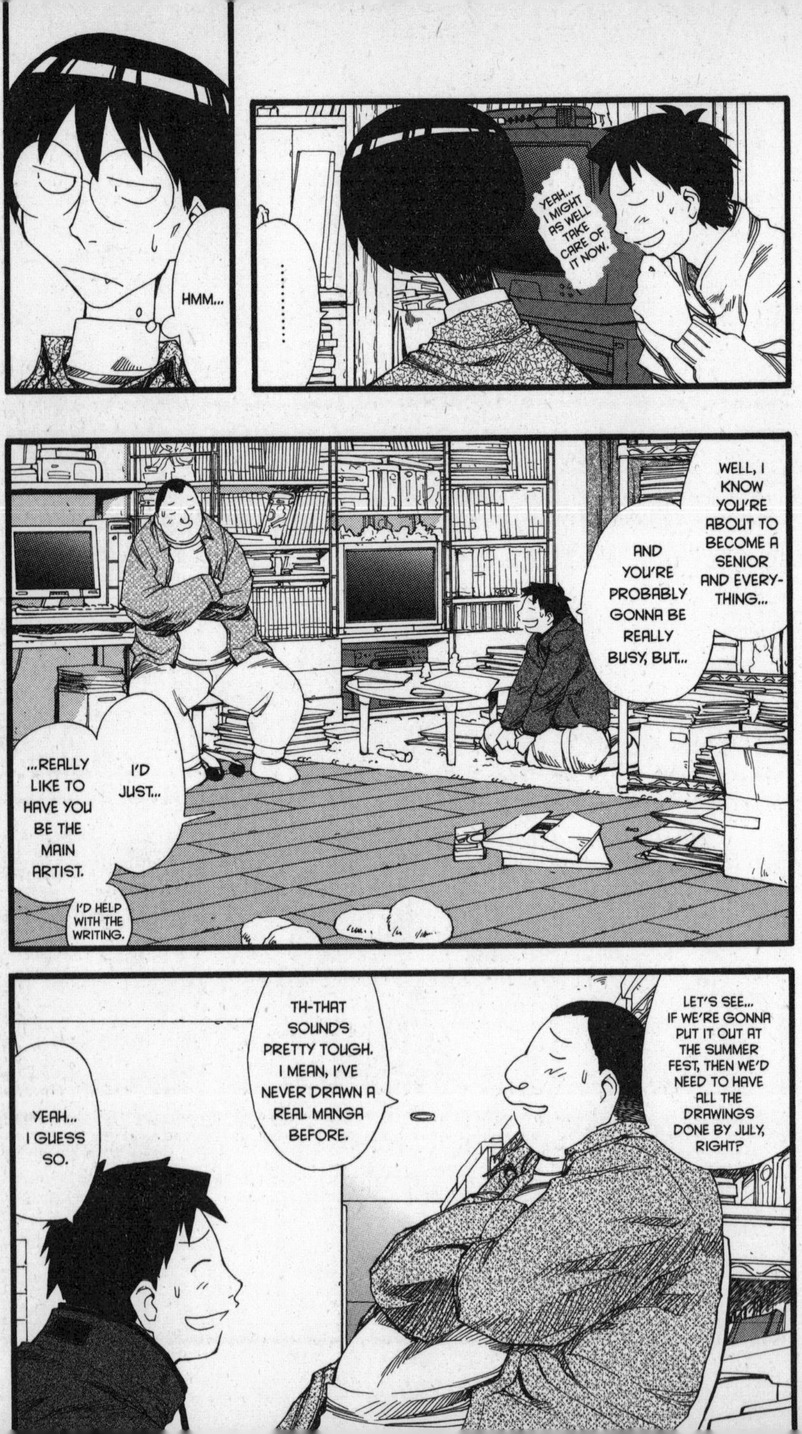
YEAH... I MIGHT AS WELL TAKE CARE OF IT NOW.
......
HMM...
WELL, I KNOW YOU'RE ABOUT TO BECOME A SENIOR AND EVERYTHING...
AND YOU'RE PROBABLY GONNA BE REALLY BUSY, BUT...
I'D JUST...
...REALLY LIKE TO HAVE YOU BE THE MAIN ARTIST.
I'D HELP WITH THE WRITING.
LET'S SEE... IF WE'RE GONNA PUT IT OUT AT THE SUMMER FEST, THEN WE'D NEED TO HAVE ALL THE DRAWINGS DONE BY JULY, RIGHT?
TH-THAT SOUNDS PRETTY TOUGH. I MEAN, I'VE NEVER DRAWN A REAL MANGA BEFORE.
YEAH... I GUESS SO.

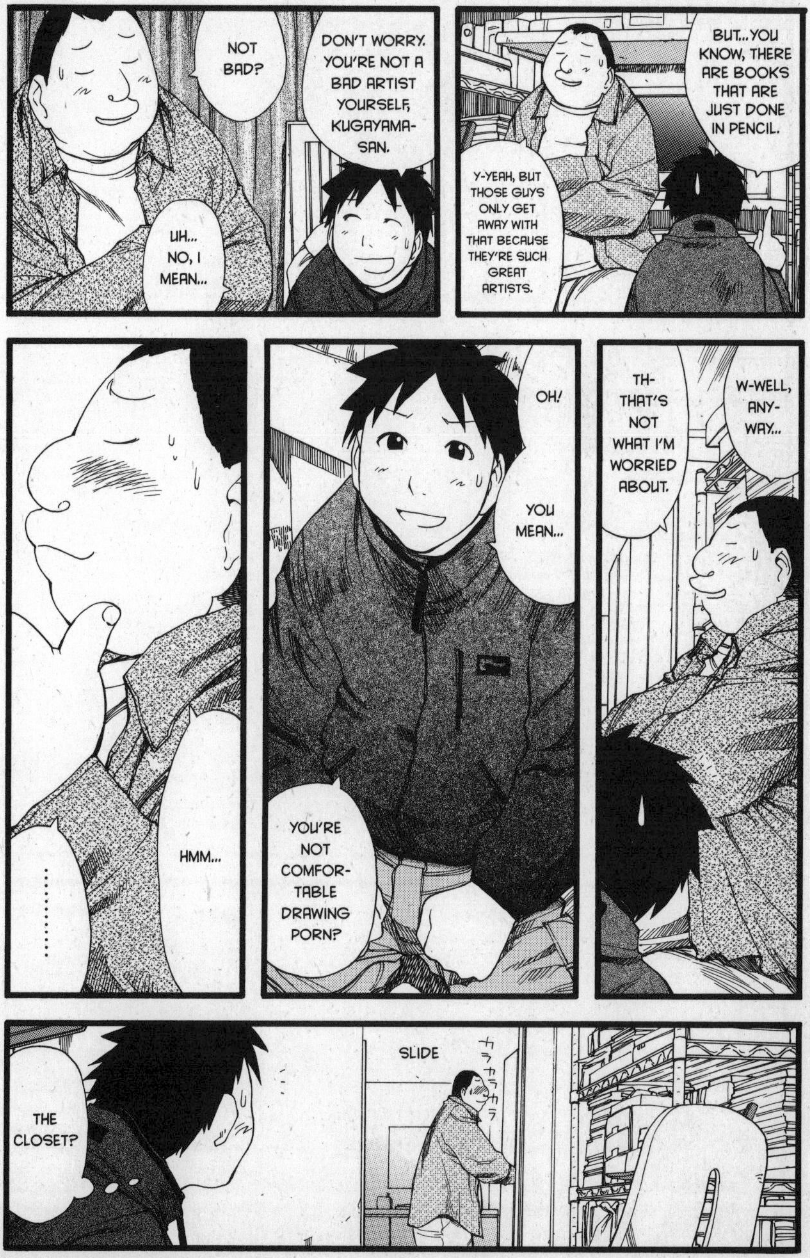
BUT...YOU KNOW, THERE ARE BOOKS THAT ARE JUST DONE IN PENCIL.
Y-YEAH, BUT THOSE GUYS ONLY GET AWAY WITH THAT BECAUSE THEY'RE SUCH GREAT ARTISTS.
DON'T WORRY. YOU'RE NOT A BAD ARTIST YOURSELF, KUGAYAMA-SAN.
NOT BAD?
UH... NO, I MEAN...
W-WELL, ANY-WAY...
TH-THAT'S NOT WHAT I'M WORRIED ABOUT.
OH!
YOU MEAN...
YOU'RE NOT COMFOR-TABLE DRAWING PORN?
HMM...
............
カラカラ
SLIDE
THE CLOSET?

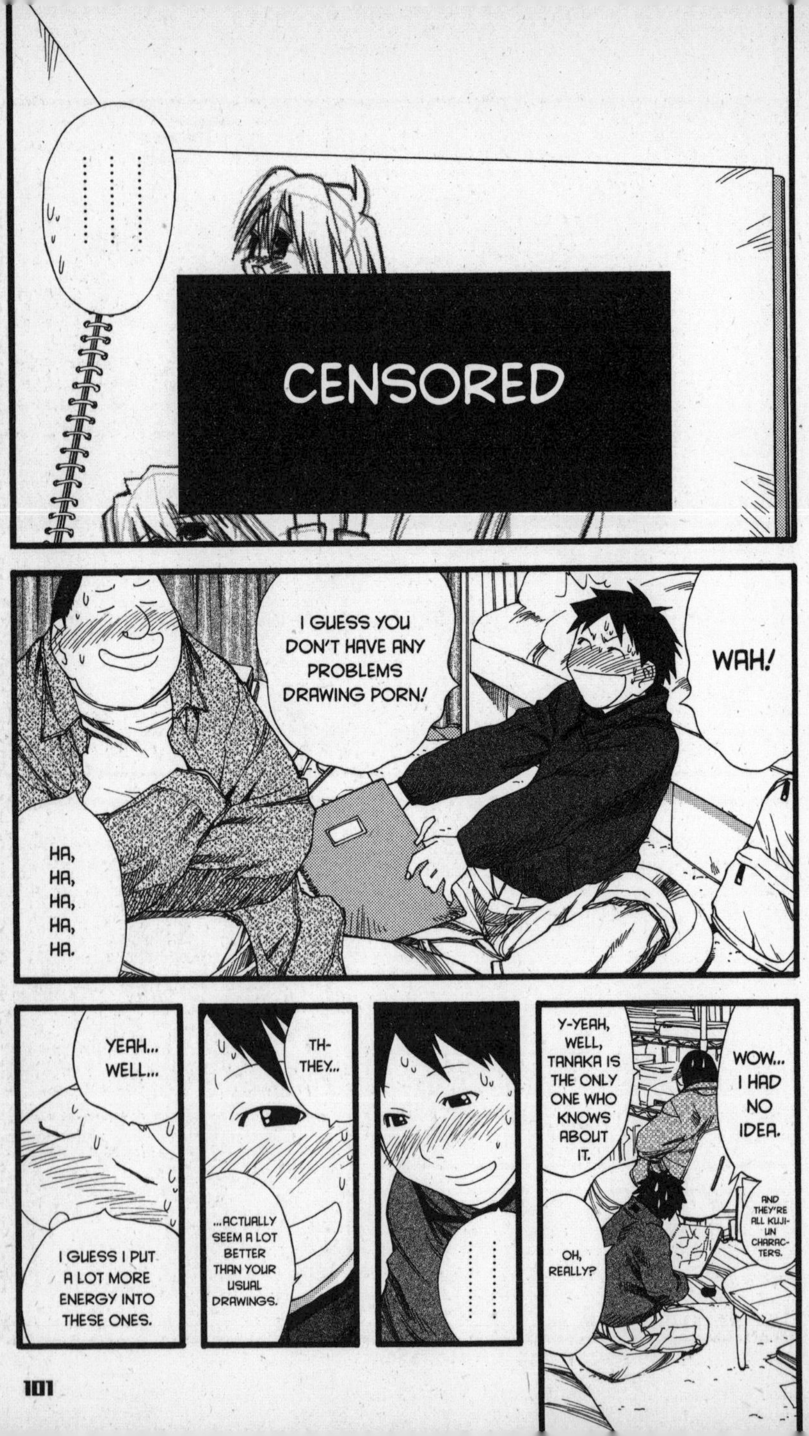
……
CENSORED
WAH!
I GUESS YOU DON'T HAVE ANY PROBLEMS DRAWING PORN!
HA, HA, HA, HA, HA.
WOW... I HAD NO IDEA.
Y-YEAH, WELL, TANAKA IS THE ONLY ONE WHO KNOWS ABOUT IT.
AND THEY'RE ALL KUJI-UN CHARACTERS.
OH, REALLY?
……
TH- THEY...
...ACTUALLY SEEM A LOT BETTER THAN YOUR USUAL DRAWINGS.
YEAH... WELL...
I GUESS I PUT A LOT MORE ENERGY INTO THESE ONES.

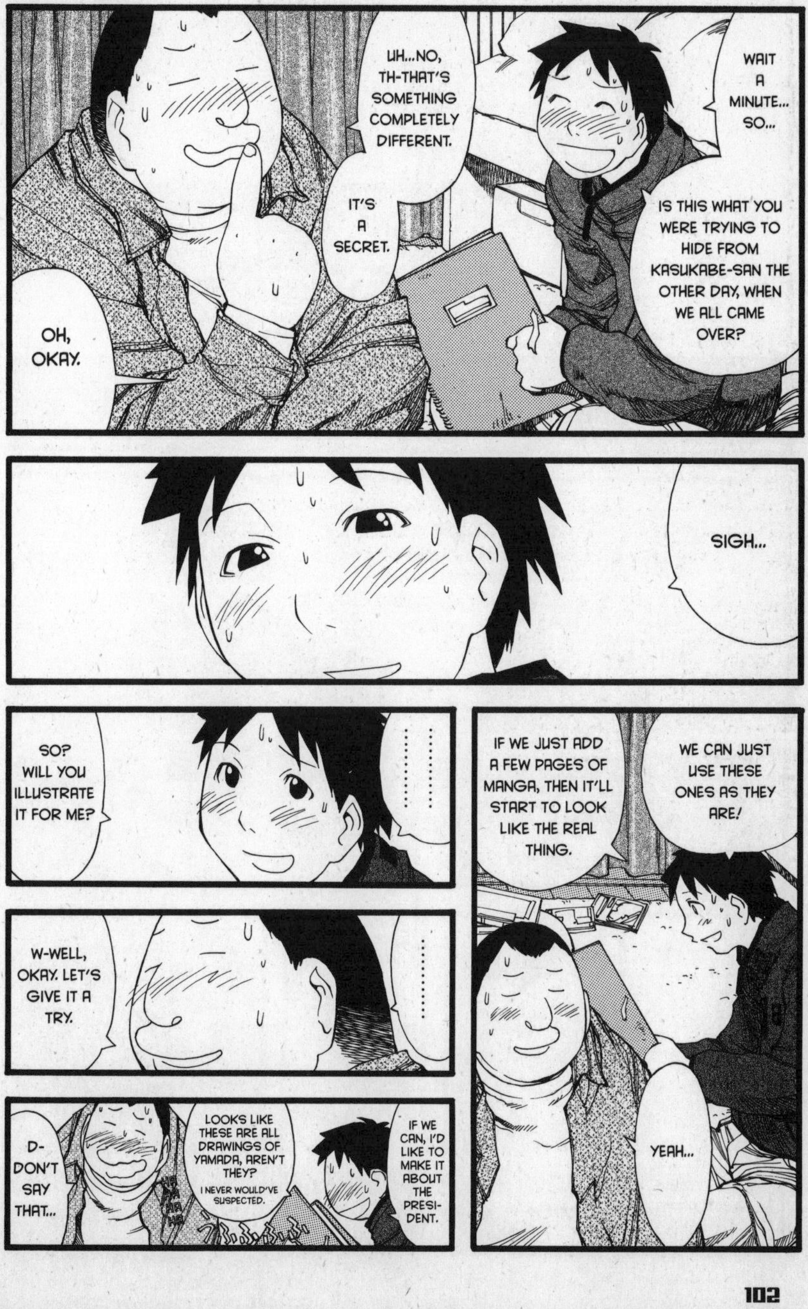
WAIT A MINUTE... SO...
IS THIS WHAT YOU WERE TRYING TO HIDE FROM KASUKABE-SAN THE OTHER DAY, WHEN WE ALL CAME OVER?
UH...NO, TH-THAT'S SOMETHING COMPLETELY DIFFERENT.
IT'S A SECRET.
OH, OKAY.
SIGH...
WE CAN JUST USE THESE ONES AS THEY ARE!
IF WE JUST ADD A FEW PAGES OF MANGA, THEN IT'LL START TO LOOK LIKE THE REAL THING.
YEAH...
......
SO? WILL YOU ILLUSTRATE IT FOR ME?
......
W-WELL, OKAY. LET'S GIVE IT A TRY.
IF WE CAN, I'D LIKE TO MAKE IT ABOUT THE PRESIDENT.
LOOKS LIKE THESE ARE ALL DRAWINGS OF YAMADA, AREN'T THEY?
I NEVER WOULD'VE SUSPECTED.
D-DON'T SAY THAT...

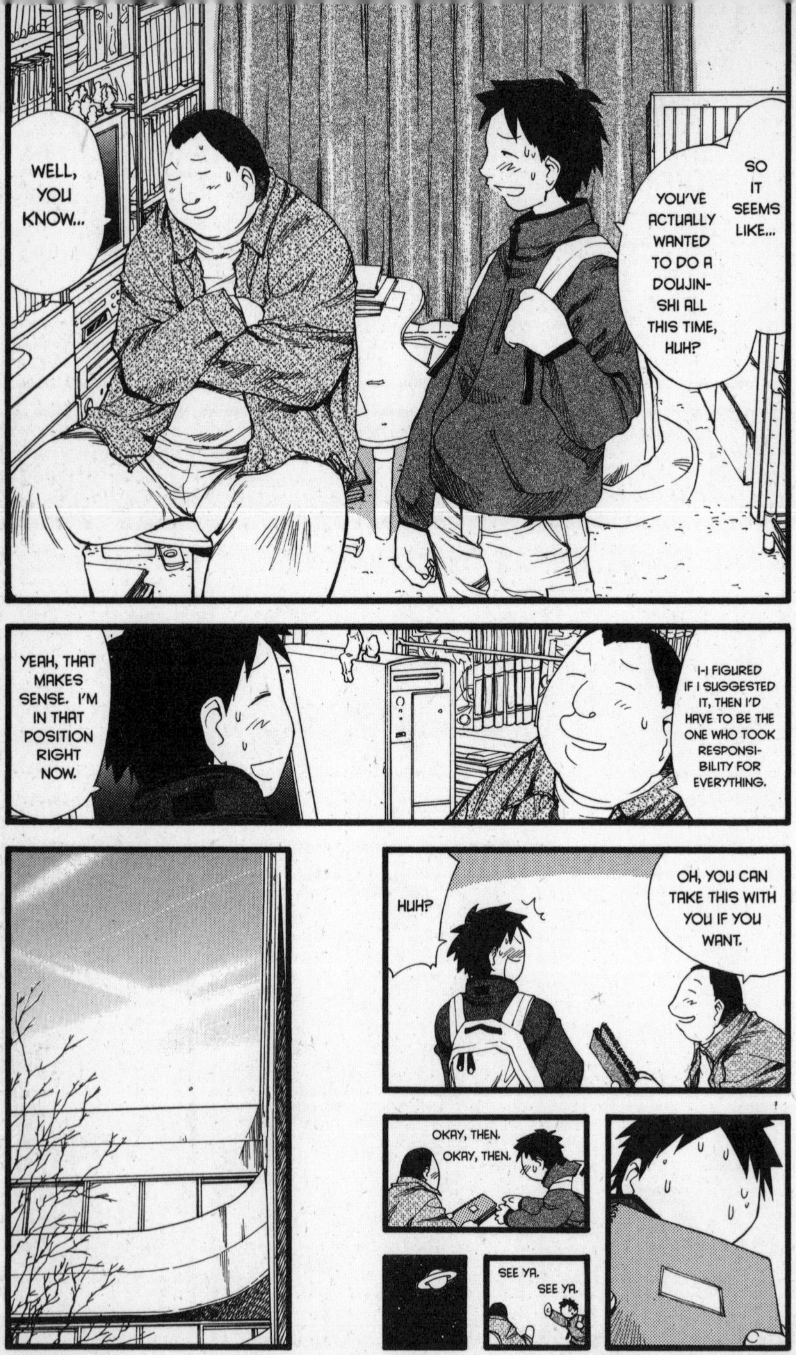
SO IT SEEMS LIKE...
YOU'VE ACTUALLY WANTED TO DO A DOUJIN-SHI ALL THIS TIME, HUH?
WELL, YOU KNOW...
I-I FIGURED IF I SUGGESTED IT, THEN I'D HAVE TO BE THE ONE WHO TOOK RESPONSI-BILITY FOR EVERYTHING.
YEAH, THAT MAKES SENSE. I'M IN THAT POSITION RIGHT NOW.
OH, YOU CAN TAKE THIS WITH YOU IF YOU WANT.
HUH?
OKAY, THEN.
OKAY, THEN.
SEE YA.
SEE YA.

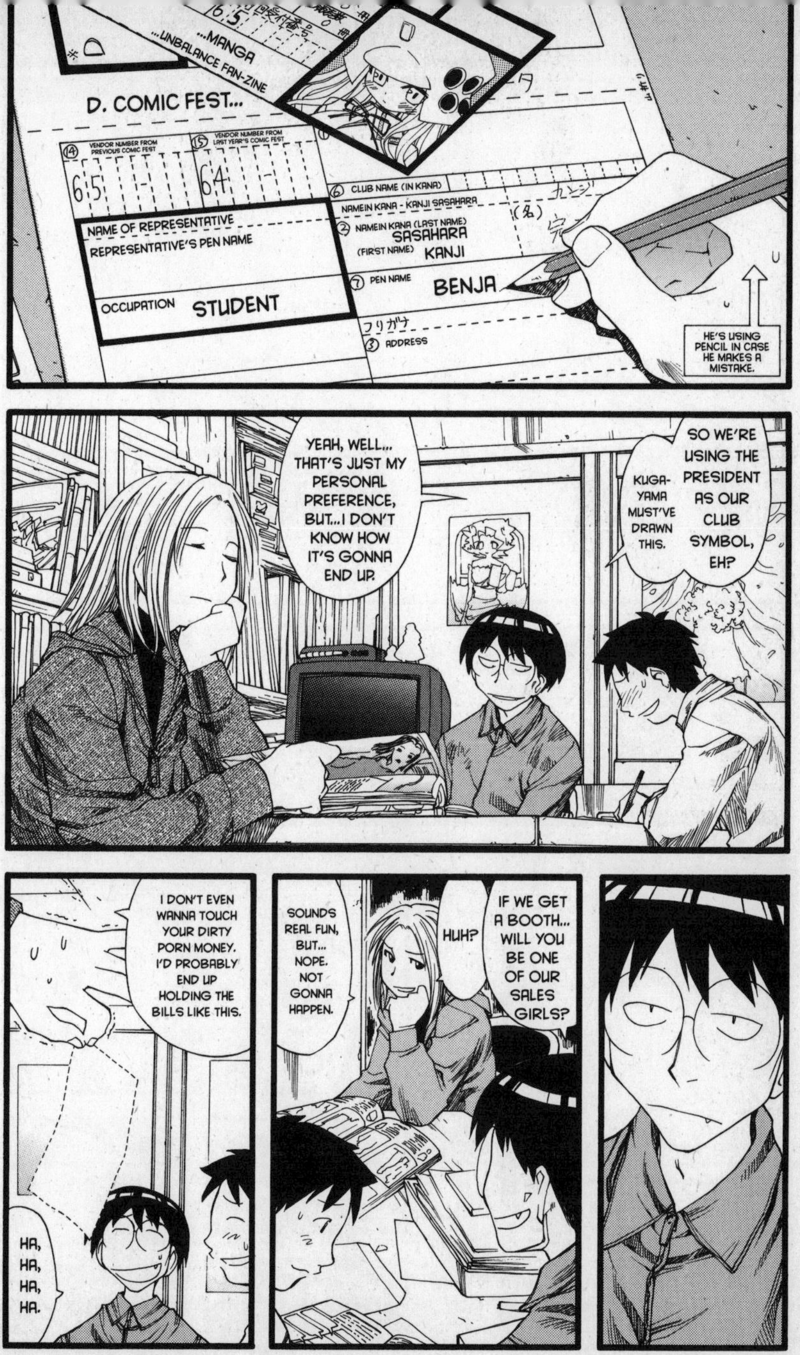
...MANGA
...UNBALANCE FAN-ZINE
D. COMIC FEST...
HE'S USING PENCIL IN CASE HE MAKES A MISTAKE.
14 VENDOR NUMBER FROM PREVIOUS COMIC FEST
65
15 VENDOR NUMBER FROM LAST YEAR'S COMIC FEST
64
6 CLUB NAME (IN KANA)
NAMEIN KANA - KANJI SASAHARA
NAME OF REPRESENTATIVE
REPRESENTATIVE'S PEN NAME
2 NAMEIN KANA (LAST NAME) SASAHARA
(FIRST NAME) KANJI
7 PEN NAME BENJA
OCCUPATION STUDENT
フリガナ
3 ADDRESS
SO WE'RE USING THE PRESIDENT AS OUR CLUB SYMBOL, EH?
KUGA-YAMA MUST'VE DRAWN THIS.
YEAH, WELL... THAT'S JUST MY PERSONAL PREFERENCE, BUT...I DON'T KNOW HOW IT'S GONNA END UP.
IF WE GET A BOOTH... WILL YOU BE ONE OF OUR SALES GIRLS?
HUH?
SOUNDS REAL FUN, BUT... NOPE. NOT GONNA HAPPEN.
I DON'T EVEN WANNA TOUCH YOUR DIRTY PORN MONEY. I'D PROBABLY END UP HOLDING THE BILLS LIKE THIS.
HA, HA, HA, HA.

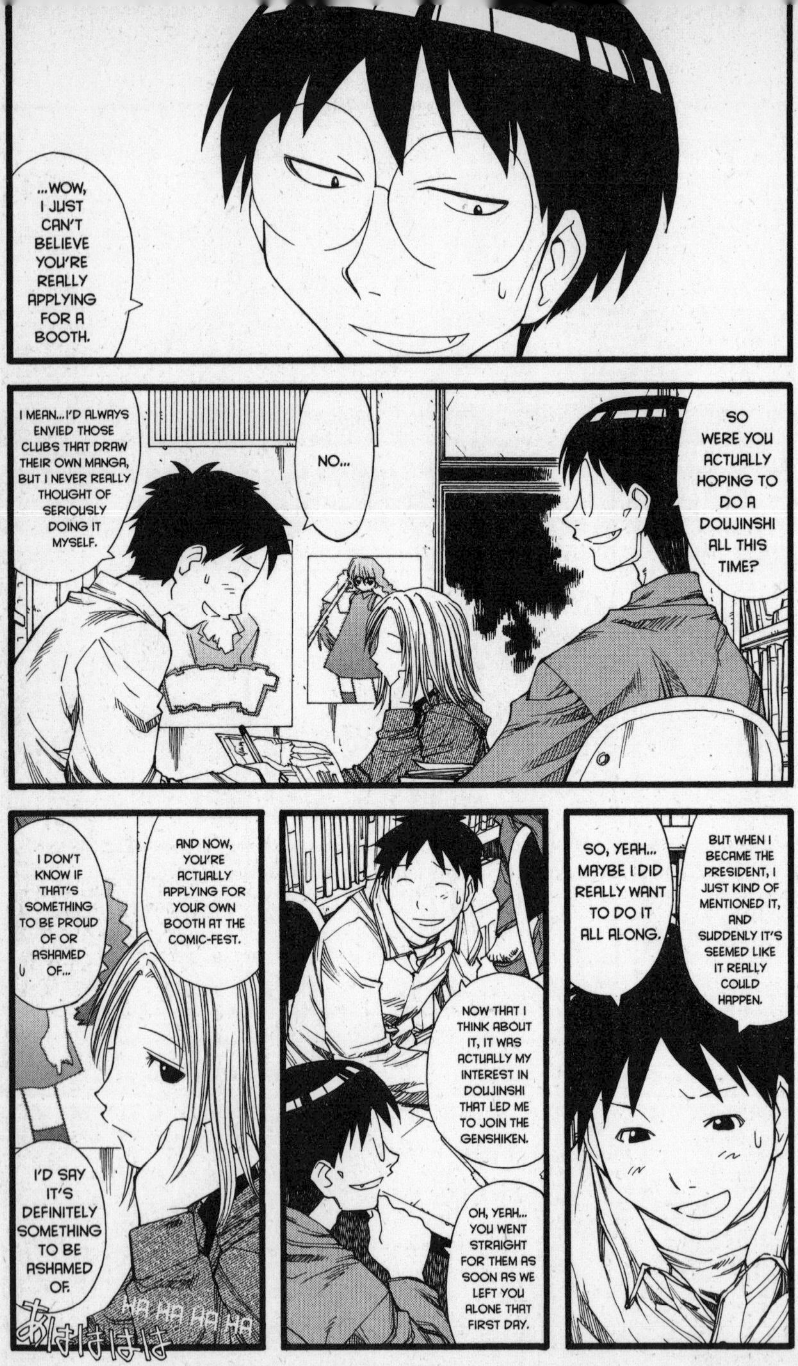
...WOW, I JUST CAN'T BELIEVE YOU'RE REALLY APPLYING FOR A BOOTH.
SO WERE YOU ACTUALLY HOPING TO DO A DOUJINSHI ALL THIS TIME?
NO...
I MEAN...I'D ALWAYS ENVIED THOSE CLUBS THAT DRAW THEIR OWN MANGA, BUT I NEVER REALLY THOUGHT OF SERIOUSLY DOING IT MYSELF.
BUT WHEN I BECAME THE PRESIDENT, I JUST KIND OF MENTIONED IT, AND SUDDENLY IT'S SEEMED LIKE IT REALLY COULD HAPPEN.
SO, YEAH... MAYBE I DID REALLY WANT TO DO IT ALL ALONG.
NOW THAT I THINK ABOUT IT, IT WAS ACTUALLY MY INTEREST IN DOUJINSHI THAT LED ME TO JOIN THE GENSHIKEN.
OH, YEAH... YOU WENT STRAIGHT FOR THEM AS SOON AS WE LEFT YOU ALONE THAT FIRST DAY.
AND NOW, YOU'RE ACTUALLY APPLYING FOR YOUR OWN BOOTH AT THE COMIC-FEST.
I DON'T KNOW IF THAT'S SOMETHING TO BE PROUD OF OR ASHAMED OF...
I'D SAY IT'S DEFINITELY SOMETHING TO BE ASHAMED OF.
あははははは
HA HA HA HA

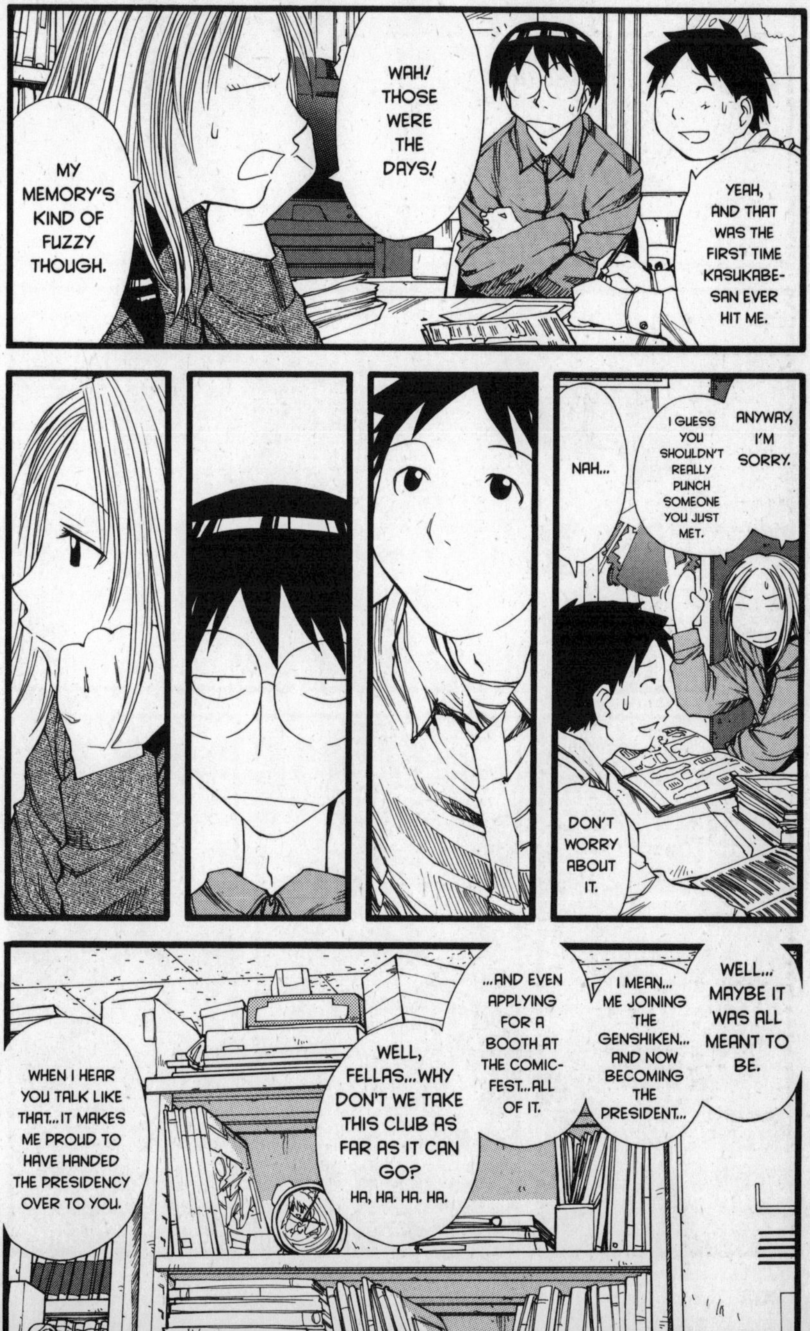
YEAH, AND THAT WAS THE FIRST TIME KASUKABE-SAN EVER HIT ME.
WAH! THOSE WERE THE DAYS!
MY MEMORY'S KIND OF FUZZY THOUGH.
ANYWAY, I'M SORRY.
I GUESS YOU SHOULDN'T REALLY PUNCH SOMEONE YOU JUST MET.
NAH...
DON'T WORRY ABOUT IT.
WELL... MAYBE IT WAS ALL MEANT TO BE.
I MEAN... ME JOINING THE GENSHIKEN... AND NOW BECOMING THE PRESIDENT...
...AND EVEN APPLYING FOR A BOOTH AT THE COMIC-FEST...ALL OF IT.
WELL, FELLAS...WHY DON'T WE TAKE THIS CLUB AS FAR AS IT CAN GO?
HA, HA. HA. HA.
WHEN I HEAR YOU TALK LIKE THAT...IT MAKES ME PROUD TO HAVE HANDED THE PRESIDENCY OVER TO YOU.

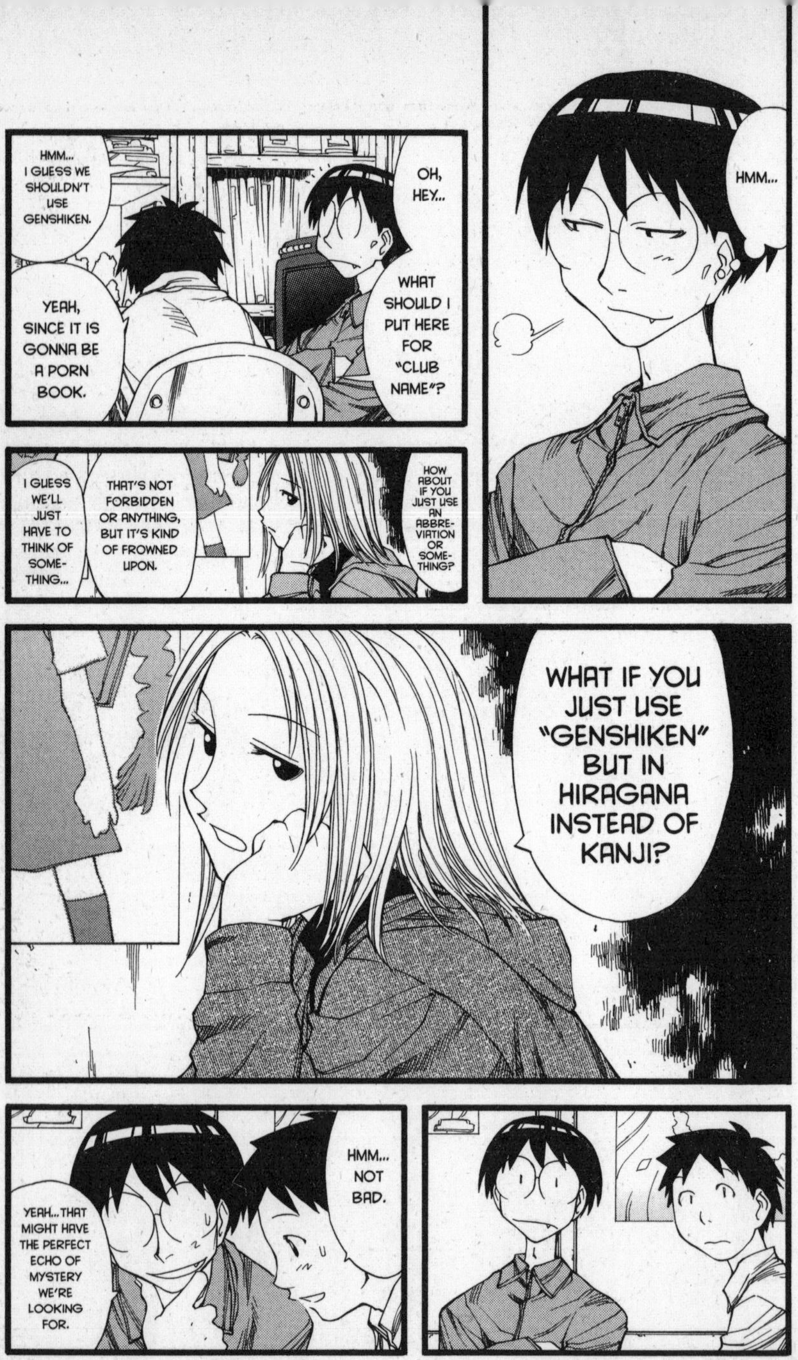
HMM...
OH, HEY...
WHAT SHOULD I PUT HERE FOR "CLUB NAME"?
HMM... I GUESS WE SHOULDN'T USE GENSHIKEN.
YEAH, SINCE IT IS GONNA BE A PORN BOOK.
HOW ABOUT IF YOU JUST USE AN ABBREVIATION OR SOMETHING?
THAT'S NOT FORBIDDEN OR ANYTHING, BUT IT'S KIND OF FROWNED UPON.
I GUESS WE'LL JUST HAVE TO THINK OF SOMETHING...
WHAT IF YOU JUST USE "GENSHIKEN" BUT IN HIRAGANA INSTEAD OF KANJI?
HMM... NOT BAD.
YEAH...THAT MIGHT HAVE THE PERFECT ECHO OF MYSTERY WE'RE LOOKING FOR.

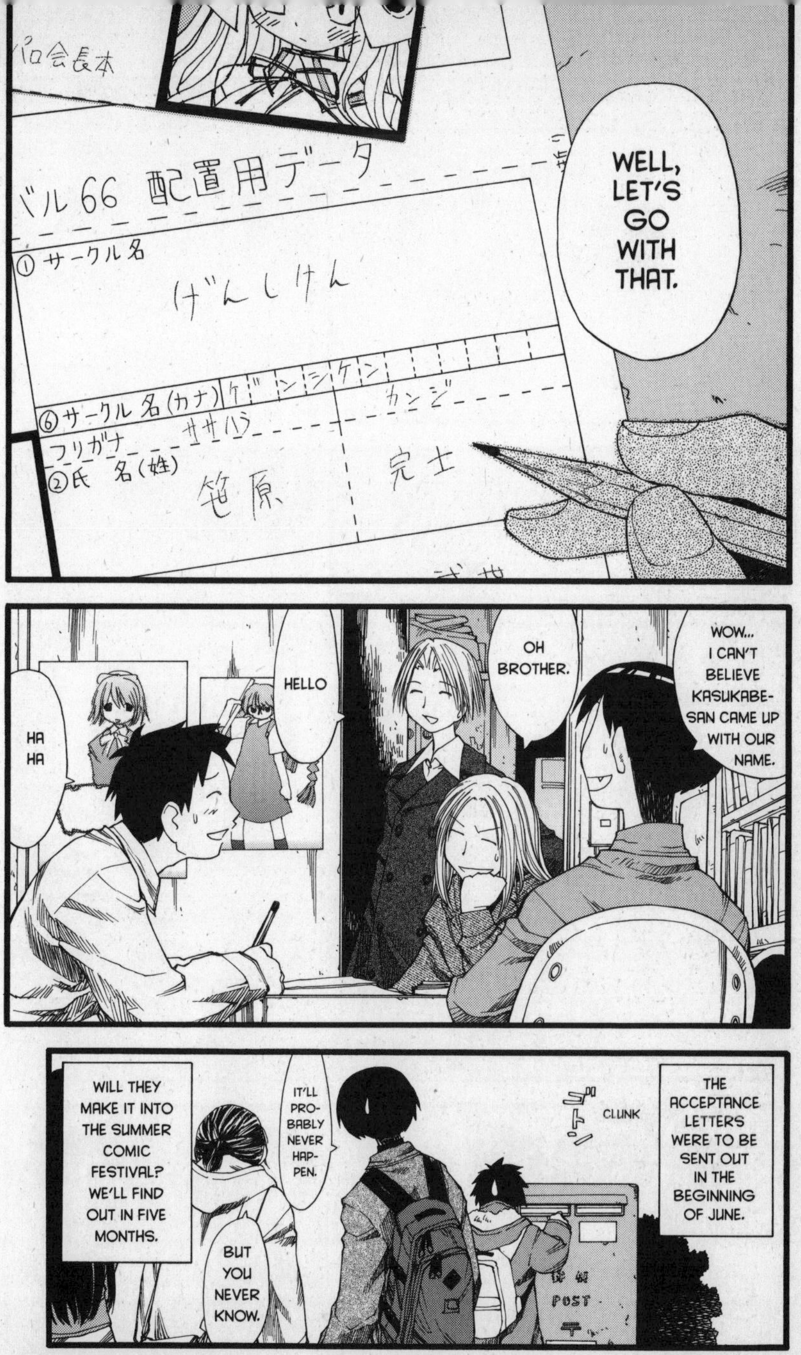
パロ会長本
バル66 配置用データ
①サークル名
げんしけん
⑥サークル名(カナ) ゲンシケン
フリガナ ササハラ カンジ
②氏 名(姓) 笹原 完士
WELL, LET'S GO WITH THAT.
WOW... I CAN'T BELIEVE KASUKABE-SAN CAME UP WITH OUR NAME.
OH BROTHER.
HELLO
HA HA
THE ACCEPTANCE LETTERS WERE TO BE SENT OUT IN THE BEGINNING OF JUNE.
ゴトン
CLUNK
IT'LL PRO-BABLY NEVER HAP-PEN.
BUT YOU NEVER KNOW.
WILL THEY MAKE IT INTO THE SUMMER COMIC FESTIVAL? WE'LL FIND OUT IN FIVE MONTHS.
POST

END OF CHAPTER 22

# OUR FAVORITE GAME ANOTHER STORIES

STORY 4

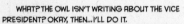

KASUMI KISARAGI

REVIEWED BY KODAMA

WHAT? THE OWL ISN'T WRITING ABOUT THE VICE PRESIDENT? OKAY, THEN...I'LL DO IT.

IN A WAY, THE VICE PRESIDENT'S SCENARIO IS THE ONE THAT IS THE MOST DIFFERENT FROM THE ORIGINAL MANGA. [HA HA] EVEN IN DOUJINSHI YOU ALMOST NEVER SEE THE VICE PRESIDENT VS. CHIHIRO. OF COURSE IN THIS GAME'S VERSION, CHIHIRO IS SORT OF LIKE YOUR TYPICAL MALE CHARACTER IN A PORN GAME. HE'S SORT OF STRIPPED DOWN OF ALL DEFINING CHARACTERISTICS...OR MAYBE THAT'S HOW HE ALWAYS WAS. [HA HA]

SINCE IT'S SORT OF HARD TO INCREASE HER POPULARITY POINTS, IT CAN BE DIFFICULT TO ATTACK AS A TEAM WITH OTHER CHARACTERS. THE BALANCE IS ESPECIALLY DIFFICULT TO ACHIEVE WITH THE PRESIDENT. ACTUALLY, AT FIRST, WHEN YOU PLAY USING BOTH THE PRESIDENT AND THE VICE PRESIDENT, YOU'LL GET A LOT OF POPULARITY POINTS, BUT IF YOU'RE NOT CAREFUL, THE GAME WILL END UP MORPHING INTO THE PRESIDENT'S SCENARIO. TO BE HONEST, YOU'LL PROBABLY HAVE TO USE A STRATEGY GUIDEBOOK, OR YOU'LL NEVER GET ANYWHERE.

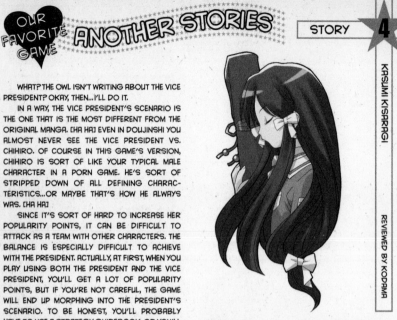

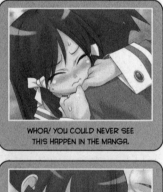

WHOA! YOU COULD NEVER SEE THIS HAPPEN IN THE MANGA.

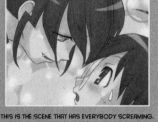

THIS IS THE SCENE THAT HAS EVERYBODY SCREAMING. "STOP, STOP, STOP!" IT'S SERIOUSLY AROUSING.

THERE SEEMS TO BE A WALL BETWEEN THE TWO CHARACTERS, BUT THEY GRADUALLY START TO GET ALONG. THAT ACTUALLY MAKES THE GAME MORE REALISTIC. YOU GET TO SEE BOTH HER DARK, ADULT SIDE AS WELL AS HER VULNERABLE, CHILDLIKE SIDE. THE DIFFERENCE IS ASTONISHING. IN THIS SCENARIO, ALEX MAKES AN APPEARANCE VERY QUICKLY, EVEN BEFORE SUMMER BEGINS. CHIHIRO AND ALEX ARE RIVALS, BUT DURING THE BATTLE WITH THE KIKYUU GANG, THEY BECOME FRIENDS. THIS ADDS A WHOLE NEW TWIST TO THE SCENARIO. [HA HA] IT CREATES A LOVE TRIANGLE BETWEEN THE TWO GUYS AND THE PRESIDENT, WHICH PUTS A BURDEN ON THEIR RELATIONSHIP, AND ALSO ADDS ANOTHER EXCITING ELEMENT TO THE SCENARIO. IF YOU GET CLOSE TO THE PRESIDENT'S CHARACTER, YOU'LL GET A CHANCE TO ENJOY THE ROMANCE COMIC STYLE STORY LINE. THE FUNNY THING IS THAT WHEN THE VICE PRESIDENT SEES PEOPLE BEING NICE TO THE PRESIDENT, IT MAKES HER HAPPY.

OH, YEAH...AND SHE GRADUALLY STARTS TO OVERCOME HER "FEAR OF HUMAN CONTACT"...WITH AROUSING RESULTS. [HA HA] WELL, I KNOW THAT'S A TYPICAL STORYLINE, BUT THE DETAILS ARE REALLY AMAZING, AND SO IS THE FINAL SCENE, WHERE WE SEE HER IN A WEDDING DRESS. [K]

★

WELL, WHAT ABOUT YOU? WHY DIDN'T YOU CHOOSE YAMADA? YAMADA'S IN THE SAME CLASS AS CHIHIRO, SO YOU COULD'VE WRITTEN ALL ABOUT THEIR "CLASSROOM LOVE STORY." CHOOSE MORE CAREFULLY NEXT TIME.

## CHAPTER 22 - MOMENTS LATER

**IS IT BECAUSE YOU NEVER WEAR PANTS?**

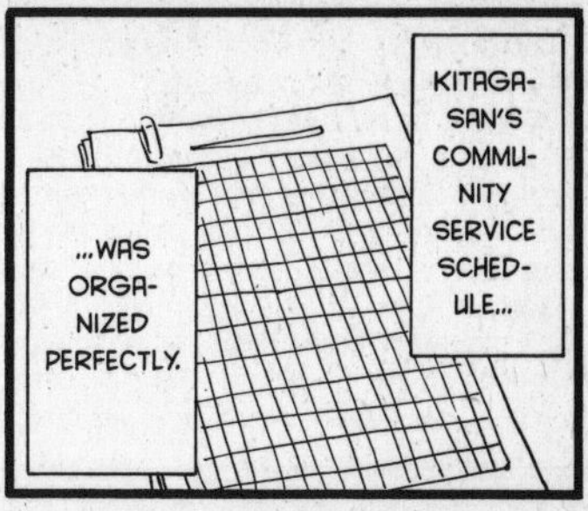
KITAGA-SAN'S COMMUNITY SERVICE SCHEDULE...
...WAS ORGANIZED PERFECTLY.

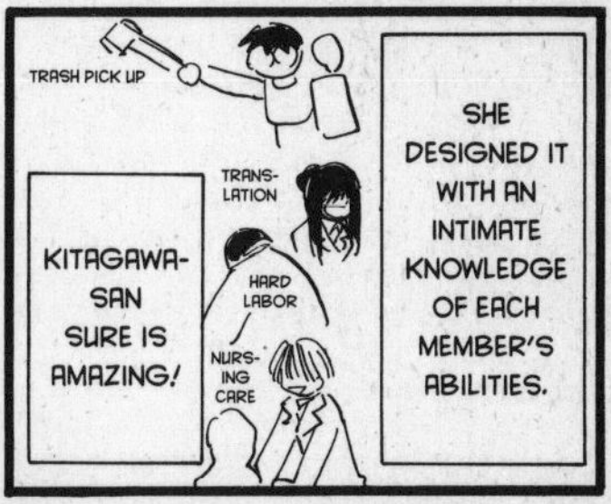
SHE DESIGNED IT WITH AN INTIMATE KNOWLEDGE OF EACH MEMBER'S ABILITIES.
TRASH PICK UP
TRANSLATION
HARD LABOR
NURSING CARE
KITAGAWA-SAN SURE IS AMAZING!

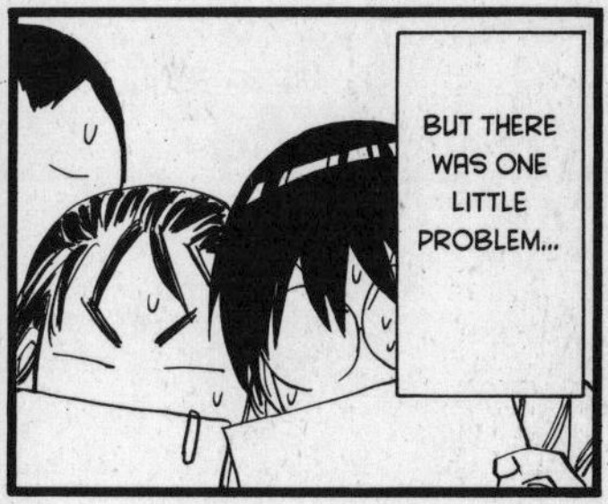
BUT THERE WAS ONE LITTLE PROBLEM...

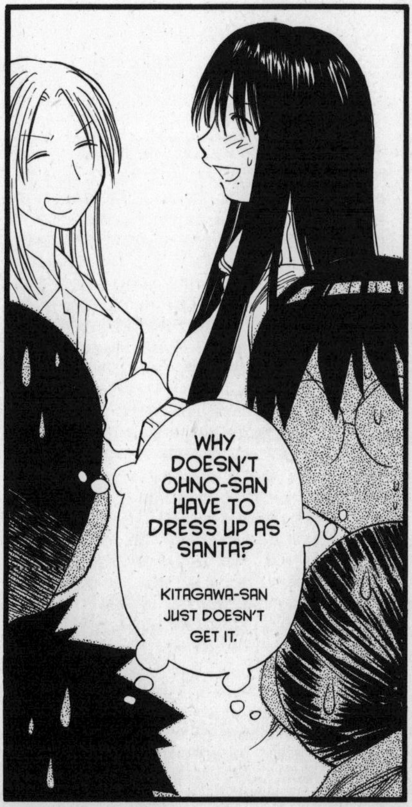
WHY DOESN'T OHNO-SAN HAVE TO DRESS UP AS SANTA?
KITAGAWA-SAN JUST DOESN'T GET IT.

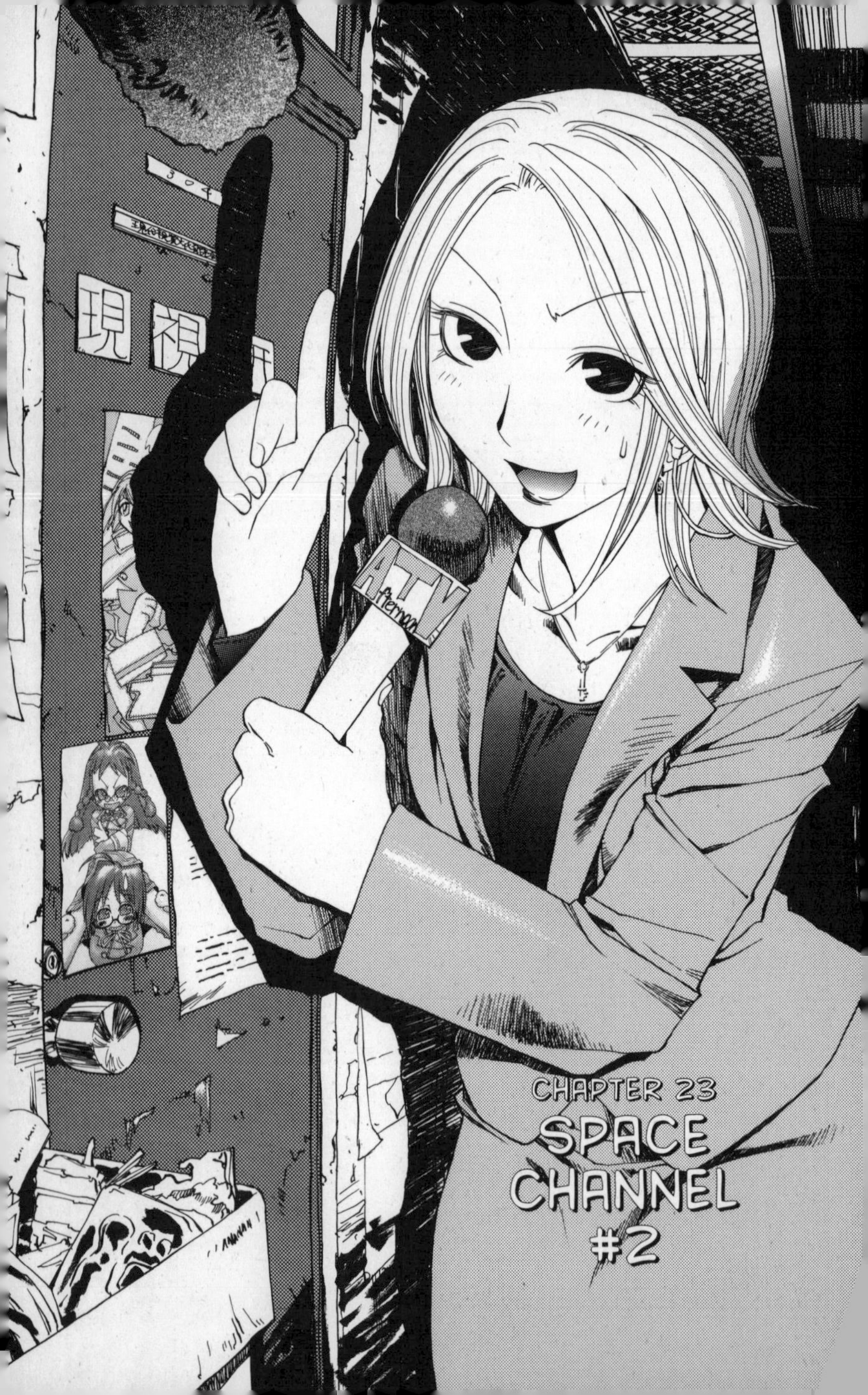
CHAPTER 23
SPACE
CHANNEL
#2

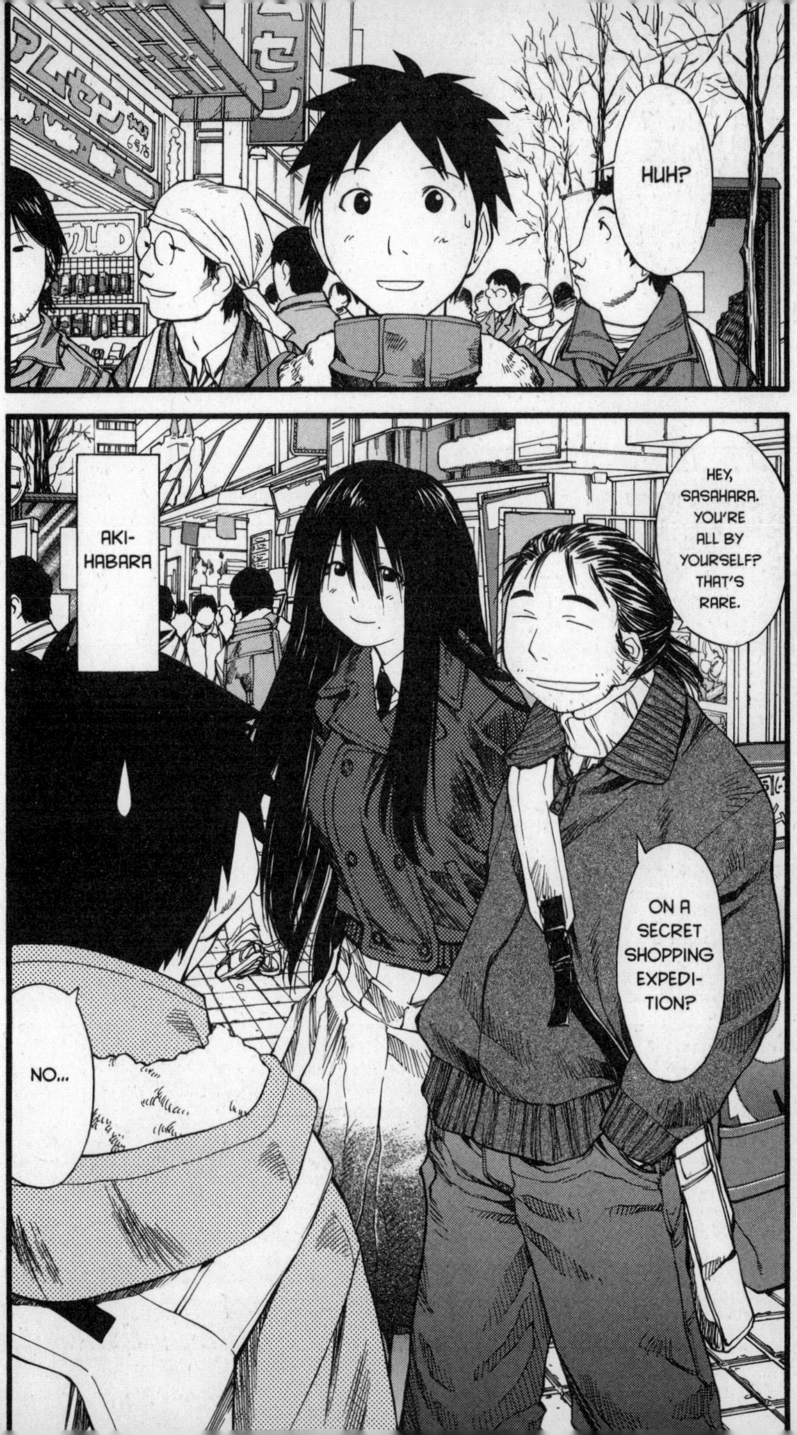
HUH?
HEY, SASAHARA. YOU'RE ALL BY YOURSELF? THAT'S RARE.
AKI-HABARA
ON A SECRET SHOPPING EXPEDI-TION?
NO...

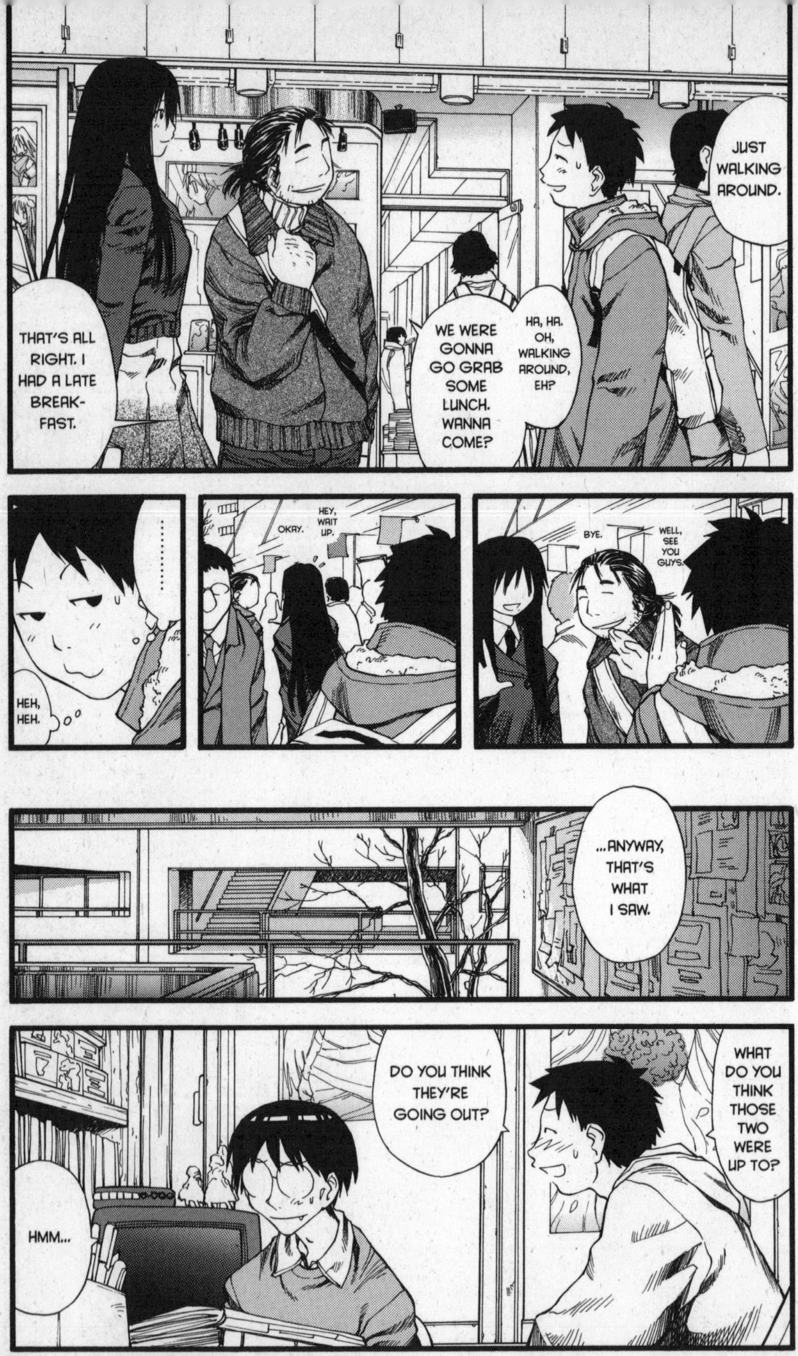
JUST WALKING AROUND.
HA, HA. OH, WALKING AROUND, EH?
WE WERE GONNA GO GRAB SOME LUNCH. WANNA COME?
THAT'S ALL RIGHT. I HAD A LATE BREAK-FAST.
WELL, SEE YOU GUYS.
BYE.
HEY, WAIT UP.
OKAY.
......
HEH, HEH.
...ANYWAY, THAT'S WHAT I SAW.
WHAT DO YOU THINK THOSE TWO WERE UP TO?
DO YOU THINK THEY'RE GOING OUT?
HMM...

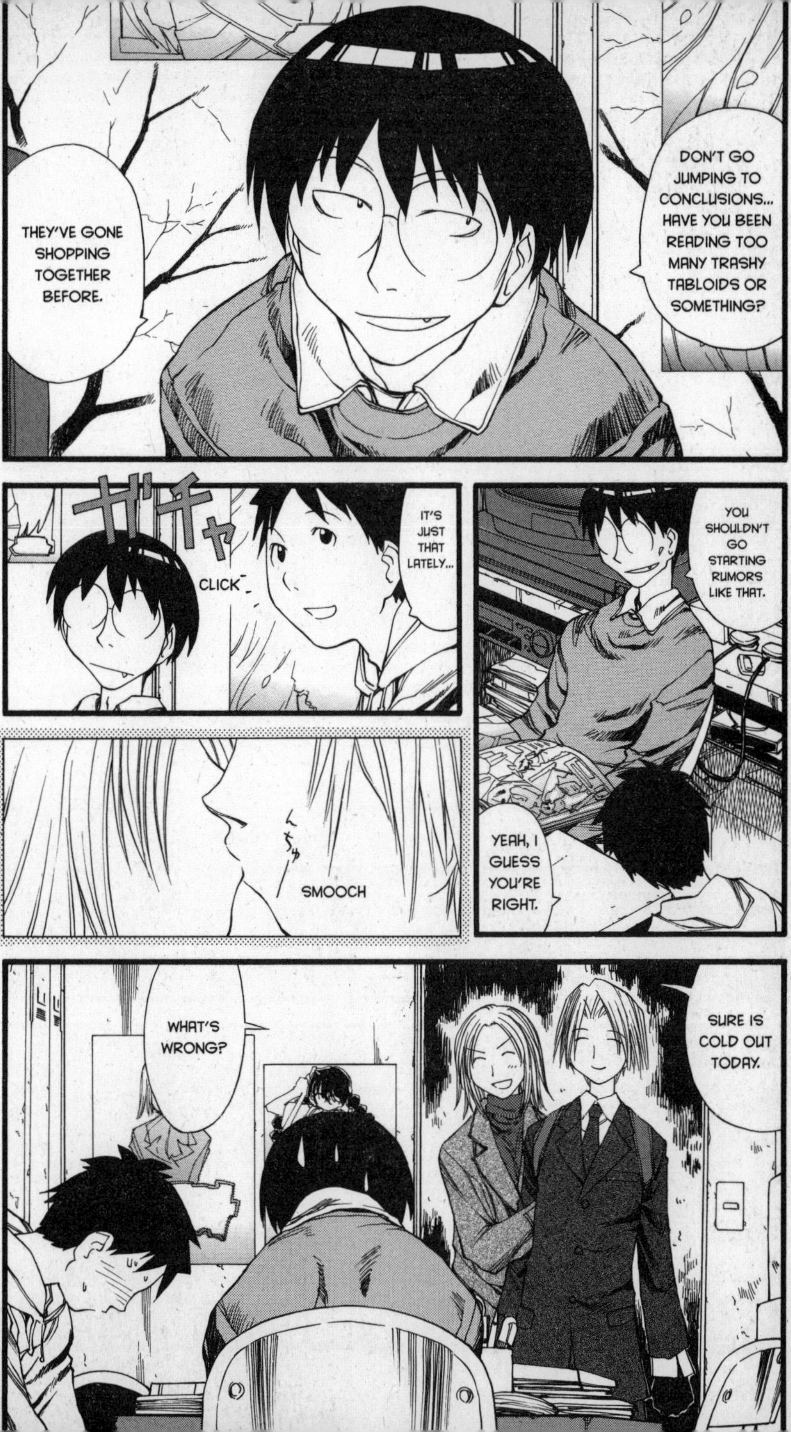
DON'T GO JUMPING TO CONCLUSIONS... HAVE YOU BEEN READING TOO MANY TRASHY TABLOIDS OR SOMETHING?
THEY'VE GONE SHOPPING TOGETHER BEFORE.
YOU SHOULDN'T GO STARTING RUMORS LIKE THAT.
YEAH, I GUESS YOU'RE RIGHT.
IT'S JUST THAT LATELY...
ガチャ
CLICK
んちゅ
SMOOCH
SURE IS COLD OUT TODAY.
WHAT'S WRONG?

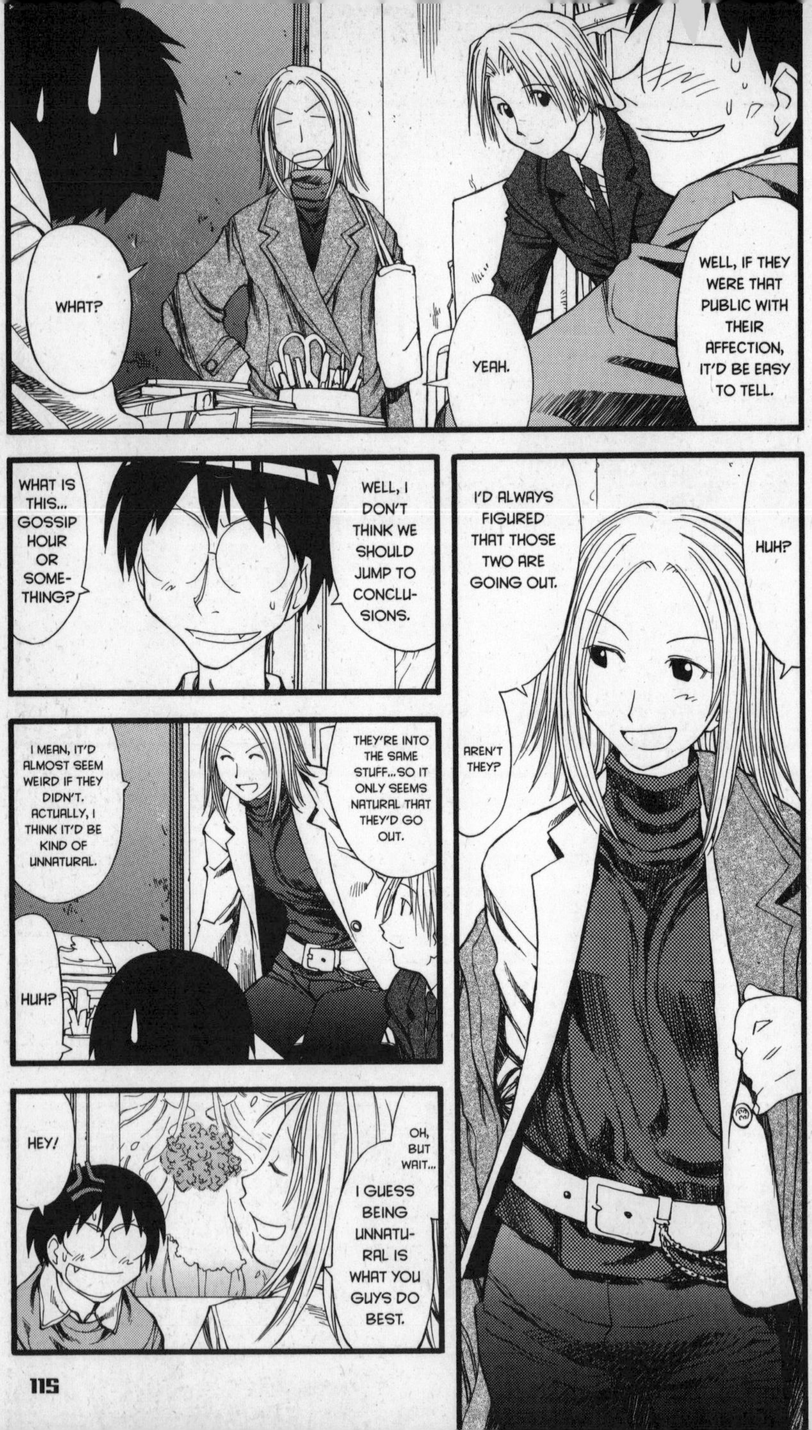

WELL, IF THEY WERE THAT PUBLIC WITH THEIR AFFECTION, IT'D BE EASY TO TELL.
YEAH.
WHAT?
HUH?
I'D ALWAYS FIGURED THAT THOSE TWO ARE GOING OUT.
AREN'T THEY?
WELL, I DON'T THINK WE SHOULD JUMP TO CONCLUSIONS.
WHAT IS THIS... GOSSIP HOUR OR SOMETHING?
THEY'RE INTO THE SAME STUFF...SO IT ONLY SEEMS NATURAL THAT THEY'D GO OUT.
I MEAN, IT'D ALMOST SEEM WEIRD IF THEY DIDN'T. ACTUALLY, I THINK IT'D BE KIND OF UNNATURAL.
HUH?
OH, BUT WAIT...
I GUESS BEING UNNATURAL IS WHAT YOU GUYS DO BEST.
HEY!

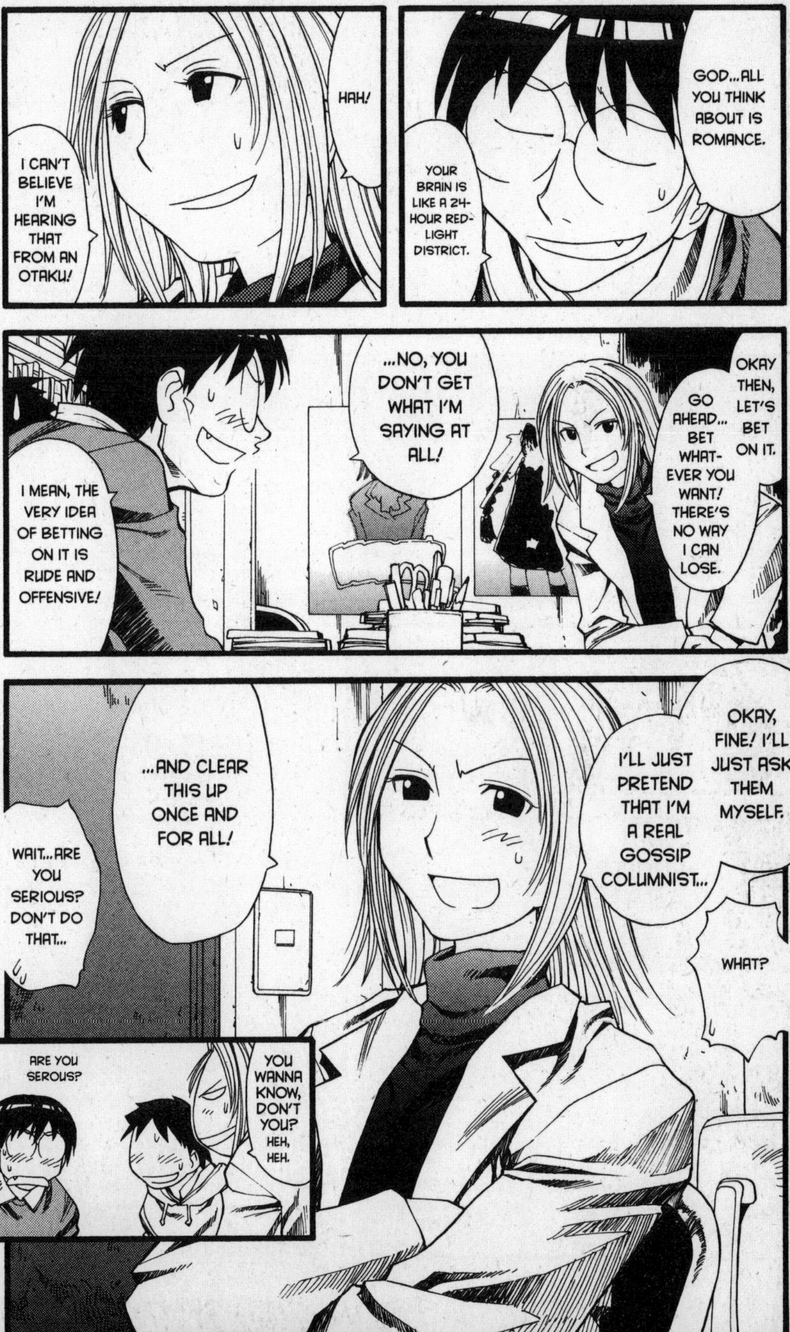
GOD...ALL YOU THINK ABOUT IS ROMANCE.
YOUR BRAIN IS LIKE A 24-HOUR RED-LIGHT DISTRICT.
HAH!
I CAN'T BELIEVE I'M HEARING THAT FROM AN OTAKU!
OKAY THEN, LET'S BET ON IT.
GO AHEAD... BET WHAT-EVER YOU WANT! THERE'S NO WAY I CAN LOSE.
...NO, YOU DON'T GET WHAT I'M SAYING AT ALL!
I MEAN, THE VERY IDEA OF BETTING ON IT IS RUDE AND OFFENSIVE!
OKAY, FINE! I'LL JUST ASK THEM MYSELF.
I'LL JUST PRETEND THAT I'M A REAL GOSSIP COLUMNIST...
...AND CLEAR THIS UP ONCE AND FOR ALL!
WAIT...ARE YOU SERIOUS? DON'T DO THAT...
WHAT?
YOU WANNA KNOW, DON'T YOU? HEH, HEH.
ARE YOU SEROUS?

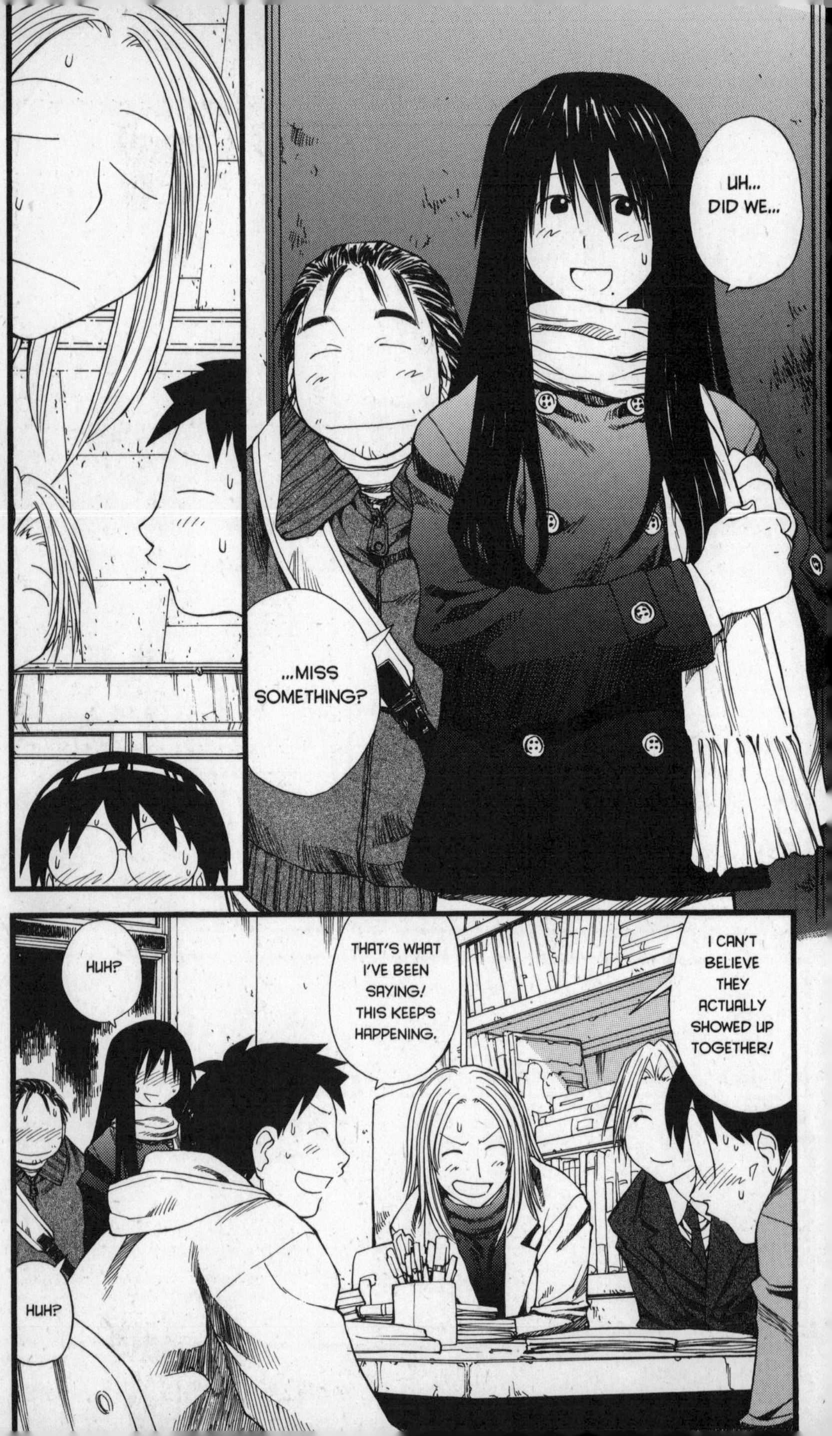
UH... DID WE...
...MISS SOMETHING?
I CAN'T BELIEVE THEY ACTUALLY SHOWED UP TOGETHER!
THAT'S WHAT I'VE BEEN SAYING! THIS KEEPS HAPPENING.
HUH?
HUH?

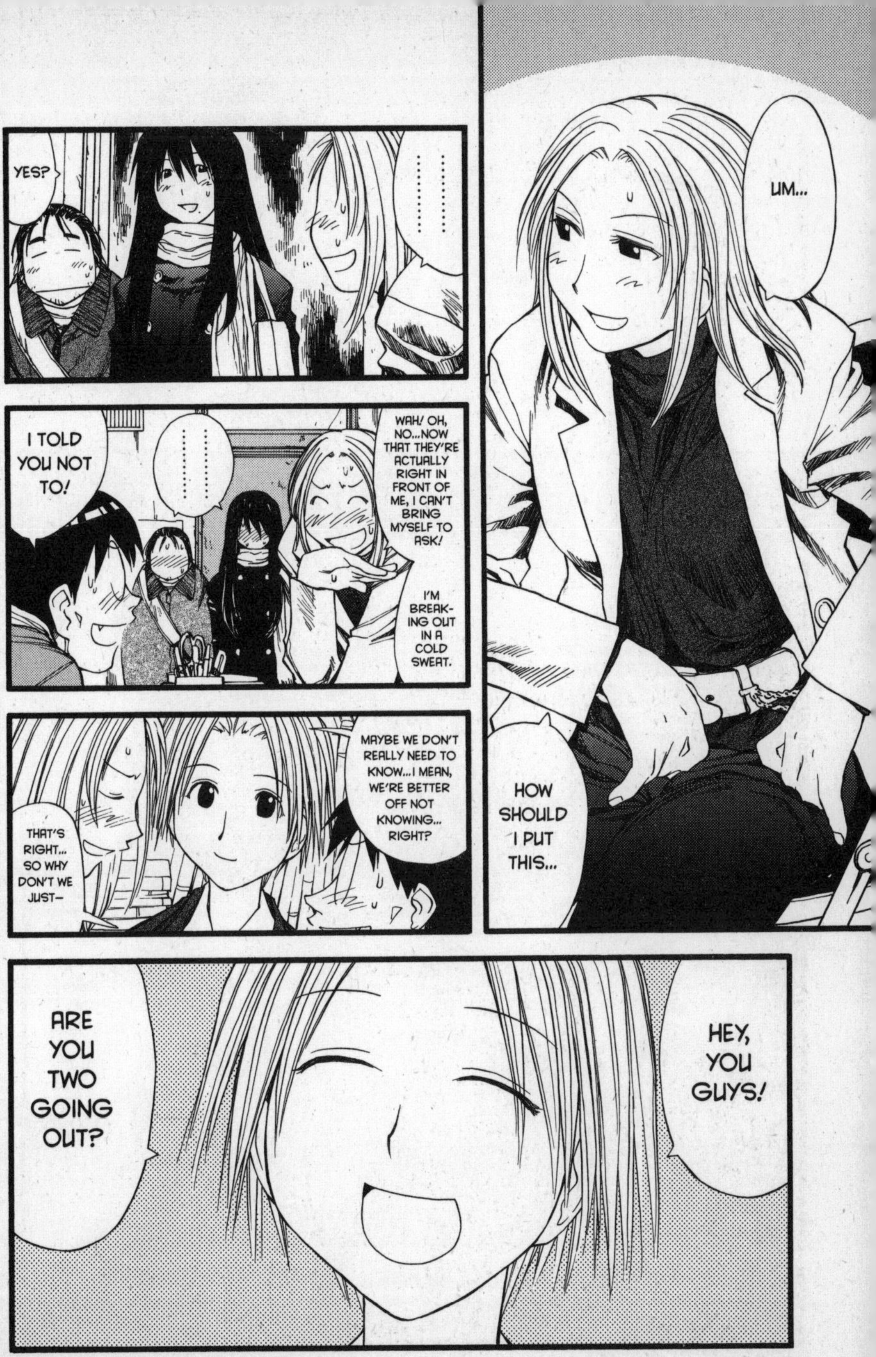
UM...
HOW SHOULD I PUT THIS...
......
YES?
WAH! OH, NO...NOW THAT THEY'RE ACTUALLY RIGHT IN FRONT OF ME, I CAN'T BRING MYSELF TO ASK!
I'M BREAKING OUT IN A COLD SWEAT.
......
I TOLD YOU NOT TO!
MAYBE WE DON'T REALLY NEED TO KNOW...I MEAN, WE'RE BETTER OFF NOT KNOWING... RIGHT?
THAT'S RIGHT... SO WHY DON'T WE JUST—
HEY, YOU GUYS!
ARE YOU TWO GOING OUT?

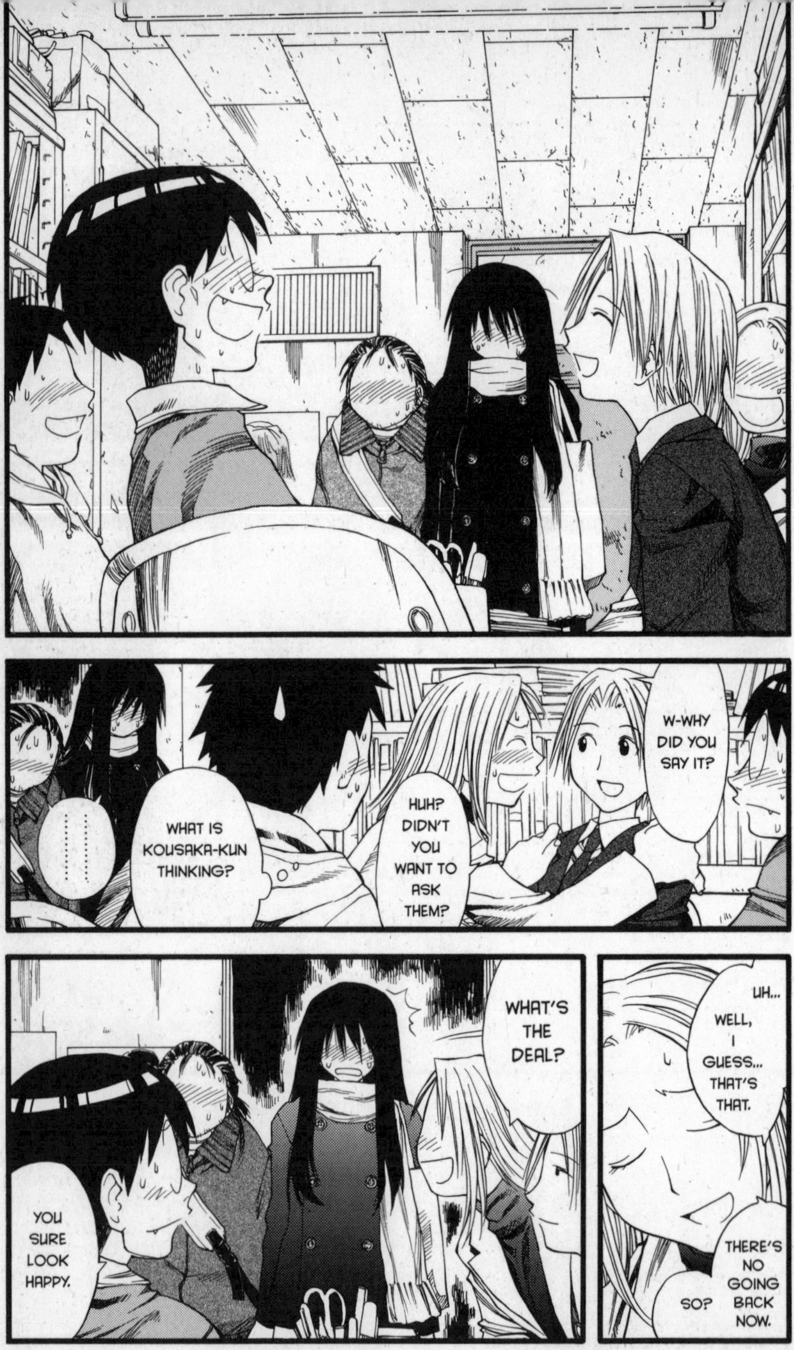
W-WHY DID YOU SAY IT?
HUH? DIDN'T YOU WANT TO ASK THEM?
WHAT IS KOUSAKA-KUN THINKING?
......
UH... WELL, I GUESS... THAT'S THAT.
THERE'S NO GOING BACK NOW.
SO?
WHAT'S THE DEAL?
YOU SURE LOOK HAPPY.

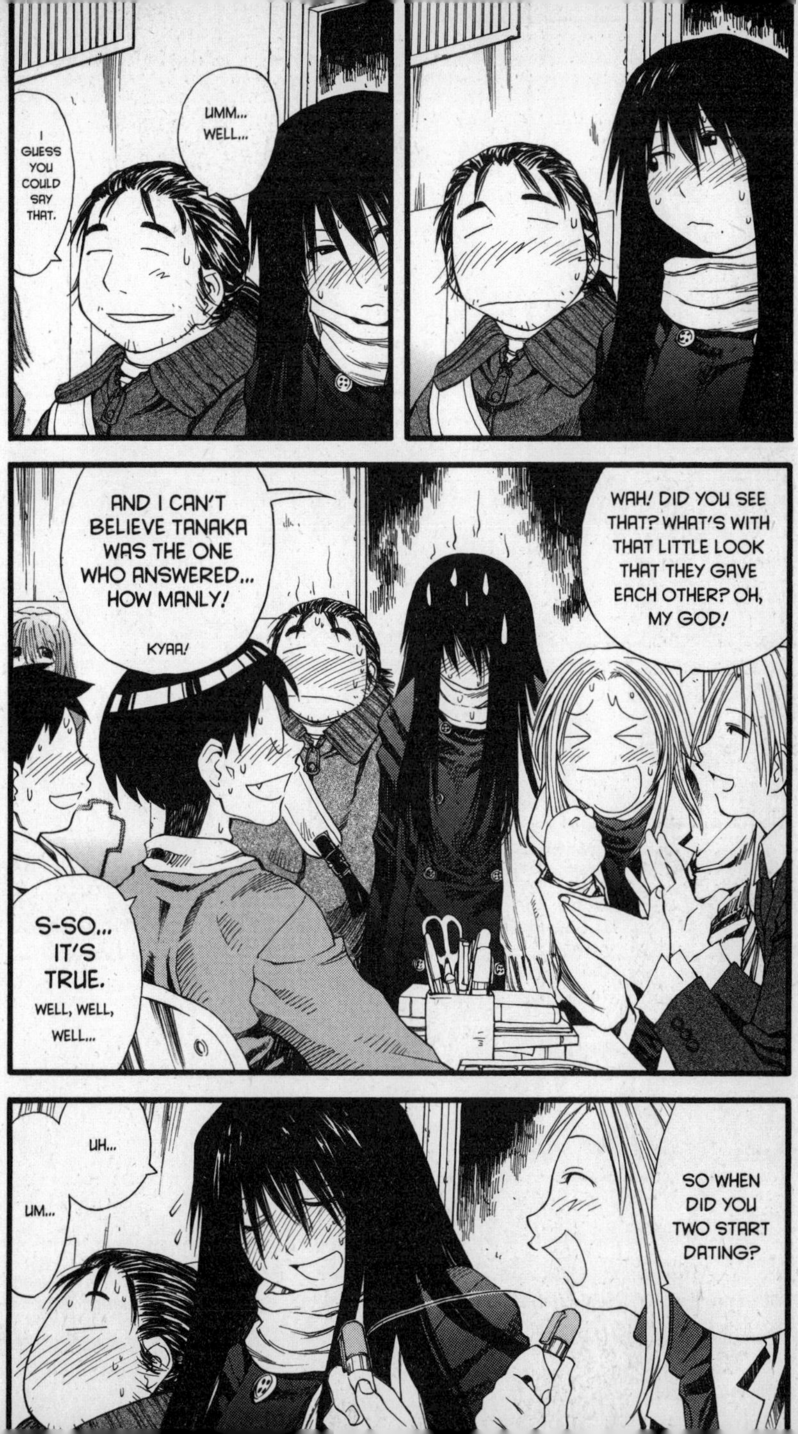
UMM... WELL...
I GUESS YOU COULD SAY THAT.
WAH! DID YOU SEE THAT? WHAT'S WITH THAT LITTLE LOOK THAT THEY GAVE EACH OTHER? OH, MY GOD!
AND I CAN'T BELIEVE TANAKA WAS THE ONE WHO ANSWERED... HOW MANLY!
KYAA!
S-SO... IT'S TRUE.
WELL, WELL, WELL...
SO WHEN DID YOU TWO START DATING?
UH...
UM...

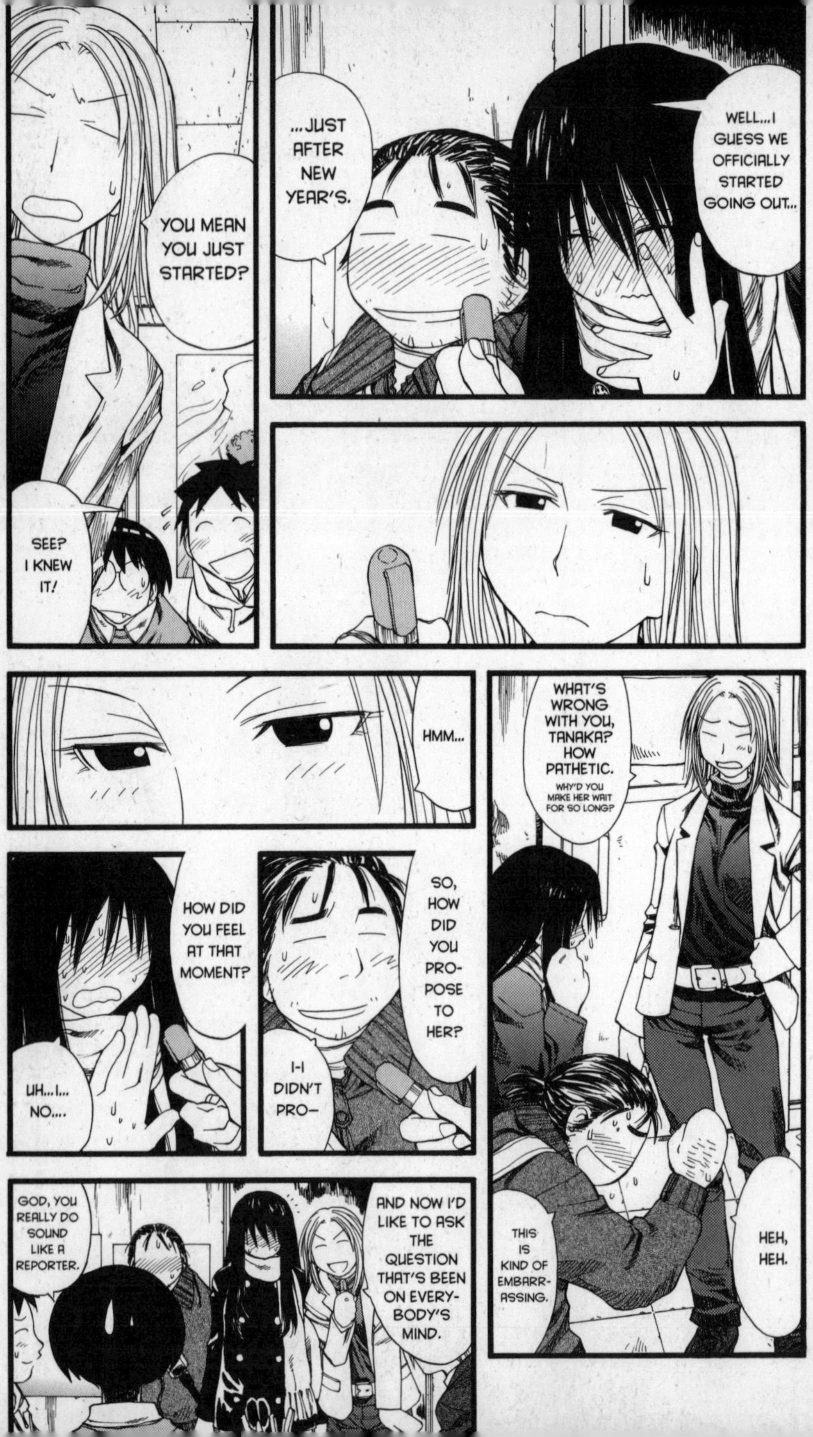
WELL...I GUESS WE OFFICIALLY STARTED GOING OUT...
...JUST AFTER NEW YEAR'S.
YOU MEAN YOU JUST STARTED?
SEE? I KNEW IT!
WHAT'S WRONG WITH YOU, TANAKA? HOW PATHETIC.
WHY'D YOU MAKE HER WAIT FOR SO LONG?
HEH, HEH.
THIS IS KIND OF EMBARR-ASSING.
HMM...
SO, HOW DID YOU PRO-POSE TO HER?
I-I DIDN'T PRO—
HOW DID YOU FEEL AT THAT MOMENT?
UH...I... NO....
AND NOW I'D LIKE TO ASK THE QUESTION THAT'S BEEN ON EVERY-BODY'S MIND.
GOD, YOU REALLY DO SOUND LIKE A REPORTER.

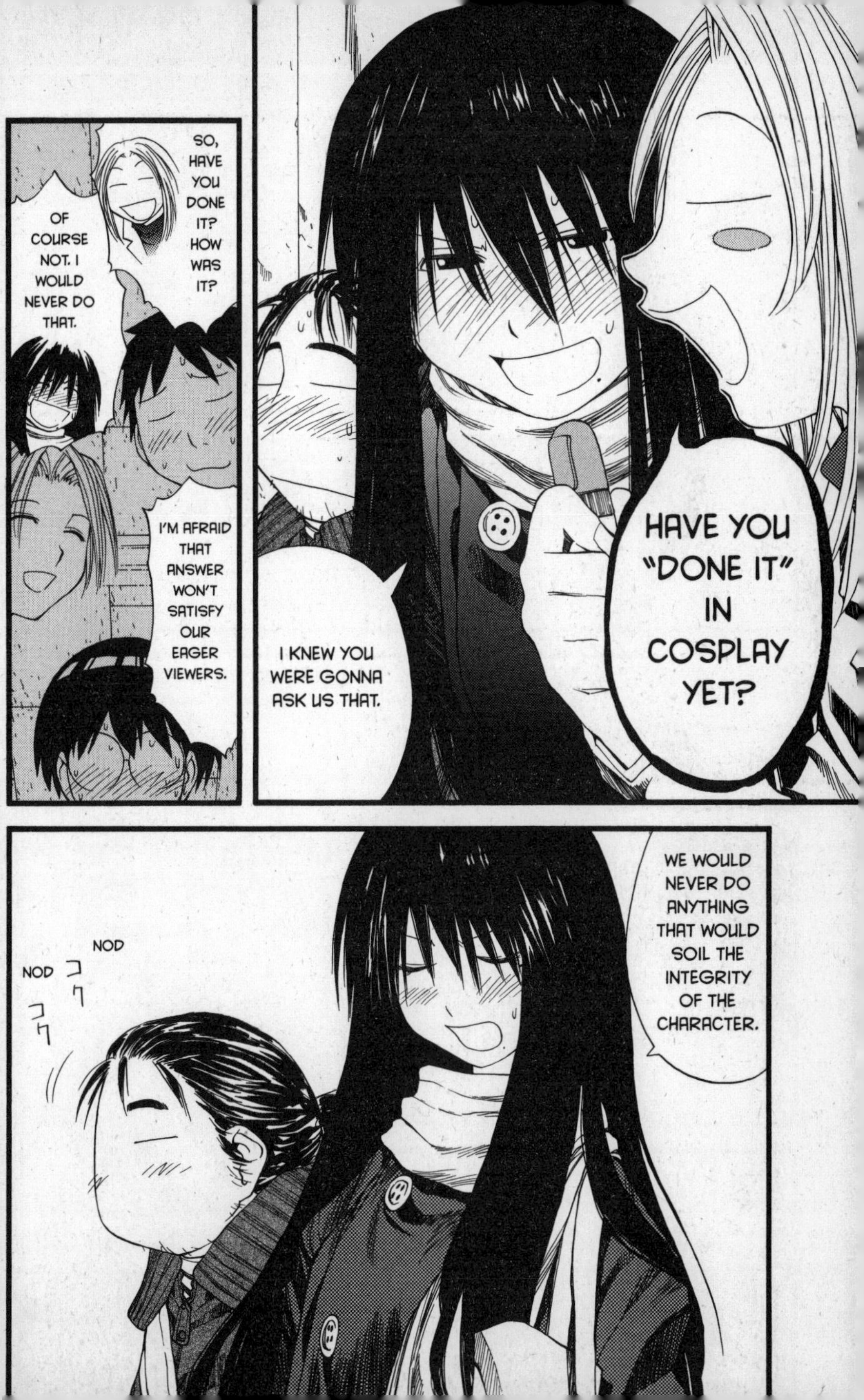
HAVE YOU "DONE IT" IN COSPLAY YET?
I KNEW YOU WERE GONNA ASK US THAT.
SO, HAVE YOU DONE IT? HOW WAS IT?
OF COURSE NOT. I WOULD NEVER DO THAT.
I'M AFRAID THAT ANSWER WON'T SATISFY OUR EAGER VIEWERS.
WE WOULD NEVER DO ANYTHING THAT WOULD SOIL THE INTEGRITY OF THE CHARACTER.
NOD コク
NOD コク

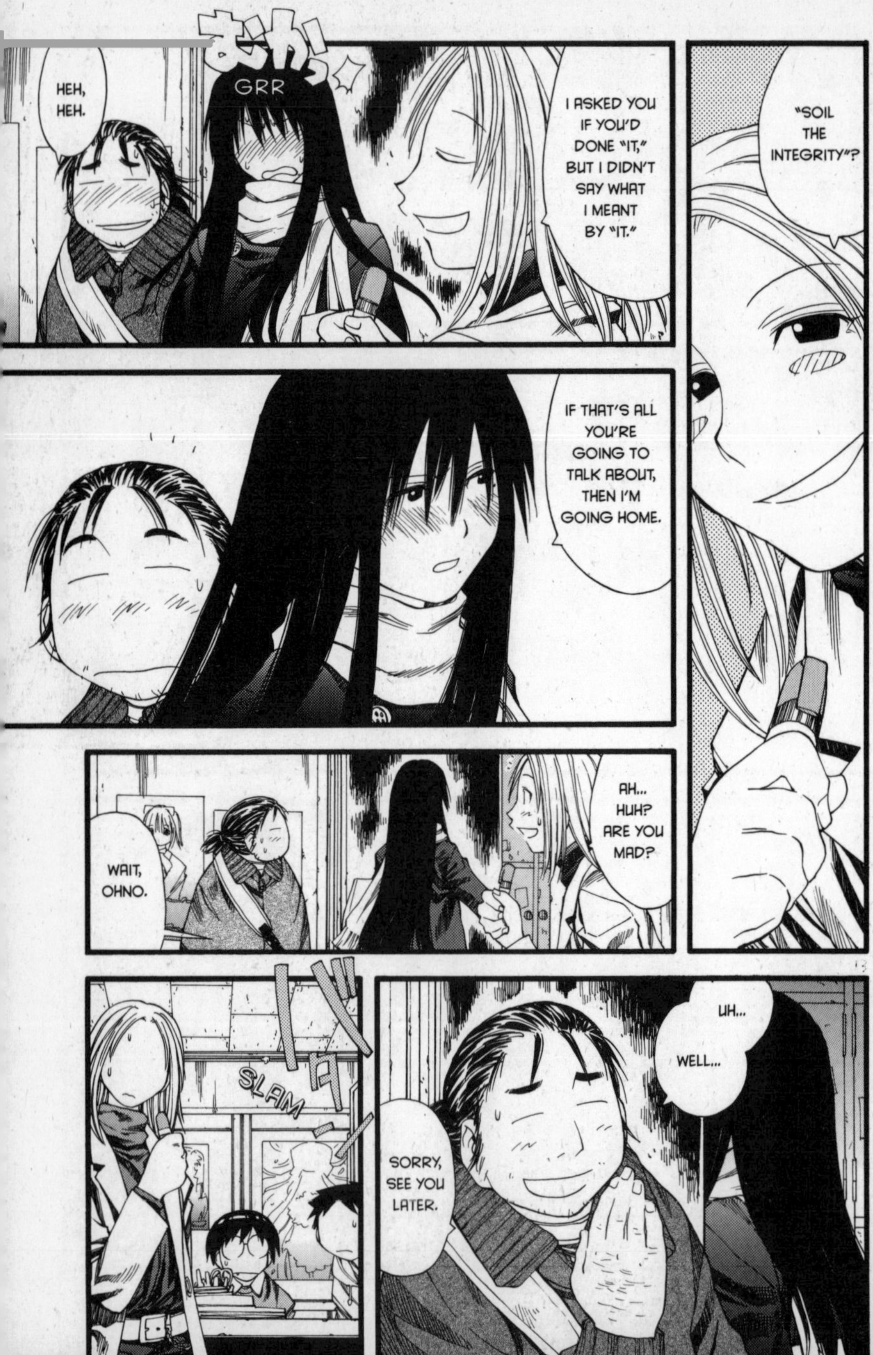
"SOIL THE INTEGRITY"?
I ASKED YOU IF YOU'D DONE "IT," BUT I DIDN'T SAY WHAT I MEANT BY "IT."
GRR
HEH, HEH.
IF THAT'S ALL YOU'RE GOING TO TALK ABOUT, THEN I'M GOING HOME.
AH... HUH? ARE YOU MAD?
WAIT, OHNO.
UH...
WELL...
SORRY, SEE YOU LATER.
SLAM

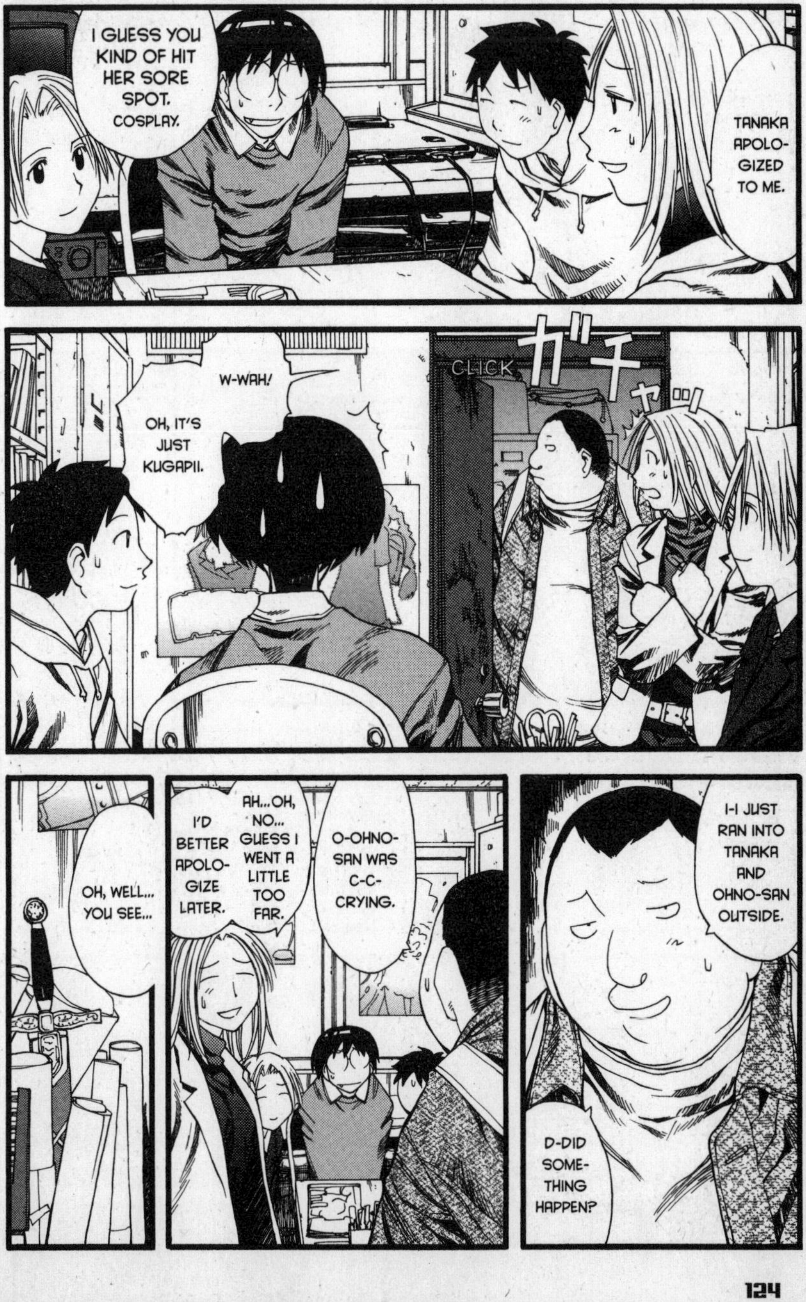
TANAKA APOLOGIZED TO ME.
I GUESS YOU KIND OF HIT HER SORE SPOT. COSPLAY.
ガチャッ
CLICK
W-WAH!
OH, IT'S JUST KUGAPII.
I-I JUST RAN INTO TANAKA AND OHNO-SAN OUTSIDE.
D-DID SOMETHING HAPPEN?
O-OHNO-SAN WAS C-C-CRYING.
AH...OH, NO... GUESS I WENT A LITTLE TOO FAR.
I'D BETTER APOLOGIZE LATER.
OH, WELL... YOU SEE...

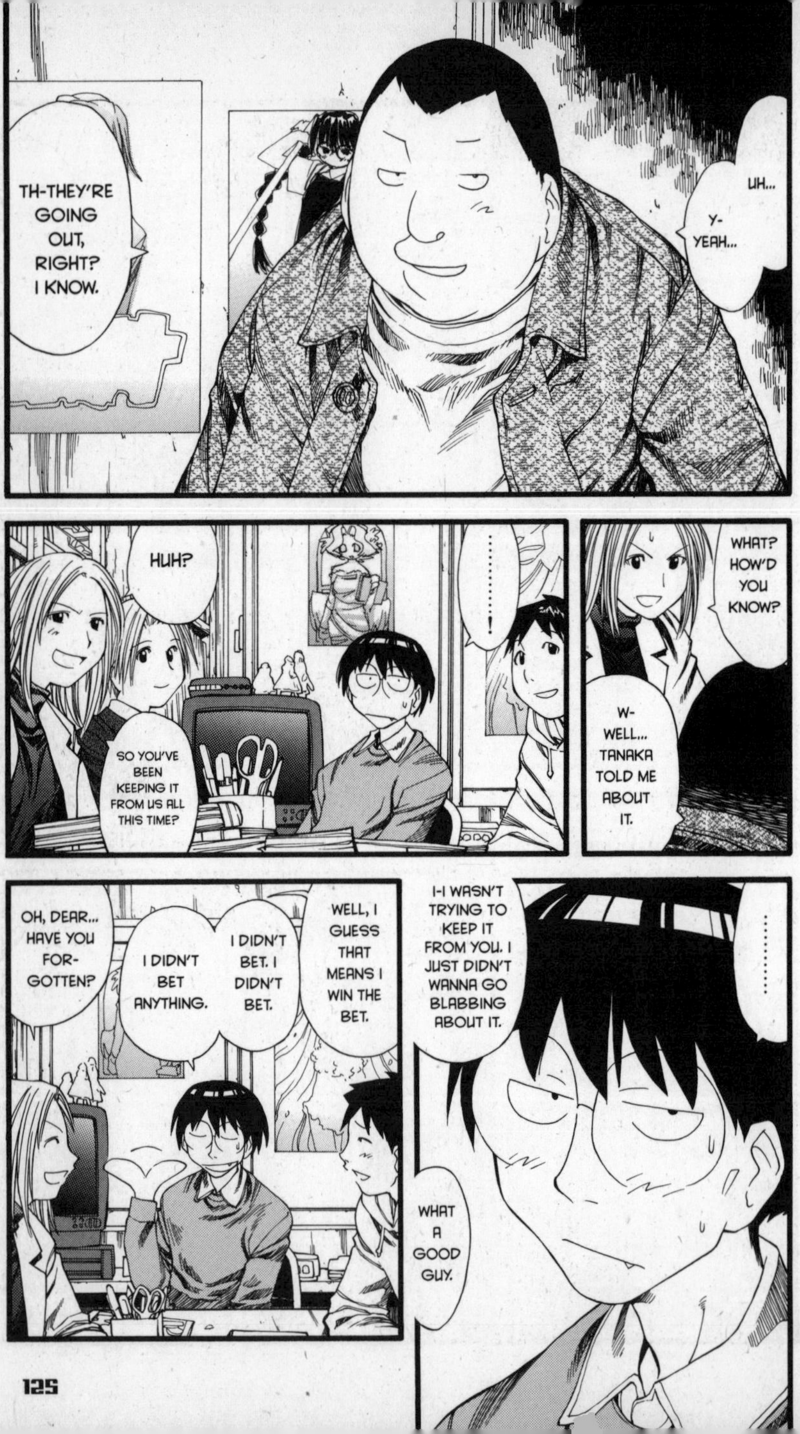

UH... Y-YEAH...
TH-THEY'RE GOING OUT, RIGHT? I KNOW.
WHAT? HOW'D YOU KNOW?
W-WELL... TANAKA TOLD ME ABOUT IT.
......!
HUH?
SO YOU'VE BEEN KEEPING IT FROM US ALL THIS TIME?
......
I-I WASN'T TRYING TO KEEP IT FROM YOU. I JUST DIDN'T WANNA GO BLABBING ABOUT IT.
WHAT A GOOD GUY.
WELL, I GUESS THAT MEANS I WIN THE BET.
I DIDN'T BET. I DIDN'T BET.
I DIDN'T BET ANYTHING.
OH, DEAR... HAVE YOU FOR-GOTTEN?

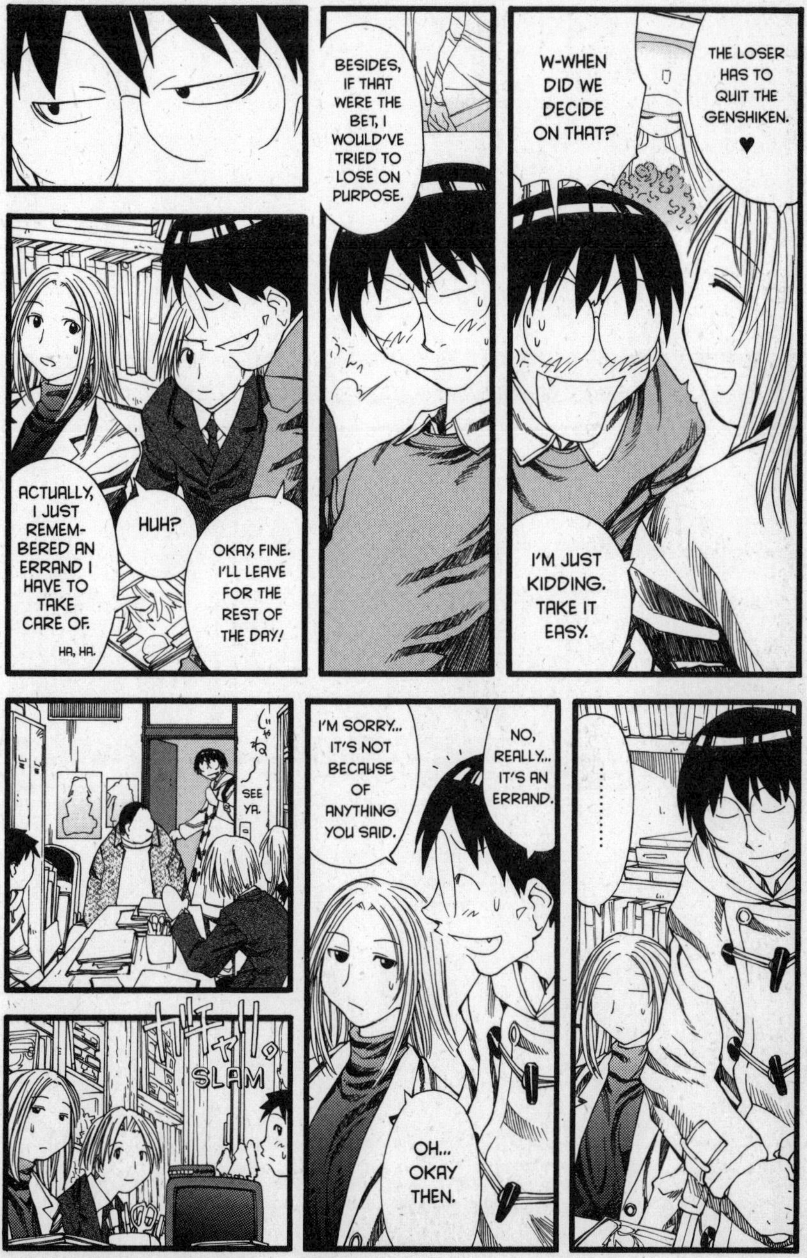
THE LOSER HAS TO QUIT THE GENSHIKEN. ♥
W-WHEN DID WE DECIDE ON THAT?
I'M JUST KIDDING. TAKE IT EASY.
BESIDES, IF THAT WERE THE BET, I WOULD'VE TRIED TO LOSE ON PURPOSE.
OKAY, FINE. I'LL LEAVE FOR THE REST OF THE DAY!
HUH?
ACTUALLY, I JUST REMEMBERED AN ERRAND I HAVE TO TAKE CARE OF.
HA, HA.
......
I'M SORRY... IT'S NOT BECAUSE OF ANYTHING YOU SAID.
NO, REALLY... IT'S AN ERRAND.
OH... OKAY THEN.
SEE YA.
SLAM

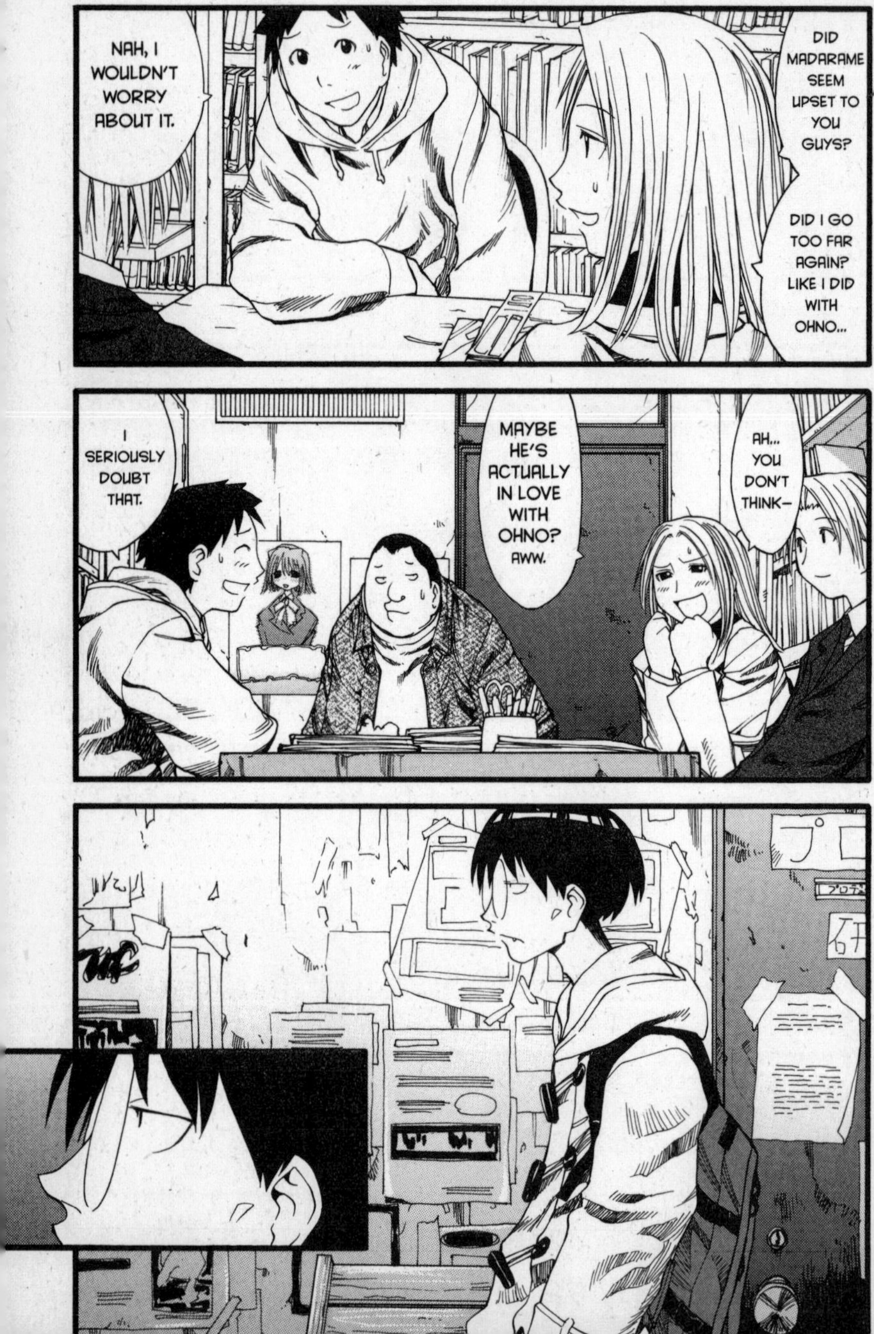
DID MADARAME SEEM UPSET TO YOU GUYS?
DID I GO TOO FAR AGAIN? LIKE I DID WITH OHNO...
NAH, I WOULDN'T WORRY ABOUT IT.
AH... YOU DON'T THINK—
MAYBE HE'S ACTUALLY IN LOVE WITH OHNO? AWW.
I SERIOUSLY DOUBT THAT.

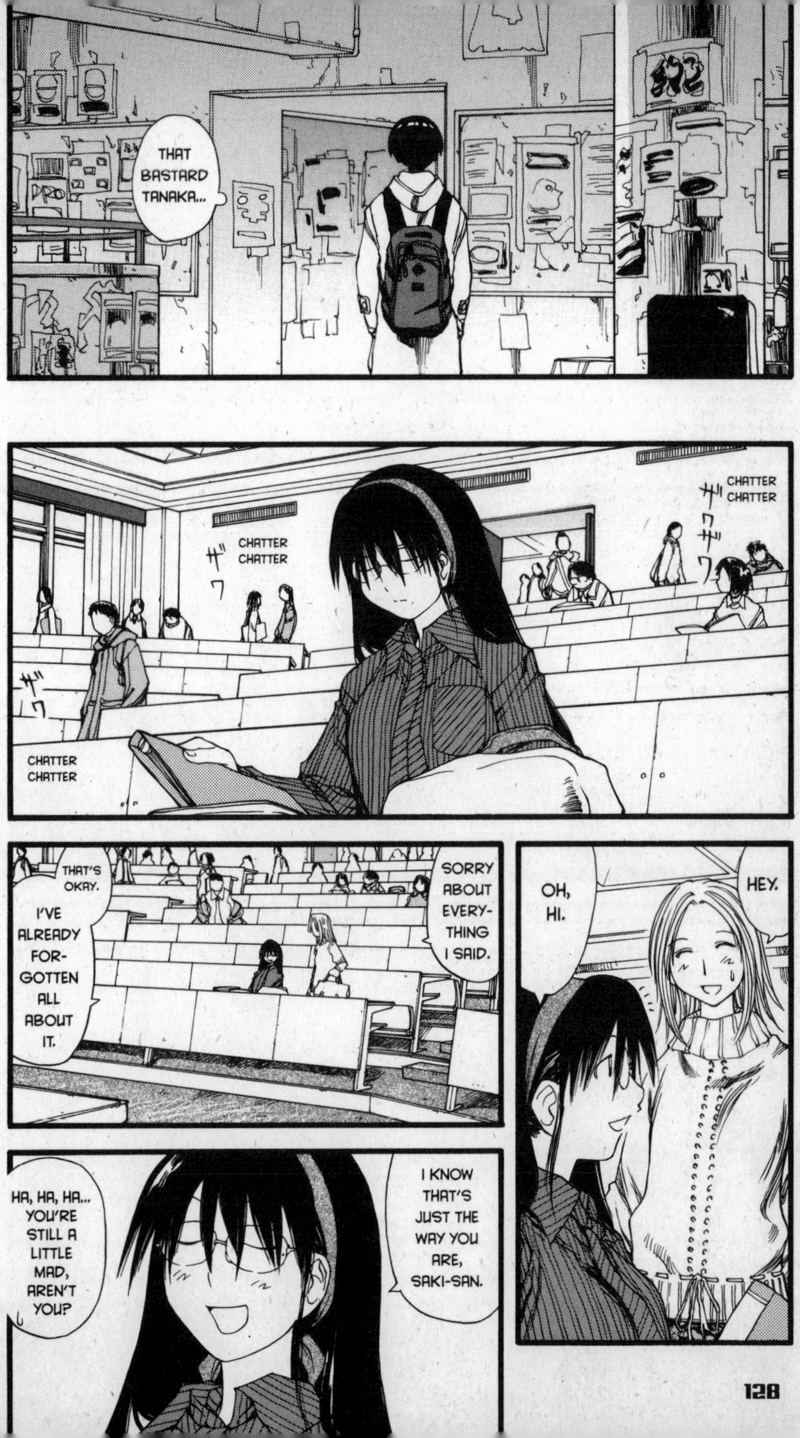
THAT BASTARD TANAKA...
CHATTER CHATTER
ザワザワ
CHATTER CHATTER
ザワ
ザワ
CHATTER CHATTER
HEY.
OH, HI.
SORRY ABOUT EVERY-THING I SAID.
THAT'S OKAY.
I'VE ALREADY FOR-GOTTEN ALL ABOUT IT.
I KNOW THAT'S JUST THE WAY YOU ARE, SAKI-SAN.
HA, HA, HA... YOU'RE STILL A LITTLE MAD, AREN'T YOU?

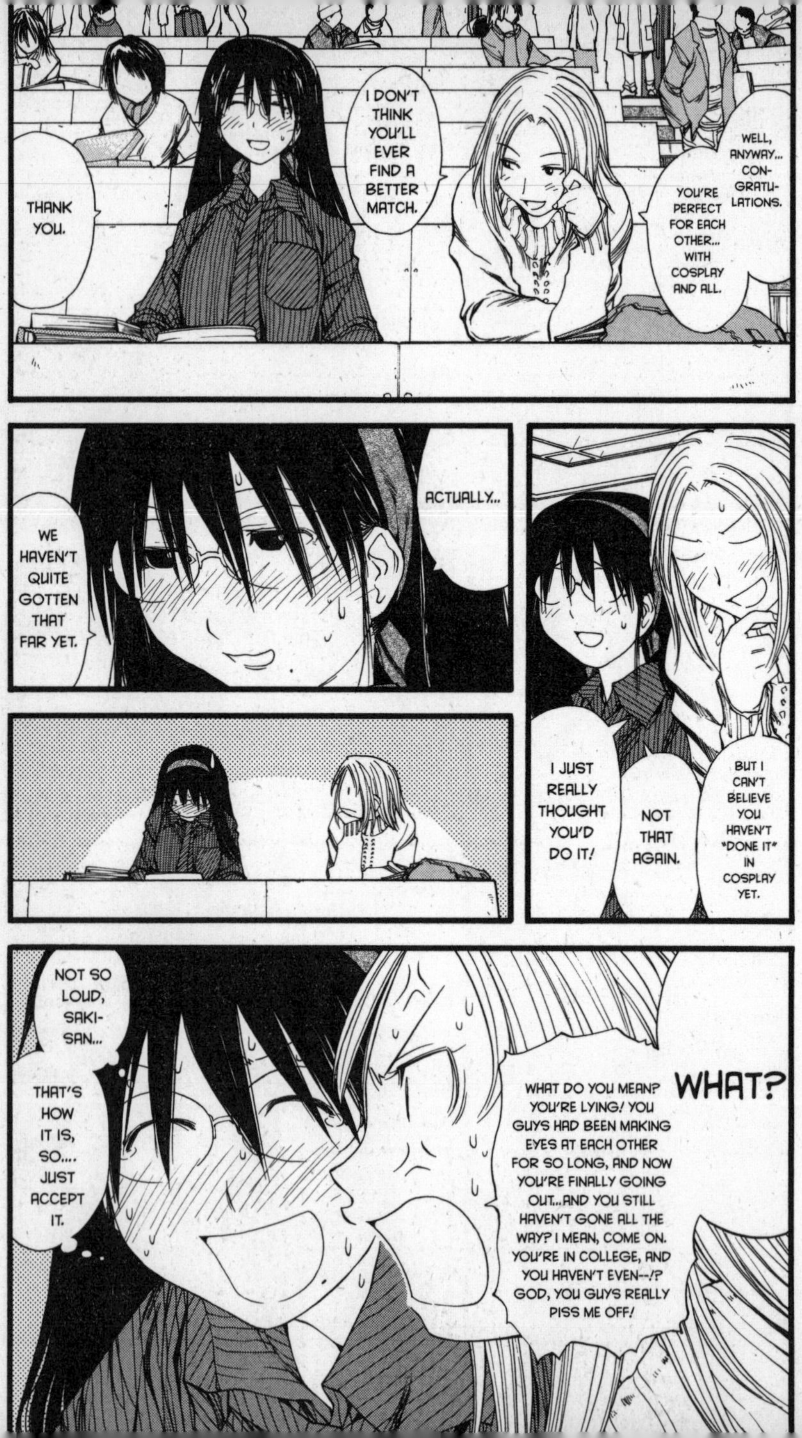
WELL, ANYWAY... CON-GRATU-LATIONS.
YOU'RE PERFECT FOR EACH OTHER... WITH COSPLAY AND ALL.
I DON'T THINK YOU'LL EVER FIND A BETTER MATCH.
THANK YOU.
ACTUALLY...
WE HAVEN'T QUITE GOTTEN THAT FAR YET.
BUT I CAN'T BELIEVE YOU HAVEN'T "DONE IT" IN COSPLAY YET.
I JUST REALLY THOUGHT YOU'D DO IT!
NOT THAT AGAIN.
WHAT?
WHAT DO YOU MEAN? YOU'RE LYING! YOU GUYS HAD BEEN MAKING EYES AT EACH OTHER FOR SO LONG, AND NOW YOU'RE FINALLY GOING OUT...AND YOU STILL HAVEN'T GONE ALL THE WAY? I MEAN, COME ON. YOU'RE IN COLLEGE, AND YOU HAVEN'T EVEN--!? GOD, YOU GUYS REALLY PISS ME OFF!
NOT SO LOUD, SAKI-SAN...
THAT'S HOW IT IS, SO.... JUST ACCEPT IT.

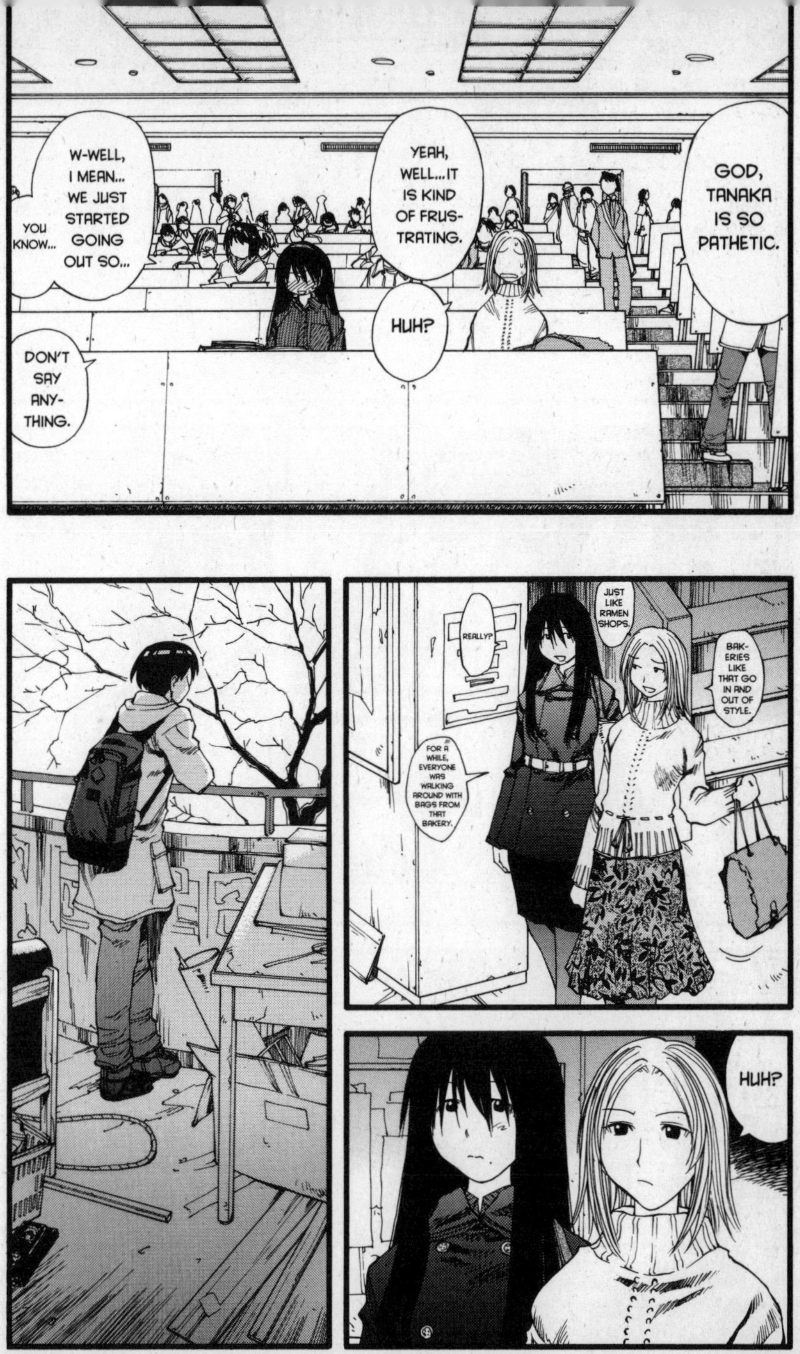
GOD, TANAKA IS SO PATHETIC.
YEAH, WELL...IT IS KIND OF FRUS-TRATING.
HUH?
W-WELL, I MEAN... WE JUST STARTED GOING OUT SO...
YOU KNOW...
DON'T SAY ANY-THING.
BAK-ERIES LIKE THAT GO IN AND OUT OF STYLE.
JUST LIKE RAMEN SHOPS.
REALLY?
FOR A WHILE, EVERYONE WAS WALKING AROUND WITH BAGS FROM THAT BAKERY.
HUH?

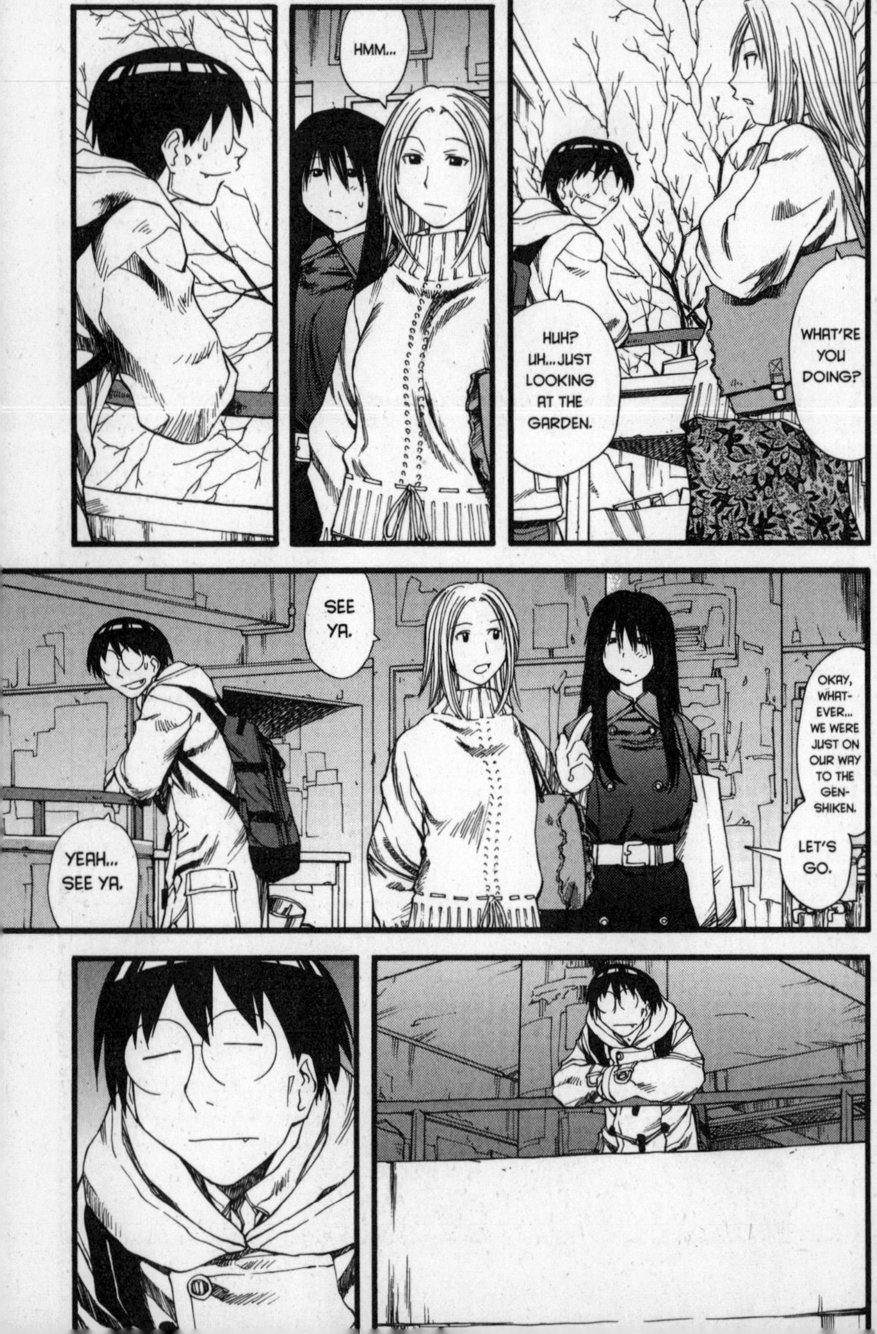
WHAT'RE YOU DOING?
HUH? UH...JUST LOOKING AT THE GARDEN.
HMM...
OKAY, WHAT-EVER... WE WERE JUST ON OUR WAY TO THE GEN-SHIKEN.
LET'S GO.
SEE YA.
YEAH... SEE YA.

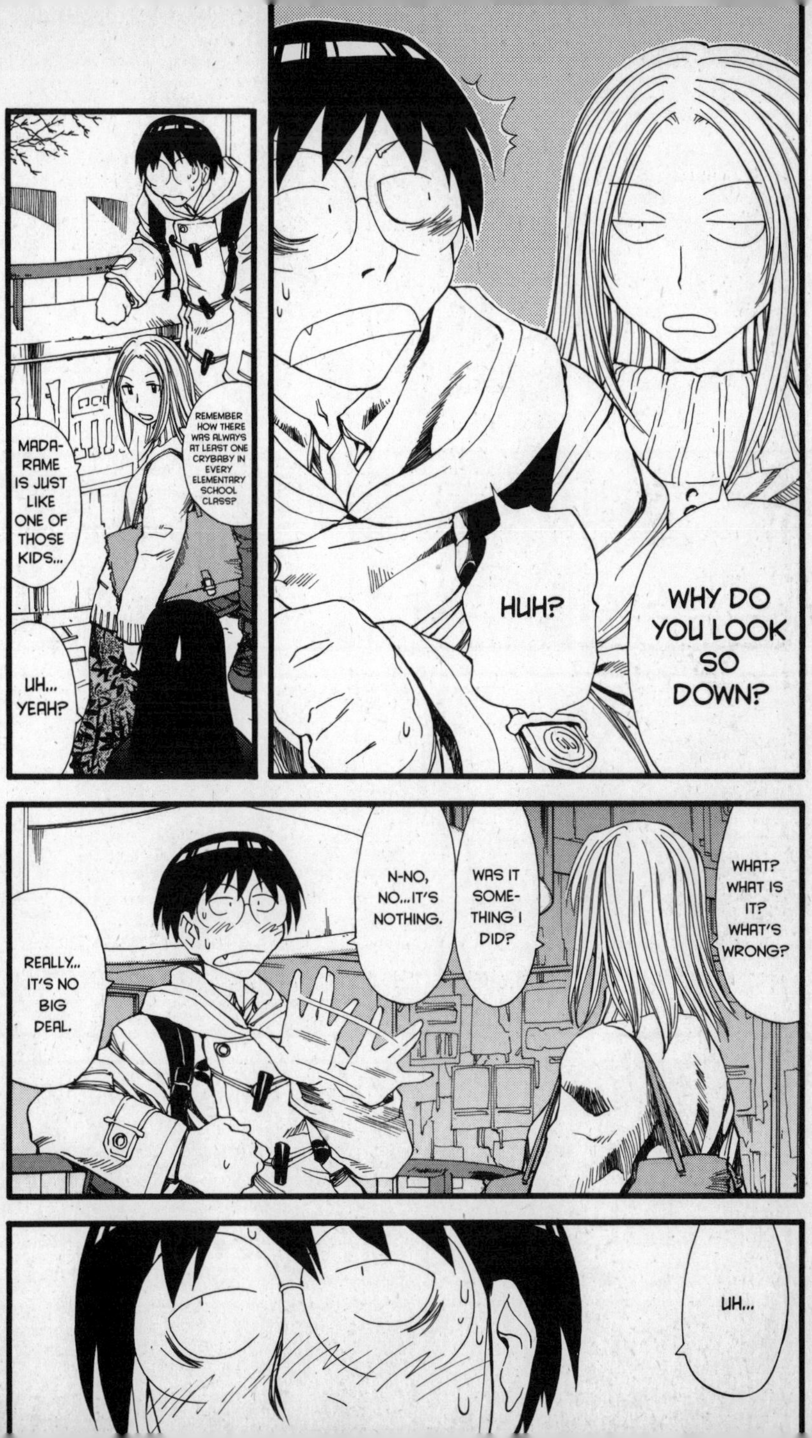
WHY DO YOU LOOK SO DOWN?
HUH?
REMEMBER HOW THERE WAS ALWAYS AT LEAST ONE CRYBABY IN EVERY ELEMENTARY SCHOOL CLASS?
MADA-RAME IS JUST LIKE ONE OF THOSE KIDS...
UH... YEAH?
WHAT? WHAT IS IT? WHAT'S WRONG?
WAS IT SOME-THING I DID?
N-NO, NO...IT'S NOTHING.
REALLY... IT'S NO BIG DEAL.
UH...

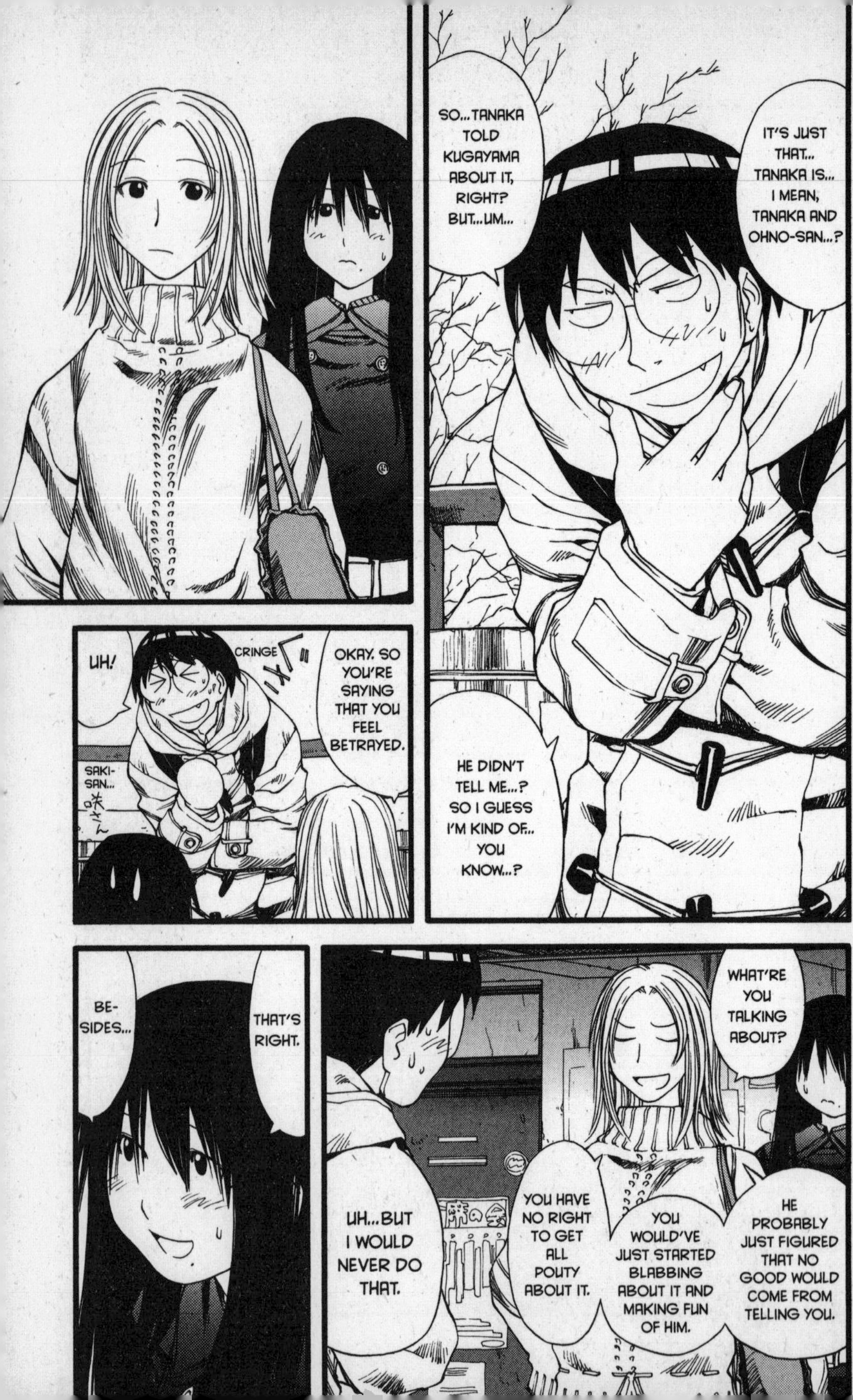
IT'S JUST THAT... TANAKA IS... I MEAN, TANAKA AND OHNO-SAN...?
SO...TANAKA TOLD KUGAYAMA ABOUT IT, RIGHT? BUT...UM...
HE DIDN'T TELL ME...? SO I GUESS I'M KIND OF... YOU KNOW...?
OKAY. SO YOU'RE SAYING THAT YOU FEEL BETRAYED.
CRINGE
UH!
SAKI-SAN...
咲さん
WHAT'RE YOU TALKING ABOUT?
HE PROBABLY JUST FIGURED THAT NO GOOD WOULD COME FROM TELLING YOU.
YOU WOULD'VE JUST STARTED BLABBING ABOUT IT AND MAKING FUN OF HIM.
YOU HAVE NO RIGHT TO GET ALL POUTY ABOUT IT.
UH...BUT I WOULD NEVER DO THAT.
THAT'S RIGHT.
BE-SIDES...

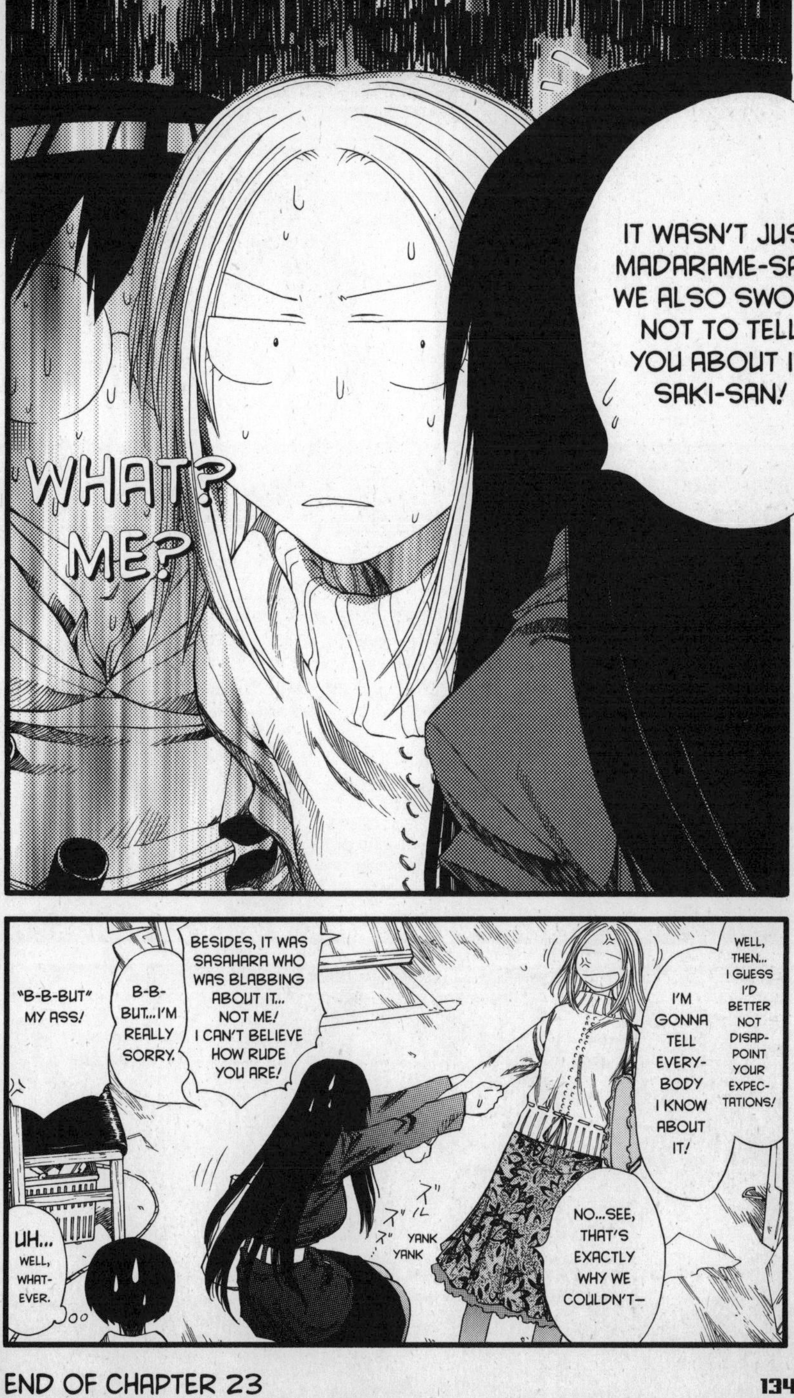
IT WASN'T JUST MADARAME-SAN. WE ALSO SWORE NOT TO TELL YOU ABOUT IT, SAKI-SAN!
WHAT? ME?
WELL, THEN... I GUESS I'D BETTER NOT DISAPPOINT YOUR EXPECTATIONS!
I'M GONNA TELL EVERYBODY I KNOW ABOUT IT!
BESIDES, IT WAS SASAHARA WHO WAS BLABBING ABOUT IT... NOT ME! I CAN'T BELIEVE HOW RUDE YOU ARE!
B-B-BUT...I'M REALLY SORRY.
"B-B-BUT" MY ASS!
NO...SEE, THAT'S EXACTLY WHY WE COULDN'T—
YANK YANK
UH... WELL, WHATEVER.

END OF CHAPTER 23

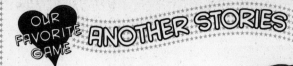

STORY 5

## KOYUKI ASAGIRI

REVIEWED BY TOSHIZO

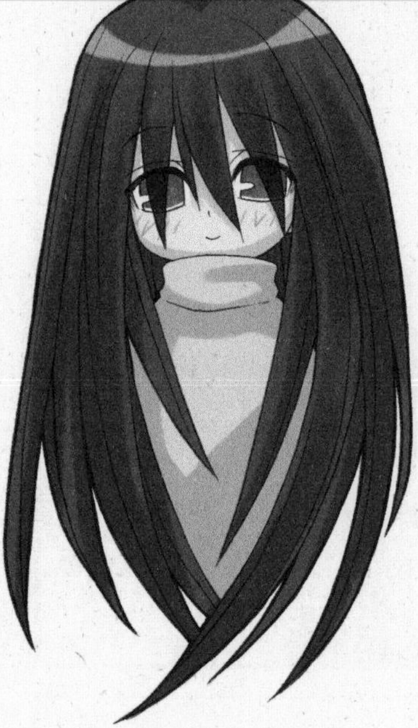

SHE'S KOMAKI'S LITTLE SISTER, AND SHE'S ACTUALLY ONE OF THE CHARACTERS YOU CAN USE IN THE GAME. I CHOSE HER BECAUSE I THOUGHT IT WAS COOL THEY INCLUDED HER.

HER SCENARIO SPLITS PATHS WITH KOMAKI'S. KOYUKI DOESN'T REQUIRE POPULARITY POINTS TO WIN, SO IT'S ACTUALLY QUITE EASY. I GUESS THAT'S BECAUSE SHE'S REALLY JUST A BONUS CHARACTER.

THE TIME FRAME OF THE GAME IS REALLY SHORT TOO. IT'S OVER BY WINTER. THE ENDING SCENE TAKES US 15 YEARS INTO THE FUTURE. AND OF COURSE, YOU GET TO SEE HOW SHE'S MATURED. THAT IS DEFINITELY THIS SCENARIO'S MAIN SELLING POINT. PLUS, WHEN YOU FIGURE THAT CHIHIRO MUST BE 30 YEARS OLD, IT'S OVERWHELMINGLY MOVING. [TOSHIZO]

NO, IT ISN'T. NO, IT ISN'T. IT MOST DEFINITELY IS NOT. [HA HA] KOYUKI-CHAN... YEAH, I LIKE TO USE HER TOO. THERE'S JUST SOMETHING ABOUT HER CHARACTER THAT MAKES ME WANT TO HELP HER FIND TRUE HAPPINESS. BUT PERSONALLY, I THINK THE IMAGE OF KOYUKI IN THE FUTURE IS...HOW SHALL I PUT THIS...UH...I MEAN, SHE'S REALLY GORGEOUS, RIGHT? AND OF COURSE, I WANTED TO SEE HOW SHE'D LOOK GROWN UP, BUT THE TRUTH IS...I JUST WANT TO YELL OUT LOUD "PLEASE, DON'T EVER GROW UP!" I GUESS THAT'S THE CALL OF A MAN WITH A TRUE LOLITA COMPLEX.

...BUT POOR KOMAKI NEVER GETS THE SUCCESS SHE DESERVES. [HA HA] EVEN THOUGH SHE'S SUCH A GOOD PERSON. POOR THING.

DESPITE HER CHEERFUL GOOD LOOKS, SHE'S ACTUALLY LED A VERY HARD LIFE. HER FATHER, A TRUCK DRIVER, WAS KILLED IN AN ACCIDENT, AND HER MOTHER, THE NURSE, IS ALWAYS BUSY AT WORK. KOMAKI HAS TO LOOK AFTER HER LITTLE BROTHERS (TRIPLETS) AND KOYUKI, AND YET SHE STILL MANAGES TO GET GOOD GRADES.

★

I REALLY LIKE THE WAY THAT KOMAKI'S SCENARIO FOCUSES ON THE SIMPLE EVENTS OF HER EVERYDAY LIFE. [PIT VIPER]

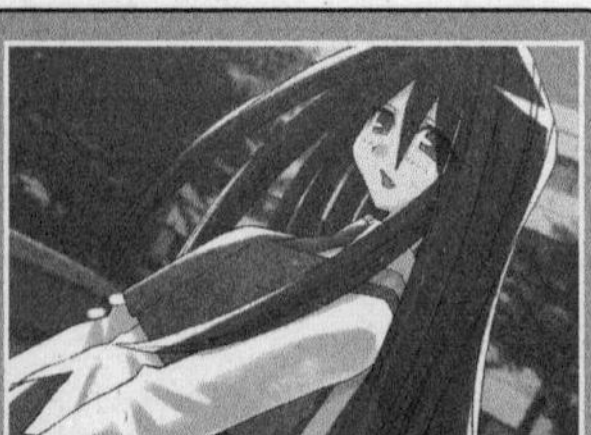

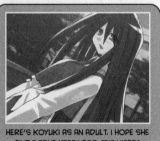

HERE'S KOYUKI AS AN ADULT. I HOPE SHE FINDS TRUE HAPPINESS. [PIT VIPER]

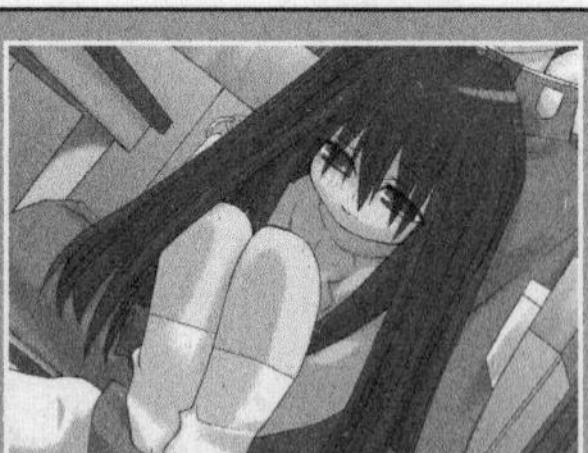

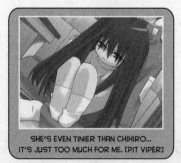

SHE'S EVEN TINIER THAN CHIHIRO... IT'S JUST TOO MUCH FOR ME. [PIT VIPER]

## CHAPTER 23 - MOMENTS LATER

### GUYS WILL SAY ANYTHING

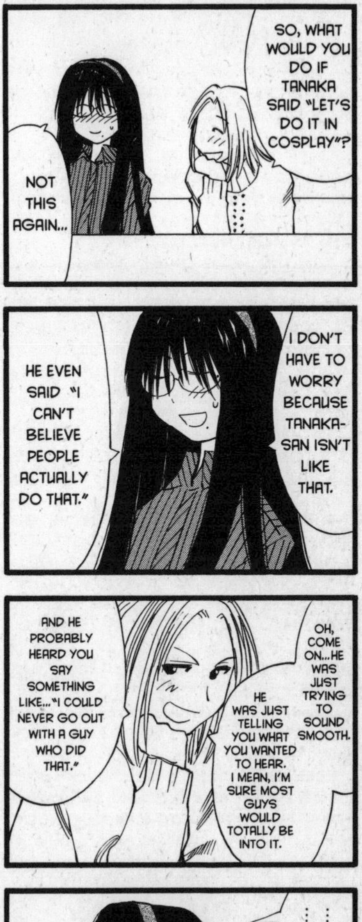
SO, WHAT WOULD YOU DO IF TANAKA SAID "LET'S DO IT IN COSPLAY"?
NOT THIS AGAIN...
I DON'T HAVE TO WORRY BECAUSE TANAKA-SAN ISN'T LIKE THAT.
HE EVEN SAID "I CAN'T BELIEVE PEOPLE ACTUALLY DO THAT."
OH, COME ON...HE WAS JUST TRYING TO SOUND SMOOTH.
HE WAS JUST TELLING YOU WHAT YOU WANTED TO HEAR. I MEAN, I'M SURE MOST GUYS WOULD TOTALLY BE INTO IT.
AND HE PROBABLY HEARD YOU SAY SOMETHING LIKE..."I COULD NEVER GO OUT WITH A GUY WHO DID THAT."
......
AM I RIGHT OR WHAT?
NO...

### ACTUALLY, THEY'VE ALREADY...

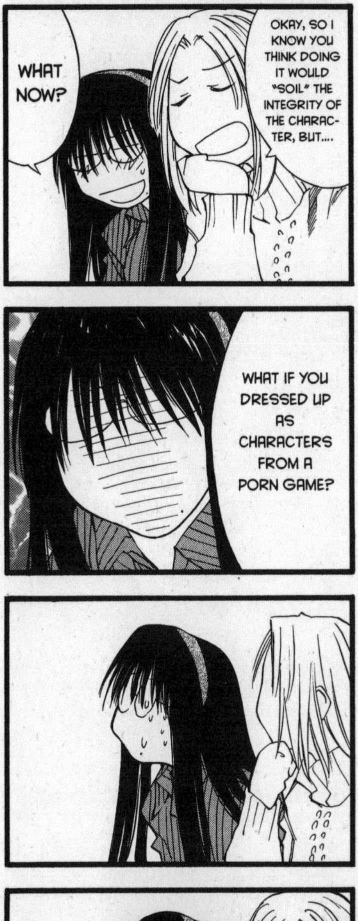
OKAY, SO I KNOW YOU THINK DOING IT WOULD "SOIL" THE INTEGRITY OF THE CHARACTER, BUT....
WHAT NOW?
WHAT IF YOU DRESSED UP AS CHARACTERS FROM A PORN GAME?
WAS IT SOMETHING I SAID?

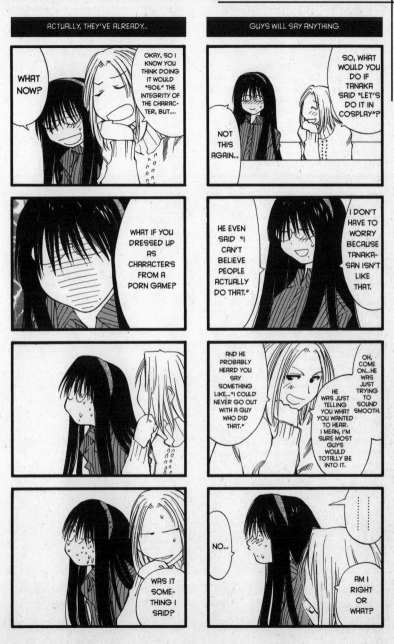

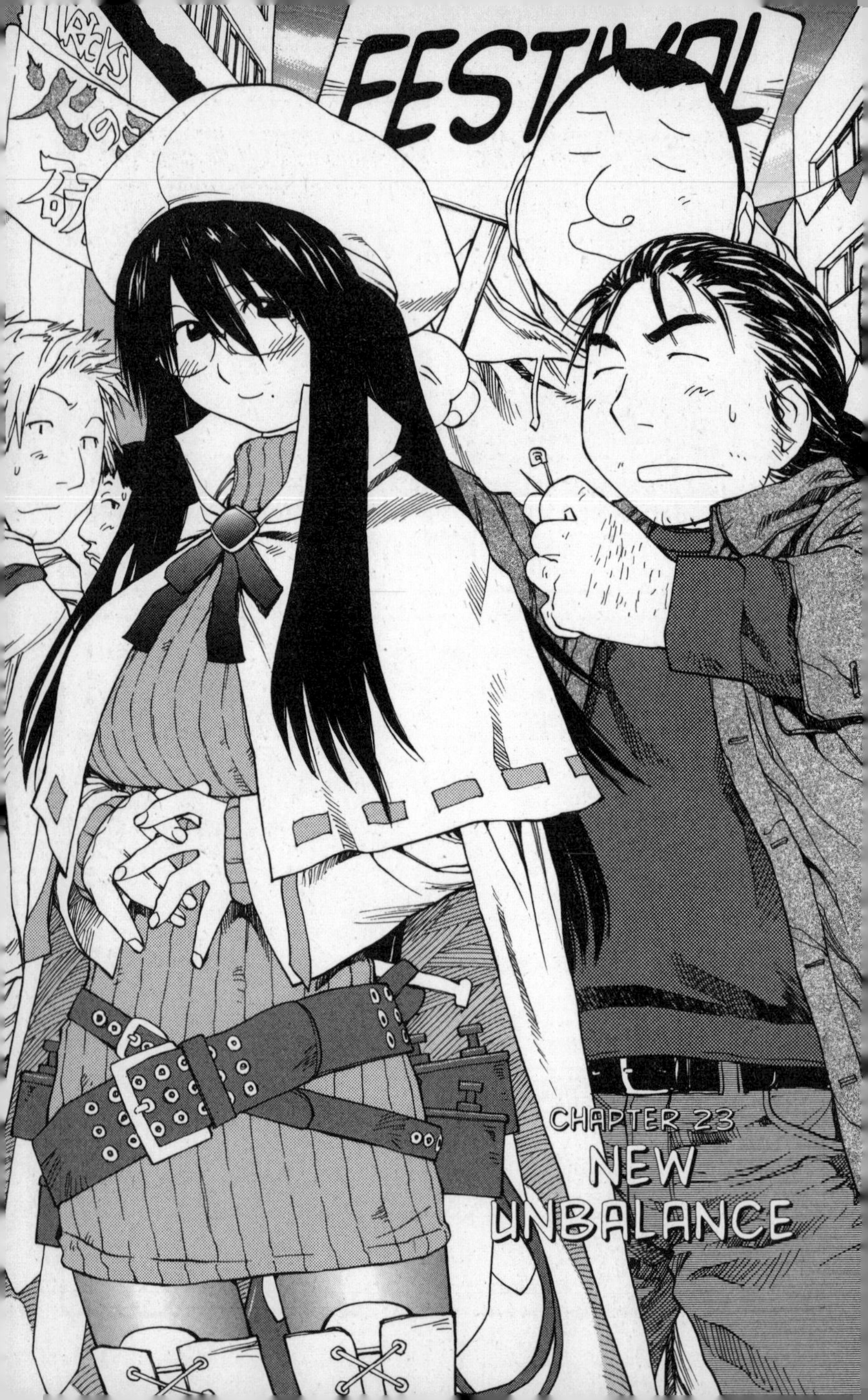
CHAPTER 23
NEW
UNBALANCE

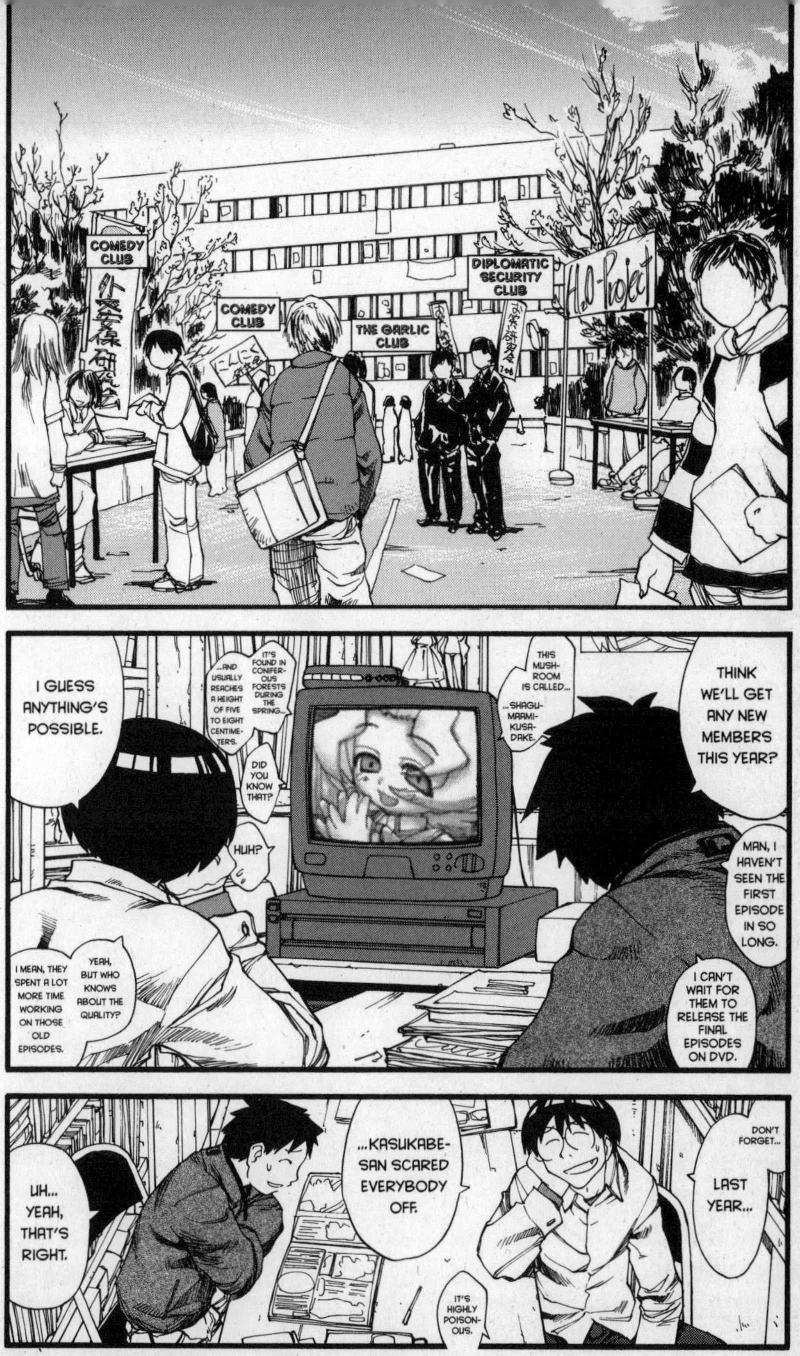
H2O-Project
DIPLOMATIC SECURITY CLUB
THE GARLIC CLUB
COMEDY CLUB
COMEDY CLUB
THINK WE'LL GET ANY NEW MEMBERS THIS YEAR?
THIS MUSHROOM IS CALLED...
...SHAGU-MAAMI-KUSA-DAKE.
IT'S FOUND IN CONIFER-OUS FORESTS DURING THE SPRING...
...AND USUALLY REACHES A HEIGHT OF FIVE TO EIGHT CENTIME-TERS.
DID YOU KNOW THAT?
I GUESS ANYTHING'S POSSIBLE.
HUH?
MAN, I HAVEN'T SEEN THE FIRST EPISODE IN SO LONG.
I CAN'T WAIT FOR THEM TO RELEASE THE FINAL EPISODES ON DVD.
YEAH, BUT WHO KNOWS ABOUT THE QUALITY?
I MEAN, THEY SPENT A LOT MORE TIME WORKING ON THOSE OLD EPISODES.
DON'T FORGET...
LAST YEAR...
...KASUKABE-SAN SCARED EVERYBODY OFF.
IT'S HIGHLY POISON-OUS.
UH... YEAH, THAT'S RIGHT.

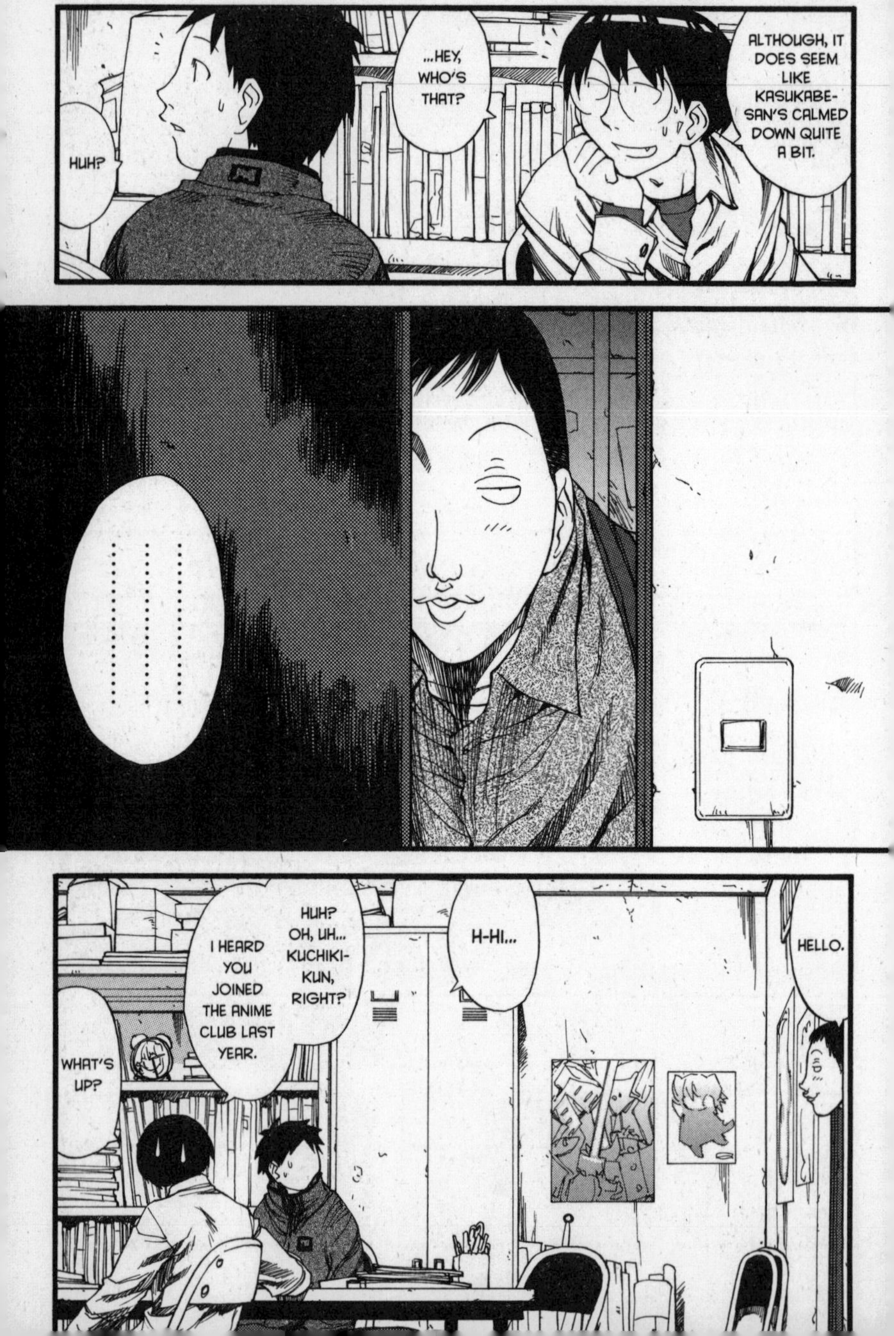
ALTHOUGH, IT DOES SEEM LIKE KASUKABE-SAN'S CALMED DOWN QUITE A BIT.
...HEY, WHO'S THAT?
HUH?
......
HELLO.
H-HI...
HUH? OH, UH... KUCHIKI-KUN, RIGHT?
I HEARD YOU JOINED THE ANIME CLUB LAST YEAR.
WHAT'S UP?

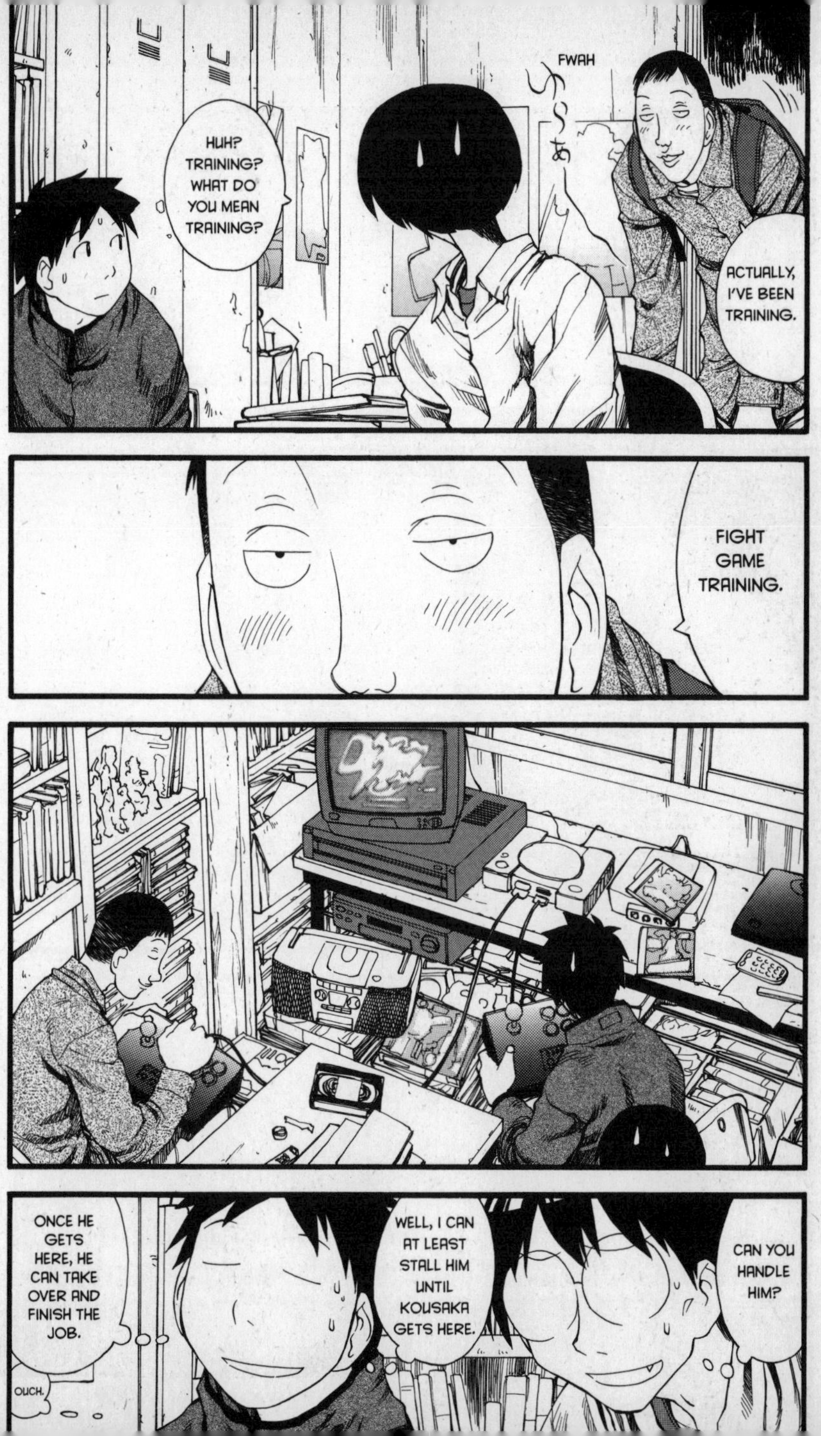
FWAH
ゆらぁ
ACTUALLY, I'VE BEEN TRAINING.
HUH? TRAINING? WHAT DO YOU MEAN TRAINING?
FIGHT GAME TRAINING.
CAN YOU HANDLE HIM?
WELL, I CAN AT LEAST STALL HIM UNTIL KOUSAKA GETS HERE.
ONCE HE GETS HERE, HE CAN TAKE OVER AND FINISH THE JOB.
OUCH.

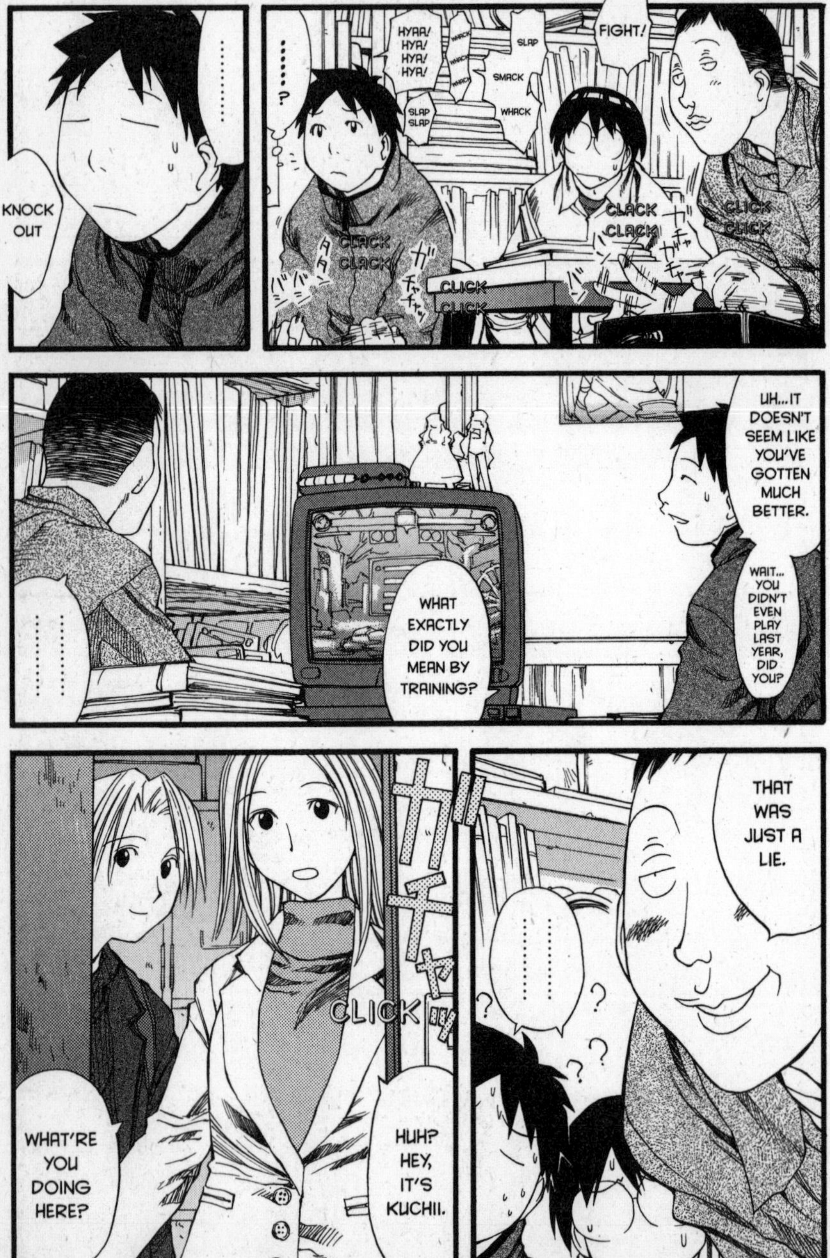
FIGHT!
HYAA! HYA! HYA! HYA!
WHACK
WHACK
WHACK
SLAP
SMACK
WHACK
SLAP SLAP
......?
CLACK CLACK
CLICK CLICK
CLACK CLACK
CLICK CLICK
......
KNOCK OUT
UH...IT DOESN'T SEEM LIKE YOU'VE GOTTEN MUCH BETTER.
WAIT... YOU DIDN'T EVEN PLAY LAST YEAR, DID YOU?
WHAT EXACTLY DID YOU MEAN BY TRAINING?
......
THAT WAS JUST A LIE.
......
CLICK
HUH? HEY, IT'S KUCHII.
WHAT'RE YOU DOING HERE?

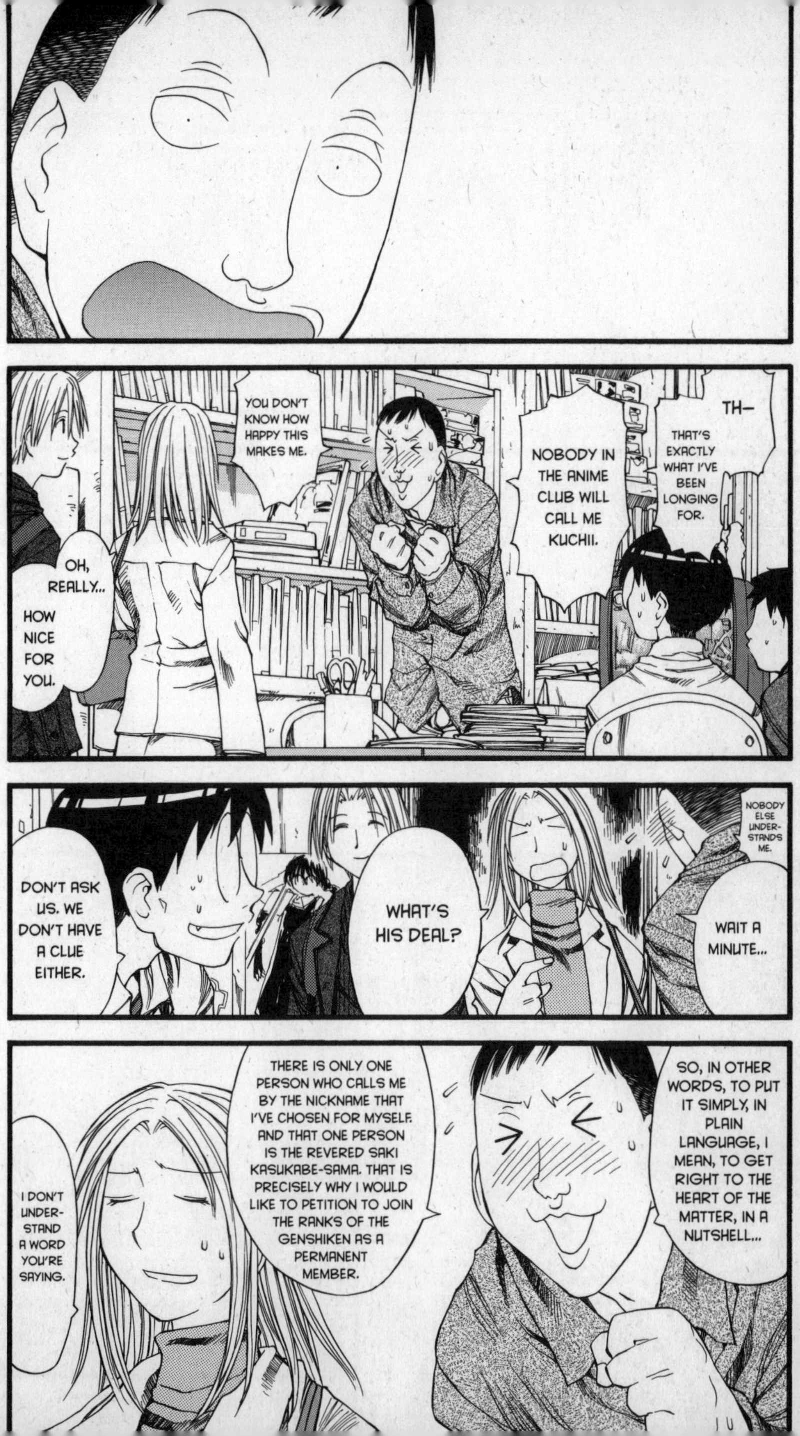
TH—
THAT'S EXACTLY WHAT I'VE BEEN LONGING FOR.
NOBODY IN THE ANIME CLUB WILL CALL ME KUCHII.
YOU DON'T KNOW HOW HAPPY THIS MAKES ME.
OH, REALLY... HOW NICE FOR YOU.
NOBODY ELSE UNDER-STANDS ME.
WAIT A MINUTE...
WHAT'S HIS DEAL?
DON'T ASK US. WE DON'T HAVE A CLUE EITHER.
SO, IN OTHER WORDS, TO PUT IT SIMPLY, IN PLAIN LANGUAGE, I MEAN, TO GET RIGHT TO THE HEART OF THE MATTER, IN A NUTSHELL...
THERE IS ONLY ONE PERSON WHO CALLS ME BY THE NICKNAME THAT I'VE CHOSEN FOR MYSELF. AND THAT ONE PERSON IS THE REVERED SAKI KASUKABE-SAMA. THAT IS PRECISELY WHY I WOULD LIKE TO PETITION TO JOIN THE RANKS OF THE GENSHIKEN AS A PERMANENT MEMBER.
I DON'T UNDER-STAND A WORD YOU'RE SAYING.

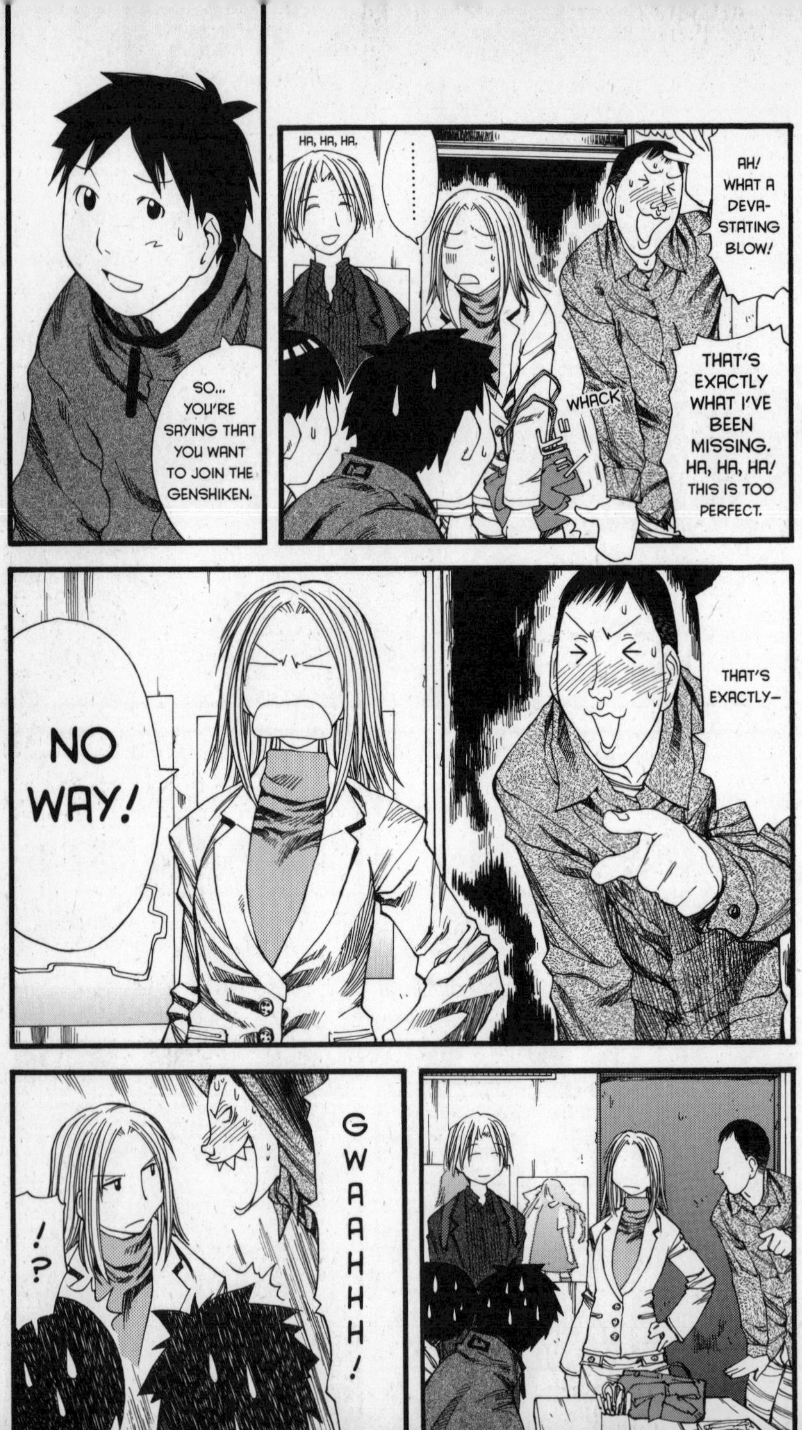
AH! WHAT A DEVA-STATING BLOW!
......
HA, HA, HA.
THAT'S EXACTLY WHAT I'VE BEEN MISSING. HA, HA, HA! THIS IS TOO PERFECT.
WHACK
SO... YOU'RE SAYING THAT YOU WANT TO JOIN THE GENSHIKEN.
THAT'S EXACTLY—
NO WAY!
GWAAHHH!
!?

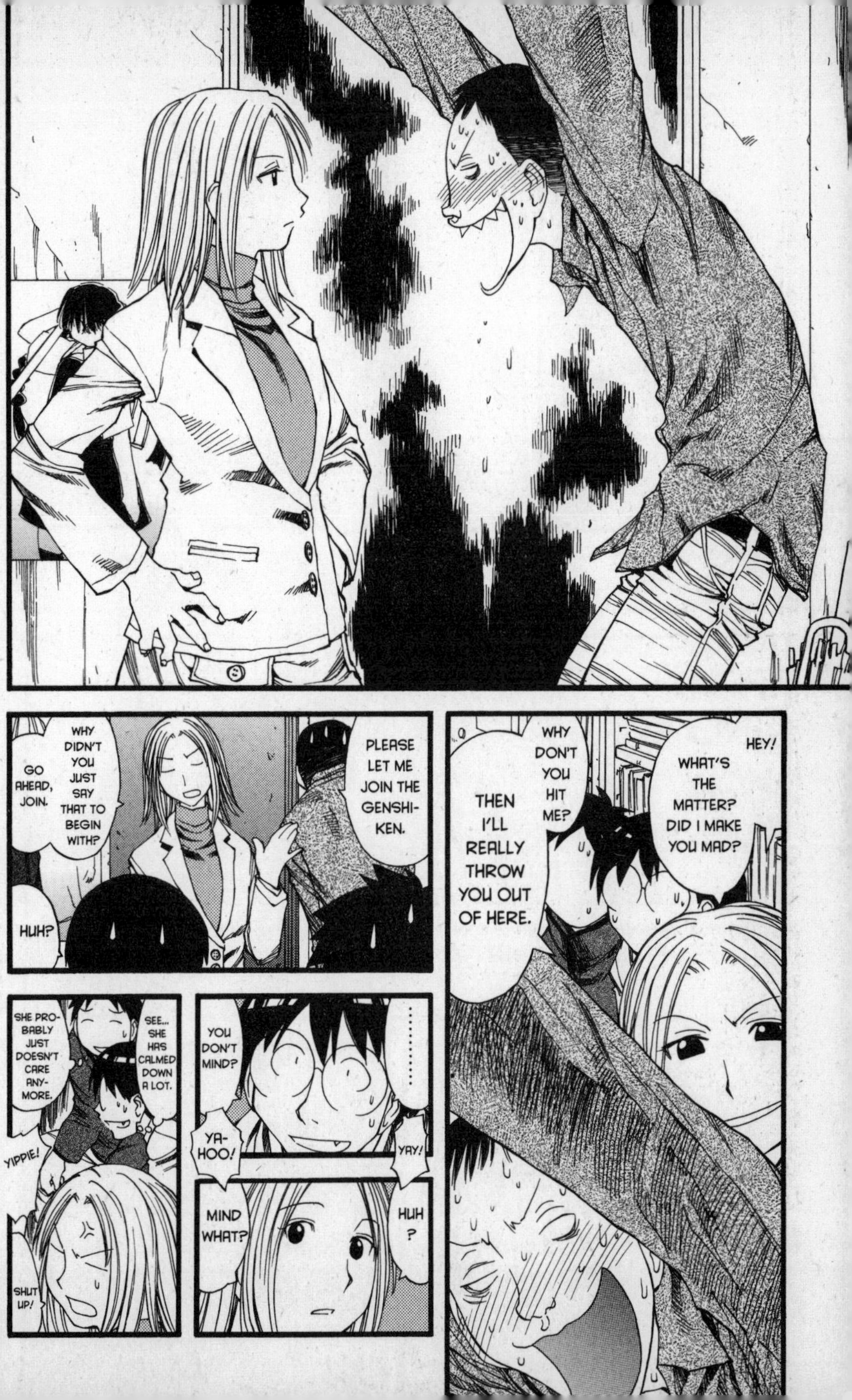
HEY!
WHAT'S THE MATTER? DID I MAKE YOU MAD?
WHY DON'T YOU HIT ME?
THEN I'LL REALLY THROW YOU OUT OF HERE.
PLEASE LET ME JOIN THE GENSHI-KEN.
WHY DIDN'T YOU JUST SAY THAT TO BEGIN WITH?
GO AHEAD, JOIN.
HUH?
......
YOU DON'T MIND?
YAY!
YA-HOO!
SEE... SHE HAS CALMED DOWN A LOT.
SHE PRO-BABLY JUST DOESN'T CARE ANY-MORE.
YIPPIE!
SHUT UP!
HUH?
MIND WHAT?

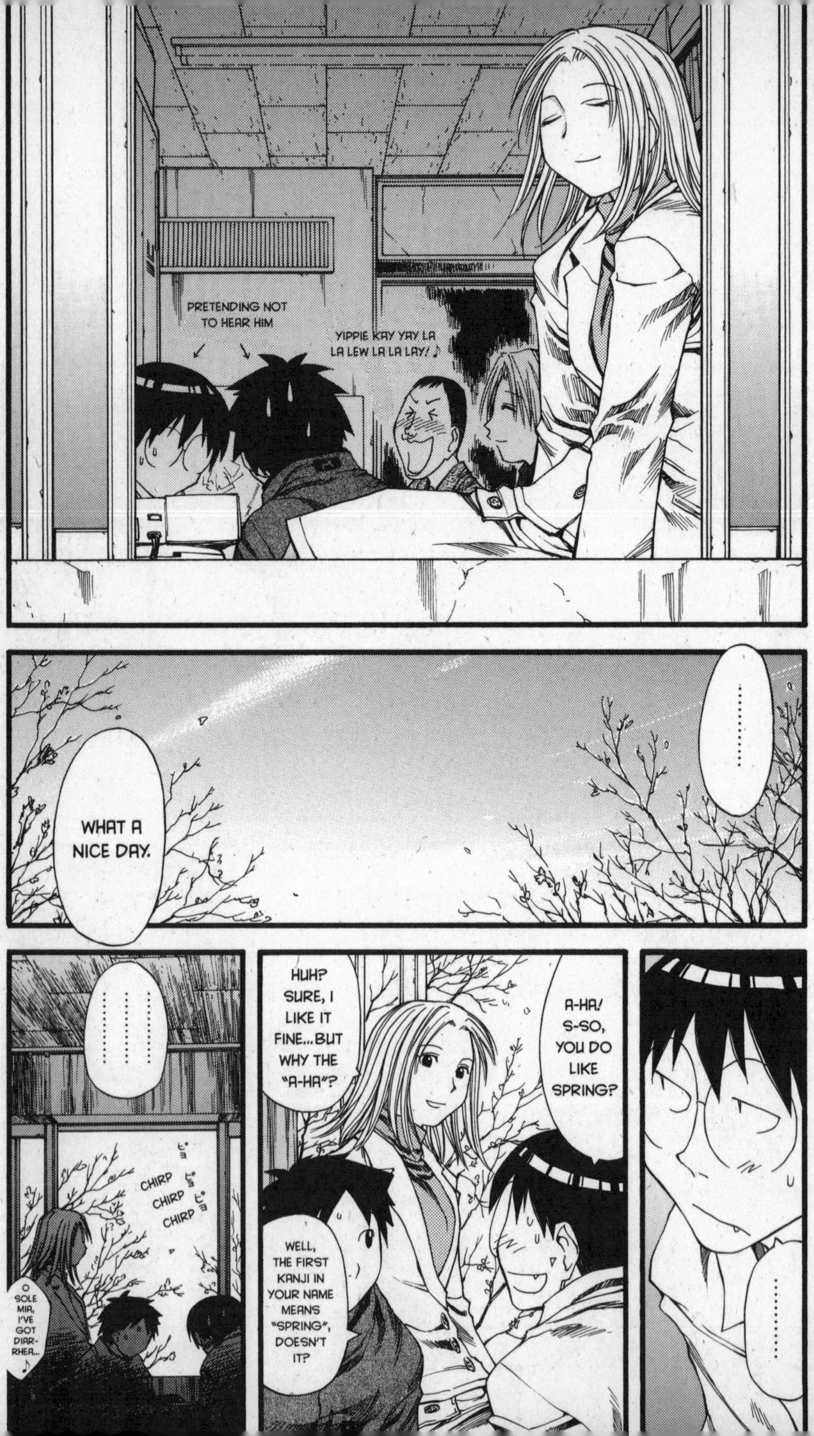
YIPPIE KAY YAY LA LA LEW LA LA LAY! ♪
PRETENDING NOT TO HEAR HIM
......
WHAT A NICE DAY.
......
A-HA! S-SO, YOU DO LIKE SPRING?
HUH? SURE, I LIKE IT FINE...BUT WHY THE "A-HA"?
WELL, THE FIRST KANJI IN YOUR NAME MEANS "SPRING", DOESN'T IT?
......
ピヨ ピヨ ピヨ
CHIRP CHIRP CHIRP
O SOLE MIA, I'VE GOT DIARRHEA... ♪

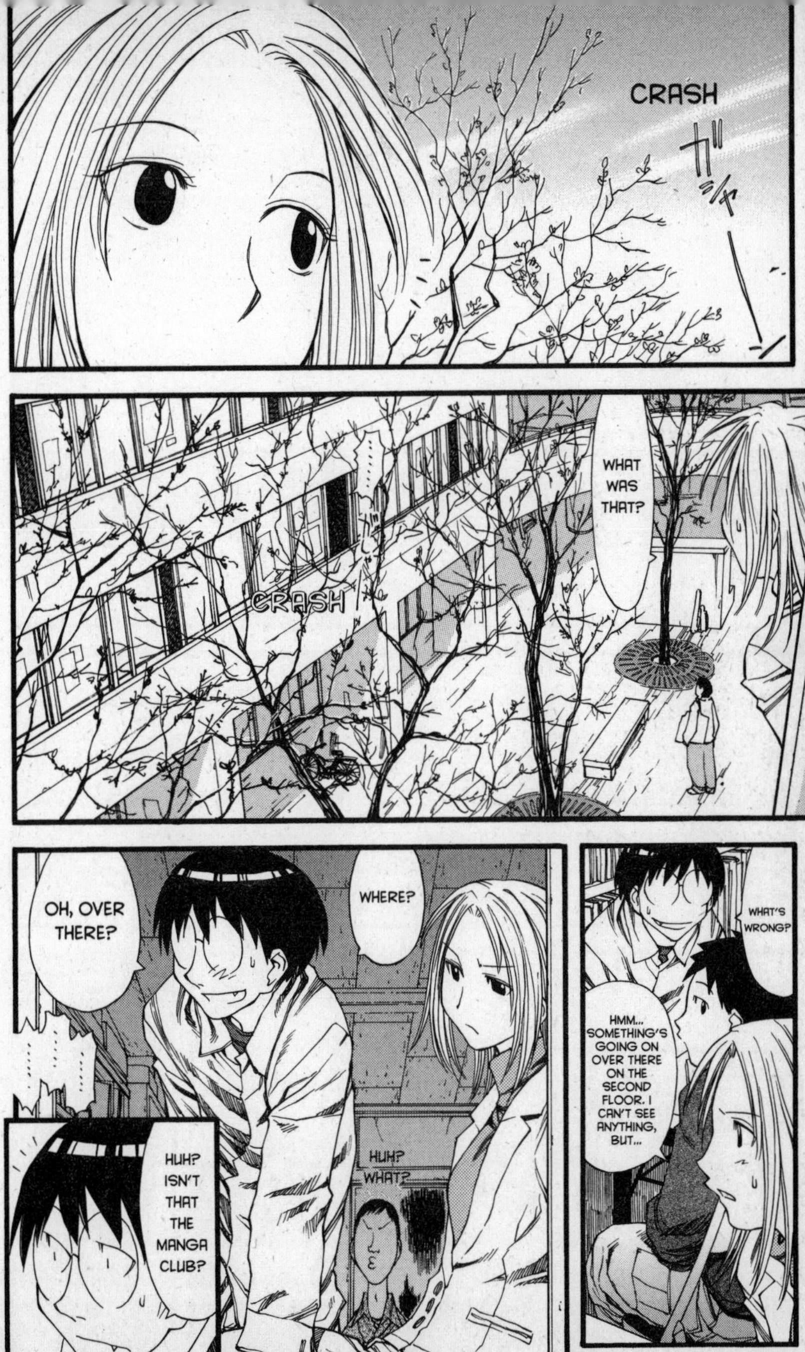
CRASH
ガシャー
CRASH
WHAT WAS THAT?
WHAT'S WRONG?
HMM... SOMETHING'S GOING ON OVER THERE ON THE SECOND FLOOR. I CAN'T SEE ANYTHING, BUT...
WHERE?
OH, OVER THERE?
HUH? ISN'T THAT THE MANGA CLUB?
HUH? WHAT?

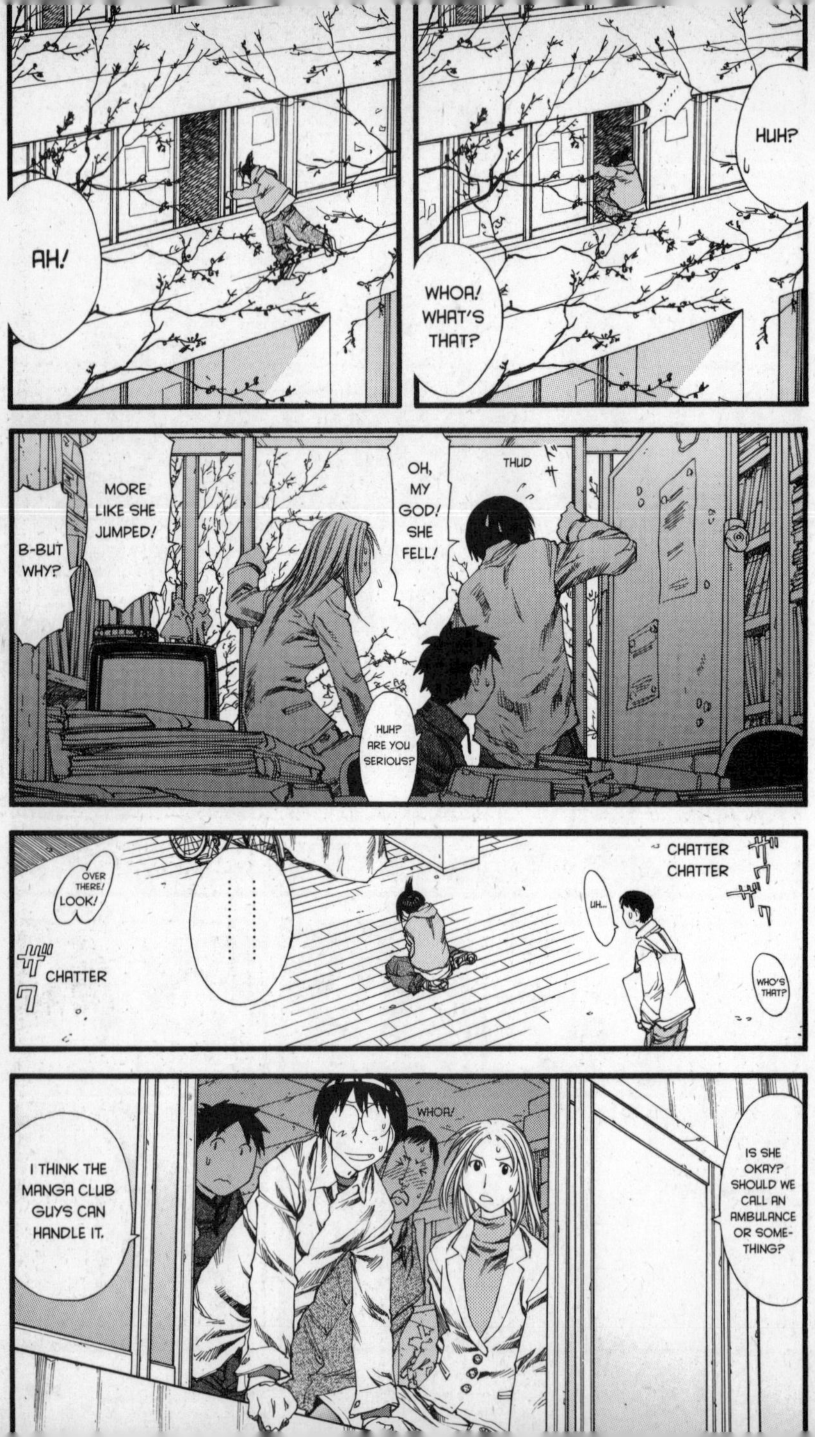
HUH?
WHOA! WHAT'S THAT?
AH!
THUD
OH, MY GOD! SHE FELL!
MORE LIKE SHE JUMPED!
B-BUT WHY?
HUH? ARE YOU SERIOUS?
CHATTER CHATTER
UH...
WHO'S THAT?
......
OVER THERE! LOOK!
CHATTER
IS SHE OKAY? SHOULD WE CALL AN AMBULANCE OR SOME-THING?
WHOA!
I THINK THE MANGA CLUB GUYS CAN HANDLE IT.

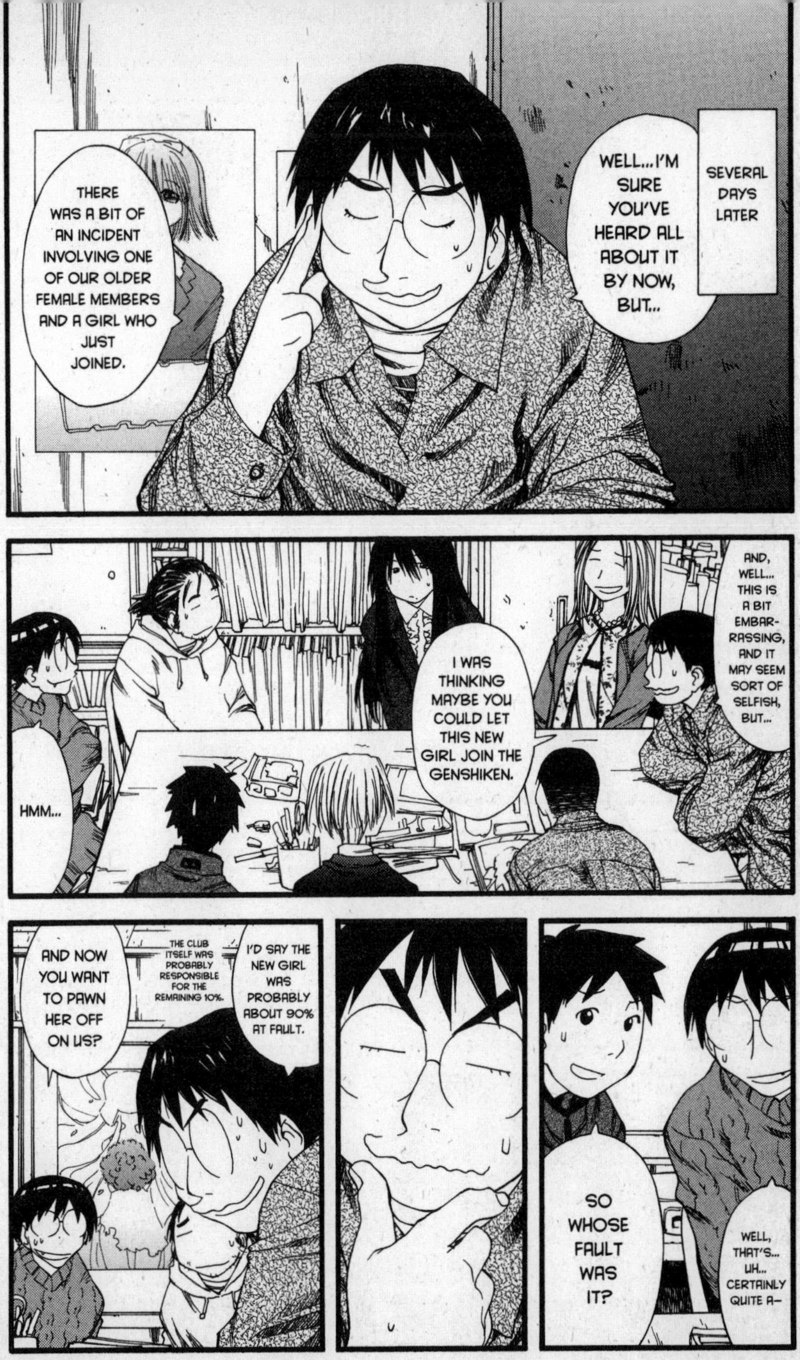
SEVERAL DAYS LATER
WELL...I'M SURE YOU'VE HEARD ALL ABOUT IT BY NOW, BUT...
THERE WAS A BIT OF AN INCIDENT INVOLVING ONE OF OUR OLDER FEMALE MEMBERS AND A GIRL WHO JUST JOINED.
AND, WELL... THIS IS A BIT EMBARRASSING, AND IT MAY SEEM SORT OF SELFISH, BUT...
I WAS THINKING MAYBE YOU COULD LET THIS NEW GIRL JOIN THE GENSHIKEN.
HMM...
SO WHOSE FAULT WAS IT?
WELL, THAT'S... UH... CERTAINLY QUITE A—
I'D SAY THE NEW GIRL WAS PROBABLY ABOUT 90% AT FAULT.
THE CLUB ITSELF WAS PROBABLY RESPONSIBLE FOR THE REMAINING 10%.
AND NOW YOU WANT TO PAWN HER OFF ON US?

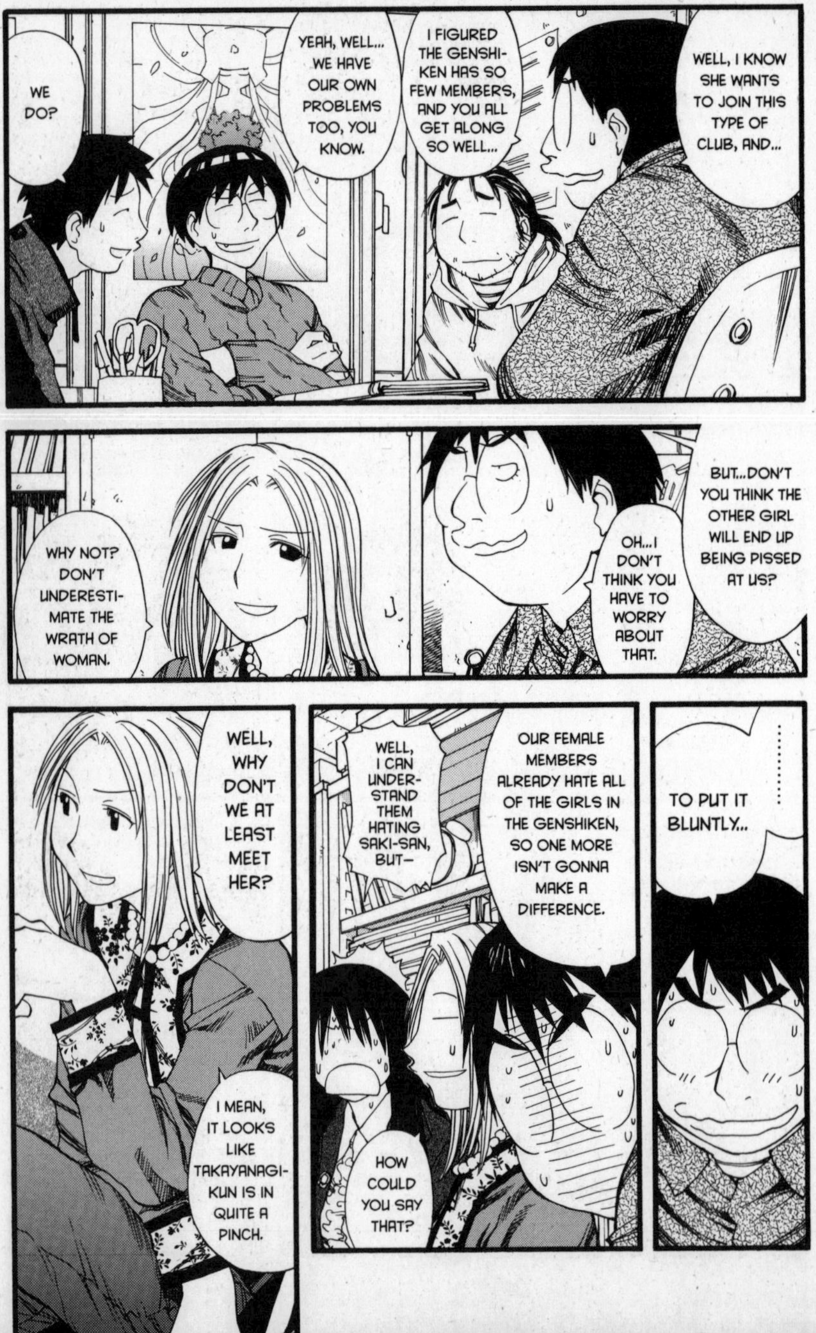
WELL, I KNOW SHE WANTS TO JOIN THIS TYPE OF CLUB, AND...
I FIGURED THE GENSHIKEN HAS SO FEW MEMBERS, AND YOU ALL GET ALONG SO WELL...
YEAH, WELL... WE HAVE OUR OWN PROBLEMS TOO, YOU KNOW.
WE DO?
BUT...DON'T YOU THINK THE OTHER GIRL WILL END UP BEING PISSED AT US?
OH...I DON'T THINK YOU HAVE TO WORRY ABOUT THAT.
WHY NOT? DON'T UNDERESTIMATE THE WRATH OF WOMAN.
......
TO PUT IT BLUNTLY...
OUR FEMALE MEMBERS ALREADY HATE ALL OF THE GIRLS IN THE GENSHIKEN, SO ONE MORE ISN'T GONNA MAKE A DIFFERENCE.
WELL, I CAN UNDERSTAND THEM HATING SAKI-SAN, BUT—
HOW COULD YOU SAY THAT?
WELL, WHY DON'T WE AT LEAST MEET HER?
I MEAN, IT LOOKS LIKE TAKAYANAGI-KUN IS IN QUITE A PINCH.

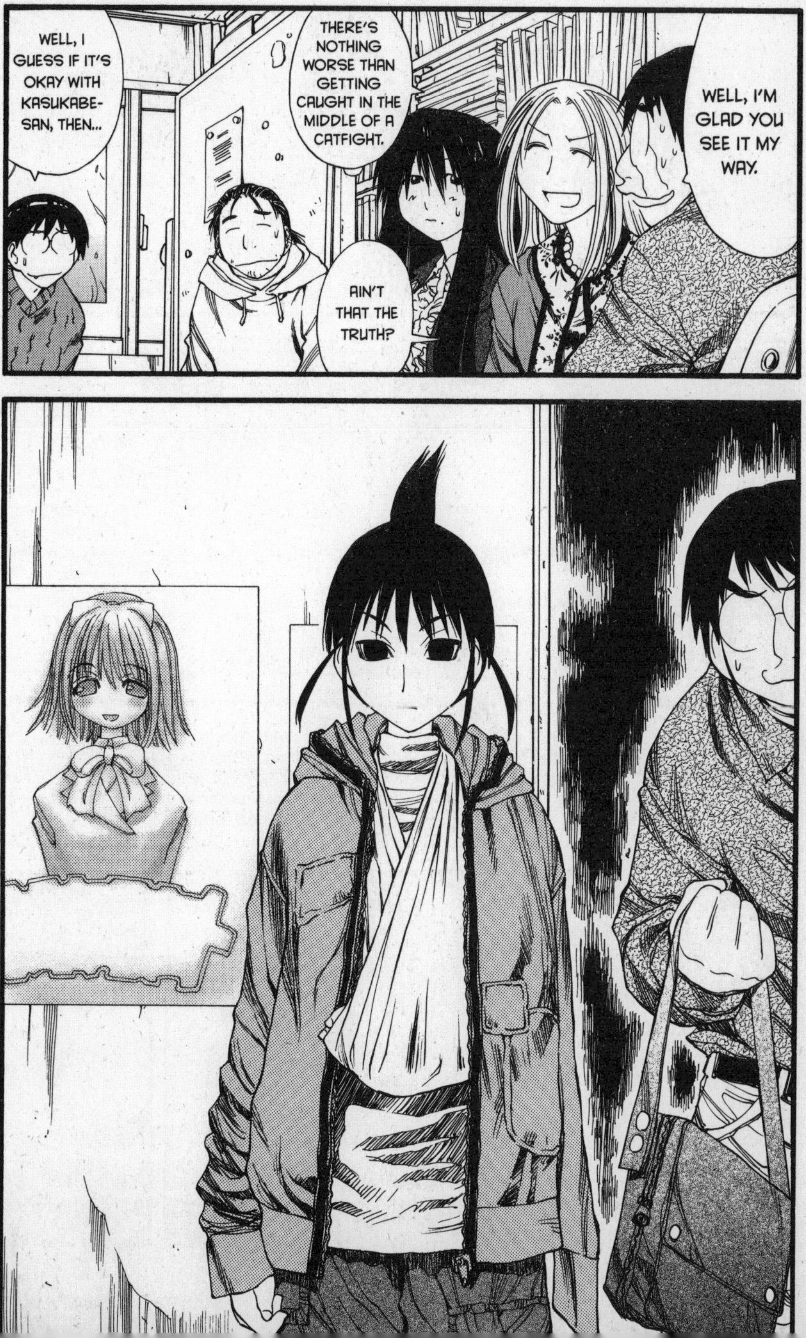
WELL, I'M GLAD YOU SEE IT MY WAY.
THERE'S NOTHING WORSE THAN GETTING CAUGHT IN THE MIDDLE OF A CATFIGHT.
AIN'T THAT THE TRUTH?
WELL, I GUESS IF IT'S OKAY WITH KASUKABE-SAN, THEN...

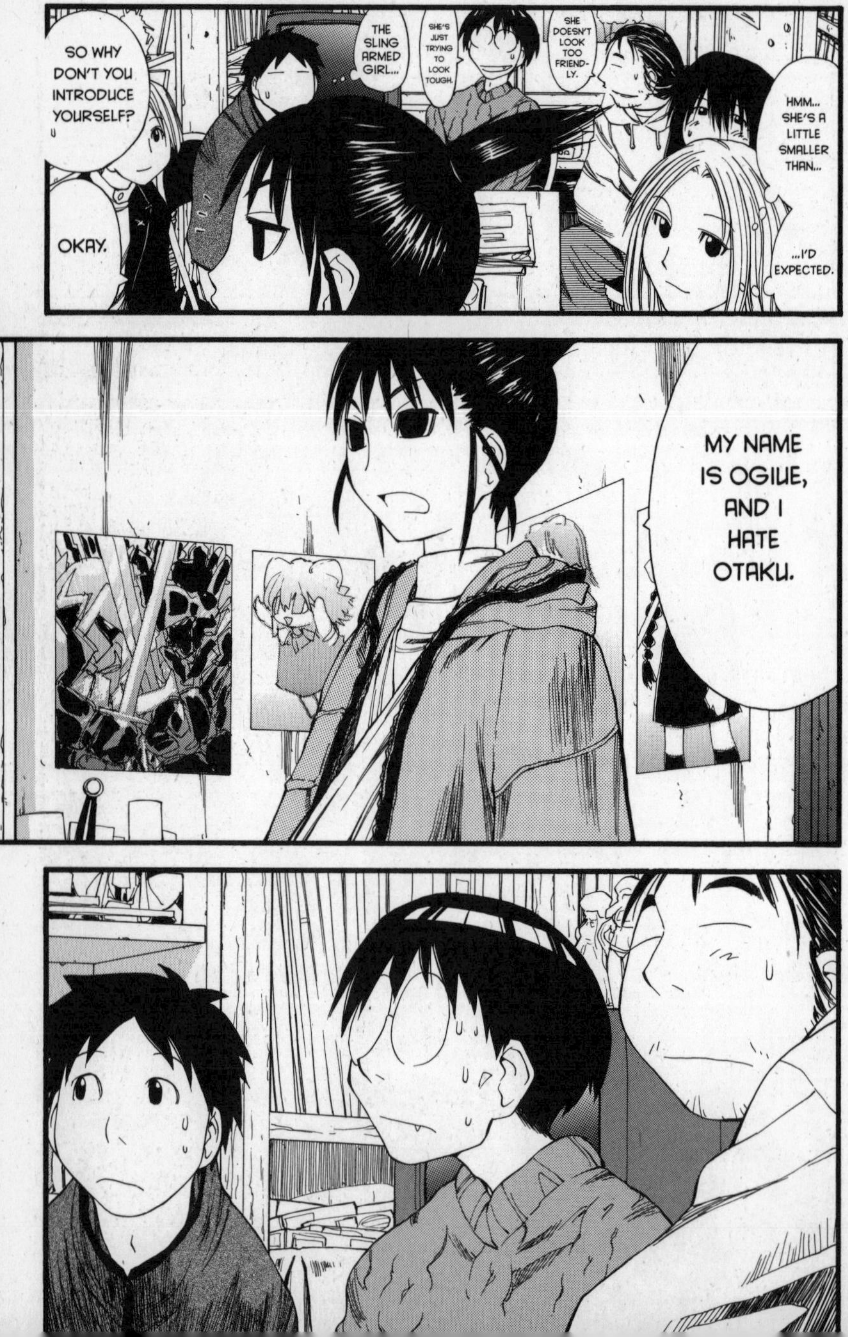
HMM... SHE'S A LITTLE SMALLER THAN...
...I'D EXPECTED.
SHE DOESN'T LOOK TOO FRIEND-LY.
SHE'S JUST TRYING TO LOOK TOUGH.
THE SLING ARMED GIRL...
SO WHY DON'T YOU INTRODUCE YOURSELF?
OKAY.
MY NAME IS OGIUE, AND I HATE OTAKU.

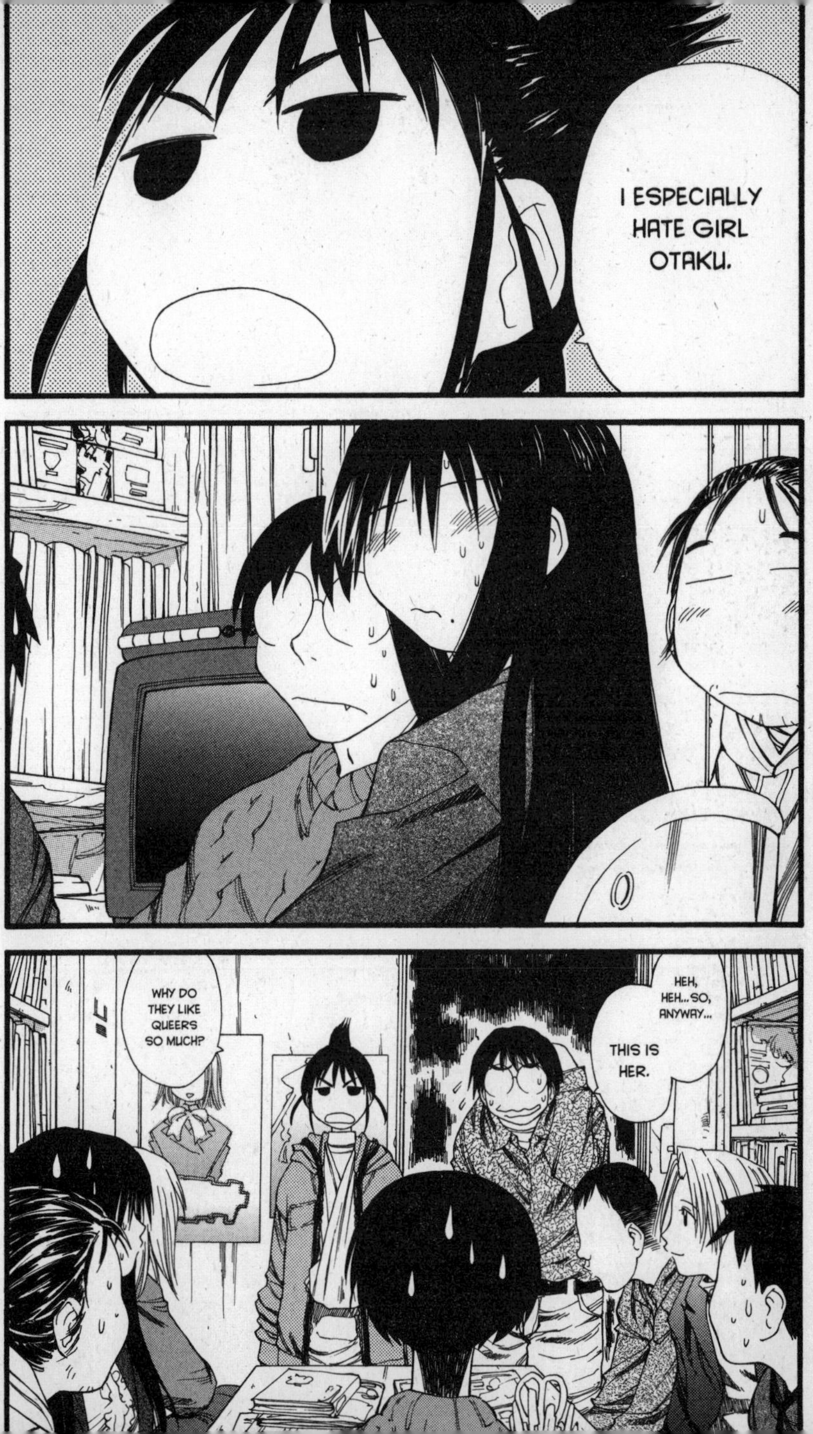
I ESPECIALLY HATE GIRL OTAKU.
HEH, HEH...SO, ANYWAY...
THIS IS HER.
WHY DO THEY LIKE QUEERS SO MUCH?

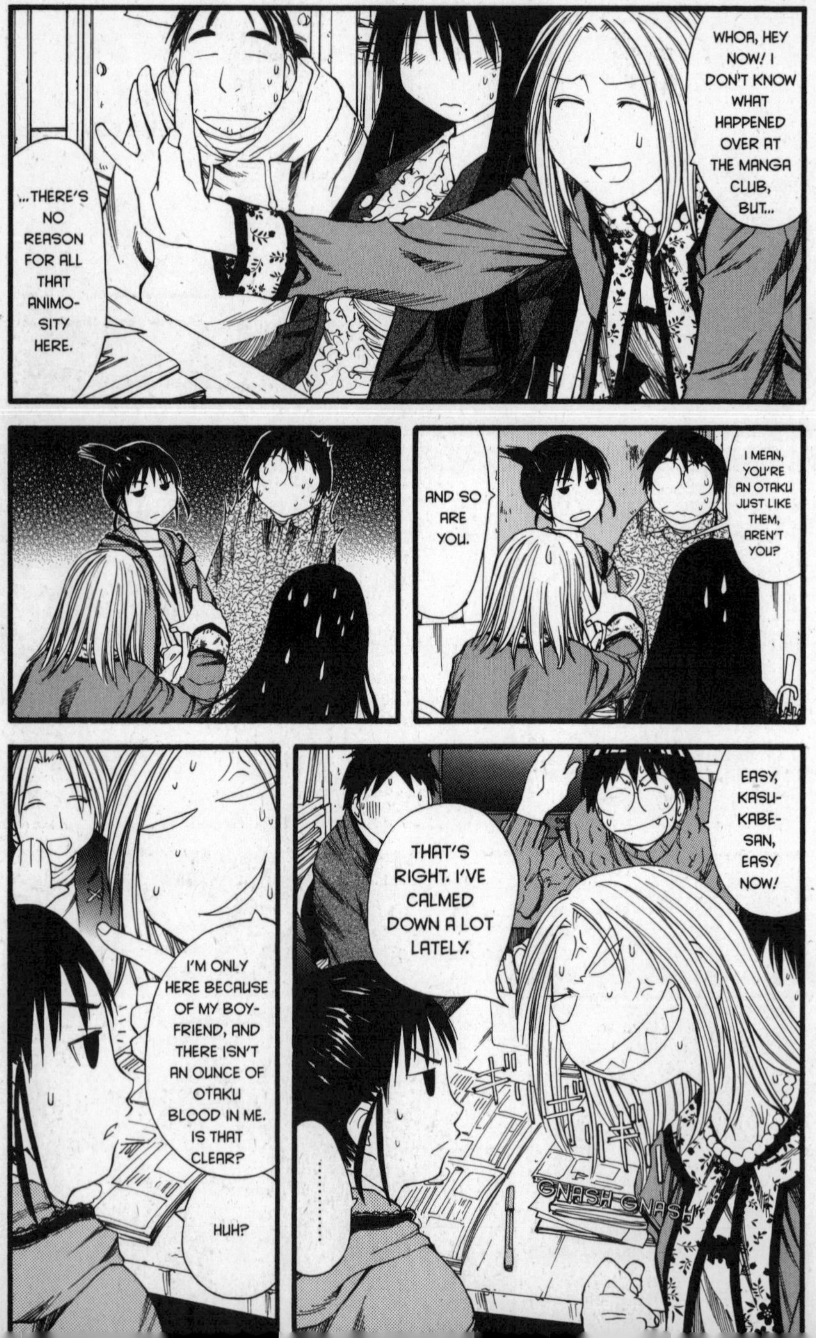
WHOA, HEY NOW! I DON'T KNOW WHAT HAPPENED OVER AT THE MANGA CLUB, BUT...
...THERE'S NO REASON FOR ALL THAT ANIMO-SITY HERE.
I MEAN, YOU'RE AN OTAKU JUST LIKE THEM, AREN'T YOU?
AND SO ARE YOU.
EASY, KASU-KABE-SAN, EASY NOW!
THAT'S RIGHT. I'VE CALMED DOWN A LOT LATELY.
GNASH GNASH
......
I'M ONLY HERE BECAUSE OF MY BOY-FRIEND, AND THERE ISN'T AN OUNCE OF OTAKU BLOOD IN ME. IS THAT CLEAR?
HUH?

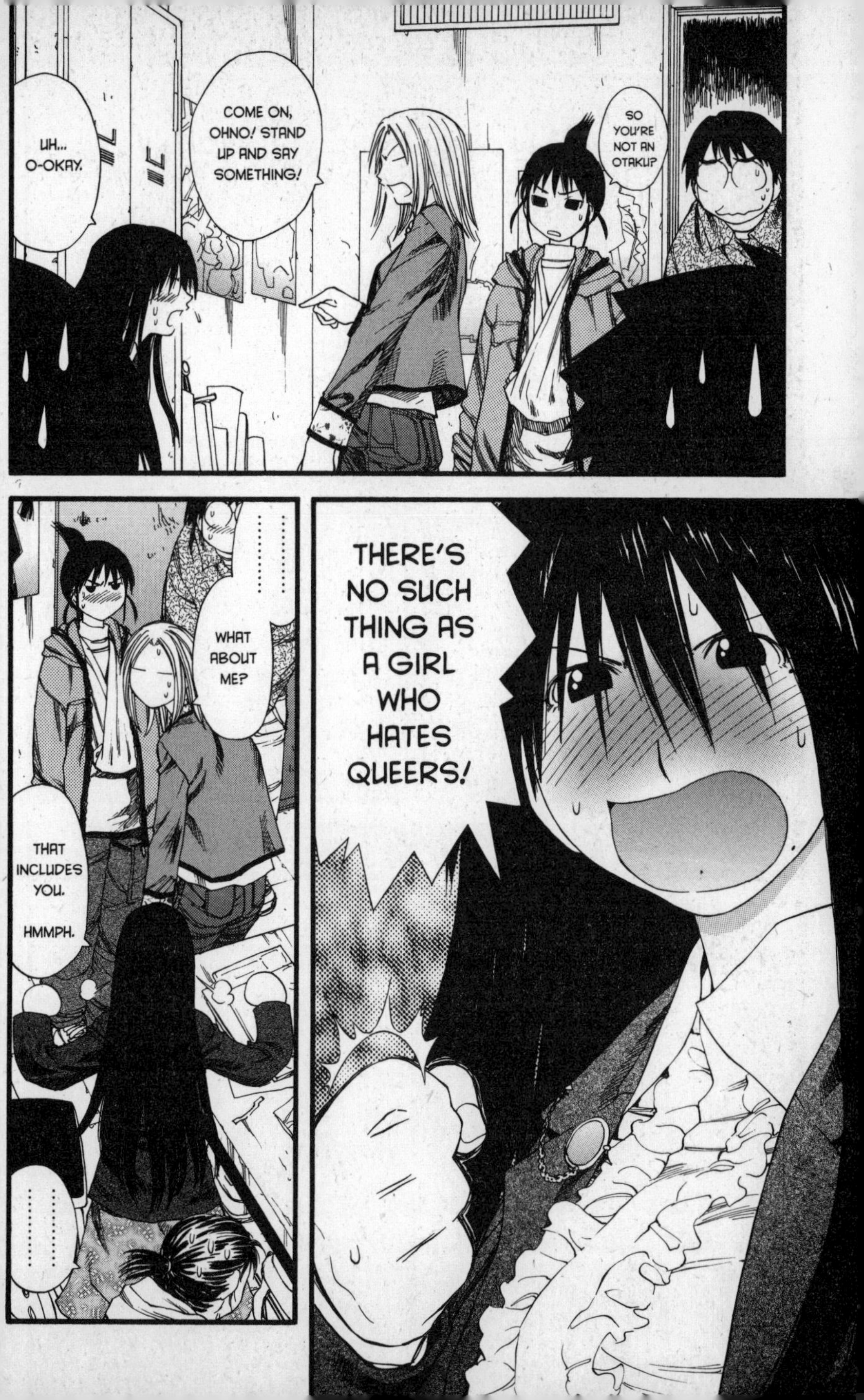
SO YOU'RE NOT AN OTAKU?
COME ON, OHNO! STAND UP AND SAY SOMETHING!
UH... O-OKAY.
THERE'S NO SUCH THING AS A GIRL WHO HATES QUEERS!
......
WHAT ABOUT ME?
THAT INCLUDES YOU.
HMMPH.
......

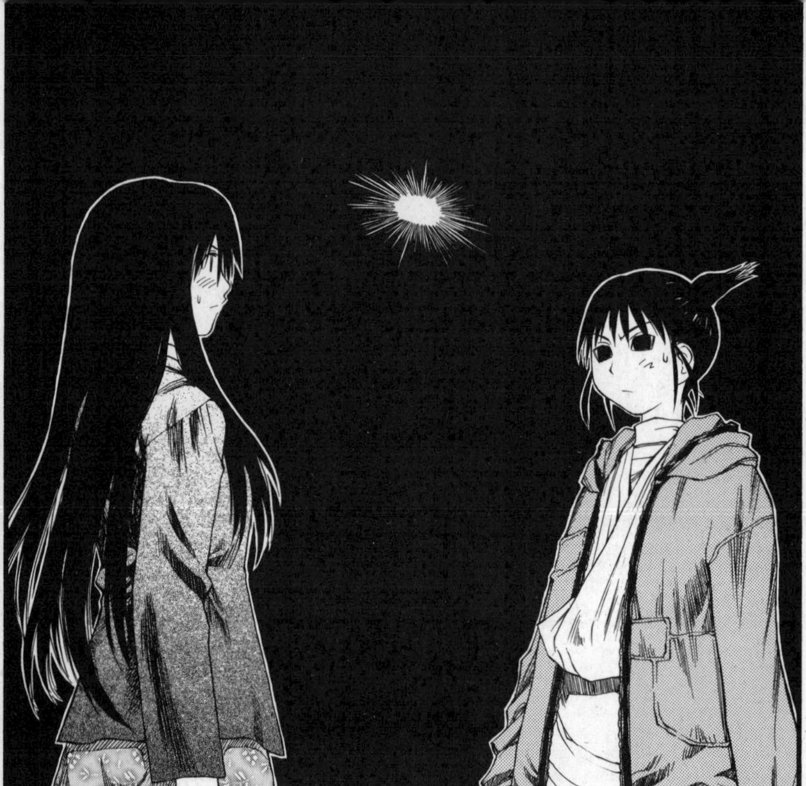

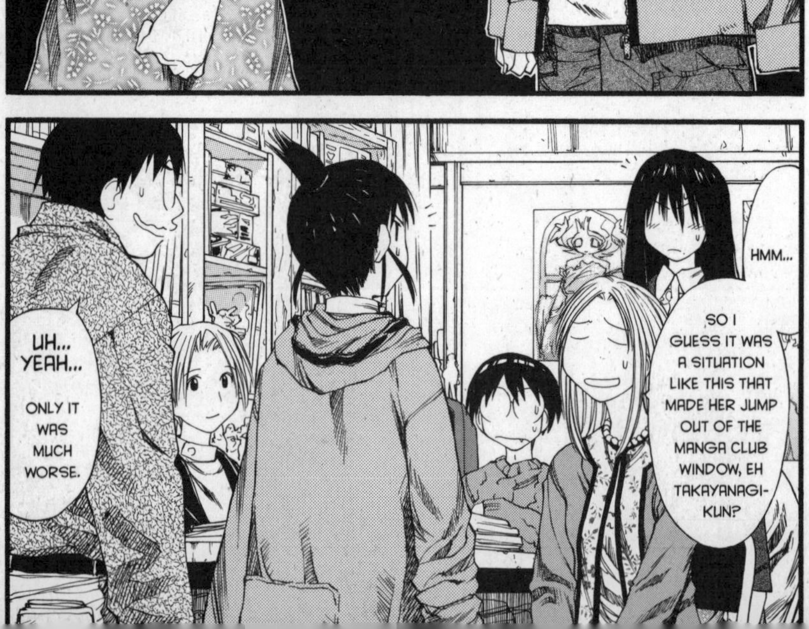
HMM...
SO I GUESS IT WAS A SITUATION LIKE THIS THAT MADE HER JUMP OUT OF THE MANGA CLUB WINDOW, EH TAKAYANAGI-KUN?
UH... YEAH...
ONLY IT WAS MUCH WORSE.

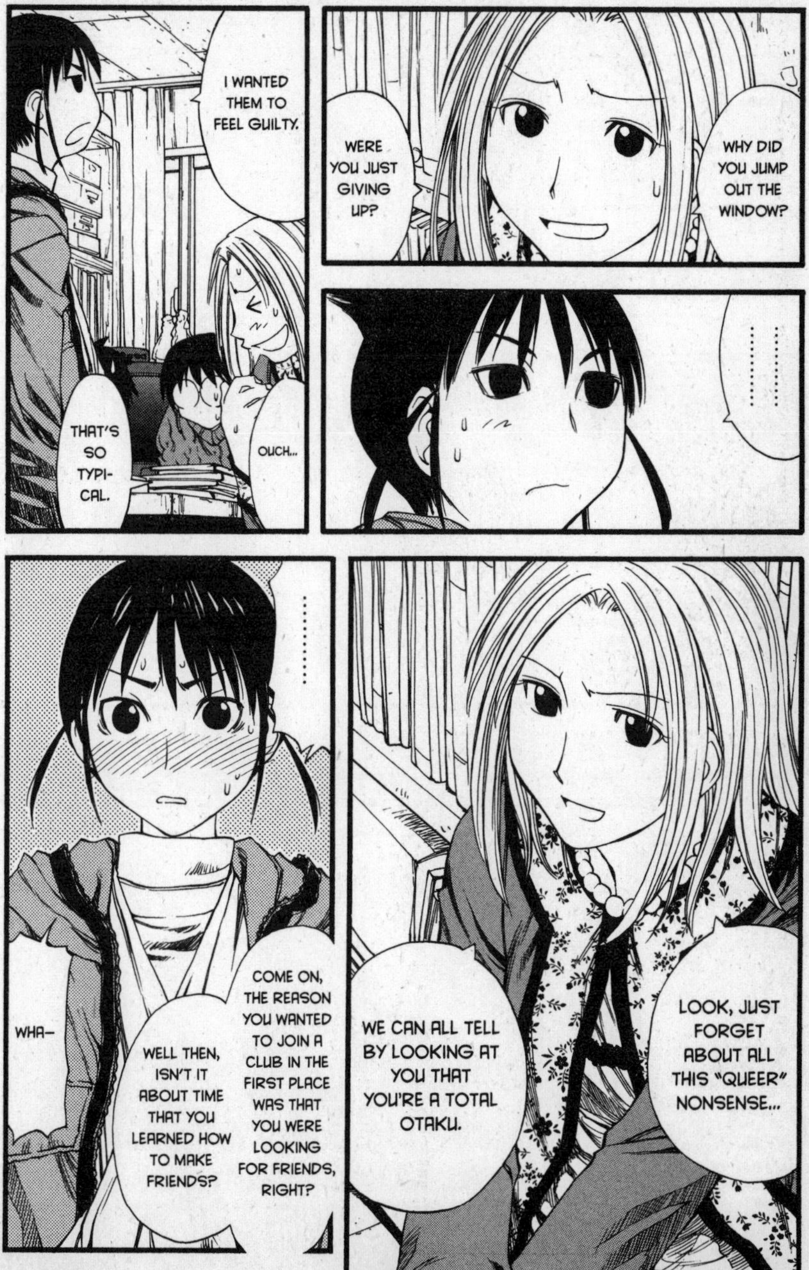
WHY DID YOU JUMP OUT THE WINDOW?
WERE YOU JUST GIVING UP?
......
I WANTED THEM TO FEEL GUILTY.
OUCH...
THAT'S SO TYPI-CAL.
LOOK, JUST FORGET ABOUT ALL THIS "QUEER" NONSENSE...
WE CAN ALL TELL BY LOOKING AT YOU THAT YOU'RE A TOTAL OTAKU.
......
COME ON, THE REASON YOU WANTED TO JOIN A CLUB IN THE FIRST PLACE WAS THAT YOU WERE LOOKING FOR FRIENDS, RIGHT?
WELL THEN, ISN'T IT ABOUT TIME THAT YOU LEARNED HOW TO MAKE FRIENDS?
WHA—

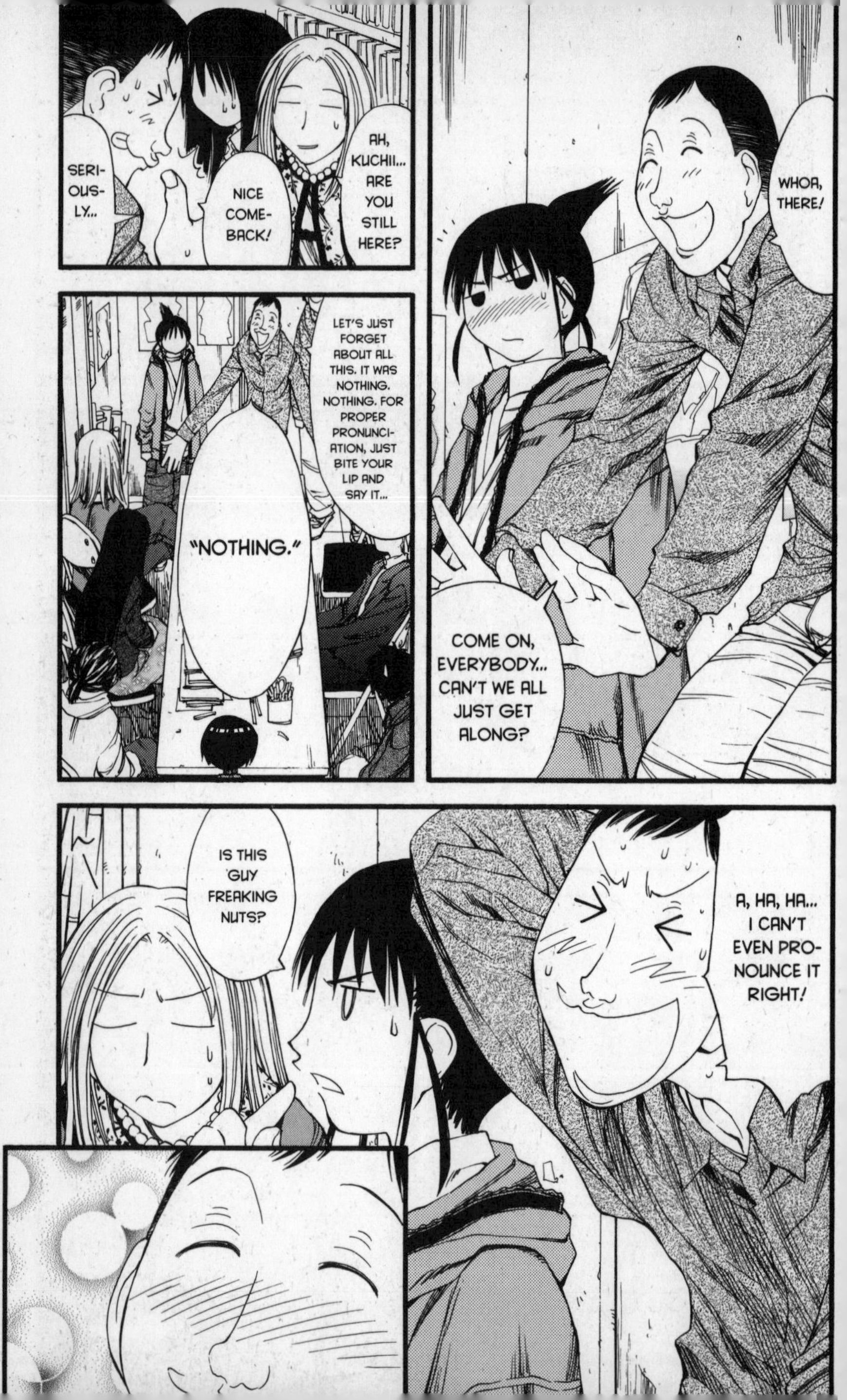
WHOA, THERE!
COME ON, EVERYBODY... CAN'T WE ALL JUST GET ALONG?
AH, KUCHII... ARE YOU STILL HERE?
NICE COME-BACK!
SERI-OUS-LY...
LET'S JUST FORGET ABOUT ALL THIS. IT WAS NOTHING. NOTHING. FOR PROPER PRONUNCI-ATION, JUST BITE YOUR LIP AND SAY IT...
"NOTHING."
A, HA, HA... I CAN'T EVEN PRO-NOUNCE IT RIGHT!
IS THIS GUY FREAKING NUTS?

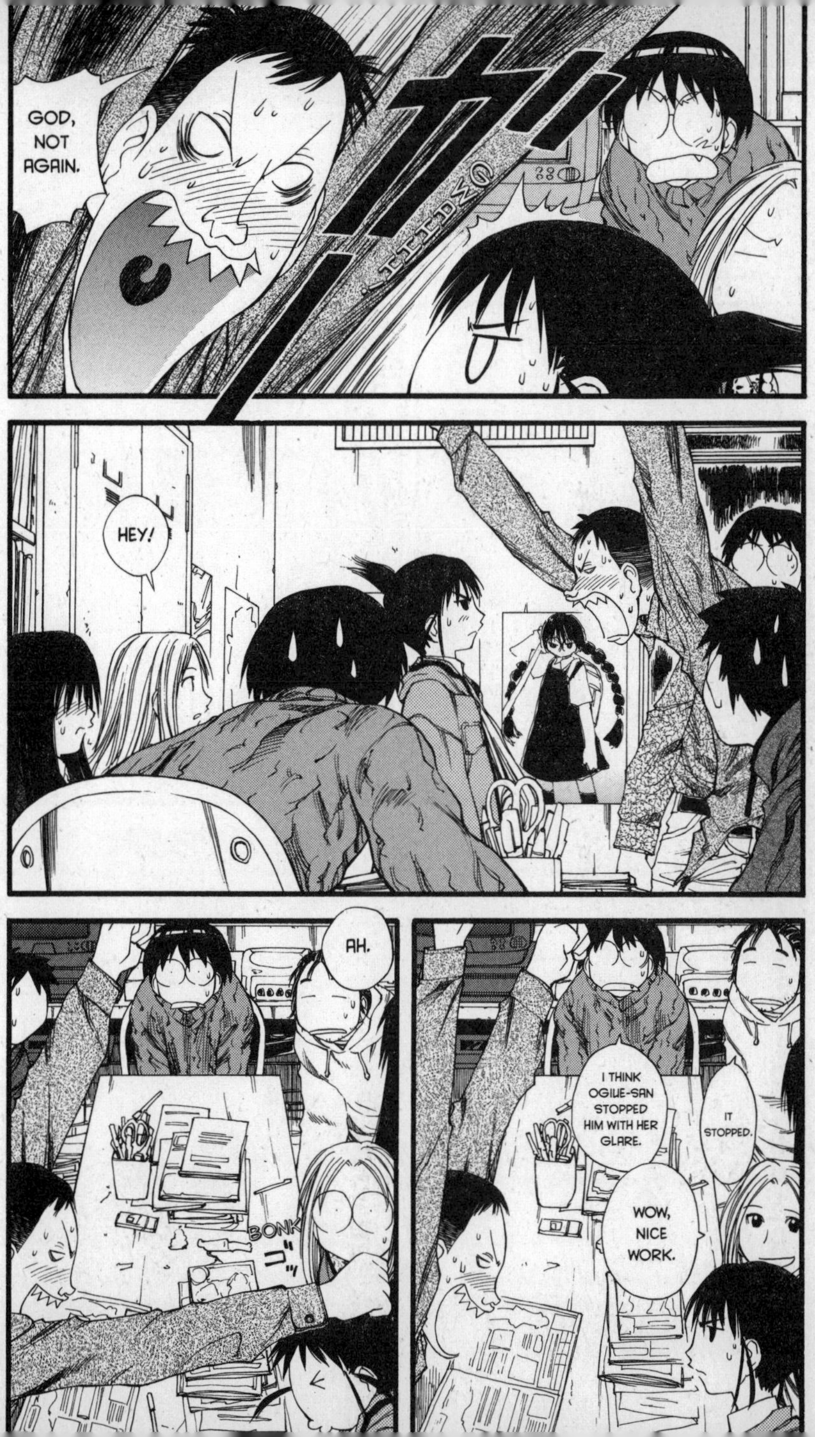
GOD, NOT AGAIN.
HEY!
IT STOPPED.
I THINK OGIUE-SAN STOPPED HIM WITH HER GLARE.
WOW, NICE WORK.
AH.
BONK

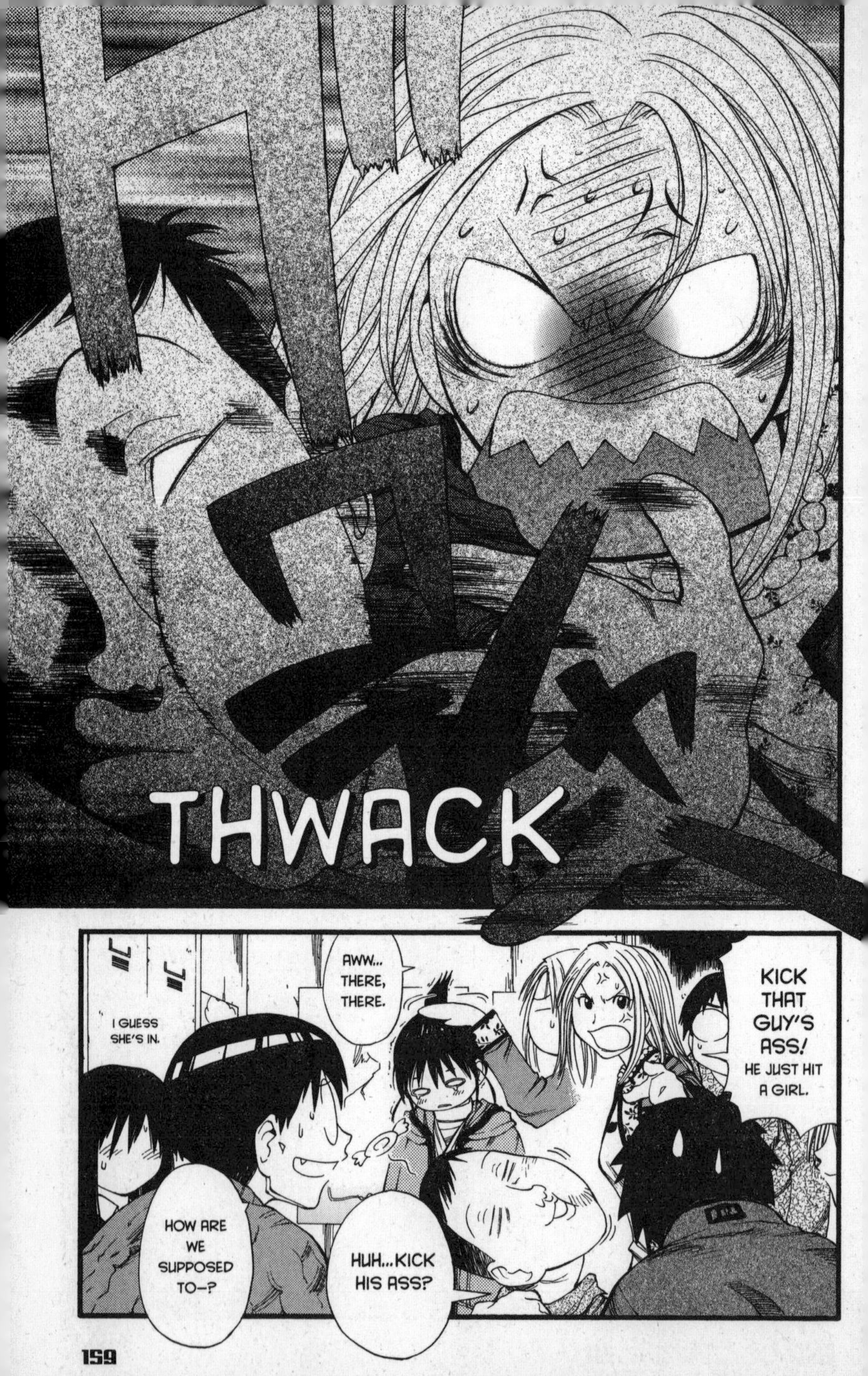
THWACK
KICK THAT GUY'S ASS!
HE JUST HIT A GIRL.
AWW... THERE, THERE.
I GUESS SHE'S IN.
HUH...KICK HIS ASS?
HOW ARE WE SUPPOSED TO—?

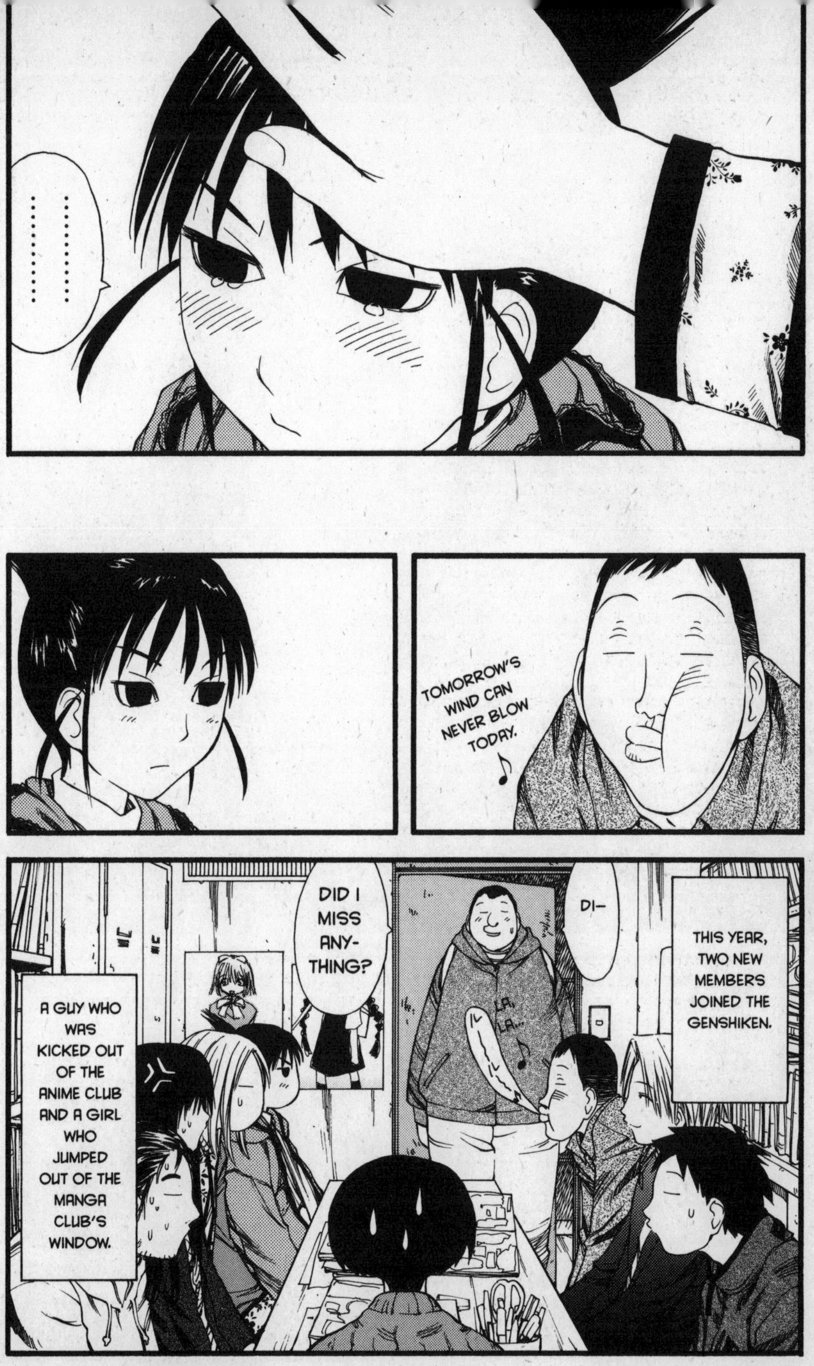
......
TOMORROW'S WIND CAN NEVER BLOW TODAY. ♪
THIS YEAR, TWO NEW MEMBERS JOINED THE GENSHIKEN.
DI–
LA, LA... ♪
DID I MISS ANY-THING?
A GUY WHO WAS KICKED OUT OF THE ANIME CLUB AND A GIRL WHO JUMPED OUT OF THE MANGA CLUB'S WINDOW.

END OF CHAPTER 24

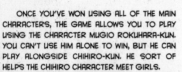

# OUR FAVORITE GAME ANOTHER STORIES

STORY 6

CHIHIRO ENOMOTO

REVIEWED BY YOKO KANNAZUKI

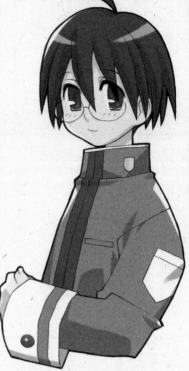

ONCE YOU'VE WON USING ALL OF THE MAIN CHARACTERS, THE GAME ALLOWS YOU TO PLAY USING THE CHARACTER MUGIO ROKUHARA-KUN. YOU CAN'T USE HIM ALONE TO WIN, BUT HE CAN PLAY ALONGSIDE CHIHIRO-KUN. HE SORT OF HELPS THE CHIHIRO CHARACTER MEET GIRLS.

BUT BE CAREFUL, BECAUSE HE CAN ALSO GET IN THE WAY OF CHIHIRO'S RELATIONSHIPS. THE ROKUHARA-KUN CHARACTER WAS DESIGNED TO INTERFERE WITH CHARACTERS WHO WEREN'T A GOOD MATCH, BUT SOMEHOW HE ENDED UP BEING ABLE TO GET IN THE WAY OF ALL THE CHARACTERS. OF COURSE, EVERYBODY'S GONNA TAKE ADVANTAGE OF THAT. [HA HA] HALFWAY THROUGH THE GAME, CHIHIRO-KUN STARTS HAVING ALL OF THESE ROMANTIC DATES. EVEN IF HE JUST GOES TO HANG OUT WITH SOMEONE, IT TURNS INTO A DATE. HE KEEPS BRUSHING OFF ALL THE GIRLS THAT HIT ON HIM, AND GOES HEADLONG INTO THE FINAL SCENE. OF COURSE, CHIHIRO LEAVES HOME AFTER HIS OLDER SISTER GETS MARRIED, AND HE ENDS UP RENTING A ROOM WITH ROKUHARA-KUN. OH, DEAR...WHO CAME UP WITH THAT?

IF THIS GAME WERE A BIT MORE DEMENTED, ROKUHARA-KUN WOULD PROBABLY KEEP STEALING AWAY ALL OF CHIHIRO'S FEMALE FRIENDS. HE'D PROBABLY END UP KILLING CHIHIRO OR SOMETHING. I'D RATHER PLAY A GAME LIKE THAT. [HEART] [HA HA] [YOKO]

★

WHAT'RE YOU LAUGHING ABOUT? IS SOMETHING WRONG WITH YOU? ARE YOU THAT UPSET THAT YOU CAN'T WIN THE GAME WITH ROKUHARA-KUN ALONE? ROKUHARA-KUN GETS A LOT OF ACTION IN THE IZUMI SCENARIO AND THE VICE PRESIDENT SCENARIO. ISN'T THAT ENOUGH FOR YOU? [PIT VIPER]

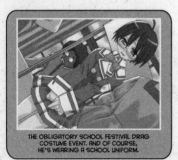

THE OBLIGATORY SCHOOL FESTIVAL DRAG COSTUME EVENT. AND OF COURSE, HE'S WEARING A SCHOOL UNIFORM.

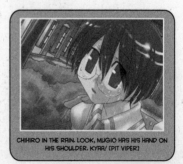

CHIHIRO IN THE RAIN. LOOK, MUGIO HAS HIS HAND ON HIS SHOULDER. KYAA! [PIT VIPER]

HOWL FROM THE HEART

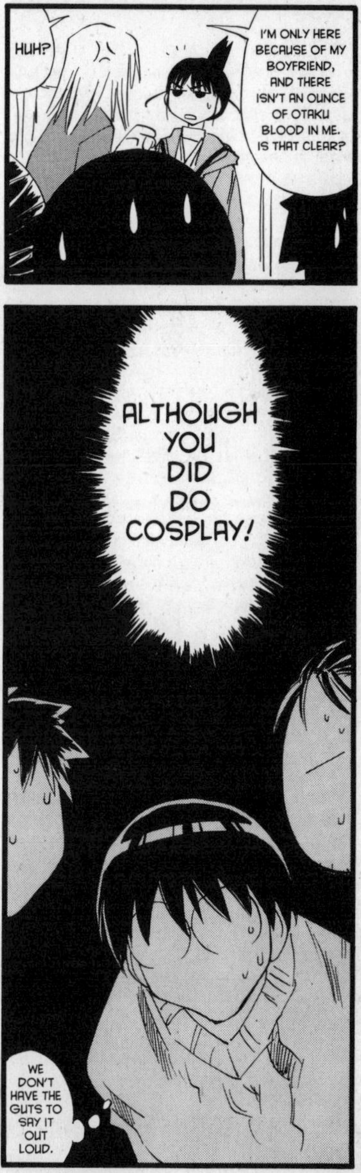
I'M ONLY HERE BECAUSE OF MY BOYFRIEND, AND THERE ISN'T AN OUNCE OF OTAKU BLOOD IN ME. IS THAT CLEAR?
HUH?
ALTHOUGH YOU DID DO COSPLAY!
WE DON'T HAVE THE GUTS TO SAY IT OUT LOUD.

THREE IF YOU INCLUDE HER TRIP TO THE TRAIN STATION

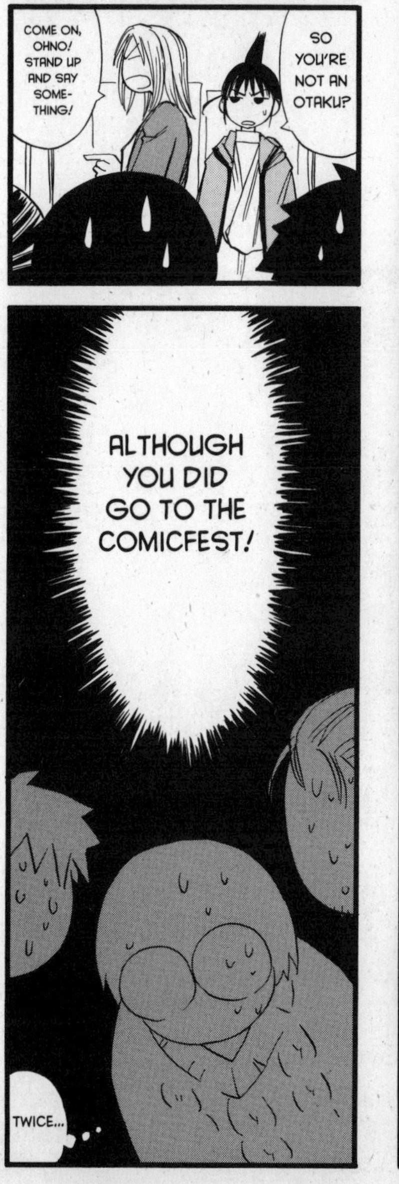
SO YOU'RE NOT AN OTAKU?
COME ON, OHNO! STAND UP AND SAY SOME-THING!
ALTHOUGH YOU DID GO TO THE COMICFEST!
TWICE...

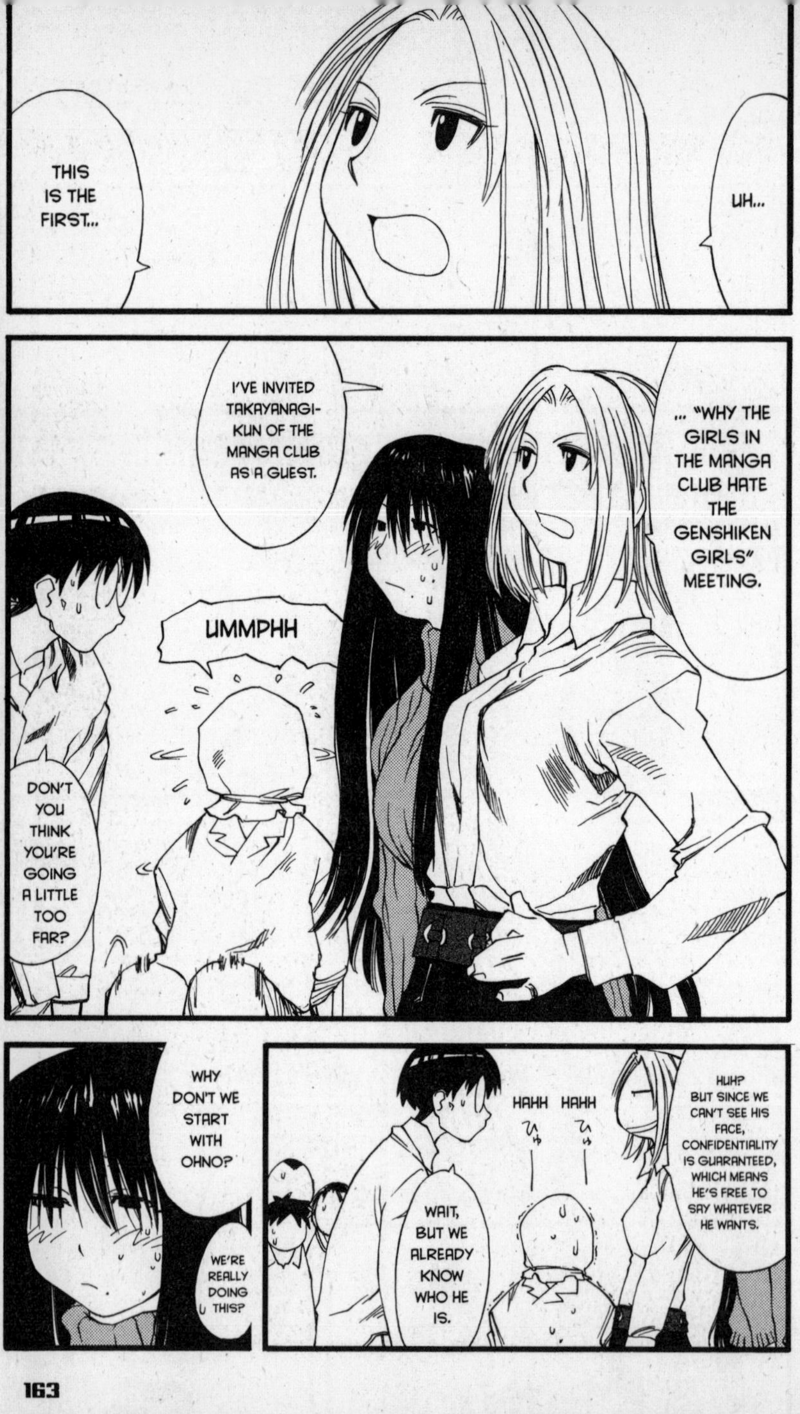
UH...
THIS IS THE FIRST...
... "WHY THE GIRLS IN THE MANGA CLUB HATE THE GENSHIKEN GIRLS" MEETING.
I'VE INVITED TAKAYANAGI-KUN OF THE MANGA CLUB AS A GUEST.
UMMPHH
DON'T YOU THINK YOU'RE GOING A LITTLE TOO FAR?
HUH? BUT SINCE WE CAN'T SEE HIS FACE, CONFIDENTIALITY IS GUARANTEED, WHICH MEANS HE'S FREE TO SAY WHATEVER HE WANTS.
HAHH HAHH
WAIT, BUT WE ALREADY KNOW WHO HE IS.
WHY DON'T WE START WITH OHNO?
WE'RE REALLY DOING THIS?

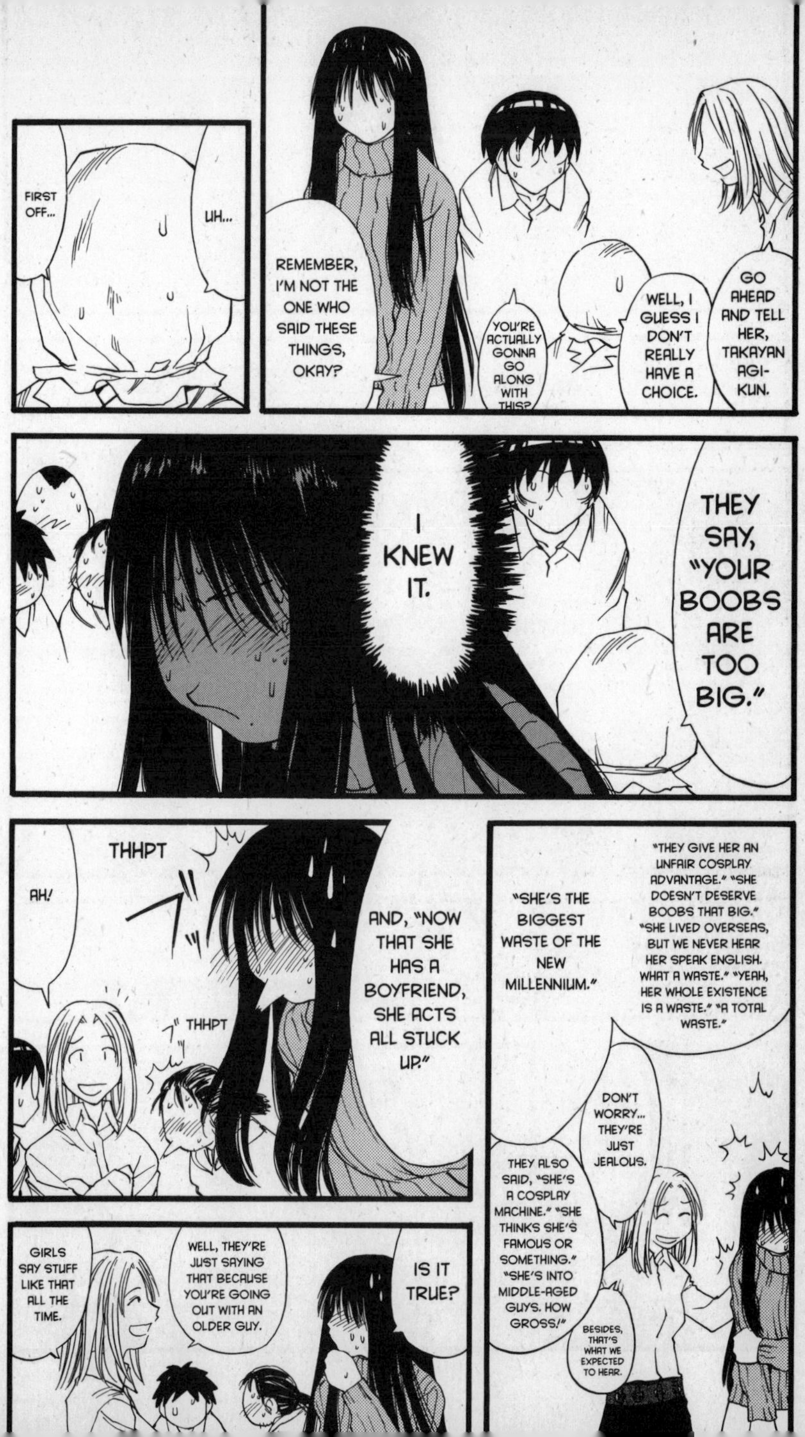
GO AHEAD AND TELL HER, TAKAYANAGI-KUN.
WELL, I GUESS I DON'T REALLY HAVE A CHOICE.
YOU'RE ACTUALLY GONNA GO ALONG WITH THIS?
REMEMBER, I'M NOT THE ONE WHO SAID THESE THINGS, OKAY?
UH...
FIRST OFF...
THEY SAY, "YOUR BOOBS ARE TOO BIG."
I KNEW IT.
"THEY GIVE HER AN UNFAIR COSPLAY ADVANTAGE." "SHE DOESN'T DESERVE BOOBS THAT BIG." "SHE LIVED OVERSEAS, BUT WE NEVER HEAR HER SPEAK ENGLISH. WHAT A WASTE." "YEAH, HER WHOLE EXISTENCE IS A WASTE." "A TOTAL WASTE."
"SHE'S THE BIGGEST WASTE OF THE NEW MILLENNIUM."
DON'T WORRY... THEY'RE JUST JEALOUS.
THEY ALSO SAID, "SHE'S A COSPLAY MACHINE." "SHE THINKS SHE'S FAMOUS OR SOMETHING." "SHE'S INTO MIDDLE-AGED GUYS. HOW GROSS!"
BESIDES, THAT'S WHAT WE EXPECTED TO HEAR.
AND, "NOW THAT SHE HAS A BOYFRIEND, SHE ACTS ALL STUCK UP."
THHPT
AH!
THHPT
IS IT TRUE?
WELL, THEY'RE JUST SAYING THAT BECAUSE YOU'RE GOING OUT WITH AN OLDER GUY.
GIRLS SAY STUFF LIKE THAT ALL THE TIME.

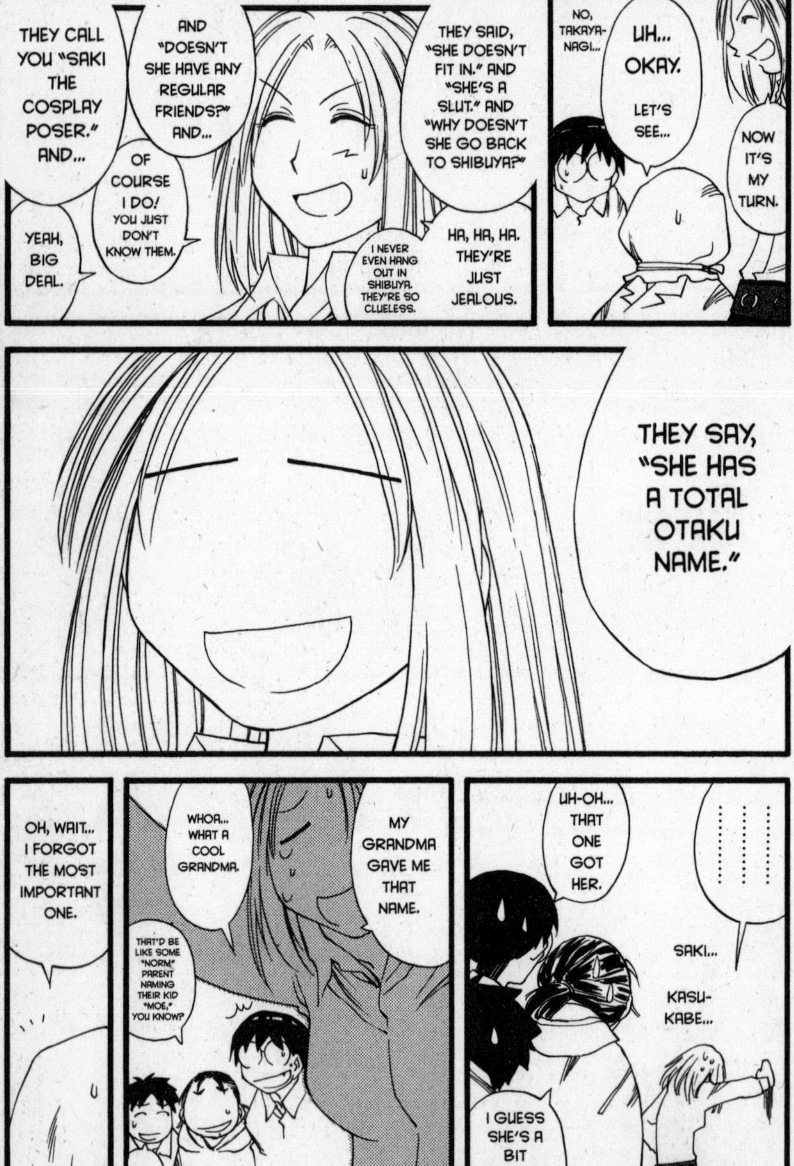
NOW IT'S MY TURN.
UH... OKAY. LET'S SEE...
NO, TAKAYA-NAGI...
THEY SAID, "SHE DOESN'T FIT IN." AND "SHE'S A SLUT." AND "WHY DOESN'T SHE GO BACK TO SHIBUYA?"
HA, HA, HA. THEY'RE JUST JEALOUS.
I NEVER EVEN HANG OUT IN SHIBUYA. THEY'RE SO CLUELESS.
AND "DOESN'T SHE HAVE ANY REGULAR FRIENDS?" AND...
OF COURSE I DO! YOU JUST DON'T KNOW THEM.
THEY CALL YOU "SAKI THE COSPLAY POSER." AND...
YEAH, BIG DEAL.
THEY SAY, "SHE HAS A TOTAL OTAKU NAME."
......
UH-OH... THAT ONE GOT HER.
SAKI... KASU-KABE...
I GUESS SHE'S A BIT SENSITIVE ABOUT HER NAME.
MY GRANDMA GAVE ME THAT NAME.
WHOA... WHAT A COOL GRANDMA.
THAT'D BE LIKE SOME "NORM" PARENT NAMING THEIR KID "MOE," YOU KNOW?
NOT QUITE.
OH, WAIT... I FORGOT THE MOST IMPORTANT ONE.

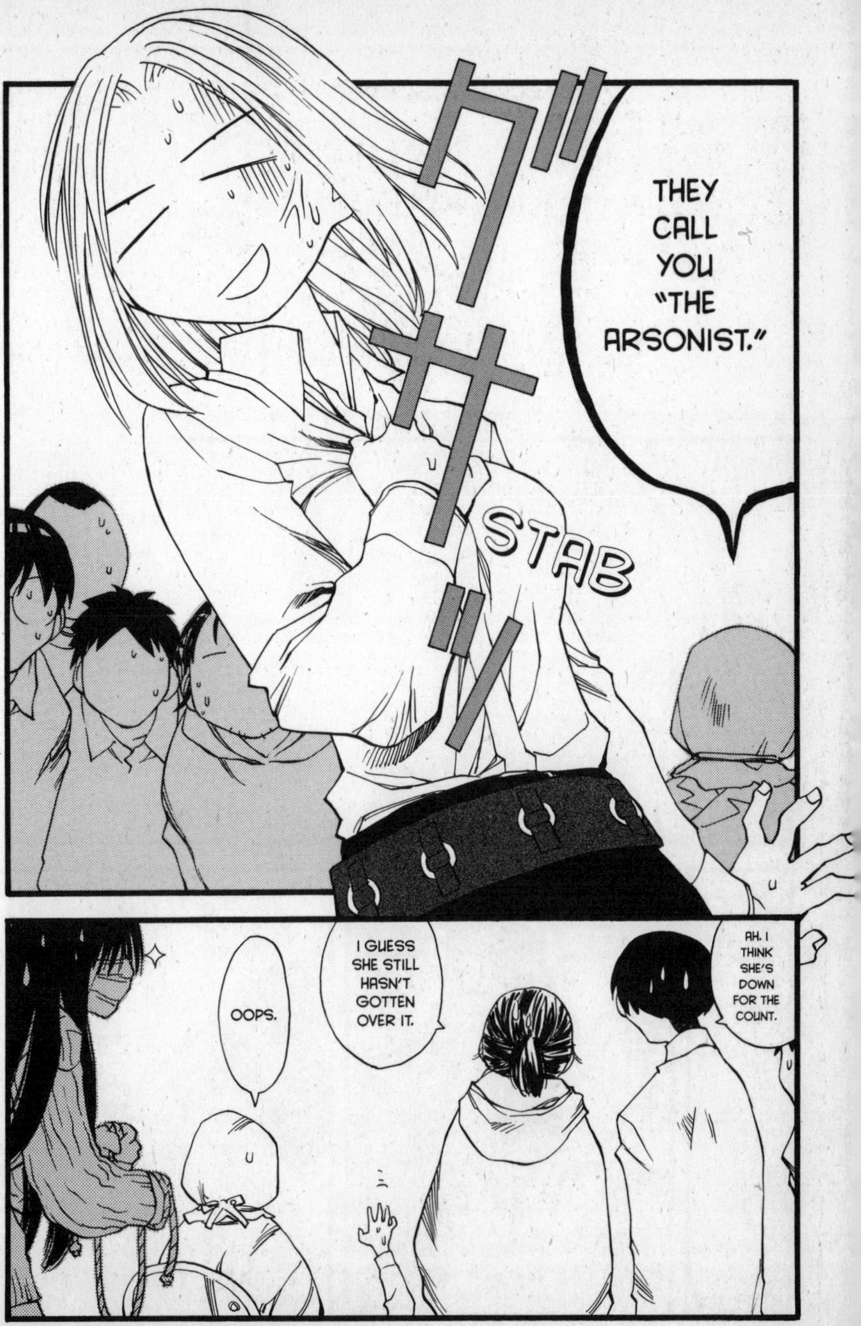
THEY CALL YOU "THE ARSONIST."
グサッ
STAB
AH. I THINK SHE'S DOWN FOR THE COUNT.
I GUESS SHE STILL HASN'T GOTTEN OVER IT.
OOPS.

END OF GENSHIKEN BOOK 4

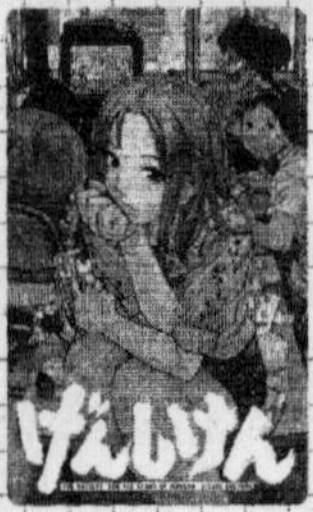
げんしけん

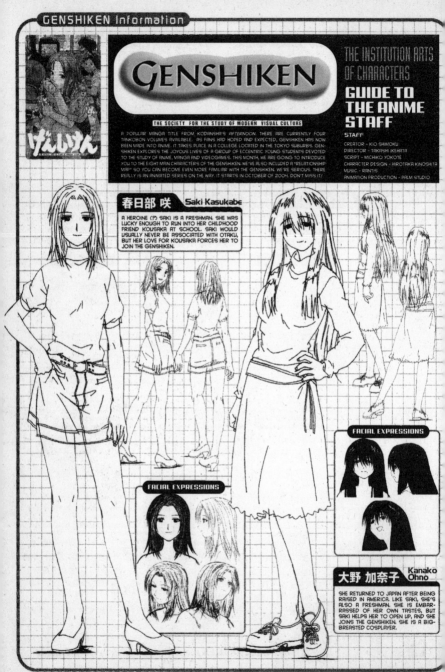

# GENSHIKEN

THE SOCIETY FOR THE STUDY OF MODERN VISUAL CULTURE

A POPULAR MANGA TITLE FROM KODANSHA'S *AFTERNOON*. THERE ARE CURRENTLY FOUR TANKOBON VOLUMES AVAILABLE. AS FANS HAD HOPED AND EXPECTED, GENSHIKEN HAS NOW BEEN MADE INTO ANIME. IT TAKES PLACE IN A COLLEGE LOCATED IN THE TOKYO SUBURBS. GENSHIKEN EXPLORES THE JOYOUS LIVES OF A GROUP OF ECCENTRIC YOUNG STUDENTS DEVOTED TO THE STUDY OF ANIME, MANGA AND VIDEOGAMES. THIS MONTH, WE ARE GOING TO INTRODUCE YOU TO THE EIGHT MAIN CHARACTERS OF THE GENSHIKEN. WE'VE ALSO INCLUDED A "RELATIONSHIP MAP" SO YOU CAN BECOME EVEN MORE FAMILIAR WITH THE GENSHIKEN. WE'RE SERIOUS. THERE REALLY IS AN ANIMATED SERIES ON THE WAY. IT STARTS IN OCTOBER OF 2004. DON'T MISS IT!

## THE INSTITUTION ARTS OF CHARACTERS

## GUIDE TO THE ANIME STAFF

STAFF

CREATOR - KIO SHIMOKU
DIRECTOR - TAKASHI IKEHATA
SCRIPT - MICHIKO YOKOTE
CHARACTER DESIGN - HIROTAKA KINOSHITA
MUSIC - RANTIS
ANIMATION PRODUCTION - PALM STUDIO

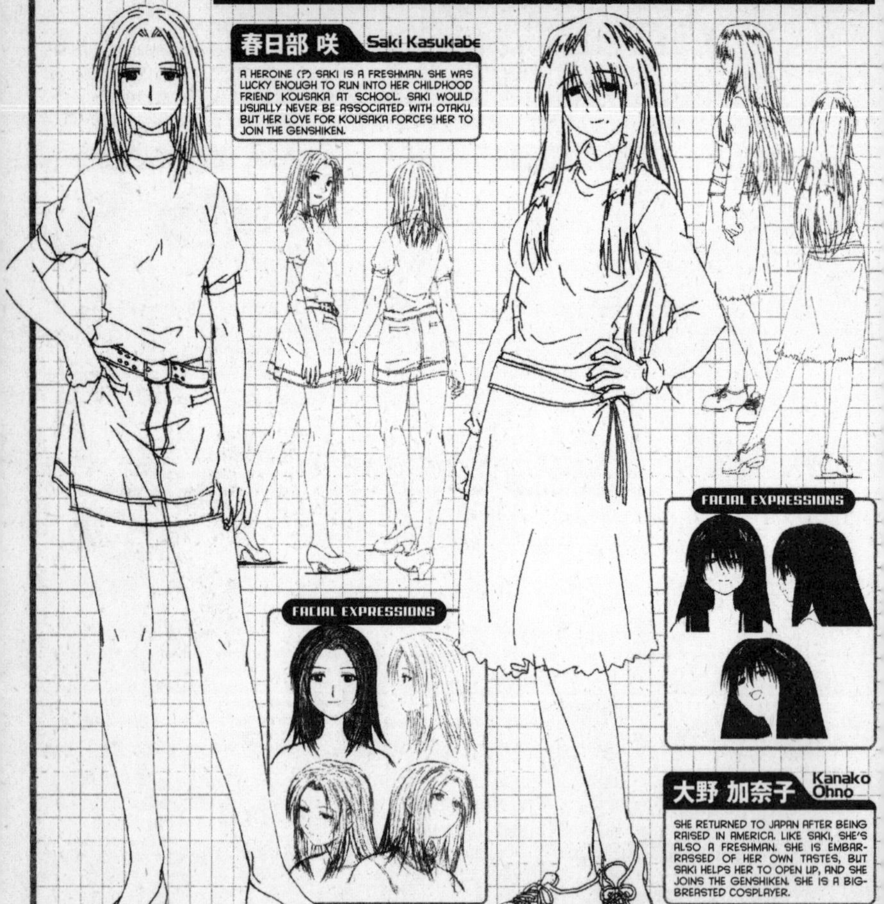
FACIAL EXPRESSIONS
FACIAL EXPRESSIONS

### 春日部 咲 Saki Kasukabe

A HEROINE (?) SAKI IS A FRESHMAN. SHE WAS LUCKY ENOUGH TO RUN INTO HER CHILDHOOD FRIEND KOUSAKA AT SCHOOL. SAKI WOULD USUALLY NEVER BE ASSOCIATED WITH OTAKU, BUT HER LOVE FOR KOUSAKA FORCES HER TO JOIN THE GENSHIKEN.

### 大野 加奈子 Kanako Ohno

SHE RETURNED TO JAPAN AFTER BEING RAISED IN AMERICA. LIKE SAKI, SHE'S ALSO A FRESHMAN. SHE IS EMBARRASSED OF HER OWN TASTES, BUT SAKI HELPS HER TO OPEN UP, AND SHE JOINS THE GENSHIKEN. SHE IS A BIG-BREASTED COSPLAYER.

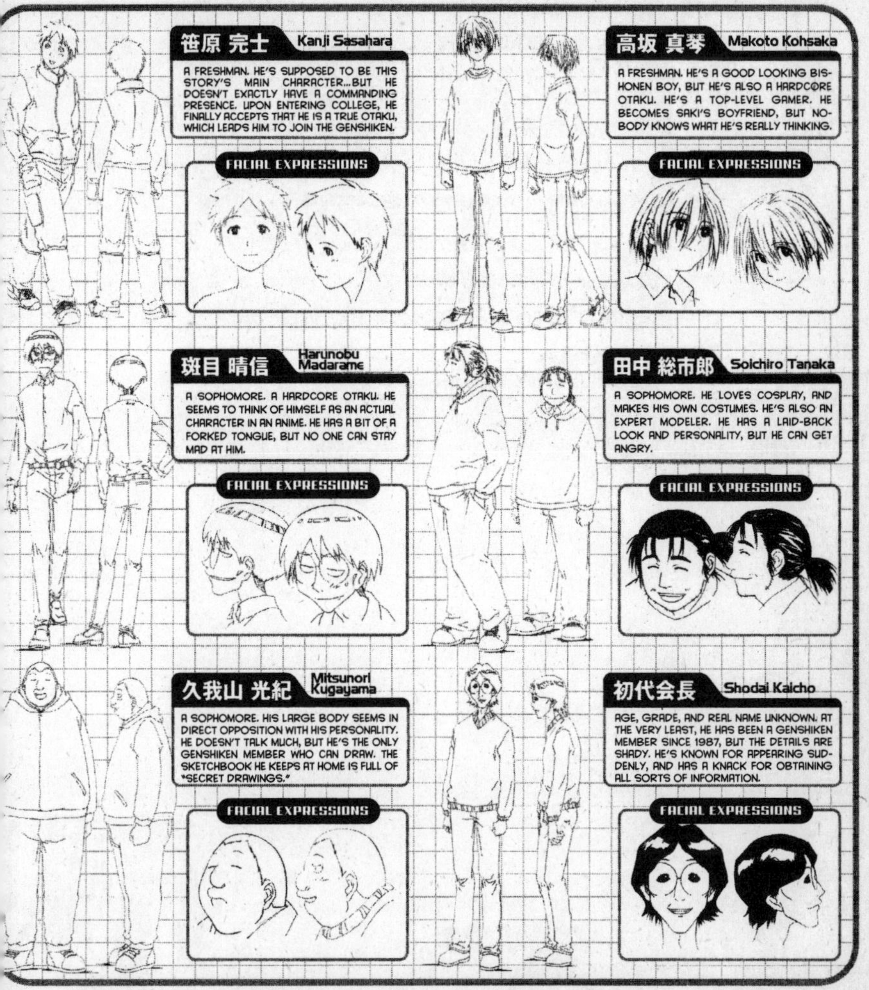

笹原 完士 Kanji Sasahara
A FRESHMAN. HE'S SUPPOSED TO BE THIS STORY'S MAIN CHARACTER...BUT HE DOESN'T EXACTLY HAVE A COMMANDING PRESENCE. UPON ENTERING COLLEGE, HE FINALLY ACCEPTS THAT HE IS A TRUE OTAKU, WHICH LEADS HIM TO JOIN THE GENSHIKEN.
FACIAL EXPRESSIONS
高坂 真琴 Makoto Kohsaka
A FRESHMAN. HE'S A GOOD LOOKING BISHONEN BOY, BUT HE'S ALSO A HARDCORE OTAKU. HE'S A TOP-LEVEL GAMER. HE BECOMES SAKI'S BOYFRIEND, BUT NOBODY KNOWS WHAT HE'S REALLY THINKING.
FACIAL EXPRESSIONS
斑目 晴信 Harunobu Madarame
A SOPHOMORE. A HARDCORE OTAKU. HE SEEMS TO THINK OF HIMSELF AS AN ACTUAL CHARACTER IN AN ANIME. HE HAS A BIT OF A FORKED TONGUE, BUT NO ONE CAN STAY MAD AT HIM.
FACIAL EXPRESSIONS
田中 総市郎 Soichiro Tanaka
A SOPHOMORE. HE LOVES COSPLAY, AND MAKES HIS OWN COSTUMES. HE'S ALSO AN EXPERT MODELER. HE HAS A LAID-BACK LOOK AND PERSONALITY, BUT HE CAN GET ANGRY.
FACIAL EXPRESSIONS
久我山 光紀 Mitsunori Kugayama
A SOPHOMORE. HIS LARGE BODY SEEMS IN DIRECT OPPOSITION WITH HIS PERSONALITY. HE DOESN'T TALK MUCH, BUT HE'S THE ONLY GENSHIKEN MEMBER WHO CAN DRAW. THE SKETCHBOOK HE KEEPS AT HOME IS FULL OF "SECRET DRAWINGS."
FACIAL EXPRESSIONS
初代会長 Shodai Kaicho
AGE, GRADE, AND REAL NAME UNKNOWN. AT THE VERY LEAST, HE HAS BEEN A GENSHIKEN MEMBER SINCE 1987, BUT THE DETAILS ARE SHADY. HE'S KNOWN FOR APPEARING SUDDENLY, AND HAS A KNACK FOR OBTAINING ALL SORTS OF INFORMATION.
FACIAL EXPRESSIONS


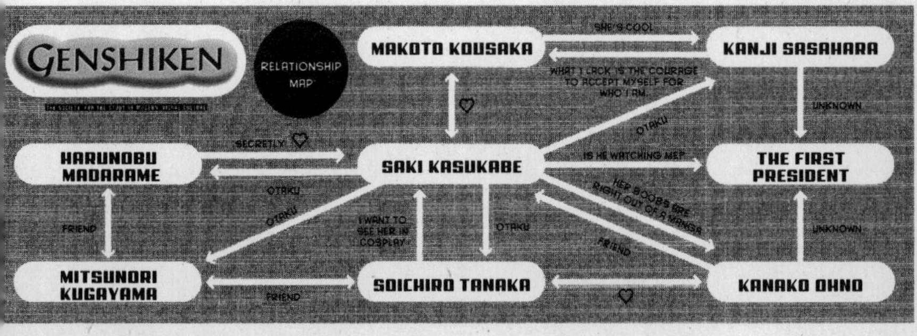

GENSHIKEN
RELATIONSHIP MAP
MAKOTO KOUSAKA
KANJI SASAHARA
SHE'S COOL
WHAT I LACK IS THE COURAGE TO ACCEPT MYSELF FOR WHO I AM.
UNKNOWN
OTAKU
SECRETLY
HARUNOBU MADARAME
SAKI KASUKABE
IS HE WATCHING ME?
THE FIRST PRESIDENT
OTAKU
OTAKU
HER BOOBS ARE RIGHT OUT OF A MANGA
FRIEND
I WANT TO SEE HER IN COSPLAY
OTAKU
FRIEND
UNKNOWN
MITSUNORI KUGAYAMA
SOICHIRO TANAKA
KANAKO OHNO
FRIEND

# About the Author

Kio Shimoku was born in 1974.
In 1994 his debut work, *Ten No Ryoiki*, received
second place in the "Afternoon Shiki Prize"
contest. Other past works include *Kagerounikii*,
*Yonensei*, and *Gonensei*, all of which
appeared in *Afternoon* magazine.
He has been working on *Genshiken*
since 2002.

# Translation Notes

Japanese is a tricky language for most Westerners, and translation is often more art than science. For your edification and reading pleasure, here are notes on some of the places where we could have gone in a different direction in our translation of the work, or where a Japanese cultural reference is used.

## *Face mask, page 4*

You will notice that Ohno-san is wearing a kind of surgical mask throughout much of this chapter. These masks are a familiar sight during the flu season in Japan and are used to prevent spreading your illness to those around you. Masks are also marketed as a method of relieving sore throats and dry nasal passages by recycling the moisture produced by the breath.

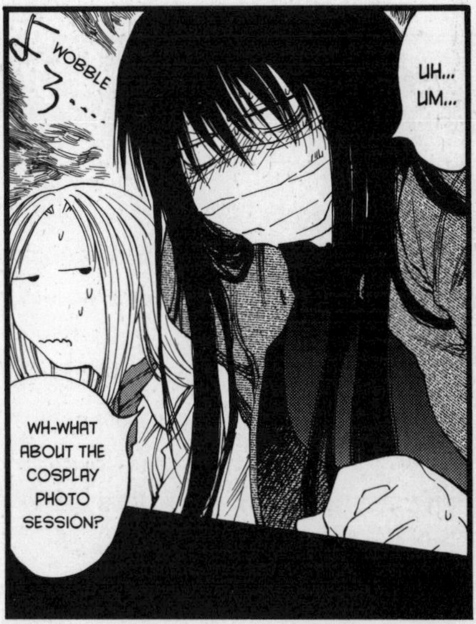
UH... UM...
WOBBLE
WH-WHAT ABOUT THE COSPLAY PHOTO SESSION?

## *I've been sick..., page 5*

This is a reference to *Genshiken* volume 3 (page 158), in which Saki tossed stagnant, dirty water on Ohno while trying to put out a fire.

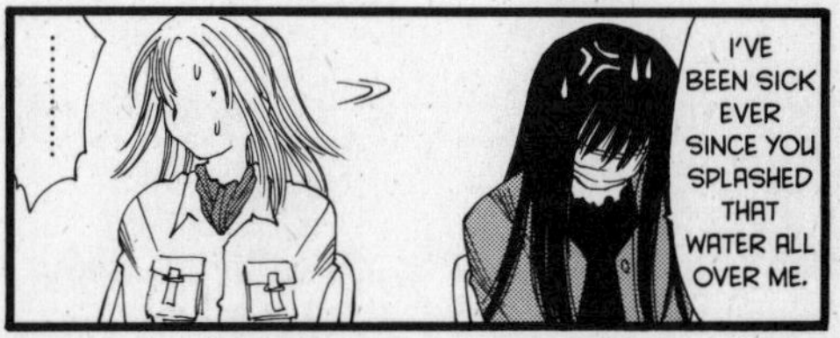
I'VE BEEN SICK EVER SINCE YOU SPLASHED THAT WATER ALL OVER ME.

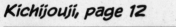

## *Kichijouji, page 12*

......
SHE'S HAD HER HEAD DOWN LIKE THAT ALL DAY.
SHE TRIED TO GET OUT OF IT BY RUNNING AWAY TO KICHIJOJI (A PART OF TOWN WHERE SHE ALMOST NEVER GOES) AND HIDING OUT IN A TINY, LITTLE CAFÉ TUCKED AWAY IN A LONELY ALLEY. SHE WAS EATING HER CHICKEN AND EGG OVER RICE WHEN SHE WAS CAUGHT BY KOUSAKA.
WHEN THE GUYS ASKED HIM HOW HE FOUND HER, HE REPLIED, "I JUST FOL-LOWED MY INSTINCTS."


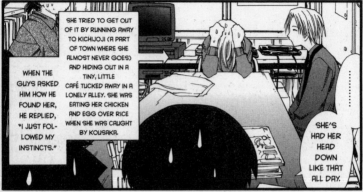

Kichijouji is a hip section of Tokyo with lots of bars, music and clothing stores. (It's also the former home of your humble translator.) That's where Saki was found eating a bowl of *oyako donburi,* a delicious combination of chicken and egg over rice.

## *Looking for a job, page 91*

In Japan, the job search system for soon-to-be college graduates is very formal. Most students begin their job hunt at the beginning of their senior year.

LISTEN, I HAVE TO START LOOKING FOR A JOB THIS YEAR.
A JOB?

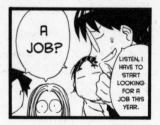

## *Kanji vs. kana, page 104*

...MANGA
...UNBALANCE FAN-ZINE
D. COMIC FEST...
VENDOR NUMBER FROM PREVIOUS COMIC FEST
VENDOR NUMBER FROM LAST YEAR'S COMIC FEST
65
64
CLUB NAME (IN KANA)
NAMEIN KANA - KANJI SASAHARA
NAMEIN KANA (LAST NAME) SASAHARA
(FIRST NAME) KANJI
PEN NAME BENJA
NAME OF REPRESENTATIVE
REPRESENTATIVE'S PEN NAME
OCCUPATION STUDENT
フリガナ
ADDRESS
HE'S USING PEN-CIL IN CASE HE MAKES A MIS-TAKE.

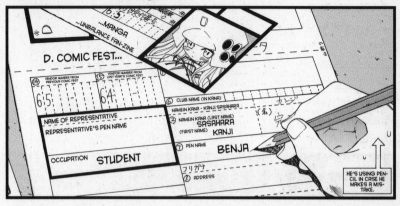

There are two main styles of script in Japanese: kanji (based on Chinese characters) and kana (hiragana and katakana which are syllabic). Since the readings for kanji used in people's names can often vary, the form asks for the applicant's name in both kanji and kana.

BUT WHEN I BECAME THE PRESIDENT, I JUST KIND OF MENTIONED IT, AND SUDDEN-LY IT'S SEEMED LIKE IT REALLY COULD HAP-PEN.
SO, YEAH... MAYBE I DID REALLY WANT TO DO IT ALL ALONG.

## *Hazing the newbies, page 105*

Refers to *Genshiken* volume 1, pages 21 - 26. As part of his initiation into the Genshiken, the guys leave Kanji alone in the club room and spy on him from the window of another building. Once he's alone, Kanji immediately begins looking for porn.

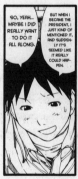

## *The other meaning of Genshiken, page 107*

"Genshiken" is typically written using three kanji symbols. Genshiken is short for "Gendai Shikaku Bunka Kenkyuukai" (The Society for the Study of Modern Visual Culture). Saki proposes writing Genshiken in hiragana. Hiragana is the syllabic form of Japanese writing. Unlike in kanji, the hiragan symbols have no inherent meaning.

## *Starbucks in Japan, page 130*

When Starbucks first appeared in Japan, it suddenly became the height of fashion. Many people kept their Starbucks bags and used them every day. Saki is probably referring to a similar phenomenon.

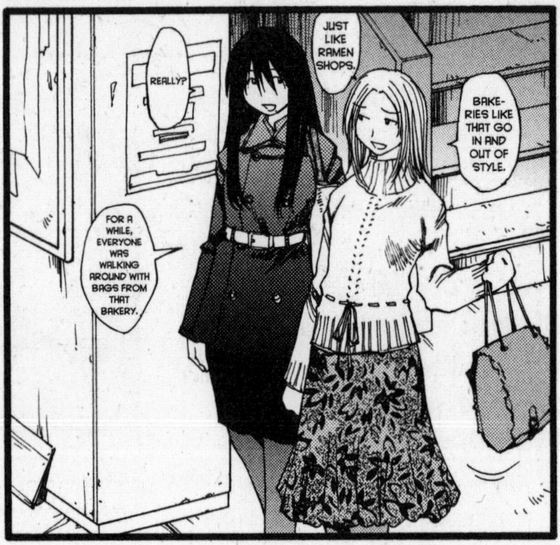
BAKERIES LIKE THAT GO IN AND OUT OF STYLE.
JUST LIKE RAMEN SHOPS.
REALLY?
FOR A WHILE, EVERYONE WAS WALKING AROUND WITH BAGS FROM THAT BAKERY.

## *Nooooothing, page 157*

Kuchiki is saying the word "nothing" in English. Apparently, his method of pronouncing the word correctly involves biting down on his lip.

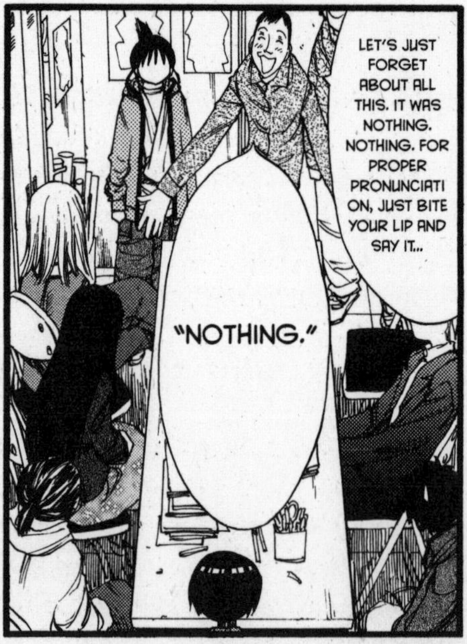
LET'S JUST FORGET ABOUT ALL THIS. IT WAS NOTHING. NOTHING. FOR PROPER PRONUNCIATI ON, JUST BITE YOUR LIP AND SAY IT...
"NOTHING."

## *Moe, page 165*

The word "moe/moeru" literally means "bud" or "sprout," but otaku use the word to refer to certain anime/manga character attributes which they are fixated on or aroused by. Most non-otaku have no idea of this alternative meaning. In the normal world "moe" is sometimes used as a girl's name, but to otaku it would have a very different connotation.

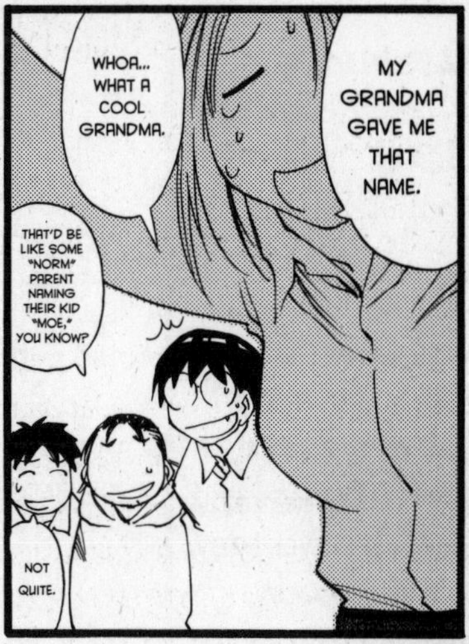
MY GRANDMA GAVE ME THAT NAME.
WHOA... WHAT A COOL GRANDMA.
THAT'D BE LIKE SOME "NORM" PARENT NAMING THEIR KID "MOE," YOU KNOW?
NOT QUITE.

# Honorifics

Throughout the Del Rey Manga books, you will find Japanese honorifics left intact in the translations. For those not familiar with how the Japanese use honorifics and, more importantly, how they differ from American honorifics, we present this brief overview.

Politeness has always been a critical facet of Japanese culture. Ever since the feudal era, when Japan was a highly stratified society, use of honorifics—which can be defined as polite speech that indicates relationship or status—has played an essential role in the Japanese language. When addressing someone in Japanese, an honorific usually takes the form of a suffix attached to one's name (example: "Asuna-san"), or as a title at the end of one's name or in place of the name itself (example: "Negi-sensei," or simply "Sensei!").

Honorifics can be expressions of respect or endearment. In the context of manga and anime, honorifics give insight into the nature of the relationship between characters. Many translations into English leave out these important honorifics, and therefore distort the "feel" of the original Japanese. Because Japanese honorifics contain nuances that English honorifics lack, it is our policy at Del Rey not to translate them. Here, instead, is a guide to some of the honorifics you may encounter in Del Rey Manga.

*-san:* This is the most common honorific and is equivalent to Mr., Miss, Ms., or Mrs. It is the all-purpose honorific and can be used in any situation where politeness is required.

*-sama:* This is one level higher than "-san" and is used to confer great respect.

*-dono:* This comes from the word "tono," which means "lord." It is an even higher level than "-sama" and confers utmost respect.

**-kun:** This suffix is used at the end of boys' names to express familiarity or endearment. It is also sometimes used by men among friends, or when addressing someone younger or of a lower station.

**-chan:** This is used to express endearment, mostly toward girls. It is also used for little boys, pets, and even among lovers. It gives a sense of childish cuteness.

**Bozu:** This is an informal way to refer to a boy, similar to the English term "kid" or "squirt."

**Sempai/Senpai:** This title suggests that the addressee is one's senior in a group or organization. It is most often used in a school setting, where underclassmen refer to their upperclassmen as "sempai." It can also be used in the workplace, such as when a newer employee addresses an employee who has seniority in the company.

**Kohai:** This is the opposite of "sempai" and is used toward underclassmen in school or newcomers in the workplace. It connotes that the addressee is of a lower station.

**Sensei:** Literally meaning "one who has come before," this title is used for teachers, doctors, or masters of any profession or art.

**[blank]:** Usually forgotten in these lists, but perhaps the most significant difference between Japanese and English. The lack of honorific means that the speaker has permission to address the person in a very intimate way. Usually, only family, spouses, or very close friends have this kind of permission. Known as *yobisute,* it can be gratifying when someone who has earned the intimacy starts to call one by one's name without an honorific. But when that intimacy hasn't been earned, it can also be very insulting.

# Preview of Volume 5

We're pleased to present you a preview from Volume 5.
This volume is available in English now!

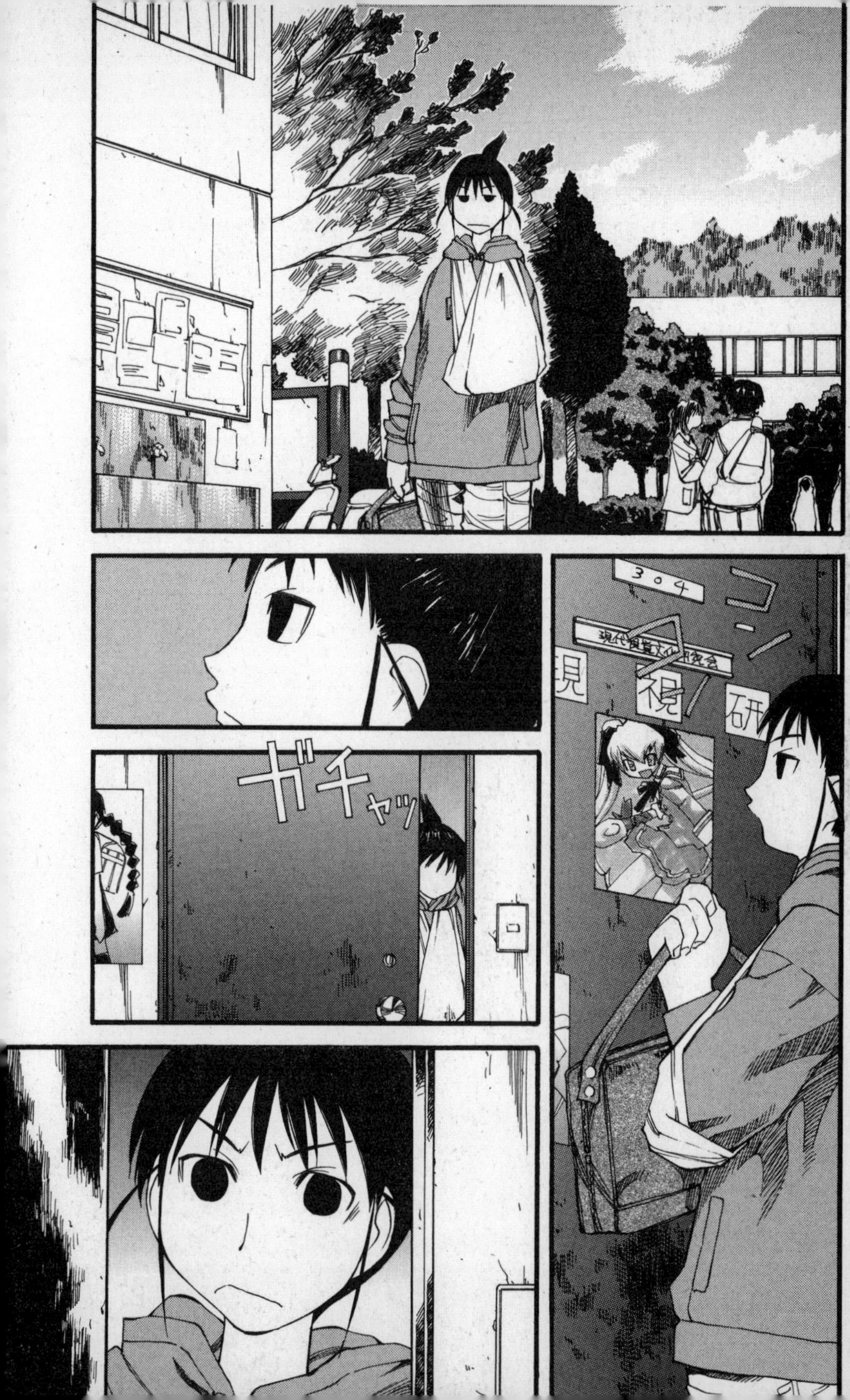
304
現代視覚文化研究会
現視研
ガチャッ

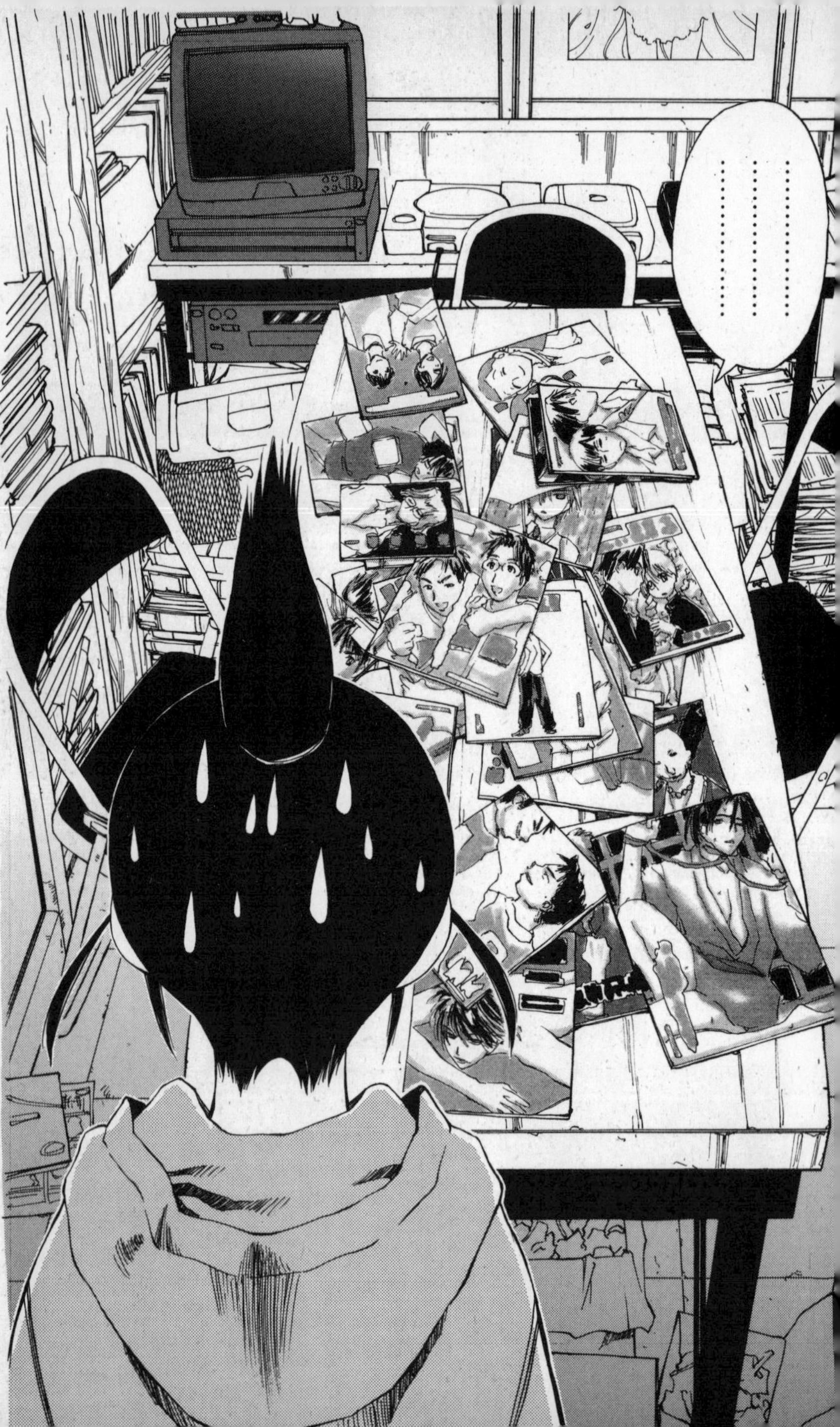
…………

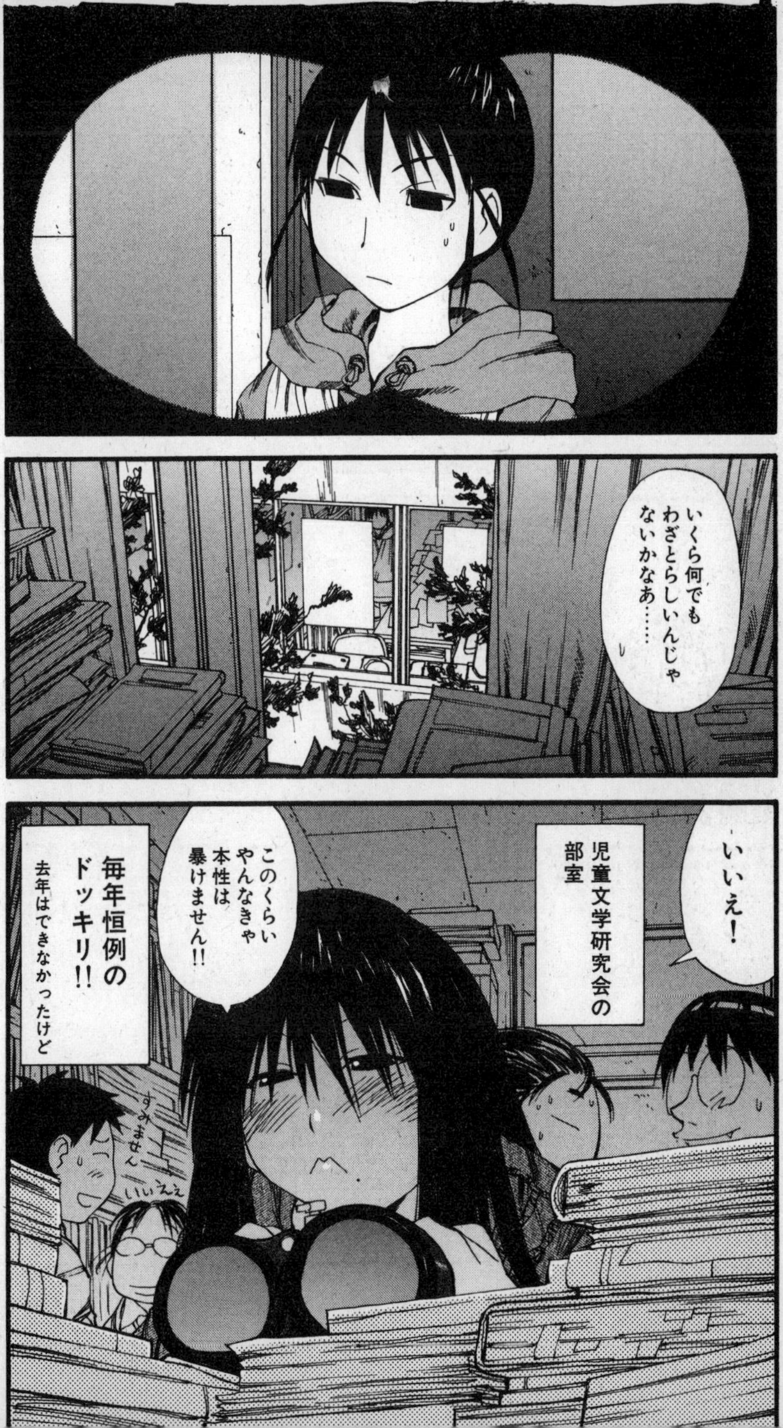
いくら何でもわざとらしいんじゃないかなあ……
いいえ!
児童文学研究会の部室
このくらいやんなきゃ本性は暴けません!!
毎年恒例のドッキリ!!
去年はできなかったけど
すみません
いいえぇ

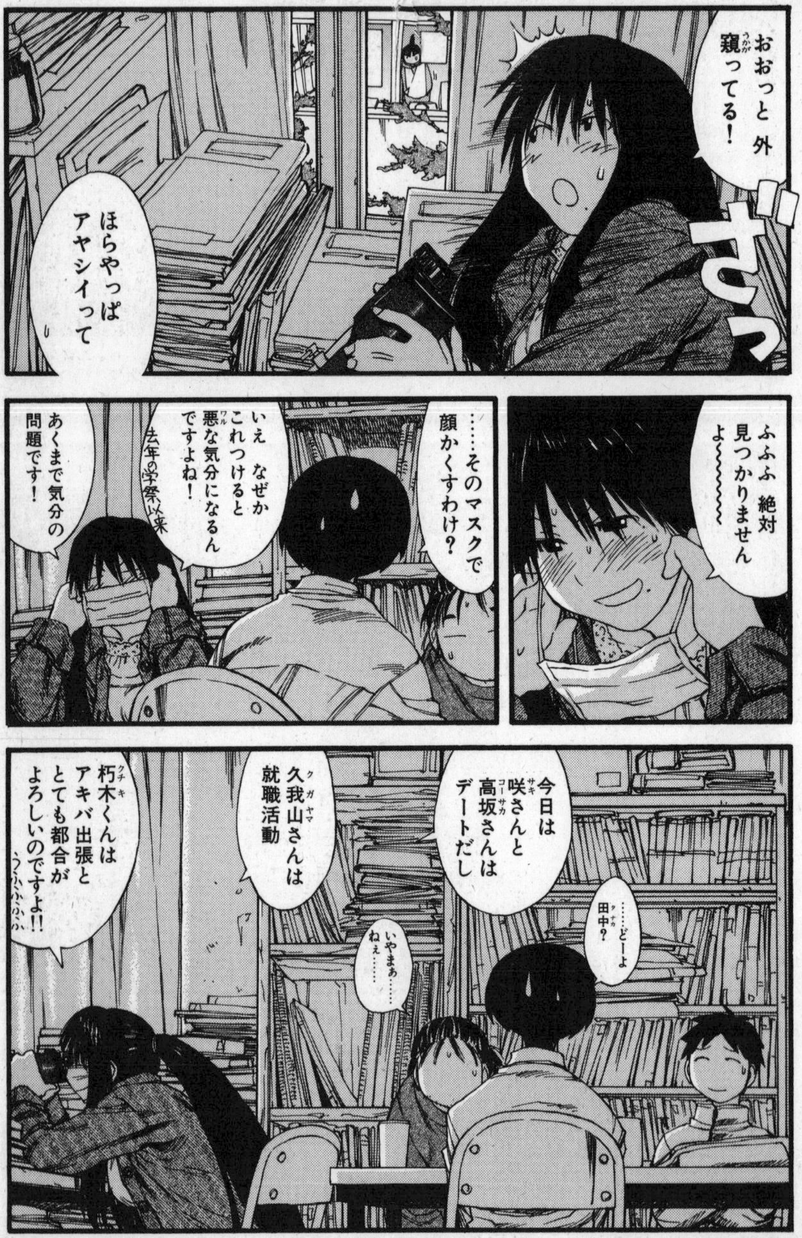

おおっと 外 窺(うかが)ってる!
ざっ
ほらやっぱ アヤシイって
ふふふ 絶対 見つかりませんよ〜〜〜〜〜
……そのマスクで 顔かくすわけ?
いえ なぜか これつけると 悪(ワル)な気分になるん ですよね!
去年の学祭以来
あくまで気分の 問題です!
今日は 咲(サキ)さんと 高坂(コーサカ)さんは デートだし
久我山(クガヤマ)さんは 就職活動
朽木(クチキ)くんは アキバ出張と とても都合が よろしいのですよ!!
うふふふふ
……どーよ 田中(タナカ)?
いやまぁ…… ねぇ……

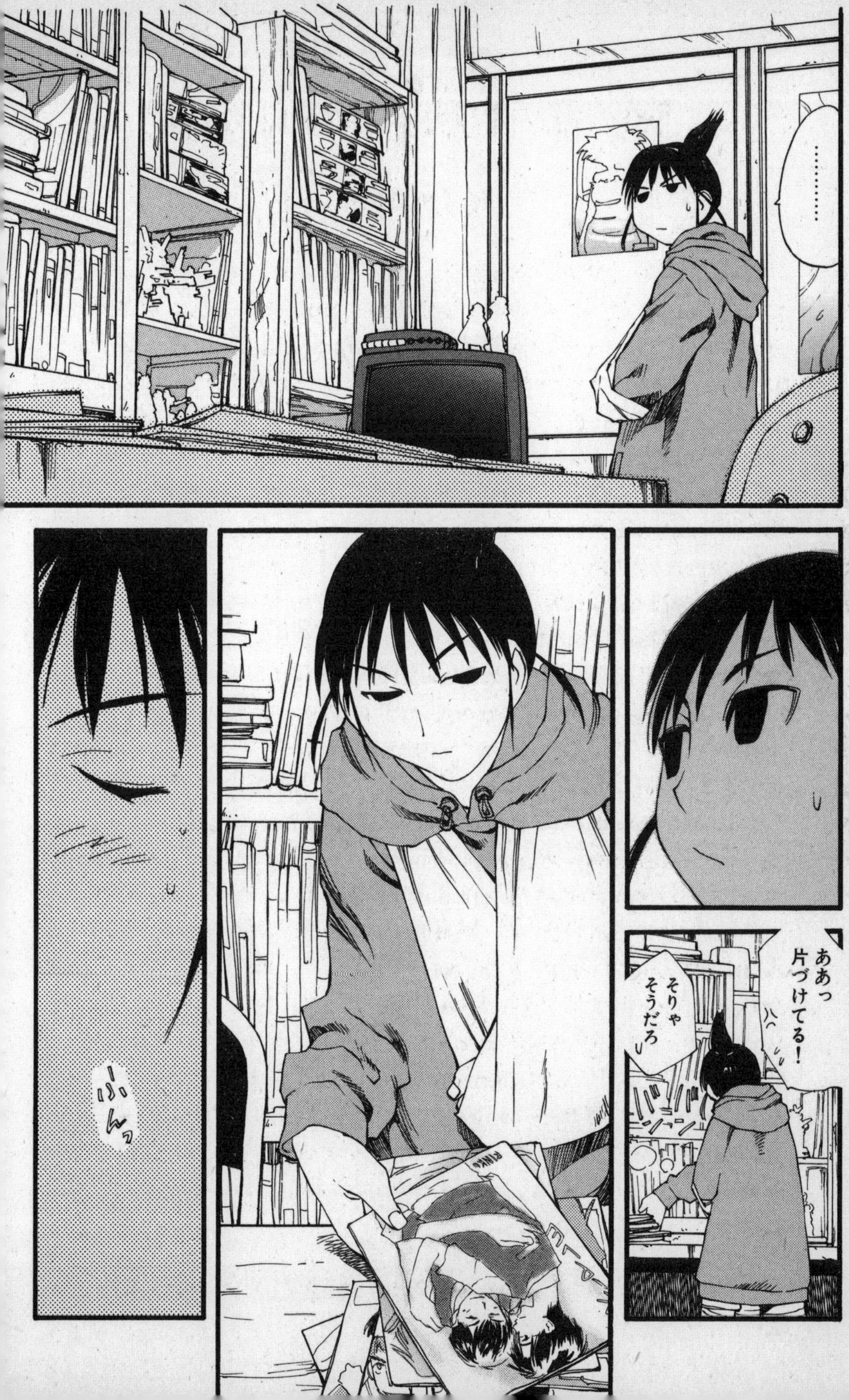
……
ああっ片づけてる!
そりゃそうだろ
ふんっ

# My Visit to Akihabara

By David Ury

Akihabara—Japan's most famous electronics paradise. The streets are lined with camera and video stores. Hawkers stand out front, luring passersby with freebies and discounts. I'd often ventured to Akihabara in search of the latest electronic gizmo, but I was completely unaware of the dark, otaku underbelly that lay hidden within Akihabara's streets.

Following in the footsteps of Kanji Sasahara, I decided to seek out Akihabara's doujinshi fan-zine specialty shops. Accompanied only by my tattered copy of Genshiken volume 1 and my helpful female Japanese companion, Mamiko, I set out on my quest. The first sight that caught my eye was a buxom young girl in a Santa cosplay outfit. She stood in front of a neon sign that read Kingdom of Porn*. Mamiko let out an embarrassed giggle as the sexy Santa led us inside. The "Kingdom," Santa informed us, was five stories high and packed with adult toys, DVDs, magazines and sexy cosplay kits. What about doujinshi, I asked. Santa tilted her head and gave me a puzzled look. "Dou-what- shi?" Hmmm, apparently even some porn professionals hadn't heard of doujinshi.

It was time for Plan B. Mamiko and I scoured the streets for otaku who might show us the way. I locked in on a gaunt Madarame lookalike. Too embarrassed to ask myself, I pushed Mamiko towards him. In her cute, girl-next-door way, she asked "Can you help us find a doujinshi shop?" Madarame stepped back in silent shock, his lips puckered tightly. Finally he turned his gaze toward the ground and slithered away, taking shelter in a nearby arcade. I pointed out a few more likely candidates and Mamiko repeated the question, but always with similar results.

*The name has been altered to protect the guilty...ur...innocent.

Finally, a friendly Tanaka-esque fellow boldly led us to what could only be described as an Otaku paradise. Models, toys, manga, anime DVDs, even anime song CDs, it was all there. The top floor was devoted solely to doujinshi. The zines were sealed in plastic, making perusal impossible. But, fear not! Attached to the back of each 'zine, a single page depicted a sample of the erotic mayhem contained within. "Eww," Mamiko gagged, pushing the 'zine away. "This is what you made me ask about? No wonder those guys ran away."

"Huh?" I muttered, my eyes glued to the titillating sample page of another doujinshi, a bit of drool collecting on my lower lip. "Did you say something?"

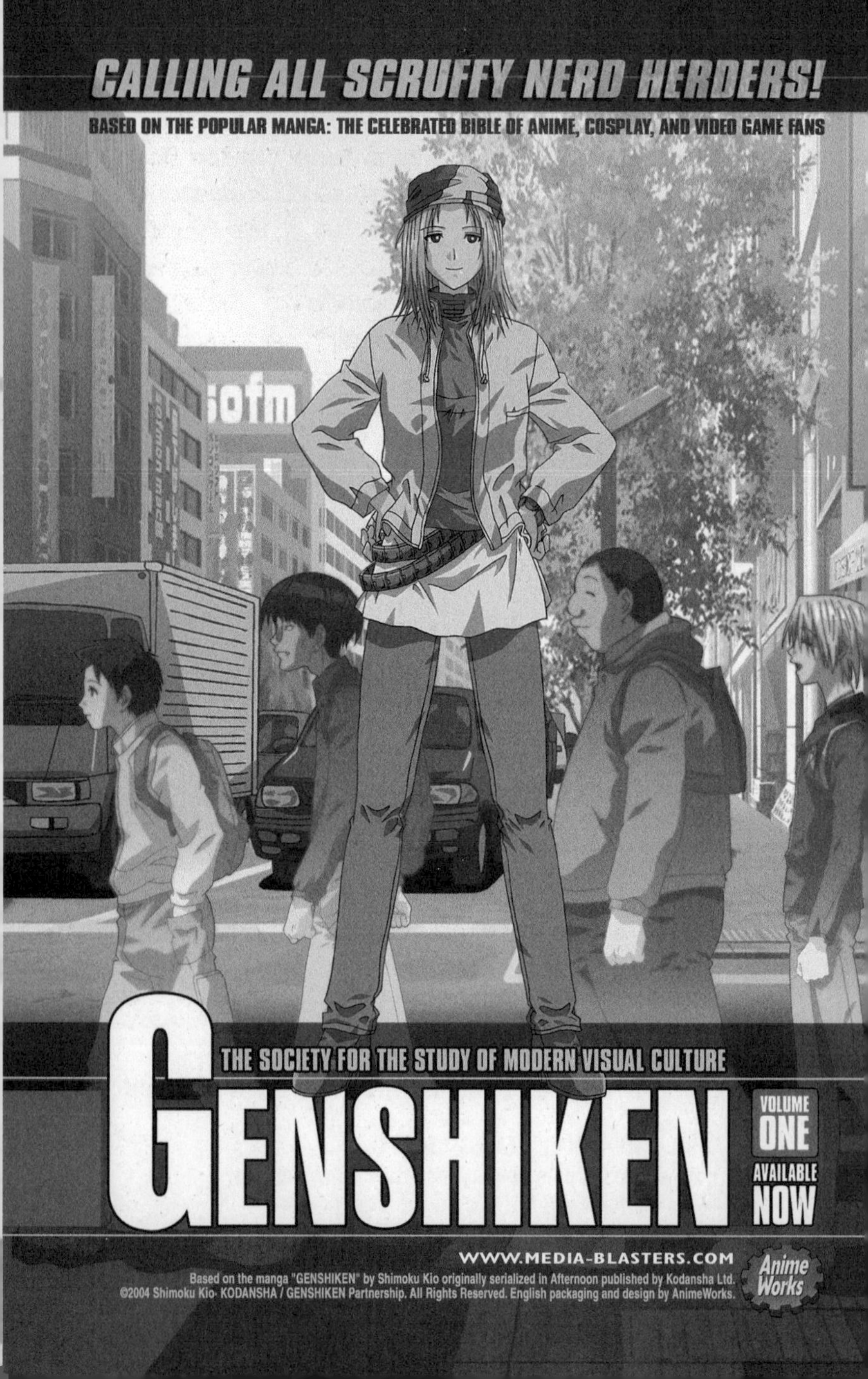

CALLING ALL SCRUFFY NERD HERDERS!
BASED ON THE POPULAR MANGA: THE CELEBRATED BIBLE OF ANIME, COSPLAY, AND VIDEO GAME FANS
THE SOCIETY FOR THE STUDY OF MODERN VISUAL CULTURE
GENSHIKEN
VOLUME ONE
AVAILABLE NOW
WWW.MEDIA-BLASTERS.COM
Anime Works
Based on the manga "GENSHIKEN" by Shimoku Kio originally serialized in Afternoon published by Kodansha Ltd.
©2004 Shimoku Kio· KODANSHA / GENSHIKEN Partnership. All Rights Reserved. English packaging and design by AnimeWorks.

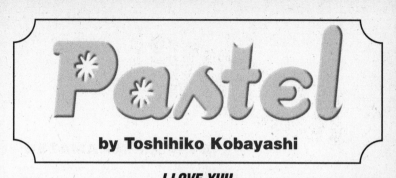

# Pastel

## by Toshihiko Kobayashi

### *I LOVE YUU*

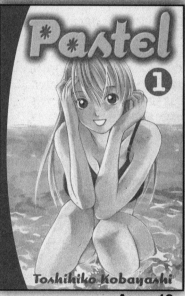

Poor 16-year-old Mugi Tadano is left heartbroken after his girlfriend moves away. A summer job at his friend Kazuki's beachside snack bar/hotel seems like the perfect way to get his mind off the breakup. Soon Kazuki sets Mugi up on a date with a girl named Yuu, who's supposed to be...well...a little less than perfect. But when Yuu arrives, she's not the monster that either of the boys had imagined. In fact, Yuu is about the cutest girl that Mugi has ever seen. But after Mugi accidentally walks in on Yuu while she's in the bath, Yuu is furious. When Mugi goes to apologize the next day, he learns that Yuu has left the island. Mugi vows to search high and low for her, but will he ever see the beautiful Yuu again?

**Ages: 16 +**

### *Special extras in each volume! Read them all!*

**DEL REY**

VISIT WWW.DELREYMANGA.COM TO:
• View release date calendars for upcoming volumes
• Sign up for Del Rey's free manga e-newsletter
• Find out the latest about new Del Rey Manga series

Pastel © 2006 Toshihiko Kobayashi / KODANSHA LTD. All rights reserved.

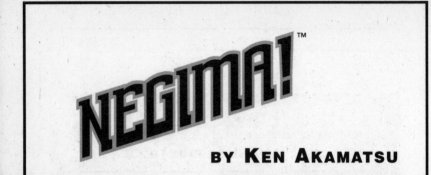

# NEGIMA!™

### BY KEN AKAMATSU

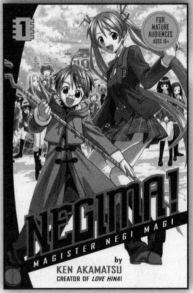

**N**egi Springfield is a ten-year-old wizard teaching English at an all-girls Japanese school. He dreams of becoming a master wizard like his legendary father, the Thousand Master. At first his biggest concern was concealing his magic powers, because if he's ever caught using them publicly, he thinks he'll be turned into an ermine! But in a world that gets stranger every day, it turns out that the strangest people of all are Negi's students! From a librarian with a magic book to a centuries-old vampire, from a robot to a ninja, Negi will risk his own life to protect the girls in his care!

Ages: 16+

*Special extras in each volume! Read them all!*

**DEL REY**

VISIT WWW.DELREYMANGA.COM TO:
• View release date calendars for upcoming volumes
• Sign up for Del Rey's free manga e-newsletter
• Find out the latest about new Del Rey Manga series

Negima © 2004 Ken Akamatsu / KODANSHA LTD. All rights reserved.

Subscribe to

# DEL REY'S MANGA
## e-newsletter—

and receive all these exciting exclusives directly in your e-mail inbox:

- Schedules and announcements about the newest books on sale

---

- Exclusive interviews and exciting behind-the-scenes news

---

- Previews of upcoming material

---

- A manga reader's forum, featuring a cool question-and-answer section

For more information and to sign up for Del Rey's manga e-newsletter, visit www.delreymanga.com

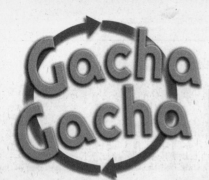

# Gacha Gacha

### By Hiroyuki Tamakoshi

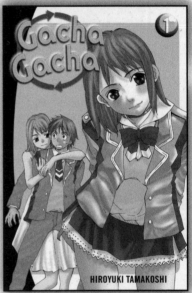

**K**ouhei is your typical Japanese high school student—he's usually late, he loves beef bowls, he pals around with his buddies, and he's got his first-ever crush on his childhood friend Kurara. Before he can express his feelings, however, Kurara heads off to Hawaii with her mother for summer vacation. When she returns, she seems like a totally different person . . . and that's because she is! While she was away, Kurara somehow developed an alternate personality: Arisa! And where Kurara has no time for boys, Arisa isn't interested in much else. Now Kouhei must help protect his friend's secret, and make sure that Arisa doesn't do anything Kurara would regret!

HIROYUKI TAMAKOSHI

**Ages: 16+**

*Special extras in each volume! Read them all!*

**DEL REY**

VISIT WWW.DELREYMANGA.COM TO:
- View release date calendars for upcoming volumes
- Sign up for Del Rey's free manga e-newsletter
- Find out the latest about new Del Rey Manga series

Gacha Gacha © 2002 Hiroyuki Tamakoshi / KODANSHA LTD. All rights reserved.

HRYA

# TOMARE!

## [STOP!]

**You're going the wrong way!**

**Manga is a completely different type of reading experience.**

**To start at the *beginning*, go to the *end*!**

That's right! Authentic manga is read the traditional Japanese way—from right to left. Exactly the *opposite* of how American books are read. It's easy to follow: Just go to the other end of the book, and read each page—and each panel—from right side to left side, starting at the top right. Now you're experiencing manga as it was meant to be!